Critical Human Geography

'Critical Human Geography' is an international series which provides a critical examination and extension of the concepts and consequences of work in human geography and the allied social sciences and humanities. The volumes are written by scholars currently engaged in substantive research, so that, wherever possible, the discussions are empirically grounded as well as theoretically informed. Existing studies and the traditions from which they derive are carefully described and located in their historically specific context, but the series at the same time introduces and explores new ideas and insights from the human sciences as a whole. The series is thus not intended as a collection of synthetic reviews, but rather as a cluster of considered arguments which are accessible enough to engage geographers at all levels in the development of geography. The series therefore reflects the continuing methodological and philosophical diversity of the subject, and its books are united only by their common commitment to the prosecution of a genuinely human geography.

Department of Geography   MARK BILLINGE
University of Cambridge   DEREK GREGORY
England   RON MARTIN

Critical Human Geography

PUBLISHED

Recollections of a Revolution: Geography as Spatial Science
Mark Billinge. Derek Gregory and Ron Martin (*editors*)

Capitalist Development: A Critique of Radical Development Geography
Stuart Corbridge

The European Past: Social Evolution and Spatial Order
Robert A. Dodgshon

The Arena of Capital
Michael Dunford and Diane Perrons

Regional Transformation and Industrial Revolution:
A Geography of the Yorkshire Woollen Industry
Derek Gregory

Social Relations and Spatial Structures
Derek Gregory and John Urry (*editors*)

Geography and the State: An Essay in Political Geography
R. J. Johnston

Long Waves of Regional Development
Michael Marshall

The Geography of De-industrialisation
Ron Martin and Bob Rowthorn (*editors*)

Spatial Divisions of Labour: Social Structures and the Geography of
Production
Doreen Massey

Conceptions of Space in Social Thought: A Geographic Perspective
Robert David Sack

The Urban Arena: Capital, State and Community in Contemporary Britain
John R. Short

FORTHCOMING

A Cultural Geography of Industrialisation in Britain
Mark Billinge

Regions and the Philosophy of the Human Sciences
Nicholas Entrikin

Strategies for Geographical Enquiry
Derek Gregory and Ron Martin

The European Past

Social Evolution and Spatial Order

Robert A. Dodgshon

MACMILLAN
EDUCATION

First published 1987

Published by
MACMILLAN EDUCATION LTD
Houndmills, Basingstoke, Hampshire RG21 2XS
and London
Companies and representatives
throughout the world

Distributed in the United States of America by
Sheridan House Inc, 145 Palisade Street, Dobbs
Ferry, New York, NY 10522, U.S.A.

Printed in Hong Kong

British Library Cataloguing in Publication Data
Dodgshon, Robert A.
The European past: social evolution and
spatial order. — (Critical human geography)
1. Anthropo-geography
I. Title   II. Series
304.2   GF95
ISBN 0–333–28107–1 (hardcover)
ISBN 0–333–28109–8 (paperback)

For Clare and Lucy
A version of the past for two of the future

Contents

vii

List of Figures

Preface

I have always had a deeply felt conviction that the range of geographical concepts and ideas can be greatly enriched by drawing on the experience of the past. This conviction is founded on the belief that the principles which govern the organisation of human spatial order have changed in step with the substantive or qualitative changes that have occurred in the organisation of society itself. The aim of this book is to prompt a greater interest in this historical phasing of human spatial order over the very long term and also in the means by which one system gave way to another. I want to stress that I do not see the study of such high-order problems as a substitute for the basic task of reconstructing past landscapes. What I am suggesting is that a healthy and vibrant historical geography needs to pursue both levels of approach, the one nourishing the other. My early thoughts on a history of spatial systems in the very long term took shape during the late 1970s partly through the stimulus of my interest in the institutional forms of early Celtic landscape, and their manifest differences with those of more recent landscapes, and partly through the stimulus of reading through the work of scholars like K. Polanyi, E. L. Jones, D. C. North and C. Renfrew. These thoughts matured through a specialist course which I have put on at Aberystwyth since the academic year, 1979–80, a course which has constantly served to remind me that any debate over the way that spatial systems have evolved in the very long term must strive to see the problem at its own level and in its own terms.

I have no doubt that some will see any attempt to produce such high-order generalisations as a fruitless exercise. For this reason, it has been of some reassurance to find that the pool of relevant ideas on societal evolution has expanded impressively in recent years. This eruption of interest, though, has made the process of producing an 'interim' history of spatial systems a slower, more laborious affair. I am extremely grateful to my editors and publisher for their patience and tolerance during the book's gestation. Special thanks are due to Derek Gregory and two anonymous referees for their helpful comments on the manuscript. Written without the benefit of study-leave, its demands have also placed a greater than usual burden on my wife, Katherine, and daughters, Clare and Lucy. Struggling to produce an acceptable draft was a case of spurning delights and living laborious days as much for them as for me. At the cost of another trip to the rich delights of Trasqua, they generously funded the electronic fun-machine on which the second and third drafts were produced. Although I am acutely conscious of the gaps and flaws in my text, I have chosen to dedicate it to my daughters in the hope that they will accept it as a product of honest labour. Being a mild determinist at heart, I have often reflected on whether working from a study that looks out across Cardigan Bay has encouraged me in my abstractions about the broader horizons of historical geography. It would be a source of satisfaction if my daughters too, found pleasure in moving between the busy detail of close, Brueghelian landscapes and those which, as in the paintings of Caspar David Friedrich, lead to higher, mistier planes or out to far horizons.

Aberystwyth   ROBERT A. DODGSHON

1
Introduction

The aim of this book is to show how the organising principles behind human spatial order have changed in the very long term. It embodies a philosophy of the way that historical geography might make a greater contribution to geographical concept. This philosophy is guided by the belief that historical geography can gain more from a substantivist than from a formalist approach to its problems. By this is meant that we should work from the premise that modern concepts of human spatial organisation are inapplicable outside the specific socio-historical context in which they have been formulated and that we should seek to clarify how the unfolding human landscape records the successive imprint of different systems of spatial order. These systems of spatial order are defined through the variables and interactions which determined the organisation of society in space. Change from one system to another is taken to mean a qualitative change in the nature of the system, a change which could involve different levels or spheres of determination, control mechanisms or goals and, in consequence, effects.

There have always been historical geographers willing to think their problems out on a very large scale or in the very long term, to write what Jones has called 'big-picture history' (Jones, 1981, p. 239). The most epic attempt has surely been Peake and Fleure's *Corridors of Time*, a ten-volumed study of human history down to the first civilizations (Peake and Fleure, 1927–56). A more enduring attempt at large-scale synthesis and one which successfully demonstrated the need for high order generalisation at this scale of analysis was Smith's *Historical Geography of Western Europe Before 1800* (1966). Closer in spirit to my own approach, is Bobek's short but suggestive review of socio-cultural evolution from a geographical perspective (Bobeck, 1962, pp. 218–47). Latterly, major thematic studies of long-term change have been published by Grigg on agriculture (1974 and 1982) and by Vance (1977) and Carter (1983) on urban systems, all accomplished examples of this genre of historical geography writ large. Nor should we exclude Jones' *The European Miracle*. Although written ostensibly from the standpoint of an economic historian, it ranks as a seminal study in historical geography no less than in economic history. To pen a history of spatial systems in the very long term then, is hardly to break new ground. It is a scale of analysis that already has an established tradition behind it.

The real challenge is the interpretative framework through which we conceive the history of spatial systems and the insights to be derived from it. Of course, there are some geographers who would argue that whatever interpretative framework is employed, these insights can hardly be original in what they contribute to geographical concept. For them, there is only one spatial system. Since the ultimate character of this spatial system is construed as timeless, beyond chronology, it follows that an historical perspective can have no special or privileged role in the production of theory. Indeed, forced to approach this apparently omnipresent system of spatial order through the chance-grab samples of early documentary sources or through the lancet-like windows on the past offered by early census data, historical geography is reduced to the role of illustrating rather than originating theory. In a universe of time–space substitutes, it is far easier for the student of spatial order to overcome distance than it is to overcome time.

Such an ahistorical view of spatial order though, is surely developed in ignorance rather than knowledge of the past. In fact, it is inconceivable that one could have an ahistorical view of spatial systems. Given that the primary concerns of a spatial perspective are the way societal systems disposed themselves in space, the way their social, economic, political and ritual behaviour is configurated through space and the way they coped with the problem of exploiting and consuming geographically-uneven resources, it is difficult to see how such systems can be problematised from anything other than a materialist viewpoint. Admittedly, materialism has of late become a veritable bean-bag of a concept, shaped by a whole variety of ideological needs into dialectical, historical, economic and cultural variants (Harris, 1980). All of them, however, share the belief that societal formations are not devised by society in isolation from the practical problems of living in the world, as an exercise in pure idealism, but develop out of the material conditions of existence. As Marx put it, life determines thought, not vice versa. Our explanatory framework of societal change in the very long term must embrace and incorporate the progressive and substantive adjustments which have taken place between societal formations and their material bases. The study of spatial systems can hardly exempt itself here. As an attempt to problematise the very plane of intersection between societal systems and their material world, it too is compelled to set its conclusions within their specific socio-historical context and to seek an evolutionary frame of reference for them.

Can we expect this historical schema for spatial systems to be constituted entirely in its own terms or can it be interfaced to the wider debate by historians, archaeologists, anthropologists and sociologists on the evolution of societal systems? It is an uncomfortable fact that fellow-historians and social scientists have not always appreciated the geographer's curiously flat and occasionally transparent interpretations of societal structures and processes. For them, the geographer is too often concerned with mere shadows and reflections rather than the substance or body of societal formations. The problem is that there is no such thing as an exclusively or innately geographical process, one that falls to the geographer alone to elucidate. Rather, it is his task to show how interactions and processes, whether social, economic, political or ritualistic, are configured in space and how their configuration in space is intrinsic or prejudicial to their meaning and effect. Whether this configuration in space was intentional or unintentional does not matter. Whether it was part of the way things operated does. In a sense, the spatial perspective can be likened to the stage management of the human play, a contribution concerned with establishing the arena of action, with working out stage directions and with actualising interactions and processes in space as a necessary part of why they occurred and to what effect. Seen in this way, the spatial perspective can no more constitute its problems in isolation from the more basic issues of societal formations than a play can be staged without a plot. The one is integral to the other, enabling the content and meaning of the human play to be more fully realised when subjected to critical analysis (Gregory, 1978, p. 120). It also follows from this last point that a spatial perspective on societal systems is far from being a geographer's fetish or a viewpoint without value. Even a cursory examination of the literature on the long-term development of societal systems reveals that a number of historians and social scientists have grasped this point and have incorporated a spatial dimension into the structuring of their argument. The history of spatial systems then, offers no uncharted journey into *terra incognito*, but guides the geographer through the wider debate on the history of societal formations, reciprocally contributing as much as it derives from this debate.

The Need for an Organisational Approach

The only meaningful way in which we can construct an evolutionary perspective on spatial systems is through an organisational approach. Of late, there has been a renewed interest, primarily among anthropologists, political scientists and prehistorians, in the systems of order through which society has evolved. Apart from a lone review by Newson of the particular contribution made by Sahlins and Service (Newson, 1976, pp. 239–55) and a more general survey by the political geographer Taylor (Taylor, 1971, pp. 115–30; Taylor, 1973, pp. 31–68), this literature has generally been ignored by geographers. And yet, as Newson and Taylor demonstrate, and as Renfrew (Renfrew, 1977, pp. 89–114) has recently confirmed in a more abstract review aimed at prehistorians and anthropologists, the ideas and concepts of an organisational approach translate readily into spatial order. In part, the avoidance of such an approach reflects the sharp antagonism which some geographers have felt towards it. They have argued that by its explicit or implicit invocation of organisational imperatives or needs, it strips societal systems of their humanity, their capacity to decide for themselves. In Giddens's words, it reduces human agents to 'cultural dopes' (Giddens, 1981, p. 18). One is never quite sure whether these critics are rejecting the fact that societal organisation is affected by variables like the scale of societal integration or whether they are really lamenting the fact that they do play a part. Other reservations over an organisational approach have arisen through its heavy reliance on systems theory for most of its conceptual apparatus. There seems to be a feeling that to apply systems theory, especially General Systems Theory, to the problem of societal formations is to reduce our interpretation to a mechanical or deterministic analysis, since it squeezes our interpretation into a predetermined strait-jacket of concepts, and involves a loss of art or feeling akin to painting by numbers! (see for example, Gregory, 1978, pp. 44–5; Gregory, 1980, pp. 327–42; Hodder, 1984, pp. 25–32). And yet, there are those troubled precisely by its lack of numbers. With relatively few exceptions (Renfrew and Cooke, 1979), most scholars who have made use of a systems approach have not quantified their variables or the relationships identified between them. But even in the light of Langton's strictures on the empty use of the mere terminology of systems theory (Langton, 1972b, p. 159) I would suggest that there is profit in such an approach to societal formations and their correlates of spatial order. To define the relevant variables, establish those that were linked and the nature of their interaction, and locate areas of negative and positive feedback – to do all this at the level of societal systems – is not to define the obvious but to isolate one interpretative structure from a wide range of possibilities and to make an assay of its worth and significance (cf. Taylor, 1973, pp. 56–7). Yes, the quantification of variables would make for greater insight but lack of it does not undermine our appreciation of its systemic structure any more than a failure to quantify the stresses and strains on each pillar, on each arch, of the Ponte Vecchio undermines our appreciation of it as an architectural form that sustains life.

Approached via an organisational perspective, societal systems can be seen as evolving through a succession of increasingly complex forms, moving from homogeneity to heterogeneity and from uniformity to hierarchy (White, 1959, especially pp. 142–236; Sahlins and Service, 1960; Parsons, 1966, especially pp. 21–5; Flannery, 1976, pp. 96–118; Renfrew, 1977, pp. 89–112; Segraves, 1982, pp. 287–300). In broad terms, we can typify this growing complexity as a trend towards larger systems of societal order, larger systems always requiring a more elaborate organisation if they are to achieve stability (Carneiro, 1967, p. 239). In the process, society became progressively more differentiated into sub-systems which, in time, acquired functional specialisation. With differentiation and specialisation came a more intense adaptation to prevailing opportunities, a trend to which Parsons refers as the adaptive upgrading of sub-systems (Parsons, 1966, p. 22, though see also, Wenke, 1981, pp. 111–12). Step by step with the increasing number of subsystems and with their functional specialisation, there also developed a hierarchy of control functions, the progressive elaboration of the latter matching the growing scale and elaboration of the former. Segraves has expressed these organisational trends in terms of a simple succession:

$$A > AAAAAA > AABBCCDD$$

with the whole system being overlaid with a higher tier of control once sub-systems became specialised (Segraves, 1982, p. 288; see also, Parsons, 1966, p. 24; Carneiro, 1967, p. 240 and, for a critique, Blute, 1979, p. 50). Put crudely, such trends have direct biological analogues. So too, does the way in which their growing organisational complexity has been seen in thermodynamic terms. Sahlins and Service saw elaboration occurring through an increasing level of energy capture, though they were careful to stress that they had in mind an increase in the gross level of energy capture not an increase in the efficiency of its capture (Sahlins and Service, 1960, p. 34, though cf. White, 1975, p. 19). Anxious not to violate the second law of thermodynamics by defining societal systems as negentropic, as if they were actually creating energy, others have preferred to rephrase this thermodynamic trend in terms of an increasing level of energy use and, therefore, dissipation (see for example, Adams, 1975, pp. 122–3).

Societal systems do not exist in a vacuum. Although some portray them as structured entirely within their own terms, as somehow being in the world but not of it, the view maintained here is that we can best construe them as adaptations to the problems of living in a material world, problems that arise from the need to exploit the resources of their environment and to organise their social relationships in space. Adaptation is taken to mean those phases during which societal systems establish a relatively stable relationship with the environment and space which they occupy, with various regulators (for instance, cultural norms, institutions, administrators, etc.) maintaining the relationship in a state of homeostasis by means of governing loops that use negative feedback to control the various sub-systems within acceptable limits (Butzer, 1982, pp. 281–6). The idea that societal systems can be profitably viewed as adaptations does have its critics. Giddens, for instance, dismisses it as a 'vacuous concept' that must not be instated as a driving force of societal development (Giddens, 1984, pp. 233–6). The force of his criticism is directed at the way some schemes of societal adaptation seem to externalise the factors controlling societal order, reducing it to a functional exigency rather than a matter of human choice. He himself prefers to stress the knowledgeability of human agents, rather than to treat them as mere *fantocinni* activated by forces and functions beyond their control. Yet such criticism would only be valid if societal adaptation was defined in narrow and crudely deterministic terms, with a given habitat or mode of production always producing a given societal response, the one shaped exclusively by the other. There are passages where Giddens certainly sees it in these terms. However, the notion of societal adaptation fits just as comfortably into a possibilist framework: this assumes that having to cope with the manifold problems of living in a material world is the prior consideration for any societal system but admits that precisely how it copes with such problems – how, therefore, it designs its societal order – is a matter of choice, a choice about which society as a whole has been increasingly knowledgeable.

In fact, seen in this way, the notion of adaptation appears similar to those elements in Giddens's own ideas that stress the need for seeing societal order as determined contextually, a product of concrete historical processes and situations. To this extent, his notion of seeing societal systems in terms of their time–space distanction – their extension and integration through specific durations of time and over specific blocks of space – can easily be implanted into arguments based on adaptation. For Giddens, this would still be a flawed argument because – as one based on adaptation – it would depend heavily on society's technical command over its material world. Again, though, much depends on how adaptation is defined. To restate what I said earlier, adaptation can be broadened so as to embrace the way a society organises its relations in space as well as the way it mapped itself onto its resource base. This compound meaning is crucial, for Giddens sees the restriction of its meaning to the way in which societies exploited their resource base as a fundamental weakness precisely because it omits consideration of the way societies exercised social control over themselves. His own interpretation of the way societal systems were structured is developed around what he calls the intersection between their allocative and authoritative resources: the former being based on what they extracted from their material world and the latter on the means by which they exercised social control over themselves through time and space. Clearly, there need be no real conflict of meaning between Giddens's notion of a society ordered around the intersection between its allocative and authoritative resources and one which stresses the way in which it adapted itself to the practical conditions of living in a material world. However, one major point of disagreement must remain. Giddens rejects the possibility that his structures of domination, that is, the interplay between allocative and authoritative resources, provide the basis for an evolutionary perspective. 'Human history', he declared, 'does not have an evolutionary shape and positive harm can be done by attempting to compress it into one' (Giddens, 1984, p. 236). The opposite view is taken here, with the growing scale and integration of societal systems combining with their increasing command over their material resources to impart an evolutionary drift to societal development, one that can be measured in terms of increasing societal complexity and increasing energy capture.

The question of how one level of societal complexity is transformed or quantised into a higher form can be broken down into three lines of approach. First, there are those who see the problem in terms of maladaptation. Stress is placed on the fact that some variables or sub-systems may have a capacity for runaway growth (Bateson, 1972, p. 447). Under normal conditions, society institutes control functions that regulate the behaviour of its sub-systems within tolerable limits, the overall system being maintained in a steady state via negative feedback (Bateson, 1972, p. 447; Rappaport, 1977, p. 49). To this extent, they can be classed as essentially 'conservative' systems (Bateson, 1972, p. 447). Occasionally, however, the amplitude of variation may become excessive, so much so that the entire system becomes relocated, via positive feedback and irreversible change, around a wholly new equilibrium (Bateson, 1972, p. 355; Taylor, 1973, pp. 56–7; Rappaport, 1977, pp. 49–71). Rappaport describes the failure of regulators to cope with excessive variation or deviant behaviour within sub-systems as maladaptation. Significantly, some of the prime causes of maladaptation discussed by Rappaport are factors which affect the organisation of societal systems in space. Thus, significant shifts in the scale of societal systems, the spread of all-purpose money and the introduction of high-energy technology were each capable of interfering with the work of system regulators or of causing runaway growth in particular sub-systems, thereby initiating a shift towards more complex systems of areal integration and specialisation (Rappaport, 1977, pp. 65–6).

The second line of approach dispenses with the notion of societal order moving through successive equilibria and, instead, makes use of Prigogine's ideas on how order can result from non-equilibrium systems. In effect, such a view holds to the stock idea that societal systems move through contrasting phases of stability and flux but they read its meaning in quite different terms. Particular forms of societal order are not explained as stable systems of energy capture functioning – albeit temporarily – in a state of equilibrium, but are seen as dissipative structures (Prigogine *et al*, 1977, pp. 1–23; Segraves, 1982, pp. 289–95; Friedman, 1982, pp. 177–9; Wallerstein, 1983, pp. 30–1). The attraction of such a view lies in its ability to accommodate more effectively the lineal, ongoing nature of societal change. This avoids what some see as a prime weakness of an organisational approach to change. Its stress on society passing through successive equilibria means that the very control functions and regulators that are seen as maintaining societal order in some form of steady state have to be suppressed if change to a new equilibrium is to occur. In other words, a strict organisational approach contains no theory of change. It offers a theory of persistence but not one of change. Indeed, the very principles invoked to explain societal order have to be abandoned in order to explain the appearance of new systems (Bock, 1963, especially pp. 232–3; Nisbet, 1969, especially pp. 251–67).

The third line of approach sees the problem not so much in terms of change from within, as something immanent within society, but in terms of how societal systems coped with or reacted to what was going on around them. White, for instance, and latterly, Renfrew, have proposed that systemic change takes place through the integration of whole systems, with the systems of one level being fused together so as to form the sub-systems of the next higher level of order. Such a view stresses the interaction that exists between adjacent systems and their associative or reciprocating effect on each other's development (White, 1959, p. 147; Renfrew, 1977, pp. 47–8; see also, Elias, 1982, p. 88). As a process, systemic change in this fashion has been given a staged form by Adams. Systems start off by acquiring identity, one from another. Through exchange and other types of interaction, they become co-ordinated. Finally, coupled as interacting systems, they become centralised into single system (Adams, 1975, pp. 208–11). Some of the precise mechanisms by which they become more centralised have been outlined by Flannery. Two, in particular, need to be noted: promotion, whereby lower-order sub-systems acquire a higher ranking within the total system, and linearisation, whereby higher-order sub-systems take over the functions of lower-order sub-systems. Through the operation of such mechanisms, Flannery discerns an overall evolutionary trend whereby new sub-systems or institutions are continually generated which then, in time, undergo a gradual metamorphosis from being system-serving to being self-serving (Flannery, 1976, pp. 103–12). Such a trend, of course, is only possible in a system that *in toto* tends towards greater complexity and greater centralisation.

Is there a Geographical Dimension to Societal Change?

Although exceptions can be cited, such as Berry's laudable attempt to distinguish between evolutionary, revolutionary and involutionary change (Berry, 1973, pp. 3–21) an increasing number of geographers have framed their understanding of societal or institutional change solely in terms of dialectical change, that is, the transformation from one system to another through the resolution of internal conflict and the struggle between class groups. To the cry of 'come the revolution' has been added the geographer's new mystery of 'where is the revolution?'. But even fortified (or should it be sobered?) by the reminder that 500 years of peace in Switzerland produced the cuckoo-clock whilst 500 years of warring, of family feuding and factional strife in Italy produced the Renaissance, I find myself unable to share the same unequivocal faith in the sufficiency of internal conflict as the sole basis for analysing societal change in the very long term or to accept that change is something immanent within society. Admittedly, part of my misgivings are rooted in matters of definition, over what we can define as internal as opposed to external, rather than over whether social conflict breeds change. Yet even allowing for these matters of definition, there are still disagreements over substance. Societal organisation can be stressed in ways other than through its inner contradictions.

It is inconceivable, for instance, that the geographer should understate the relationship between society and environment and the way this relationship can move between adaptation and maladaptation. To start with, mention might be made of the ecological contrast which Jones has drawn between the diverse chequerboard environments in which the state systems of Europe evolved and the vast, fertile but uniform riverine environments in which the exploitive empires of the Middle and Far East developed: the former favouring societies 'moulded by the forest' and localised if not decentralised power systems and the latter, large centralised power systems based on arable and coercion (Jones, 1981, pp. 10–11). Adapting a slogan of women's liberation movements, some might reply that topography is not destiny. I would prefer myself to see Jones's text as a forceful reminder that societal organisation is, in part, an adaptation to the possibilities of its environment. By the same token, environmental change can be seen as precipitating organisational adjustments. Reasoning of this sort has been used as a source of explanation for the transformation of bands into tribes, with the richer habitats of the post-glacial period encouraging a more intensive use of smaller territories; this, in turn, is seen as reducing mobility and, thereby, as undermining traditional mechanisms of birth control so that population began to grow quickly. Faced with a growth of population, bands had to adopt more intensive systems of food production and a more sedentary existence, thereby creating conditions that were conducive to the formation of tribes. The further intensification of food production, though, brought fresh problems of adjustment. Farming represented a narrower, more precarious ecology than the natural habitats which it increasingly replaced. It brought with it new levels of risk and uncertainty. For some commentators, the rise of big-men and chiefs and with them, the emergence of the earliest ranked societies, can be seen as an insurance against these enhanced risks. The payment or exaction of tribute took on the meaning of an insurance premium, with dividends being paid out when harvests failed and crisis threatened. The fact that big-men and chiefs usually commanded access to different environments meant that societies which acquired this sort of control or managerial function invariably had greater reliability over those without. In effect, the emergent systems of redistributive exchange provided a form of social storage, enabling communities, albeit at a price, to lay down a long-term supply of food.

A strong case can also be marshalled for seeing the increasing size of societal systems, their size in terms of both population and spatial extension, as a relevant variable, with each new jump in scale injecting fresh problems of conflict and maladjustment into prevailing forms of societal organisation and integration. Considered in this way, the ongoing changes in societal systems represent adjustments to scalar stress (White, 1975, p. 45; Johnson, 1982, pp. 388–421; Segraves, 1982, p. 291). Such an approach relies, in part, on biological analogues, especially for its central belief that as system size moves beyond certain critical thresholds, adjustments in organisation become necessary. System size can be seen as an amalgam of both spatial extension and population. 'For qualitative system change to occur', writes Segraves, 'critical spatial dimensions must be exceeded' (Segraves, 1982, p. 291). Later in the same discussion, she phrases it as a problem of population mass, arguing that socio-cultural evolution at a very general level can be seen as an 'adaptation to the imperatives of an increasing population' (Segraves, 1982, p. 293). Although the actual environment obviously played a part in determining what these size thresholds were for particular forms of societal integration, this aspect is almost impossible to derive as a statistical measure. Crude indices of population size and spatial extension have proved easier to construct. To date, most work of this nature has focused on the threshold size at which bands tried to regulate themselves or at which states came into being though there have been some valiant attempts to consider whether size thresholds can be devised for all the different phases of socio-cultural evolution (see for example, Carneiro, 1967, pp. 234–43; Carneiro, 1978, pp. 205–23). Whilst acknowledging that some geographers will find this sort of structural determinism entirely unacceptable or will see it as analytical corsetry of a most uncomfortable kind, I would contend that it is a perspective on the problem that the geographer cannot baulk. It helps to establish how living in a spatially-constructed world mattered materially to the organisation of the societal system. It is not something that we can dismiss as incidental, a geographer's perversion.

An indisputable fact of societal evolution is that when we examine individual societies or cultures, their history appears characterised by collapses, discontinuities, catastrophes and disjunctions. On the face of it, such breaks and reversals would seem to quash any hopes of establishing a broad evolutionary trend towards greater societal complexity. A solution to this dilemma, though, was published by Sahlins and Service as long ago as 1960. As Newson has pointed out, their argument is of great potential interest to the geographer. In relation to what will be argued here, part of its importance stems from the light which it sheds on the twin questions of how the process of societal change was organised in space and how this organisation in space contributed to the very process of change. At the core of their argument is their distinction between two forms of cultural evolution: specific and general. Specific evolution consists of the developments that we can see taking place amongst specific cultures in particular areas or environments, and represents a process of cultural adaptation and, therefore, of divergence. At this level, cultural change could be as much about regress as about progress. Indeed, at this level, there need not be change of any sort after a point, only stagnation. General evolution meanwhile, is a more abstracted concept and deals with the overall movement of societal systems towards greater complexity of order, a complexity measured in terms of higher forms of organisation and higher forms of energy capture. In their own words, whilst 'specific evolution is the production of diverse species, general evolution is the production of higher forms' (Sahlins and Service, 1960, p. 19). By making this simple distinction, Sahlins and Service were able to resolve a paradox that had inhibited earlier attempts to build 'progressive' models of socio-cultural evolution, a paradox created by the misguided attempts to create models of general evolution through the narrative history of individual or specific cultures. The latter comprises a catalogue of breaks, collapses and reverses in addition to phases of progress towards greater societal complexity. Only at the more general aggregate level do we find the basis for defining a continuous curve (possibly curvilinear) of increasing societal complexity.

The contrast between general and specific evolution has important implications for the geographical basis of societal change. These geographical implications are so germaine to the very process of societal change that Sahlins and Service drew out some of them for us. In other words, they are not implications that the geographer is left to infer entirely on his own or solely for his own ends. We can begin to understand what these implications are by restating a central proposition of their argument: that is, that societal evolution at the specific level is non-lineal – and in two senses.

It is non-lineal because of what is called the phylogenetic discontinuity of progress. The most advanced forms of societal organisation do 'not naturally beget the next stage of progress', so that the next stage sometimes 'begins in a different line' (Sahlins and Service, 1960, p. 99). Behind this principle of societal descent stands the belief that more highly organised forms of society are less adaptable than less organised forms, so that change has more potential and is more easily accomplished amongst the latter. Sahlins and Service make the comparison with Trotsky's 'privilege of historic backwardness' in an effort to convey the point that some of the really significant bifurcations in societal development – those that led on towards new levels of societal complexity – occurred just below rather than on the topmost branches of the societal tree.

But because specific cultures occupy specific territories, it also follows that not only are 'successive stages of progress not likely to go from one species to its next descendant' but they are 'not likely to occur in the same locality' (Sahlins and Service, 1960, p. 99). We are thus provided with a principle not just of phylogenetic discontinuity, but also, of local or geographical discontinuity. In a critical revaluation of Sahlins and Service's work, Segraves has suggested that this 'leap-frog' effect was flawed. Instead, she argues that the tendency for more advanced systems to be more ecologically generalised, that is, to rely on a wider array of resources would have made them more structurally stable and; therefore, more likely to advance to the next higher stage, thus directly challenging Sahlins and Service's ideas on evolutionary potential (Segraves, 1974, pp. 537–44). However, without disputing her assertion that more advanced socio-cultural systems are associated with higher levels of ecological generalisation and that this conferred greater structural stability, I would read a quite opposite conclusion from it. The weakness of Segraves's interpretation is that she talks solely in terms of a static system. Greater ecological generalisation does, indeed, mean greater structural stability and greater survival probability at this level of organisation. But when base conditions alter radically – perhaps through environmental change or the development of new technologies – this greater stability becomes a greater handicap because adaptability to new conditions and opportunities can be inversely related to the structural stability gained by being more ecologically adapted. In what Bateson called the economics of flexibility, the exploitation of all possible niches leaves ecologically generalised societies with few areas of 'unused freedom', no budget of flexibility (Bateson, 1972, p. 505). It is this fact, coupled with the ongoing change in base conditions, that explains the tendency, sooner or later, for new lead areas of socio-cultural advancement to come from behind.

We should note that Sahlins and Service did not see these principles of phylogenetic and local discontinuity as offering us a deterministic view of cultural evolution, a principle that enables us to determine the exact moment when cultures flowered or wilted. They simply acknowledged the inescapable fact that when the record of cultural evolution is surveyed, it reveals that societies which might claim to be in the van of cultural development at a general level did not remain there permanently but sooner or later, yielded their position to societies that had previously been less advanced. For this reason, we cannot assume that the most advanced societies at each stage of cultural evolution necessarily conceived the organisational changes that were to typify the next highest stage of cultural evolution. This is not to deny that advanced societies underwent radical or revolutionary changes, that they could be transformed from within, but only to restate again that less advanced societies (and less advanced sectors within more advanced societies) had greater potential for implementing or adopting radical changes in organisation and that history is littered with examples of this option being seized by these less advanced, peripheral societies. From a geographical point of view, this means that each era had its own map of societies that were most advanced and those that were less advanced, the loci of those with the most complex systems of societal organisation and the highest levels of energy-capture being progressively redrawn.

This changing map of societal complexity has recently been taken up and used as the foundation for a core–periphery view of societal evolution (Friedman and Rowlands, 1977, pp. 201–76; Ekholm, 1980, pp. 155–66; Ekholm, 1981, pp. 241–61; Friedman, 1982, pp. 175–96). Unlike Wallerstein's 'European world-system', this core–periphery structure is seen as extending back deep into prehistory, with each phase of societal development having its own disposition of core and peripheral areas. But as with Wallerstein's version, its characterisation rested on different societies being arranged into core and peripheral areas and these core and peripheral areas being bonded together via a system of unequal exchange such that 'the larger network is the condition of reproduction of the local system' (Friedman and Rowlands, 1977, p. 270). The earliest forms of ranked societies (that is, chiefdoms, early states, early civilisations) are seen as depending on the mobilisation of goods over a wide area for their very formation and survival as a socio-political system (Friedman and Rowlands, 1977, p. 270). Civilisations, Ekholm argued, whether those of prehistory or more recent times, need a resource base wider than that contained within their own bounds, so that we can define a system of civilisation 'by the existence of local spaces and a supralocal space to which only the centre has access and which, as such, defines the superiority of the centre as well as the under-developed nature of peripheral areas' (Ekholm, 1981, p. 249).

As with Sahlins and Service's study, this recent debate over the core–periphery basis of all societal systems sees cultural evolution as involving discontinuity at a local or specific level but continuity at a general level. Again, this apparent paradox is explained away by dividing the problem into a combination of spatial discontinuity (specific evolution) and temporal continuity (general evolution) (Ekholm, 1981, p. 243). Taking spatial discontinuity first, core–periphery systems are seen as existing in a state of geographical flux, with new core areas growing and then decaying (Friedman and Rowlands, 1977, p. 269) and leaving what Ekholm called 'underdevelopment in its path' (Ekholm, 1981, p. 248). This shifting of core areas invariably meant that new core areas were raised out of old peripheral areas. However, there is no clear attempt to relate such change, even in a partial or contributory sense, to the greater evolutionary potential of peripheral or less advanced areas. Friedman notes only the inner conflict of core areas, conflicts that eventually precipitated their decline or collapse (Friedman, 1982, p. 182). Ekholm too, refers explicitly to the internal contradictions that afflicted core areas (Ekholm, 1981, p. 252) but he also concedes that external conflict – or conflict between cores – was equally instrumental in bringing about change (Ekholm, 1981, p. 252). As newly-emergent core areas were simply peripheral areas that had turned dependency into ascendency and as declining core areas were areas whose ascendency had given way to dependency and peripherality, we can see this competitive striving between core areas as entirely compatible with, indeed, as enlarging on, the ideas put forward by Sahlins and Service on the role of peripheral areas in the generation and propulsion of societal change.

As regards the matter of general evolution, Friedman *et al* emphasise that despite the transient nature of individual examples, core–periphery systems were always present so that we can speak of a structural continuity in the way societal systems were organised. This does not mean that they discard the whole idea of evolution. On the contrary, they use the term liberally. The meaning which they attach to it though, differs significantly from the meaning given to it by Sahlins and Service and requires careful statement. The main source of difference is not so much to do with what evolution involved – like Sahlins and Service, they talk of a shift towards more complex societies, meaning more hierarchical order, more internal differentiation, more extensive and intensive systems of exchange and greater levels of energy capture – as with what they chose to stress (Friedman and Rowlands, 1977, p. 270). What seems to matter more to them is the pervasiveness of core–periphery systems at all times in the history of socio-cultural development, with core areas or civilisations always being at the centre of wider societal systems that extended out to embrace organisationally less-advanced societies. In this sense, there is no evolution but merely reorganisation. For this reason, they reject outright any suggestion that cultural evolution can be reduced to stages based on forms of societal organisation, or bands, tribes, chiefdoms and states (Friedman and Rowlands, 1977, pp. 267–9; Ekholm, 1981, pp. 248–9). Giddens too, sees the interconnection between different types of society, across what he calls time–space edges, as invalidating the whole idea of societal order passing through distinct stages of development (Giddens, 1981, p. 83). His own response is to emphasise the need for seeing societal systems as structured around the intersection between their allocative and authoritative resources, with change occuring via historical episodes that are allowed to have a direction in themselves but not, it seems, one that consistently maintains itself from episode to episode (Giddens, 1981, p. 82). Friedman, Rowlands and Ekholm meanwhile, prefer to talk of phases or epochs when particular 'structures of processes' (Friedman and Rowlands, 1977, p. 267) or 'specific mechanisms' (Ekholm, 1981, p. 256) operated, rather than stages when the particular forms or institutions created by these processes existed. Friedman and Rowlands see their ideas as providing an epigenetic view of socio-cultural evolution, that is, a view in which the living forms (core-periphery structures) and the means by which they were established did not alter over time. Instead, society is always being reborn in the same embryonic form.

Such an analysis seems designed to frustrate the geographer. They construct an intrinsically geographical view of societal evolution, one in which core–periphery systems are being continually relocated in space, yet whilst the determining processes and mechanisms are allowed to change, the broad geographical forms are not. We are offered a geography rich in process but not appearances, a geography of static forms in which the spatial structuring of societal process is always the same. To an extent, my disagreement with such a view is simply a matter of where we place the emphasis. Friedman *et al* concede that societal systems move towards greater complexity over time, but decide that, all things considered, it is more significant that societal structure does not deviate from a core–periphery form once such a form had been established back in the third millenium BC. Yet arguably, we can only reduce societal order to an unchanging form if we talk about core–periphery structures in the crudest possible way, as a generic term for any sort of centralised system, and ignore the way such systems evolved morphogenetically into larger, more integrated forms. For the geographer, no less than for others, the emergence of these larger, more integrated, systems of spatial order must form the basis of any evolutionary perspective. Elucidating the stages or phases through which they passed also enables us to establish an explicitly geographical basis for societal change. If we take note of Sahlins and Service's principles of phylogenetic and local discontinuity, then we are provided with the assumption that change in the nature of societal order is both more likely and easier in peripheral areas – peripheral in both an organisational and geographical sense – simply because, being less complex or ordered sectors of a system, and with greater reserves of flexibility, they are better able to make forward adaptations. I stress that this sort of change at the margins, whether achieved through outward expansion into new sub-systems that prove regenerative or by an upward shift to new levels of inter-societal interaction and integration, is not to be seen as the only form of change, but it is a type with which the geographer is peculiarly well equipped to deal.

Stages of Human Spatial Order

In an important paper for the geographer entitled 'Time, Space and Polity', Renfrew has drawn attention to the historical link between the structural organisation of a society and its organisation in space (Renfrew, 1977, pp. 89–112; cf. Bobek, 1962, pp. 218–47). On this basis, we can expect anthropological schemes of societal order to double as a scheme of their spatial order. The most widely-accepted scheme conceives societal evolution in terms of a four-stage model: bands, egalitarian tribes, chiefdoms and state-systems (Service, 1971; Flannery, 1976, pp. 96–118). Each of these successive stages can be seen as constituting a quantum or qualitative jump in societal complexity over the previous stage, with increases in both the scale and elaboration of societal order and in the degree of energy-capture. It is a scheme that captures and expresses the overall trend of societal evolution towards a greater scale of integration and with it, greater differentiation, functional specialisation and hierarchisation. It is also one that can be matched with Renfrew's 'building-block' ideas on societal organisation with their emphasis on its fundamentally cellular and modular structure and on evolution through their integration into larger, more hierarchically-ordered systems (Renfrew, 1977, pp. 104–5). The idea of an organisational succession through bands, egalitarian tribes, chiefdoms and states, though, is not without its critics or its rival schemes (for summary, see Redman, 1978, pp. 201–5). A great deal of dispute, for instance, surrounds the validity of having a distinct tribal category (Fried, 1975, pp. 98–9). For some, it is a matter of whether they can be effectively distinguished from bands. For others, it is a matter of whether they can be effectively distinguished from chiefdoms. The geographer, though, cannot overlook the fact that bands are associated with a system of societal order that is constantly adjusting itself in space whilst tribes are linked to a stable, place-specific system or the fact that tribes, like bands before them, can be typified as a uniform and homogeneous system whereas chiefdoms introduce an element of hierarchy and centrality. In any scheme of historical spatial order, such differences clearly warrant distinction.

A criticism of the 'stages' approach which cannot be so easily

deflected is that whilst it provides us with a plausible scheme of
societal development down to the formation of early states, it
offers no insight into the vast accumulation of human history or
development thereafter. Its critics have argued, and reasonably so,
that if an organisational approach cannot say anything about
change in, say, European society following the emergence of the
early states system between the seventh and tenth centuries AD,
then it fails as a worthwhile approach to societal systems in
general. The way out of this impasse is to recognise the need to
adjust our perspective and to appreciate that once early states had
formed, organisational adjustments took a new direction. The
character of early states, including their spatial order, was quite
different from that which began to emerge over the sixteenth and
seventeenth centuries. States continue as political units but the
regulated character of early states and their institutional forms
began to give way as the organising force behind societal systems
and their spatial order. In time, they were transcended in this
latter role by a narrower economic mechanism, – the price-fixing
market – that worked itself out both within and beyond state
bounds, slowly integrating state systems into a still larger system.
As it did so, we find ourselves dealing with a system of societal
order that was realised through practice rather than concept. Such
a switch is best interpreted through the work of Polanyi (1944,
1968 and 1977).

Polanyi's ideas have no stated geographical dimension. Conclusions about the changing nature of spatial order, however, can be
readily inferred from them. Their central focus is the changing
nature of exchange systems and the institutional developments
that accompanied them. Adopting a perspective that encompassed
the full spectrum of societal formations, from primitive down to
modern societies, he envisaged a four-stage history of exchange:
reciprocal exchange, redistributive exchange, exchange via regulated markets and exchange via price-fixing (or self-regulating,
free or allocative) markets. Each of these different forms of
exchange can not only be correlated with a different phase or
phases of societal organisation, but can also be seen as an embodiment of the structures and processes around which the various
societal formations were developed. This was the reason why
Polanyi saw the study of exchange as being also a study of societal
integration. Thus, reciprocal systems of exchange were seen by

him as helping to bond together different sections within bands and tribes. Redistributive systems were seen as operating within the context of early ranked societies or chiefdoms, a movement of goods, people and ideas in and out of chiefly centres in such a way that it served to integrate the core and peripheral elements of the system. Likewise, the regulated market systems of the medieval period sprang from the matrix of closely defined, dependent relations between lord and vassal that lay at the heart of all feudal societies. Finally, price-fixing markets, with their allocative power over all factors of production (land, labour and commodities) signalled the emergence of societies that were structured and integrated through the market function, with the interaction of supply and demand detemining both the way in which the various factors were used and their interrelation. It was this expressed link between the prevailing system of exchange on the one hand and the dominant structures and processes of societal formations on the other, and the clear implications which these structures and processes had for spatial order, that encouraged Harvey to use Polanyi's history of exchange as the basis for his substantive history of urban spatial order (Harvey, 1973).

Polanyi's interest in the history of exchange derived from an ulterior interest in the history of the economy. His last, posthumously-published work was in fact entitled *The Livelihood of Man*. His stress on the enduring relationship between the prevailing form of exchange and societal integration has been misread by some as indicating his support for the now unfashionable Marxist view that societal structure invariably developed out of its economic base, so that change in the latter wrought change in the former. This would be incorrect. We miss a cardinal point of his entire thesis if we fail to appreciate how for Polanyi, the study of exchange in the very long term reveals a complete inversion of meaning. Although there is a sense in which he saw this inversion as under way once regulated markets began first to supplement and then to replace redistributive systems of exchange back in the medieval period, he located the critical threshold of change – the moment of capsize – in the eighteenth century when free markets began to take over rapidly from regulated markets. At this point, we move from what Polanyi saw as an economy embedded in society to a society embedded in economy (Polanyi, 1944, pp. 57–75; Polanyi, 1968, p. 149 and pp. 158–73; White, 1959, p. 329).

With this broad inversion in mind, it is difficult to accept Gregory's criticism that Polanyi saw societal evolution as the progressive realisation of a single principle, the market principle (Gregory, 1978, p. 113). The contrast between an economy embedded in society and a society embedded in economy is most sharply delineated in his comparison between the earliest systems of exchange and those of modern societies. His description of the former drew on anthropological ideas surrounding the ceremonial gift-cycle and its observed socio-politico-religious meaning. Indeed, for Polanyi, as for many anthropologists, this socio-politico-religious meaning outweighed any economic meaning, the latter being subsumed within the former. In effect, exchange was accessory to other aspects of societal organisation (Polanyi, 1968, pp. 10–11). Its structural character was that imposed on it by this wider context of meaning – a wider context which it clearly helps to signify. A slight but critical variant on this view eschews so-called levels of determination and simply assumes that the various component meanings of exchange – the social, political, religious and economic – were not yet disaggregated in the way they appear to the modern mind but were conflated into a single, gross meaning (cf. Sahlins, 1968, p. 15). By comparison, the organisation of modern societal systems is seen by Polanyi as something determined through the workings of price-fixing markets. What he calls the commodity fictions of land and labour were taken to market no less than commodities actually produced for market and control over their use allocated out between competing ends. The structuring of economic, social and spatial relations were all realised through the market-place. There is nothing controversial in this suggestion. If anything, what distinguishes Polanyi's contribution to the debate is his insistence that early society did not possess either an innate market mentality or a propensity to barter for gain. For this reason, he did not regard the emergence of price-fixing markets out of the regulated markets of the medieval period as a natural or inevitable development. Rather were they a change in the direction of development, an abberation even. Moreover, they were a late development. He sees that their penetration into land, labour and commodities only became widespread during the Industrial Revolution of the eighteenth and nineteenth centuries. In other words, the economy as we know it was 'an instituted process', a product of the eighteenth century at the earliest.

Fused together, stock ideas on the organisational development of society and Polanyi's ideas on the changing nature of societal integration provide us with a preliminary five-stage history of spatial systems: bands, egalitarian tribes, chiefdoms, the regulated or feudalised systems that emerged with the early states and, finally, the market-based systems of more recent centuries (cf. Bobek, 1962, pp. 218–42). Concerned ostensibly with the problem of economic integration, Polanyi treats bands and tribes under a single heading, since both were associated with reciprocal systems of exchange. There are, however, other organisational differences which force us to distinguish between them, including those linked directly to the fact that whereas bands were maintained as small, mobile groups, tribes formed larger, sedentary groups. Polanyi's definition of redistributive systems and definitions of chiefdoms – such as that offered by Service – pose no problems of compatibility and can be treated as a single phase. Of all Polanyi's phases of exchange, that based on regulated markets has proved the most controversial. He wrote about it at great length and produced a number of important conclusions, not least of which was his concept of the port of trade (Polanyi, 1968, pp. 238–60). The main problem with his discussion is that it is too narrowly construed. He talks of new institutions and forms of integration that were growing but which, by his own admission, were still peripheral to society. It tells us far less about the organisation of society at large than his ideas on reciprocity and redistribution. We need to depend far more heavily on the wider anthropological and historical discussion of early states for relevant ideas on their distinct form of spatial order. Given the European context in which I propose to discuss these ideas, it is also necessary to consider how feudalism fits in with organisational concepts of the early state. The final phase in this proposed succession of spatial systems is defined for us by Polanyi's free-market system, when society no less than the economy became subject to the working-out of the bid-price mechanism. Since Polanyi wrote on this problem, there has been a great deal more work on it, delineating how earlier regulated markets were broken down and replaced by free markets, how such markets penetrated into the commodity fictions of land and labour as well as into those factors actually produced for market and the effect which this penetration had on the organisation of space.

2
What Season is this Place?

The earliest system of human spatial order was that developed by
hunter–gatherer bands of the palaeolithic and mesolithic periods.
Palaeolithic hunter–gatherers first made their way into southern
Europe at least 500 000 years ago (Dennell, 1983). There are
increasing indications that their further penetration into north-
west Europe occurred much sooner than was once thought. New
finds have started to revise old chronologies drastically. A recent-
ly-discovered site ,at Westbury-sub-Mendip, for instance, has
pushed back the earliest palaeolithic site in England from the
Anglian to the Cromerian stage of the Pleistocene, whilst new
finds in north-west Wales have aged the first Welshman from
approximately 20 000 years to about 180 000 years. Establishing
when this inaugural phase of human spatial order came to an end
poses fewer problems. The well-adapted hunter–gatherer economies that had emerged with the post-Pleistocene (8300 BC+)
changes in climate, flora and fauna, and which mark out the
mesolithic from the palaeolithic, gave way to more advanced and
settled economies between circa 6000–4000 BC and, in the process, to wholly new systems of spatial order.

Hunter–gatherer bands do not inscribe their spatial order on the
landscape in any durable way. Their small-scale use of temporary,
shifting camps; their emphasis on the more or less immediate
consumption of non-husbanded resources and their pronounced
lack of material consumption all combined to make their impact
on landscape the slightest of all societal systems. When archaeologists talk of palaeolithic and mesolithic sites, they generally have
in mind no more than a cooking hearth, or an area where stone
tools have been worked or a carcase dismembered. By their
inconsequential nature, such sites are poor data files. Even when
sifted thoroughly, they afford us with a glimpse of only one out of a
number of sites or camps occupied or used by a particular hunter–
gatherer band. They also provide us with a poor sample of the

24

total number of sites or camps that might have been generated within a region. Attempts to calculate what the known palaeolithic and mesolithic sites in an area represent as a sample of the total number that must have existed have produced embarrassingly low· figures (Butzer, 1982, p. 270). With these limitations of data, it would be unrealistic to suppose that the spatial systems, devised by hunter–gatherer bands can be reconstructed via the evidence for palaeolithic and mesolithic Europe. In the discussion that follows, therefore, use has been made of ethnographic parallels. There is nothing new in this approach. Prehistorians and anthropologists have long shared their ideas on such groups, so much so that it has effectively become a common debate. This sharing of ideas has been particularly evident in surveys of how hunter–gatherer bands organised themselves in space.

Hunter–gatherer Bands: An Organisational Perspective

In terms of the scale at which they operated, hunter–gatherer bands are the smallest of all societal systems. Indeed, they appear to be the only societal system to have positively restricted its growth as a system. When bands exceeded a certain critical threshold of population (usually around 500 people), they underwent a process of fission, with families budding off to form the nuclei of new bands. In effect, bands maintained their size at the minimum necessary to sustain themselves as a closed breeding population (Wobst, 1976, pp. 49–52). They can be regarded as a level of societal order at which the forces of disaggregation predominated over those of aggregation. Their persistent drift towards sociopolitical independence at the lowest practicable level suggests that they constitute a system with anarchic tendencies, responding to population growth through disconnection and dispersion, a tendency which conferred on them a powerful space-filling potential.

Hunter–gatherer bands also rank as the least complex of all societal systems. Their organisation displays a minimum of internal differentiation and specialisation. System integration did not rely on the operation of a single dominant control mechanism or control hierarchy, but worked itself out through a blend of shared beliefs and primitive exchange schemes. This simplicity of order led Renfrew to typify the earliest layer of human spatial order as being modular or unitary, homogeneous and interchangeable, each part seemingly cloned from the same cell. Such a definition holds true whether we are talking about the internal structure of particular systems or drawing a comparison between systems.

The distinctive character of hunter–gatherer bands can be attributed to their dependence on the direct consumption of the natural yield of the environment. This being the case, we need not be surprised to learn that they exhibit a lower level of energy-capture than any other societal system. Affluent they may have been, at least in the sense of having sufficient food and time enough for leisure, but the simplicity of their needs and the absence of any extracted or socially-concentrated surplus meant that the gross amount of energy actually harnessed and used was low. For the same reason, hunter–gatherer bands manifested a more generalised degree of environmental adaptation than other societal systems, being dependent entirely on what nature provided rather than on what could be made of nature in any given locality. The environmental opportunities that confronted them, and the conditions to which they had to adapt or die out, varied in a number of critical ways. Rank productivity was an obvious source of variation. Whether this productivity was sustained by a species-thin or a species-rich ecosystem was also important. No matter how productive a particular environment may have been in energy terms, it offered far less potential (and far less satisfaction) if it supported only a few species of plant and animal compared with one that offered a rich diversity of flora and fauna, a veritable smorgasbord for the hunter–gatherer gourmet. Whether a region was dominated by a single, uniform habitat or whether it was subdivided into a range of different habitats (forest, plain, riverine, etc.) was a further source of variation. Finally, there was the question of the way that the output of particular habitats was phased. Those whose output was sudden and fleeting obviously posed problems of adaptation quite different from those in which the growth cycles of the various component species were evenly phased over a season or even over the entire year.

Although some hunter–gatherer camps might be favourably located at the junction between a number of productive and conveniently-phased ecosystems so that their catchments were able to sustain their occupants on an all-year round basis, such honeypots were hardly representative. More usually, bands had to cope with habitats that offered sustenance only on a temporary or seasonal basis. For this reason, their survival depended not just on adaptation, but equally, on flexibility. They faced the task of establishing a cycle of annual movement that linked together habitats, seasons and resources in a carefully devised strategy of survival. Not to be in the right place at the right time meant extinction. But with each place came a different problem of adaptation. Different habitats had different carrying capacities and required different procurement strategies. Some bands coped by flexing their social structure even to the extent of fissioning in some habitats and fusing in others. Environmental factors though, were not the only source of social flux. An annual cycle of fission and fusion helped hunter–gatherer groups to maintain relations with other groups, enabling basic social processes such as the exchange of marriageable women to operate and vital inter-group rituals to be performed. In effect, the spatial dispersion imposed by the conditions of economic survival were countered, annually but briefly, by a ritual of spatial agglomeration imposed by the conditions of social and biological survival.

Taking these different dimensions of flux in turn, we can construct the spatial mobility of hunter–gatherer bands at two levels: between camps and around them. Quite naturally, the range of band movements, and the number of camps which they occupied during the course of the year depended on the sort of habitats available. More in an effort to highlight the potential contrasts than to summarise what they see as standard types, prehistorians have drawn a distinction between generalised and specialised environments. The former involved a mosaic of rich, diverse, closely-packed habitats and permitted smaller ranges and a greater degree of sedentarism. The latter meanwhile, comprised ecologically simpler habitats that covered vast areas. To exploit them and survive, bands were forced to cover hundreds of kilometres each year, linking together a series of seasonal base camps with a series of transit camps. At a more localised scale, hunter–gatherer bands also needed a spatial strategy in their exploitation of the catchment that surrounded each camp, whether a base or transit camp. In so far as the different camps were designed to exploit different habitats, these strategies would have varied, some being geared to the group-hunting of large game, perhaps at a suitable trap along their migration route, whilst others might involve the systematic harvesting of fruit, berries, nuts and such like from woodland or forest. In a few cases, procurement strategies might have involved a distinction being drawn between a semi-permanent base camp and outlying satellite camps, the latter used only to exploit particular resources or to perform specialised tasks like the preparation of stone tools. Clearly, the size of catchment exploited from a single camp would have been smaller (within a radius of 10 km) than one exploited by means of a main base camp supplemented by a periphery of satellite camps.

Fluctuations in the social composition of bands were triggered by the needs of particular environmental adaptations and by more purely social mechanisms though, in practice, it is not always easy, or desirable, to distinguish between these two factors. The most-discussed studies of flux amongst hunter–gatherers are those published for the !Kung bushmen of the Kalahari and the Ik and Mbuti of the Congo. Work on the former stresses the pre-eminent role of environmental adaptation. Faced with habitats of variable potential, the !Kung bushmen freely adjusted group size so as to optimise their subsistence strategy for each habitat. Their social flux was 'a very efficient and unconstrained mapping of people on to the landscape allowing maximum utilisation of scattered and variable resources' (Yellen and Harpending, 1972–3, pp. 246–7). Although confirming the importance of flux to band organisation, work by Turnbull on the Ik and Mbuti stressed the primacy of social mechanisms as the basic cause. Although he acknowledges that the different phases of flux were also phases of ecological adaptation, nevertheless, he prefers to see it as a means of minimising conflict, a grouping and regrouping of bands along lines of dissent rather than descent (Turnbull, 1968, pp. 136–7). Yet in a sense, his own admission that the main phases of social flux correspond with the main phases of ecological adaptation raises doubts about an explanation based so exclusively on conflict minimisation. One is left feeling that he has explained how bands fissioned and fused rather than why, and that an ecological explanation is still plausible.

There are, however, other social mechanisms that we can invoke to help explain this evident flux in band organisation. Being exogamous, bands needed social contact with other bands. Their marriage alliances, and the wider exchange system within which these alliances were set, functioned as a form of diplomacy. Bands that did not marry each other, stood in greater risk of fighting each other. The choice before them was one of marrying each other or fighting each other, that is, of marrying out or dying out. Regularly, perhaps annually, bands came together. Although serving the primary task of allowing bands to exchange marriage partners, these larger assemblages had other functions. Gifts other than women might be exchanged, food might be shared and rituals essential to the well-being or survival of the group were performed. There is an obvious logic in supposing that these larger groupings and social interactions would have taken place in habitats and seasons whose plenitude could sustain greater densities. But we should not ignore the equal case for presuming that such gatherings may have taken place in seasons of dearth, since this is when food-sharing – with its spreading of risk over a number of different territories – would have had a positive effect in helping bands to survive. In such instances, a band's exchange scheme, with its obligations and counter-obligations and regular inter-band gatherings, would have been an essential part of its ecological adaptation to particular environments: the more risk-laden the environment, the more it would have relied on the insurance offered by its alliance partners and the more it would have worked to specify precisely who these partners were (cf. Yengoyan, 1968, 199)

This appreciation of the way that bands systematically adjusted their size and composition as part of an overall strategy of survival raises fresh problems of definition. If, during the course of the year, bands could range considerably in size, then what can be taken as their 'typical' form? Our dilemma here springs in large measure from the very fact that the organisation of bands was of the utmost simplicity. This organisation is constituted largely in terms of process, with only a limited structural component. By this I do not mean that its process had no form or pattern (for that would mean that it had no organisation) but that its processes produced no durable cast, no permanent residue, since such an investment of energy would have inhibited the flux in time and space that lay at the very heart of band organisation. Process creates structure, it has been said, but once created, structure inhibits process. The distinction of band organisation lies in the fact that its processes did not become reified, transformed into bricks and mortar or wattle and daub, but remained something that can only be understood in processual terms. For this same reason, it is the only societal system whose organisational form shifted or changed as part of the very process by which it continued to reproduce itself: with both its social, economic and spatial relations being redefined in regular cycles of flux. Faced with this organisational fluidity, recent reviews of the problem have followed Steward and have distinguished between minimal and maximal bands: or between bands in their most disaggregated and aggregated forms respectively. The former (minimal bands) have been widely portrayed in the literature as the archetypal unit of band organisation. The minimal band comprises a group of between 25 and 100 persons. Its lower threshold of size, or around 25, has been observed in a variety of different habitats so it is unlikely that it had any connection with the ecological adaptation of bands. Rather is it more likely to have been the minimum size of group necessary for the successful transmission of cultural data between generations. (Wobst, 1974, p. 172). In function, the minimal band served as the standard residence group for the greater portion of the year. It was also the level of organisation at which bands established their territories, devised their strategies of survival and regulated their network of relations with other bands. By virtue of this apparent self-sufficiency as a unit of social, economic and political order, the minimal band has generally been accepted as the level at which bands should be defined as a societal system.

Maximal bands represented the larger social gatherings that took shape, albeit temporarily, when a cluster of minimal bands came together for the exchange of women and gifts and for food-sharing. For Wobst, they comprised the mating network within which minimal bands intermarried and reproduced themselves. Armed with this assumption, and taking into account the distances that minimal bands had to travel in order to access other such bands he reasoned that maximal bands needed to be of the order of approximately 175–475 if they were to provide their constituent groups with sufficient opportunity of finding marriage-partners and that, since these were devised as estimates of their minimum possible size, their actual size was more likely to be closer to about 475 than to about 175 (Wobst, 1976, p. 50). In actuality, work on maximal bands and mating networks suggests they averaged around 500.

The case for defining band organisation at the level of the minimal band rests on the cardinal assumption that they are independent units of societal order. The minimal band is seen as subsisting within itself, socially, economically and politically. Its relations with other bands are seen as external relations, a form of diplomacy. This belief in the systemic independence of the minimal band, though, has recently been questioned. Surprisingly, these doubts are not directed at its political independence, but at the assumption that it could survive socially and economically within itself. The taboo on incest meant that minimal bands could only survive if they established marriage-alliance schemes with other minimal bands. In other words, the relations embodied in these mating networks, relations that were given concrete expression through the seasonal or periodic appearance of maximal bands, define a level at which bands reproduced themselves as a breeding population. If we correlate these mating networks and maximal bands with the units through which the cultural and linguistic heterogeneity between bands manifested itself (see below, pp. 4–9), then this would also be the level at which bands reproduced themselves as cultural systems. There are grounds then, for following Wobst in seeing the mating network and with it, the maximal band, as an alternative level at which band organisation might be defined as a system of societal order. We should also bear in mind the stress which Marxist anthropologists especially now place on the significance of food-sharing between bands and on the role of gift-exchange and inter-band rituals in aiding the reproduction of their symbolic order (Godelier, 1975, p. 11; Bender, 1978, p. 210).

Hunter–gatherer bands: their spatial organisation

The spatial organisation of hunter–gatherer bands is so intrinsic to their maintenance and reproduction as a societal system that we could hardly define the latter without incorporating some reference to the former. For this reason, the previous section necessarily included some ideas on their spatial organisation. In exploring this aspect further, I propose to structure what I have to say around three basic themes: first, there is the intensity of their relationship with space as expressed through their density of occupation: second, there is the intensity of this relationship as

expressed through the notion of territoriality: and third, there is
the way in which they used spatial mobility to piece together the
seasonal or fleeting productivity of different habitats so as to
ensure all-year round survival.

The Search for Density Equilibria

Many discussions repeatedly emphasise that because hunter–
gatherer bands were so dependent on the natural yield of the
environment, they survived only through a carefully devised strategy of adaptation. These adaptations were, of necessity, complex
affairs, compounded of different habitats, procurement strategies
and dietary patterns. We can, however, reduce them to a single
measure by looking at the way in which bands adjusted their
density of occupation to fit in with the carrying capacity of particular habitats. Just as carrying capacities varied widely between
habitats and seasons, so too did densities of band occupation.
Bands could approach the problem in two ways. They could adjust
the size of the band or the size of its territory. As pointed out in
the previous section, changes in the size of bands were permissible
if only within socially-defined limits: the lower limit of about 25
being the minimum size necessary to ensure the continued transmission of cultural data between generations and the upper limit of
about 500 being around the practicable threshold at which a mating
network could be established between bands. Changes in the size
of band-territories were governed by a more complex set of
variables. The productivity of habitats and whether this productivity was based on a broad or narrow range of species was an
obvious input into the equation. But there were also purely social
factors as work. Band-survival depended on interaction with other
bands. To ensure a sufficient density of communication, they
needed to adopt a sufficient density of occupation. Working in the
opposite direction was a medley of social forces that not only
avoided the undue aggregation of bands but also acted to disperse
them. Superimposed on these seasonal fluctuations in the size of
bands and their territories was a further dimension of change
induced by long-term shifts in climate. In a continent like Europe,
these climatic shifts produced sharp fluctuations in the productivity
of habitats, not just between glacial and inter-glacial periods, but
also, between the late Pleistocene and post-Pleistocene or Holo-

cene periods (Clarke, 1976, especially pp. 450–68; Dennell, 1983, pp. 124–8). Band-densities would have adjusted themselves accordingly. Occasionally, such adjustments are detectable in the archaeological evidence. Work on the Klachenalbin in southern Germany found that whereas home or base camps for the middle and upper palaeolithic were set 40 km apart, those for the mesolithic were around 20 km apart.

This combination of short- and long-term variability in band-densities makes it impossible to talk of an average density. Instead, we are faced with a wide range of density equilibria, each one adapted to a particular habitat, a particular season and a particular phase in its environmental history. If we take surviving hunter–gatherer bands as a guide, these density equilibria ranged from as low as 0.002 persons per sq. km up to 0.8 persons per sq. km (Wobst, 1974, p. 170). Expressed in relation to area they represent territories which, for minimal bands, range from as large as 9400 per sq. km down to what could only be a local (and highly productive) catchment worked by a near-sedentary band. In deciding where along this broad spectrum of density equilibria would we find the hunter–gatherer bands of early Europe, we must first distinguish those of the palaeolithic from those of the mesolithic period. Considering the inter-glacial environments inhabited by them, and their dependence as much on highly mobile herds of big game as on foraging for plant food, we can expect bands of the middle and upper palaeolithic periods to have been associated with large, extensive territories and correspondingly low densities. Bands living in similar sorts of environment today have densities ranging from 0.5 to 0.005 persons per sq. km (Wobst, 1976, p. 50). We can expect palaeolithic bands to have maintained density equilibria somewhere within this range. In fact, Wobst himself has pointed out that:

> nothing in the archaeological record suggests higher population densities than 0.05 persons per sq. km during glacial intervals, not even in those areas of Eurasia which have received most attention from palaeolithic archaeologists" (Wobst, 1976, p. 50).

Just to illustrate his point, Clark's work on the hunter–gatherers of southern Scania during the younger dryas period (ecologically, a late glacial phase) produced a population estimate for the

Lyngby–Bromme–Segrebo (roughly southern Sweden, Denmark and Schleswig-Holstein) of around 3300, a figure which yields a density of about 0.05 persons per sq. km (Clark, 1975, p. 98).

In a stimulating revision of ideas on the mesolithic, Clarke stressed the sheer productivity of the temperate woodland that spread through much of southern and western Europe at the end of the last ice-age (8300 BC+) (Clarke, 1976, especially p. 464). Although its winter-shutdown posed problems, its richly-varied floral and faunal content enabled hunter–gatherer economies to become much more intensive and for their territories to become much smaller. Clarke does not put any figures to this trend, but he acknowledges the possibility that some mesolithic habitats, such as those developed around major riverine or estuarine systems (like those of the Danube or Rhone), could have been sufficiently productive all-year round to sustain hunter–gatherer bands on a near-sedentary basis. In these circumstances, minimal bands may have lived off annual territories less than 250 sq. km and maximal bands off territories less than 5000 sq. km. However, to appreciate this corkscrew-like evolution of territories fully, with bands becoming more and more prescribed in their range of annual movements over the mesolithic, we need to take account not just of the way that mesolithic habitats offered higher yields of edible resources, but equally, of the way that hunter–gatherer bands adopted more intensive techniques, such as fire-setting and selective culling, to an extent which makes it difficult to decide whether they practised food extraction or food production (Clarke, 1976, 456–7: Dennell, 1983, pp. 149–51).

The idea that hunter–gatherer bands maintained themselves in a state of equilibrium via a series of feedback mechanisms begs the question of how they accommodated growth. The temptation is to presume that they simply adjusted to new equilibria, as happened over the mesolithic. Arguably though, what we see taking place over the mesolithic is more than just an adjustment to new levels of equilibria. By intensifying the relationship between society and space, the sheer productivity of mesolithic environments had the effect of undermining specific feedback mechanisms that had earlier operated to control band-densities. Change became self-amplifying. By the end of the mesolithic period, we are faced not simply with bands packed more closely together, but with the prospect of a new system of spatial organisation, one geared to new goals and regulated by a different set of control mechanisms. Under normal conditions, the adaptability of bands worked towards organisational stability. This stability depended on a stable relationship being established between band-densities and the carrying capacity of environments, though opinion varies over whether band-densities were set at the approximate carrying capacity of environments (Birdsell, 1968, p. 230) or below it (Harris, 1977, p. 408). We can take this favourable balance between numbers and resources as the goal of their adaptive behaviour. In addition to changes in band composition, spatial mobility and a willingness to adapt their food-procurement strategies, bands regulated their relationship to the environment by employing simple forms of population control, including prolonged weaning and infanticide. It has been argued that had they not done so, larger and more sedentary concentrations of population would have emerged much sooner over the palaeolithic period (Harris, 1977, p. 403).

In stressing how bands used a variety of feedback mechanisms to maintain themselves in equilibrium with the carrying capacity of particular habitats, we must not strip them of all traces of dynamic change. After all, they have the distinction of pioneering the colonisation of virtually all the earth's surface. What is more, as an essentially Pleistocene system of societal adaptation, their occupation retreated and re-advanced in step with glacial and inter-glacial periods. Clearly, we need to ask how their stable and dynamic elements fitted together. The answer is provided by Wobst. Band-populations maintained density equilibria in their core areas but in peripheral areas, there was a tendency for growth as new bands budded off from established ones and took up new territories in the space that beckoned beyond (Wobst, 1974, pp. 152–3; Birdsell, 1968, p. 229). It is this restriction of growth to the outer margins of the band system, or the so-called open-donor system of growth, that conferred on it such an impressive space-filling capacity. We can only speculate whether the pioneer colonisation of Europe some 500 000 years ago, when hunter–gatherer bands moved into south-west Europe, was a straightforward overflow of bands from Africa, a movement triggered by a favourable climatic change or one that awaited the moment when hominids acquired the 'ability to map landscape in terms of mobility both of resources and neighbouring groups in the same mating network' and could, in consequence, cope with a new environment in which plant food was scarce but whose faunal content was sufficient (Dennell, 1983, p. 190). Vast new areas of Eurasia, including most of central, south-east and eastern Europe together with Russia, were colonised over the late Pleistocene period, an expansion of living space which Clark offered as an 'illustration of their dynamic possibilities' (Clark, 1983, p. 73). Finally, at the end of the Pleistocene and the amelioration of environmental conditions, came the final push into Scandinavia.

This simple core–periphery structuring of band-dynamics, with those in core areas maintaining themselves at an equilibrium level and those of peripheral areas spawning new bands, eventually broke down over the mesolithic period. The rich woodland habitats that now spread over southern and western Europe during the immediate post-Pleistocene period offered a 'broad spectrum of relatively localised resources' (Harris, 1977, p. 409) and encouraged higher densities of resource exploitation, in core areas no less than in peripheral areas. These higher densities were inevitably accompanied by reduced patterns of mobility which, in turn, led to shortened birth intervals and higher rates of population growth. Harris talks of a self-amplifying system of change, with the onset of population growth fostering still more intensive strategies of resource exploitation, still less mobility and still more population growth (Harris, 1977, pp. 409–10). In effect, what scholars like Harris are suggesting is that the environmental changes of the Holocene induced systemic change, with not just a denser population but a slow drift towards sedentarism, larger tribe-like formations and food production as opposed to food extraction.

Did Bands Possess Space?

Just as the density at which bands occupied different habitats varied, so also, did their feeling of association with these habitats. Generally speaking, the greater their density of occupation, the greater their feeling or sentiment towards that space. One of the strands threaded through the argument of this book is that the changing relationship between society and space underwent a gradual intensification, one manifest through a progressive clarification of rights in land. With such an extensive relationship between society and space, bands understandably had the least-defined concept of space as something that could be both used and possessed. In so far as they habitually used an area, then they can be described as having territories. However, it does not follow that they related to these territories through a concept of territoriality. If we define territoriality as a sense of spatial closure and exclusivity of possession, then it was weakly developed or absent in those areas where bands were spread thinly. Australian aborigines, for instance, had a symbolic or totemic hearth area, their estate, to which they had a strong bond of attachment, but the rest of their territories comprised open, loosely-defined and, in some cases, overlapping or criss-crossing ranges (Stanner, 1965, p. 2; Hiatt, 1968, pp. 98–100). Lack of a strong sense of territoriality has also been noted amongst other surviving hunter–gatherers, for instance, Eskimoes and Kalahari bushmen (Martin, 1973, p. 435). This lack of a strong sense of territoriality can of course be interpreted functionally. In poor, risk-laden environments, having open territories or the license to move freely into adjacent territories served as an insurance against poor seasons. Arguably, we can expect similar sorts of loosely-defined and weakly conceptualised territories amongst the palaeolithic bands that inhabited the open, low-yield habitats of inter-glacial Europe.

We are more likely to find a developed sense of territoriality in habitats that supported a dense packing of bands. 'When localised resources became all-important they had to be defended and groups became more territorial, more exclusive and more antagonistic to others in the neighbourhood' (Reynolds, 1973, p. 472; see also Harpending and Davis, 1977, p. 275). In these more productive situations, we can expect bands to have become more overtly territorial in their behaviour, to have established clearly-defined boundary-markers, to have performed boundary rituals and to have defended their territory as an area over which they had exclusive rights of use. Without ruling out the possibility that there may have been palaeolithic bands living in select tropical ecologies whose density of spatial packing may have been sufficient to induce a strong sense of territoriality amongst them, this is unlikely to have been the case with the palaeolithic bands of Europe for the latter generally lived at low densities. Only when the richer ecologies and higher populations of the mesolithic period developed is it likely that European hunter–gatherers became sufficiently crowded to induce a strong sense of territoriality, with a clearly-signalled segmentation of the landscape into exclusive territories and their defence through boundary-markers, ritual and, if these failed, warfare. For this reason, we can see this heightened sense of territoriality as part of the intensifying relationship between society and space that marked the gradual breakdown of the European band system over the mesolithic period. It is an intensification which North and Thomas incorporated into their proposed evolution of property rights during the transition from hunting and gathering to the earliest farming, with the common open-for-all property of the former giving way to territorialised exclusive communal property of the latter (North and Thomas, 1977, p. 235). They see the population growth which triggered off this intensification and clarification of property rights as an independent variable. But whether we share this view or hold to the alternative of seeing population growth as a response to the richer ecologies of the mesolithic, it does not alter the basic assumption that hunter–gatherers developed a more intensive and territorialised relationship with their environment over the mesolithic and that this was a prelude to the emergence of farming.

How Band Territories Were Shaped

The precise strategy of resource exploitation that bands adopted obviously had a formative influence on their spatial order. Their reliance on the natural rather than a husbanded yield of the environment meant they operated within set parameters. The productivity yield of most environments is subject to seasonal fluctuations. These fluctuations are most marked in temperate and polar latitudes where seasons of relative abundance are contrasted with a 'shut-down' of the system during winter, but even in the tropics, the alternation of wet and dry seasons can redefine potential productivity quite sharply. Hunter–gatherers necessarily responded to this seasonality in their susbsistence base by being highly mobile, migrating from one area to another in order to maintain an all-year supply of food. Their movements were influenced by a number of considerations. Not unreasonably, they sought habitats that not only offered them a sufficient and reliable source of food, but equally, a diverse mix of edible resources (Schrire, 1972, p. 657; Harpending and Davis, 1977, p. 280). In practice, satisfying these expectations involved combining the resources of wholly different habitats. In seeking out different habitats, we can expect them to have operated 'at right angles, as it were, to a series of parallel ecological zones' (Schrire, 1972, p. 657), their adaptation being as much as matter of spatial discordance as of accordance. For the same reason, we can assume that extensive, specialised ecosystems meant large migratory ranges for hunter–gatherers, whereas a mosaic of small generalised ecosystems would have enabled them to survive within comparatively small migratory ranges (Harpending and Davis, 1977, p. 283). However, there would have been little gain from such spatial mobility if each of the habitats across which they moved had its productivity phased during the same part of the year. Survival for hunter–gatherers meant exploiting habitats whose output was phased in such a way as to ensure their sustenance all-year round. In the context of this sort of strategy, a habitat characterised by relatively low productivity but which provided a sufficiency of food during the lean months of winter, was just as critical as one which provided an abundance of food during the remainder of the year. (see Figure 2.1).

The exact reconstruction of these spatial strategies using evidence for palaeolithic Europe is impossible. Confronted with a scatter of camps and activity areas strewn across a variety of habitats, a scatter which is far from complete, there is no way in which we can elicit from such data the precise movements of a single band. And yet patently, to treat individual sites as closed or complete systems rather than as components of a wider system would be to misrepresent their character. Bands are as much an adaptation **through** space as **in** space. If we are unprepared to speculate on the processes of the former, the more verifiable structures of the latter – the hearths, kill-sites, work areas, chipping floors, etc. – will stand devoid of context. Impelled by a growing appreciation of the need to structure band systems in space, more and more prehistorians have offered reasoned reconstructions of band movements.

A well-researched example is provided by Butzer's study of mid-Pleistocene sites at Torralbe and Ambrone in Spain. Torralbe and Ambrone are situated in a low-level pass that strikes through the Sierras that divide Old from New Castile and which must have afforded a natural route for migrating herds of herbivores. For Butzer, the density and character of camps discovered at Torralbe

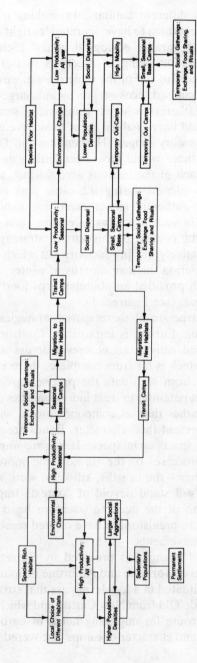

FIGURE 2.1 *Hunter-Gatherers and the Integration of Ecological Space*

and Ambrone point to them being 'a focus of seasonal camp-sites situated along this animal migration route between winter pastures (grassland and pine parkland) to the south and summer pastures (steppe grassland) to the north' (Butzer, 1982, pp. 235–6). Such camps would have been occupied during the spring and autumn when migrating herds were on the hoof. With such large and predictable movements of animals, this may have been a time of year when larger social groupings came together. During winter and summer, however, other procurement strategies were needed. Bands probably broke up into small groups that diffused themselves widely over the surrounding terrain, relying on a wide range of plant food and small mammals or birds exploited or hunted from a network of small, temporary camps (Butzer, 1982, pp. 235–7). Clark's survey of late glacial hunter–gatherers on the north German plain and in southern Scania provides a different approach to the problem. On the basis of artifact distribution, he divided the area into three broad territories: a Swidry–Chwalibogowician zone extending from the Warta to the Nieman, an Ahrensburgian zone extending from the Belgian Limbourg to Schleswig-Holstein, Mecklenburg and Brandenburg, and a Lyngby–Bromm–Segebro zone covering Schleswig-Holstein, Denmark and southern Sweden. Clark calls these 'social territories' rather than simply 'culture areas' so as to make the point that they were areas over which bands must have operated. Late glacial conditions throughout the area supported little more than tundra. The prime source of sustenance for hunter–gatherers consisted of reindeer herds supplemented by a narrow range of plant food and, along rivers and coasts, by the hunting of wildfowl, sea mammals or fishing. As a cold-climate area, we can expect hunting to have outweighed foraging as a source of food. Possibly as much an adaptation to the low productivity of the environment as to the need for mobility, Clark sees local hunter–gatherers organising themselves into fairly small bands or what he calls 'micro' bands (15–20 persons) for most of the year. Beyond these general points, he sees the annual movement of bands in each of his three zones as involving a different strategy of adaptation. Thus, writing about bands of the Hamburgian and Ahrensburgian zone, he argued for their fairly close dependence on reindeer herds 'the year round' (Clark, 1975, p. 93). The migratory movements of reindeer in this particular zone are fairly easy to predict, involving a trek southwards during autumn, possibly as far as the central or southern German Highlands, with a reciprocal movement back northwards in spring. Although site evidence does suggest a large-scale slaughtering of deer when they were *en route* for their summering and wintering grounds, but especially the latter, Clark prefers to see the annual movement of bands as mirroring those of deer, with a sequence of base-camps established along their migration routes rather than intersecting them at one or two critical moments in the year. Unlike the palaeolithic bands of central Spain, those of northern Europe had fewer alternative sources of food.

The advent of the mesolithic altered the problem in two ways. First, there is comparatively more field data. Second, recognition of the mesolithic as a separate phase of prehistory stems from the climatic amelioration that set in around 8300 BC and which marked the end of the Pleistocene. As climate improved, the ice and tundra which had covered much of central and northern Europe retreated northwards. In their place, a suite of new vegetation climaxes spread over Europe. Viewing the continent from the Mediterranean northwards, these new climaxes consisted of Mediterranean mixed woodlands, then temperate deciduous woodlands, mixed deciduous and conifers, then coniferous forests and, finally, in the far north, vestigial tundra areas (Clarke, 1976, p. 464). The emergence of these new ecologies called forth new strategies of adaptation. Instead of the relatively easy task of hunting large herds of migrating deer on open ground, or when they were funelled through narrow valley gaps, European hunter–gatherers now faced the altogether-different task of hunting in woodland or forest habitats and stalking a wider range of animals that moved in smaller groups or individually. Patience and skill were now at a premium. But these new habitats involved more than a change in skill and temperament. As Clarke has stressed, ecosystems like the Mediterranean mixed woodland and the temperate woodlands further north and west were rich in edible resources. Furthermore, they were supplemented locally or regionally by the exceptionally rich ecologies that formed around freshwater marshes (for instance, the Fens and the Hungarian marshes) and deltas (for instance, the Danube, Rhine and Rhone). These new habitats offered the hunter–gatherer an abundant and reliable supply of vegetable food. So much so, that Clarke estimated that as much as 60–80 per cent of their diet probably now came from vegetable food in one form or another (Clarke, 1976, p. 450). Only in the far north, where uniform stands of conifers and tundra preserved the species-poor environment of the late glacial period is hunting likely to have persisted as the prime source of food. Elsewhere,

> the composite abundance and interlocking seasonality of large groups of plant food-species, which meant that there was hardly a month in which a new combination of edible gums, saps, barks, shoots, stems, buds, flowers, fruits, nuts, roots, tubers, rhizomes, corns, bulbs, mosses, seaweeds, water-plants or fungi was not available, waiting immobile, predictable, for the plucking (Clarke, 1976, p. 457).

Overall, the pattern of productivity and its exploitation generated a saucer-shaped pattern of settlement in the continent as a whole, with the greatest opportunities in the central areas and poorest in the glacial or littoral environments that formed the rim (Clarke, 1976, p. 468).

These richer ecologies meant smaller annual ranges. The palaeolithic hunter–gatherers who established summer camps in the Flachenalb probably wintered in the Rhine valley, 150–200 km away. Those in the Swabian Alps may have wintered at sites over 700 km away. By comparison, the mesolithic bands that summered in the Flachenalb possibly wintered in the sheltered valley of the Donau, only 50 km away (Gamble, 1978, p. 180). Attempts to estimate the annual ranges of mesolithic communities in Britain suggest equally-limited movements (see, for example, Coles, 1971, p. 362). Such attempts to reconstruct the annual range of hunter–gatherers are, of course, conjectural. Underlying them are basic assumptions about how, in the variegated environments of post-Pleistocene Europe, hunter–gatherers' bands could best ensure their survival. Invariably, the conclusions produced juxtapose the rich, open hunting-grounds provided by the summer grazing of ungulate herds in upland areas or the easy pickings provided by their predictable migrations in and out of these areas during spring and autumn, with the well-wooded habitats of low-lying valley or littoral areas: the former offered large quantities of meat, hides and antler bone for tools, whilst the latter offered an autumnal bounty of plant food for immediate consumption plus larders of storable food like hazelnuts, and the opportunity for securing food (such as fish, molluscs, wildfowl and other small game) during the hungry gap that stretched from the time that temperate woodland ecologies shut down for winter until their renewal of growth in spring.

The annual territory ranged over by bands forms only one level at which we can discuss their mobility. There also existed a series of more localised systems pivoted on each of the base or temporary camps that they occupied during the course of the year. These localised systems were governed by two broad principles. First, there was the distance over which they were prepared to travel in order to obtain plant-food or to hunt. Resource exploitation for bands, no less than for more recent communities, was distance-dependent. Constrained by the cost of exploiting resources in terms of both the time and energy expended, the typical band tended to work within a 10-km radius of their camp, at least for those resources that were used on an habitual basis (Jarman, 1972, p. 713; Gamble, 1978, pp. 158–9). This figure will have been the same for both palaeolithic and mesolithic bands, notwithstanding the differences in the size of their annual territories. The second principle at work was their concern to maximise their returns by exploiting those resources that were most abundant or appealing. Combined, these two principles helped to determine a site-catchment or site-exploitation territory around each camp (Jarman, 1972, p. 707). They also provide us with a basis for analysing such catchments. In practice, such analyses have ranged from attempts to establish the range of food accessible within a 10-km radius (Jarman, 1972, pp. 713–16) to those which stress a more ecological approach by linking the energy expended to that obtained (Foley, 1977, pp. 163–9). Logically, only where the extraction of resources offered a positive energy balance over the energy expended, a balance measured by what Foley calls **isocals** (Foley, 1977, p. 184), can a site-catchment analysis provide any real indication of what might have been exploited as opposed to what was available.

The Socio-Cultural Consequences of Band Mobility

We have already seen how hunter–gatherer bands adjusted their size as part of their adaptation to particular habitats. Other aspects of their societal organisation can be tied to the problems posed by their organisation in space. Two aspects in particular are worth further comment: the implications which their dispersed organisation in space had for the survival of each band as a biological unit and the implications which it also had for their differentiation and survival as socio-cultural units.

Bands and the search for marriage partners

As exogamous groups, minimal bands could not survive biologically without establishing relations or alliances with other bands for the purpose of exchanging marriage partners. In fact, these marriage alliances provided the initial basis for the development of primitive exchange schemes, women being the first item of exchange, the first gift. As their exchange of marriageable women became supplemented and even complemented by the exchange of material goods (including food, stone axes, items of display like beads, feathers) so a ceremonial gift cycle emerged out of these marriage alliances. But dependent on a strategy of food extraction that required a high degree of spatial mobility, this extra need to interact periodically with other bands – no matter how briefly – obviously introduced a new constraint or distortion into their annual cycle of movements. At some point during the year or perhaps every few years, minimal bands within the same mating network or exchange system came together. It is for this reason that we can talk of maximal bands, the latter being temporary gatherings of minimal bands at which marriageable women and material gifts were exchanged. Modern band survivals are known to travel hundreds of kilometres solely to exchange women. Precisely where and when bands came together was influenced by ecological factors. Large stable groupings were possible where and when food was locally abundant though – as noted earlier – there is an equally convincing case for arguing that some bands may have used the opportunity of such gatherings as an opportunity for sharing food in precisely opposite circumstances, or when available food was scarce.

In so far as bands depended on their exchange system for a supply of marriageable women, the maintenance of contacts with other members of its mating networks was a matter of biological necessity. In environments that supported only low band densities and where, in consequence, annual ranges were extensive, the problems of sustaining these contacts were acute. Bands were able to overcome their search problems here by having alliances with each other that were fixed and determinate. With higher densities of settlement though, inter-band contact became more predictable, allowing them to have looser, more transitory alliances, though always from within the same pool of neighbouring bands. Whatever, their frequency or durability, such alliances were regulated by fixed rules as to who should be exchanged from within each band. Precisely when pair-bonding and marital exchange began can only be guessed, but we are on reasonably safe ground in inferring that most upper palaeolithic and mesolithic bands probably operated an elementary form of marriage alliance: sister-exchange or some form of cross-cousin matching. Such schemes represent direct or symmetrical forms of exchange because they involved a direct and complementary exchange between groups, either simultaneously (as with matrilateral schemes) or over time (as with patrilateral schemes). Direct or symmetrical exchange is of interest to the student of spatial order because it has generally been linked with dual organisation. Considered solely in relation to marital exchange, dual organisation consisted of pairing bands into opposed or complementary marriage classes. In some cases, it involved all the minimal bands within a mating network being assigned to opposite halves or moieties. In the celebrated case of the Australian aborigines, these moieties were further sub-divided into sections or phratries, with phratries from each moiety being tied to phratries from the opposite moiety (Yengoyan, 1968, p. 194; Fox, 1967, pp. 184–99). At those points or times in the year when they came together, bands from different moieties tended to occupy spaces within the settlement that were symbolically opposed in a corresponding manner (inner–outer, east–west), the dichotomised structure of their social order being imprinted on their spatial order. Although some regard dual organisation as 'the integral result of the inner symmetry of all social transactions, of the reciprocity of services, without which no primitive community could exist' (Malinowski, 1926, p. 25) and therefore, as something that emanates and draws its meaning from the nature of exchange systems, we cannot hope to resolve its origins without viewing it in the context of its wider use. For this reason, a fuller discussion of how dual organisation affected primitive spatial order has been reserved until later (see pp. 50–6).

Bands as 'Clusters of Idiosyncracy'

With other societal systems, their organisation in space represents only one facet of a complex multi-dimensional structure. What is more, it is not necessarily a perspective that manifests all the essential processes or relations present in the system at large. Possibly because of their organisational simplicity, this 'iceberg' factor is not such a problem with band systems, their organisation in space revealing practically everything about them as a societal system. More to the point, it can be argued that fundamental aspects of their organisation as a societal system derive from their organisation in space. This is most effectively shown by Wobst's work on the implications which their dispersion in space had for their constitution as band systems and his conclusion that such systems are likely to emerge only at certain levels of band density.

Wobst believed that mating networks needed to consist of at least eighteen minimal bands of about 25 persons each if they were to survive as a breeding population. In an ideal world, these minimal bands would have disposed themselves hexagonally within each habitat. Although this would have minimised gross distances, those located at the geographical edge of the system would have faced greater problems of access to other bands than those more centrally placed. In environments characterised by lower than average densities and large, sprawling territories, the existence of closed mating networks would have presented these geographically peripheral bands with acute problems for to gain access to bands on the geographically opposite edge of the network would have entailed movements on a prohibitive scale. A more realistic solution would be for each band to centralise itself within its own mating network, allying itself with those neighbouring bands that were most proximate. In these circumstances, we can expect to find 'continuously distributed, partially-overlapping mating networks' (Wobst, 1976, p. 53). Only where habitats supported a relatively dense packing of band territories are we likely to find closed mating networks, with groups of minimal bands interbreeding via a single mating network

The distinction between open and closed mating networks, and their direct link with band densities, is important not simply for what it tells us about mating networks *per se*, but also, for what it tells us about the flow of information between bands and their cultural differentiation. We have already seen how Renfrew has typified the most primitive form of societal organisation as being unitary, modular and homogeneous. If we concentrate solely on structural form – which is all Renfrew intended – then this typification is perfectly acceptable. Each band unit was so alike structurally, that they could be freely interchanged without endangering or altering the nature of the system as a whole. However, if we broaden our perspective, there is a sense in which their interchangeability needs qualification. The exchange of women, and the ceremony built up around it, was the prime source of communication between bands and, therefore, a prime means by which culture diffused. Wobst reasoned that open mating networks, with their complex overlapping distributions, would have tended towards cultural homogeneity. By contrast, closed mating networks would effectively have been sealed off from each other and would, in consequence, have led to cultural heterogeneity or to what Wobst himself called 'clusters of idiosyncracy' (Wobst, 1976, pp. 53–4).

This potential contrast between cultural homogeneity and heterogeneity can be interpreted either as forms of adaptation to different environments or as stages in an evolutionary trend. Because of their direct bearing on the nature of mating networks, 'poor and highly variable resources both lead to cultural homogeneity among hunter–gatherers, while rich or uniform resources favour areal differentiation and nucleation' (Yellen and Harpending, 1972–3, p. 251). Alternatively, we can see it as part of an evolutionary trend, one linked to changes in the density of band occupation over time. A number of scholars have drawn attention to the way in which the cultural homogeneity of the very earliest hunter–gatherers, as measured through their artefact assemblages, gives way to greater heterogeneity, with a markedly wider range of cultural traits and a far greater range of local assemblages, during the early stages of the upper Palaeolithic (Isaac, 1972, p. 186; Wobst, 1976, p. 55; Butzer, 1982, pp. 295–313). For Wobst, this apparent shift towards greater cultural heterogeneity signals a closer packing of bands and the emergence of closed mating networks. More controversially, he also argued that only with the emergence of these closed mating networks some 30 000 years ago and, with them, his 'clusters of idiosyncracy', did true band society emerge. In short, he asserts the 'absence of Band Society among hunter–gatherers under conditions of low population density' (Wobst, 1976, p. 54), a conclusion which he presumably would apply to poor environments at all times and to all environ-ments during the mid-palaeolithic and before. Any quibble with Wobst will not be over his assertion that the closer packing of bands during the upper Palaeolithic may have fostered a closed mating network, but with his basic assumption that band society can only be equated with his 'clusters of idiosyncracy', that is, with culturally and biologically independent groups of around 500. Owen, for instance, has taken a quite contrary view by rejecting the idea that bands were ever homogeneous groups and expressly declaring them to be hybrid groups, both culturally and biologi-cally, thanks to the overlap of mating networks (Owen, 1965, p. 675). Clearly, Wobst would not deny that open mating networks existed or that they worked against the cultural isolation of hunter–gatherers. What is in dispute is whether they should be called bands *sensu stricto.*

How Hunter–Gatherer Bands viewed the World Around Them

In this section, I want to explore how hunter–gatherer bands viewed their own spatial order. 'The advent of culture coincides with the birth of the intellect' (Lévi-Strauss, 1973, p. 174). A primary object of society's first reflective thoughts would have been the nature of the world around: this world view constitutes their cosmography. If we take the mating network of hunter–gatherer bands as the basic unit of communication and therefore, of cultural identity, then it follows that potentially, there could have been as many different cosmographies as there were mating networks. The sheer number and individuality of cosmographies is certainly a feature of their character. However, it would be mis-leading to assume that there are no grounds whatsoever for build-ing generalisations about them. For a start, primitive societies in many parts of the world tended to organise their cosmographies (like their cosmologies) through simple binary oppositions. As a rule, these binary oppositions are compounded into single, all-embracing schemes of dual classification that encompassed both their natural and social order. Arguably, these dual classifications or organisations provide us with a basis for developing powerful generalisations about the earliest cosmographies. It might also be possible to develop more limited generalisations about the actual content of these cosmographies for despite the tendency for individual versions to proliferate, themes and motifs regarding say, creation myths, can recur over wide areas. This sharing of themes and motifs is most likely to occur where bands maintained open mating networks or where bands had multiplied rapidly by fission so that just as they had spread, Adam-and-Eve-like, from a few pioneer bands, so too, had central themes and motifs of their cosmography.

A World of Two Halves

Mention has already been made of the way surviving hunter–gatherer bands generally see their social order as being organised into opposed groups or moieties. Their exchange system, ritual behaviour and even thoughts on their origin are pivoted on this dichotomy. It would be wrong, however, to see such a scheme as restricted to their social order. The way they perceive their natural order was structured in a like fashion. All the different elements of their natural world, its physiography, flora and fauna, together with its vital conditions (that is, abundance/scarcity, fertility/ sterility, wet/dry) were organised through similar binary opposi- tions. More to the point, all the different binary oppositions of their social and natural orders were combined into a single, mono- lithic scheme: their world effectively consisted of two halves, each distinct from yet essential to the other. In a seminal book on the subject, Durkheim and Mauss explained the binary structure of primitive classification and its categorical fusion of society and nature as deriving from the fact that 'the first logical categories were social categories: the first classes of things were classes of men, into which these things were integrated' so that society's most basic distinction between opposing marriage classes, or moiet- ies, 'were the first genera, clans, the first species' (Durkheim and Mauss, 1969, pp. 82–3). Their interpretation of the problem has much to commend it but it is far from being the only one. Others, for instance, see the duality that pervades the primitive view of the world as a response to the innate 'twoness' of the world (Needham, 1963, pp. vii–xlviii; Needham, 1969), whilst Lévi-Strauss has argued strongly and convincingly to persuade us that it reflects a fundamen- tal tendency for the human mind to think in terms of binary oppositions (Lévi-Strauss, 1972, pp. 135–60). An equally varied choice of explanations can be called upon to account for why the primitive mind collapsed their social and natural order into the same bilateral scheme of classification. For some, it had an objective utility. By forging what some would see as a conceptual link between society and nature, it enabled the one to act on the other. For Lévi-Strauss, it is a classificatory device and no more, enabling society to highlight and constantly reiterate the critical distinctions and oppositions that permeated society at all the different levels of its existence and thought: between culture and nature, between those one could and could not marry and so on (Lévi-Strauss, 1973).

Irrespective of how we explain their origin, the tendency for primitive cosmographies to be structured around simple binary oppositions and for them to combine social and natural order into a single scheme of dual classification and dual organisation greatly affected the cultural input to their spatial order. We can appreciate their impact by looking at the way the earliest cosmographies viewed, first, space, and second, the natural environment.

Primitive society does not abstract space as a concept separate from the capes-and-bays reality of the world. They have no word equivalent to the geographer's use of the term (Littlejohn, 1963, pp. 1–2; Hallpike, 1979, p. 285). Nor do they have any sense of Euclidean or projective space (Hallpike, 1979, p. 285). Its characterisation was based solely on 'the physiognomic aspects of space' (Hallpike, 1979, p. 285), that is, on the physical and human features that filled it and gave it appearance. The key features of this physiognomy were generally arranged into opposed pairs or attributes (for instance, sun/moon, earth/sky, light/dark, above/below, etc.); this pairing of opposites imparted a symmetry to their cosmography, each side balancing the other. Reinforcing this dual organisation of space was the way in which primitive thought transformed space through relations of proximity, separation, order, inclusion and continuity, the landscape being strongly dichotomised into regions that were either/or, inner/outer, centre/periphery, left/right, high/low, above/below, closed/open, fore/back, symmetrical/asymmetrical, bounded/non-bounded, ordered/disordered (Hallpike, 1979, pp. 283 and 285: Dodgshon, 1986a).

The integration of social and natural order into the same monolithic scheme of dual classification had the obvious effect of establishing links or bonds between those groups, elements or attributes that were assigned to each side or half of their cosmography (see, for example, Lévi-Strauss, 1969, pp. 69–83). We can see this most clearly in their confusion of personal, geographical and cosmic space. Not only do we find them establishing homologues – similarities of form and meaning – between the layout of their dwellings, settlements, surrounding environment and universe (see, for example, Griaule and Dieterlen, 1954, pp. 83–100; Hugh-Jones, 1979, pp. 237–8 and 266–9), but we also find that the primitive mind treats them as if they were one and the same, notwithstanding their differences of scale. They lived as much in a cosmic as in a geographical world, the one being indistinguishable from the other. If anything, what lay along their vertical axes of reference or what lay above, carried more force of meaning, than what lay around them, or what – to us – was mere geography. What lay above – their heavenly world – provided an archetypal model, a paradigmatic design on which the organisation of their earthly world was based in respect of both its social and physical landscapes (Eliade, 1954, pp. 6–11 and 40; Tuan, 1974, chap. 11). The conceptual force of this paradigmatic world was such as to make it more real than their earthly world. It was a 'real' world that 'transcended the pragmatic realm of texture and geometrical space and was perceived schematically in terms of extra mundane, sacred experience' (Wheatley, 1969, p. 2). The link between their heavenly and earthly worlds was the *axis mundi*, a sort of conceptual pivot for what lay above, below and around. Amongst hunter–gatherers, the *axis mundi* might take the form of a tree, or, as with the Achilpa aborigines of Australia, a sacred pole which could be carried around and erected at select sites to re-establish communication between the heavenly and earthly halves of their world (Gill, 1982, pp. 220–1).

An equally significant outcome of the bond which formed between everything within each half of these dual classificatory schemes is the link which thereby existed between the different sections of their social order and the different regions or dimensions of space. The latter were symbolically appraised through their association with particular categories of social order. The different classificatory divisions of society related to each other through spaces that were east/west, upper/lower, above/below, inner/outer and so on. In every situation where the different classificatory groups of society confronted each other, either within camp sites or during rituals, this symbolic ordination of relations would be called upon to structure actual relations in space (Lévi-Strauss, 1969, pp. 69–83; Hallpike, 1979, p. 285).

By the same means, the different social divisions within society were linked to different elements or aspects of their natural environment. For some scholars, these links are a basis for action, enabling primitive societies both to rationalise their natural world and to act upon it in their best interests. When a primitive community first settled an area, their first act was to 'cosmiscise' it, to bring it within their conceptual framework of order (Eliade, 1958, p. 10) Without this order, all would be chaos. Once reduced to order, and the proper relations between things established, then society could begin exerting its influence over nature. In what he calls the myth of the eternal return, Eliade has argued that primitive societies used ritual to re-enact the creation myths which lay at the heart of their cosmology. In so doing, they believed they were ensuring the regeneration and continuation of life (Eliade, 1954; Eliade, 1973, p. 61). In effect, ritual and the myths enacted through it were a means by which change and decay could be averted. In the primitive mind, 'time is recorded only biologically without being allowed to become history – that is, without its corrosive action being able to exert itself upon consciousness by revealing the irreversibility of events' (Eliade, 1954, p. 74). The creation of life in all its manifold dimensions was 'reactualized' through imitation. By 'continual reactualization', they were able to recreate 'the initial instant, the plentitude of a present that contains no trace of history' (Eliade, 1954, p. 76). For Eliade, the functional goal of ritual is underlined by its forms. Australian aborigines, for instance, replicated the 'dream tracks' taken by the 'culture heroes' who created their physical and human landscapes (Eliade, 1973, pp. 42–83) and performed increase rituals at select points to ensure the continued abundance of those species of flora and fauna most vital for their survival. This is what Sopher meant when he talked about primitive society's 'ritualization of ecology' (Sopher, 1967, p. 117).

For some, a necessary part of society's belief in its ability to ensure abundance were the totemic relations which it established between particular bands and particular species or attributes of their environment, a belief based not on mere sentiment but on the sincerely-held concept that these bands shared the same spirit as their totem or totems. Not everyone though, accepts that totemism had a functional basis. Durkheim and Mauss saw it as a device 'to advance understanding, to make intelligible the relations which exist between things' (Durkheim and Mauss, 1969, p. 81) but they refrained from seeing it as a means to facilitate action (Durkheim and Mauss, 1969, p. 101). Latterly, Lévi-Strauss has re-emphasised its classificatory rather than functional role. Many totems, he argues, had no objective utility (Lévi-Strauss, 1973, pp. 150–1): their only possible role being classificatory. If the totems of groups set in classificatory opposition to each other are considered, they appear ambivalent, helping not only to distinguish but also to relate. For Lévi-Strauss, this is its purpose, another means of reconciling the continuous with the discontinuous. It represents a

> particular expression, by means of a special nomenclature formed of animal and plant names . . . of correlations and oppositions which may be formalized in other ways, for example, among certain tribes of North and South America, by oppositions of the type sky/earth, war/peace, upstream/downstream, red/white, etc. (Lévi-Strauss, 1973, p. 161).

There can be little doubt that dual classificatory schemes once prevailed in Europe. However, we glimpse such a system long, long after it had disintegrated as an all-embracing and coherent system. We find little more than bits and pieces, mere mental sherds from a once complete conceptual orb. For the geographer, though, these bits and pieces are suggestive for amongst them are the vestiges of what must once have been a potent scheme of spatial differentiation. Thus, preserved amongst the folk-culture of medieval peasant societies are schemes of spatial differentiation based on simple oppositions like east/west, great/little, upper/lower or fore/back. We find them being used in relations to fields, settlements and the earliest administrative districts (Dodgshon, 1981, pp. 137–45; Dodgshon, 1986a). Of special interest are those schemes which employed a distinction between what was upper and what was lower, or between what was sunny and what was shadow. Those distinguishing between upper and lower space are distributed fairly widely, but those distinguishing between sunny and shadow space have a very specific distribution, being found in areas of Scandinavian settlement (Göransson, 1961, pp. 80–101) and in those parts of eastern Scotland occupied by the Picts (Dodgshon, 1975a, pp. 1–14). The classificatory intent behind such schemes is betrayed by the fact that the different sets of oppositions (east/west, great/little, upper/lower) are often used interchangeably: thus settlements distinguished as east/west in one source might appear as upper/lower in another. At first sight, this complementary use of distinctions measured along horizontal and vertical axes of space seems calculated to disorientate than to orientate. But seen in relation to primitive notions of spatial classification, its rationale is revealed.

That we may be dealing with the residual traces of a dual classificatory system is also borne out by evidence showing how some tribes in early medieval Britain and Ireland used such schemes not only to classify space, but also to classify themselves, so that we find them divided into east/west, great/little and upper/lower sections (Dodgshon, 1986a). In view of Lévi-Strauss's suggestion that totemism served the same end as dual classification, it is also relevant to note that there are also signs that this too, has a place in the history of early European society. Writing in 1911, MacNeill drew attention to the tribal groups that flourished in the west of Ireland during the sixth and seventh centuries AD and who presented themselves to the world as the Corcu Brihuir or beaver people, the Corcu Circe or pig people, the Boccraige or goat people, Breccaige or trout people and Corcu Tened or fire people (MacNeill, 1911, pp. 59–114; Macalister, 1921, p. 246). They stand distinctly from other tribes around them who identified themselves by the *mocu* or *maccu* principle, that is, by descent. A credible case has also been published for seeing the Picts who inhabited eastern Scotland (*floruit* third to ninth centuries AD, as totemic. It rests on their use of zoomorphic symbols on their standing stones (Jackson, 1971, pp. 121–40). Despite their patently late context, these traces of totemism link us back to the earliest stratum of human thought about the world. Not surprisingly, they relate to cultures that were not overwhelmed by the blanket of Indo-European culture that spread across Europe from the mid-Bronze age onwards (2000 BC+) but preserve elements of pre-Indo-European cultural tradition. The geographer Estyn Evans has reminded us that early Irish culture was compounded of both pre-Celtic (or pre-Indo-European) and Celtic influences, so much so, that he speculated on whether it was not so much a case of the Celts conquering Ireland but of Ireland conquering the Celts (Evans, 1973, p. 46). Likewise, the Picts have long been seen as an archaic, 'conserving society' (Thomas, 1963, pp. 68–9) whose cultural make-up also incorporated both pre-Celtic and Celtic influences.

Cosmography as Geography

Turning from the principles around which cosmographies were structured to their thematic content, we are still a long way from being able to define confidently the sort of universe – the cosmography – in which the hunter–gatherer bands of early Europe thought they lived. Interpretations are partial and subject to much dispute. The only direct contact that we have with their ideas is through palaeolithic and mesolithic rock or cave art and even with this, there is no agreement over whether it has cosmological or cosmographical significance. Art for art's sake or even graffiti say some, whilst one recent view depicts them as a means by which highly mobile bands communicated with each other about highly mobile food resources (Gamble, 1981, pp. 533–4). After what still amounts to the most exhaustive analysis yet of such sites, Leroi-Gourhan concluded that they functioned as sanctuaries, places of deep symbolic significance, and that their art served as mythograms, helping to convey a particular myth or belief. A survey by him revealed that there was a definite pattern to the position in the cave where particular animals were drawn and also in the way they were paired or grouped, either with each other or with human figures. He concluded that a dualistic scheme is discernible based on the distinction between what is male and what is female, a distinction manifest through the latent symbolism of particular animals (Leroi-Gourhan, 1968, pp. 148–50). But although there is undoubtedly pattern and purpose to such art, its precise schematic and idiomatic intentions are likely to remain obscure (Sieveking, 1979, p. 209).

A more secure basis for interpretation is provided by the increased archive of figurative drawings and motifs that appear on rock surfaces, wood and bone carvings and pottery from the neolithic period onwards. Sites like those at Capo di Ponte in northern Italy or Bohuslän in western Sweden form veritable art galleries of patently symbolic art. This vast increase in the range of artistic expression probably reflects a greater facility and willingness to express ideas than any basic change in human concept. But, this said, it must be conceded that opinion varies. Scholars like Eliade and Gimbutas see the advent of farming and its closer (if hardly new) concern with the reproductive cycles of plants and animals as contributing fresh concepts to the cosmologies of neolithic peoples. But whereas Eliade talks in terms of a complete break with earlier systems of belief (Eliade, 1958, p. 38) Gimbutas sees pre-neolithic ideas as forming central strands in these new cosmologies. Certainly, given recent thinking on the mesolithic, it is difficult to accept Eliade's argument that the shift from hunting and gathering to farming was accompanied by a stark across-the-board shift from animals to plants in the focus of primitive cosmologies. In fact, Gimbutas's categorisation of the symbols that lay at the heart of 'old' European (that is, pre-neolithic) cosmologies helps to refute it. She envisages 'two basic categories: those related to water or rain, the snake and the bird; and those associated with the moon, the vegetal life-cycle, the rotation of the seasons, the birth and growth essential to the perpetuation of life' (Gimbutas, 1982, p. 89). The first of these categories is seen by her as expressing a creation-myth that dates from the palaeolithic period and which sees life as originating from a cosmic egg enveloped in water and laid by a water bird (Gimbutas, 1982, pp. 101–2). In some versions, fish, especially the salmon, are woven into the story. Eliade's summary of what he calls these 'palaeolithic' myths shows them as making use of a variety of aquatic animals, their unifying theme from cultural group to cultural group being that they all try to structure their creation myth around a life-out-of-water concept (Eliade, 1958, p. 26). He also sees their concept of where this life-creation process began as 'built up on the basis of a fundamental centre of the world, around which space is organized' (Eliade, 1958, p. 23). How such a cosmological idea might endure and become incorporated into a later folk-tale is illustrated by an oft-cited reference to Finn, a great Celtic God. Finn became wise, all-knowing, when he ate a cooked salmon or, in one version, when he sucked a finger previously immersed in a pot of cooking salmon (Wagner, 1975, p. 3). The acquisition of knowledge at the moment when he ate the cooked salmon, or tasted its broth, recalls Lévi-Strauss's thoughts on how primitive society surrounded the art of cooking with a profound symbolic significance because it signified the fundamental distinction between what was culture (= cooked food) and what was nature (= raw food). As with Finn, human knowledge, the transposition of nature into culture, was achieved not just by eating the salmon but by cooking it. In some myths, salmon are closely and logically linked with river sources and hazelnuts. Conceivably, these two sources of food, both of critical importance to hunter–gatherer bands in early Europe, were linked because their abundance coincided at the same point in the year. But one can also imagine such bands drawing the connection between a creation-myth which saw life as emerging out of water, and a species of fish that each year, struggled upstream to river sources, the so-called eye of the river. Perhaps here too, is the reason why river or spring sources have such a deeply-rooted symbolism in north-west Europe as foci of numerous myths about their restorative or life-creative powers, a belief which could well stretch back far beyond the early Christian church's attempt to reorientate such symbolism (Ross, 1967, pp. 19–33). These are speculative thoughts. What they are designed to convey is the inescapable fact that the hunter–gatherer bands of early Europe would have perceived their world through cosmologies designed to explain how it came into being and how it continued to thrive. Furthermore, these cosmologies would have played a prominent role in integrating them together as societal systems. As Turnbull has said, with acephalous societies or societies without an instituted form of government, 'the thought binds them together' (Turnbull, 1976, p. 192). They would not have been fragmented, irrational concepts, but holistic and internally-coherent systems of thought. Our inability to reconstruct their details, does not remove their existence. However hidden and mythical they might seem to us, the cosmographies which they envisaged were very real for those who inhabited them, actually and spiritually.

The Earliest Spatial Order?

How can the spatial order of hunter-gatherer bands be summarised? Are there principles of spatial order to be abstracted from it? Two lines of approach seem important. First, there is the contribution made by hunting and gathering as a way of life. By taking their resource base as given rather than as something to be manipulated and managed, hunter–gatherers had perforce to adjust themselves to wide geographical variations in the productivity of natural ecosystems, to their seasonal rhythms in output and to the broad secular shifts in their character and distribution. Bounded by these parameters, hunter–gatherers appear to be a studied exercise in environmental adaptation. Their strategies of adaptation employed adjustments in both social structure (minimal/ maximal bands, temporary/durable alliances) and spatial structure (large/small annual ranges worked via seasonal/short-stay camps). If we are forced to talk about relations of dominance amongst hunter–gatherers, as some Marxist anthropologists have recently done, then we can credibly do so only when examining the relationship between society and its environment, not between groups within society. Altogether, the overall impression yielded by hunter–gatherer bands is one of spatial diffuseness and a minimal degree of integration and organisation. Were it not for the necessity of social interaction via their exchange system, one might be tempted to see Sahlins' portrayal of the stone-age domestic household as anarchic – though intended as a hypothetical point – as an apt summary of real conditions since it captures the drift away from aggregation and integration. Only when this drift was reversed, were the relationships within society and between society and its spatial order transformed into something different.

A second line of approach would be to grasp precisely how they transformed their real world, via cosmology, into a wholly symbolic landscape. Their concern to impose order on this world led them, as a first act, to totalise it, to create a separate universe out of their portion of it. Their sense of order though, depended on more than just myths about how their world came into being and the role played by culture heroes and supernatural beings, and on more than just the ritual behaviour through which they sort to sustain its constant regeneration. It depended equally on the way in which they structured or classified it, on the way in which they imposed a taxonomy of relationships and distinctions on it. There is suggestive if not altogether conclusive evidence for believing that as in other parts of the world, the most primitive stratum of European thought constructed its image and interpretation of the world around it through dual classificatory schemes. This would

have meant that each separate universe of cosmology, and all its
manifold dimensions of meaning, would have been organised into
two distinct but interdependent halves and all social groups, species of flora and fauna, physiognomic features and all attributes or
conditions of life assigned to each half would have been bonded
conceptually together and would have shared in each other's
distinction from the groups, species, attributes and conditions that
made up the other, opposed half of their world. The different
forms, scales and dimensions of space and spatial order were part
of this scheme, each dichotomised, homologous one with another
and each symbolically appraised through their categorical association with the classificatory divisions that ran through society itself.
It is often said that we cannot talk of hunter–gatherer bands as
having spheres of activity that we can label distinctly as social,
economic, political or religious activity. Just as their view of the
world appears crudely undifferentiated, so also, do these spheres
of activity: thus, their exchange system had social, economic,
political and religious meaning, each indistinguishable in their
mind from the other. In these circumstances, their dual organisation, with all its implications for spatial order and the way they
thought of space, takes on greater prominence as a prime organising principle.

3
Tribal Systems and the Beginnings of Spatial Structure

In a European context, the shift from hunting and gathering as the major sources of diet to economies based more wholeheartedly on farming was under way in south-east Europe by about 6000 BC. By 4000 BC, the transition had begun to affect north-west Europe, including Britain. The emergence of communities dependent on farming for their sustenance gave rise to a new system of spatial order. As a more intensive relationship between society and its resource base, it naturally fostered a relatively more intense relationship between society and the space which it occupied. This intensified relationship manifested itself in a number of ways. To start with, the higher level of energy-capture provided by husbanding crops and animals enabled larger populations to live off smaller territories and to inhabit fixed or permanent settlements. Instead of responding to growth by fissioning and dispersing more widely, bands were now able to accumulate more around specific locations. As these large, sedentary groupings took shape, there emerged new societal systems based on tribes. The critical factor behind this shift to a new societal order was not simply the enlarged scale of such systems relative to bands, but also its localisation in space. Farming introduced the possibility of relatively large groups living in social proximity to each other. It is the potential produced by this social proximity that spawned tribal systems. It did so because any significant increase in proximity between groups promoted a greater density of communication. Above all, it helped to preserve an awareness of common ancestry so that as these larger groupings emerged, they shared – indeed, were integrated by – an ideology of common descent. With this scalar increase, other areas of communication between groups, notably the exchange of women and ritual behaviour, now tended to become internalised, to be seen as an interaction between

61

discrete groups within the tribe, and, as a result, served to reinforce unity and commonality. We could argue that this was a
straightforward increase in communication with no real change of
principle or organisation. After all, many bands must have maintained belief systems and patterns of ritual behaviour in which
what they considered the 'totality' of their natural and social
orders was something defined at the level of their mating networks
or the wider grouping of bands with whom they interacted. Even
with the formation of tribes, some inner structuring would still
have been provided by the need to distinguish between classes of
potential marriage partners or to allocate ceremonial roles between major segments of the system. But there is surely a fundamental difference in ideology between a system that generates
relations with other groups through rules of exogamy and one that,
by virtue of its greater scale, is able to accommodate such relations
under rules of endogamy. One is patently more integrated as a
system than the other, both ideologically and actually, even
though there is a superficial similarity of roles and processes.
Arguably, this greater integration reflects the higher level of
communication that was possible once larger numbers of people
lived in relatively greater proximity to each other. Bringing these
points together, there is a sense in which societal organisation
must have become more segmented and more enclosed simply
because it had become more self-sufficient in social and cultural
terms.

The increasing localisation and immobilisation of society in
space was bound to produce a sharper, closer definition of territoriality. We miss the critical point though, if we see the enhanced
concept of territoriality that came with tribal systems as a product
solely of the higher energy capture that came with farming. It
mattered also that farming required a stored investment of labour
through clearing woodland, the preparation of the soil and plant-
ing the seed (Meillassoux, 1972, pp. 99–100; Dennell, 1983, p.
167). With this investment must have come a narrower, more
exclusive sense of possession. Territorial behaviour does, in fact,
increase once tribes appear and there are attempts to demarcate
property holdings physically in the landscape. The permanent
occupation of specific blocks of land also had far-reaching implications for social structure. As suitable land was colonised, access to
land and, therefore, to subsistence, became more and more con-

fined to inheritance. Regulating property may not have been the sole *raison d'être* for descent groups but as Leach has pointed out, it must have contributed substantially to the definition and constitution of the multi-generational kinship groups, or lineages, that emerged as the building-blocks of tribal society, the groups around which marriage, the gift cycle and ritual behaviour now became organised (Leach, 1961, p. 11). Despite their larger scale, tribes were still homogeneous systems, their constituent lineages or segments seeing themselves as equal in status, one with another. The extent to which struggles over access to land must, from the very beginning, have worked against such an egalitarian system, though, has caused some writers to doubt whether such segmented tribes can be distinguished from ranked societies and chiefdoms.

In so far as the advent of farming replaced a diffused and transient relationship between society and space with a more intensive and stable one, it had the effect of diminishing spatial integration. Coupled with the localisation of key societal processes – such as exchange – it might be argued that the emergence of tribal systems over the neolithic period may have witnessed, albeit temporarily, the segmentation and closure of space to a degree not evident before or since. But having said this, it also follows that since the reduced mobility of society must also have reduced the variety of resources accessible to it, then from their very beginnings, tribal societies must have been under pressure to restore variety to their material needs by restoring some degree of spatial integration: this could be achieved by establishing patterns not just of intra-tribal exchange but also, of inter-tribal exchange. Since the establishment of such flows invariably arose through 'big-men' taking over the role of tribal banker, this latent tendency of tribes to develop more extensive and more organised exchange systems is another reason why some prehistorians prefer to gloss over the differences between tribes and chiefdoms. For them, they involve the same processes or tendencies even though their forms are different (see, for example, Bender 1978, p. 209). Yet there is unquestionably a vital difference in organisation between a tribal system whose interactions and exchanges observe a strict equality between segments or lineages and one in which such processes have the instrumental value of reinforcing the superior ranking of particular lineages or persons. The difference between the two is one of principle and not merely degree. Latent tendencies towards ranking there may have been, but so long as these were held in check by levelling mechanisms and other forms of negative feedback, the impact of these tendencies would have been contained and the stability of the tribal system preserved.

The Origins of Agriculture and Sedentarism: How or Why?

The view upheld here is that the origins of agriculture and, therefore, of settled communities, can no longer be construed in terms of a Eureka-type explanation, that is, as a decisive discovery or breakthrough in human knowledge. The intimate relationship which hunter–gatherers developed with the faunal and floral content of their environment must have ensured some awareness of how resources could be managed to achieve greater outputs if the need arose (Clarke, 1976, p. 476; Harris, 1977, pp. 410–14; Bender, 1978, p. 205). Indeed, the evidence is mounting for a whole series of husbandry practices during the mesolithic. Herbivores, for instance, were selectively culled. Animals were foddered using ivy and elm leaves. There are also abundant signs that woodland was deliberately burnt, the younger, more open habitat that resulted attracting denser concentrations of animals and providing a more varied range of plant food for hunter–gatherers themselves. Plant-domesticates almost certainly originated through this sort of long-drawn-out tinkering, from harvesting wild stands to deliberately seeding or rooting plants. Clarke has stressed the artificial nature of the distinction between gathering wild plant food, and cultivation, noting that hardly any post-glacial group in Europe could have been ignorant of the 'consequences of seed and root reproduction' (Clarke, 1976, p. 459). In short, the rudiments of crop or livestock husbandry could have been no mystery to post-Pleistocene hunter–gatherers. In fact, there are even suggestions that Pleistocene hunter–gatherers husbanded some of their resources. Seen in this way, the origins of farming become more a question of why rather than how it developed. Furthermore, as both Harris and Bender have indicated, the precise question that we need to pose is one of 'why intensification?' rather than 'why domestication?' (Harris, 1977, pp. 402–4; Bender, 1978–9, p. 204).

Asking 'why intensification?' alters the problems before us radically. Instead of looking to identify moments of discovery and hearth-areas of innovation, we are now dealing with the gradual trends by which food production took over from exploitation and the broad conditions which induced this intensification. Admittedly, we cannot rule out the possibility that the shift to food production in some areas still involved a diffusion of new techniques or even colonists seeking new environments. For instance, a good case can be made out for seeing the Bandkeramik complex of central Europe as an intrusive movement of farmers, 6500–6300 BC (Dennell, 1983, pp. 169–70). The idea of a single-source model, with husbandry being irradiated across Europe from sites like Jarmo and Catal Huyuk, though, is no longer tenable. Whatever movements of ideas and colonists were taking place in Europe, 6000–4000 BC, local mesolithic communities were just as capable of effecting the transition from hunter–gatherer economies to farming on their own. They did not need the stimulus of ideas that were foreign to them, nor did they have to be replaced by those who knew better. Elaborately constructed maps of agricultural diffusion across Europe mislead. Only part of the pattern which they reveal can be put down to the movement of colonists or new techniques, though the replacement of wild cereals with high-yielding varieties like emmer wheat may have involved large-scale diffusion. Equally relevant are the conjunction and phasing of circumstances that pushed mesolithic communities to adopt intensive methods of food production.

An obvious reason for the adoption of these more intensive techniques of food production is the pressure of population growth. We need only advance the growth which set in during the mesolithic era. To recapitulate what was said in the Chapter 2, the richer ecologies which overspread much of Europe at the start of the post-glacial period would have allowed a denser packing of bands and, therefore, smaller territories: the reduced mobility involved may have disrupted traditional mechanisms for regulating band population. Still-denser patterns of band adaptation became necessary which, in turn, would have fed back more population growth. Through a process of continuous positive feedback then, bands would have slowly become less and less mobile and more and more forced to intensify food production (selective culling, fire setting, etc.). The denser pattern of bands which emerged over the mesolithic period was but one stage in this self-amplifying deviation from the equilibrium systems of the upper palaeolithic. For Harris, the eventual adoption of farming, 6000 BC, was another. Exemplifying one possible version of this 'crisis' of the late mesolithic, Jensen has described how the 'rich estuarine space' of the high Atlantic period (about 5000 BC) in Denmark may have induced greater sedentarism among hunter–gatherers. The resultant population growth turned the estuarine areas of the country into what he calls 'a propulsive area' (Jensen, 1982, p. 51), one whose expanding needs forced a more intensive exploitation of natural resources throughout the coastal zone, including that of seaward islands and inland freshwater lakes. But once the capacity of natural resources was reached, the only habitat that could be manipulated to achieve higher productivity was the forest climax of the interior. Jensen sees the husbandry techniques (for instance, fire setting) introduced into these forest zones as leading ultimately to a 'semi-agrarian economy' (Jensen, 1982, p. 52).

Clarke posits a slightly different interpretation of events. As well as describing the mosaic of richly-varied ecologies that spread over much of Europe during the immediate post-glacial period and the finely-tuned strategies with which hunter–gatherers adjusted themselves to this new chequerboard of opportunity, he highlights the way in which the new ecologies of central Europe especially, became progressively impoverished after about 4000 BC as the vegetation cover became more continental. He envisaged hunter–gatherers readjusting to these less favourable circumstances by simply emphasising the techniques of artificial food production which they carried in their ditty-bag of cultural practices. In a comment that echoed Foley's notion of the 'home range' in which the energy gained by hunting and gathering exceeded the energy expended in obtaining it, Clarke depicted the shift into farming as taking place when the energy gained through hunting and gathering failed to match the energy expended, or when their 'home range' no longer served as a sufficient catchment without the supplement of artificial food production (Clarke, 1976, especially pp. 476–9).

How Territory Became Property

It has already been observed that when localised resource use became all-important, communities responded by becoming more defensive, more territorial, more exclusive and more antagonistic towards others (Reynolds, 1973, p. 472). Being a more intensive system of food procurement, farming naturally engendered a more intense relationship between society and the space which it occupied. With the emergence of farming, we can say that territoriality acquired a sharper edge to it as territories slowly became segments of space over which groups established exclusive rights of access and use and in which they had invested labour. Through this patent intensification of society's feeling for space, we are led to the more conspicuous definition and demarcation of it (Tringham, 1973, p. 463).

Signs of this heightened sense of territoriality are provided by the appearance of man-made boundaries and boundary-markers of a more symbolic sort. How quickly these features appeared depends on how we interpret the nature of early farming. In Britain, recent discussions have favoured an initial stage of shifting cultivation, with land being cropped by means of landnam episodes, or cycles of temporary forest-clearance–cultivation–forest-regeneration (Fleming, 1972–3, p. 183; Simmons and Tooley (eds) 1981, pp. 152–91; Fowler, 1983, p. 95; Taylor, 1983, pp. 40–1). Although open grassland environments had certainly appeared in many areas by the mid-third millenium BC (see Simmons and Tooley (eds) 1981, pp. 167–73), permanently-cropped fields did not appear in any quantity until soon after 2000 BC (Fowler, 1983, pp. 94–5 and 201–5). Fowler portrays the earliest cultivators as being concerned with the extraction of food at minimum cost in terms of energy input, calling it 'shifting resource–exploiting agriculture' (Fowler, 1983, p. 95). However, straightforward analogies with standard models of agricultural intensification, such as Boserup's succession of forest- , bush- , then grass-fallow (Boserup, 1965), are invalidated by the fact that far from pointing to a progressive intensification of cultivation, the field evidence strongly suggests that after a rapid extension of shifting systems of cultivation during the opening centuries of the neolithic period (or 4500 BC+), there occurred a marked contraction of settlement and cultivation during the latter part of the fourth millenium BC. When farming eventually recovered is momentum of growth, it led to the widespread establishment of permanently-cultivated and physically-demarcated field systems especially over the early or mid-second millenium (Fowler, 1983, pp. 94–5).

With such a long opening phase of extensive cropping, the advent of farming in Britain may not have produced the immediate or profound change in prevailing notions of territoriality that we might, in theory, expect. Nor are there any grounds for believing that the earliest forms of pastoral farming showed any greater regard for closing the territories on which they must have been based by constructing artificial boundaries, though it must be admitted that pastoralism has proved notoriously more difficult to evaluate in a prehistoric context. Much depends on precisely how husbandry was organised. For instance, we could hardly expect systems based on the rotational cropping of scattered plots, with each being cultivated for five or six years in turn and the whole cycle being repeated every thirty or forty years, to have differed in its underlying concept of territoriality from the more intensive systems of hunting and gathering that evolved over the mesolithic period, especially if the later involved the manipulation of resources. Smaller territories there may have been (Taylor, 1983, p. 44) and, for this reason, a more intensive use of space, but the farming communities of the British neolithic do not appear to have immediately translated this more intensive use of space into new forms or expressions of territorial behaviour.

It is only with the phase of recovery and expansion that becomes so evident during the early or mid-second millenium BC that we find a patently new consciousness over boundaries. Once this point is reached, we find communities marking the boundaries of their territories with ditches and banks or by placing barrows and cairns along their course (Muir and Taylor, 1983, pp. 108–22). The logic behind the association between burials and boundaries is simple: when someone was buried in a boundary, it was believed that his spirit helped to protect the estate from being alienated out of the family's possession. It is a logic succinctly conveyed by a piece of Anglo-Saxon verse:

Eal waes thaet mearcland
Morde bewunden
Feondes facne

All the marches were
With death surrounded
The snares of the foe.

Attempts have been made to exploit this association between burials and boundaries by using evidence of the former (barrows, burial cairns, etc.) to reconstruct the ground-plan of early estates (Muir and Taylor, 1983, pp. 110–11). Also indicative of a possible change in the concept of territoriality during the second millenium BC is the field evidence now being assembled which shows that large areas of southern Britain appear to have been divided up into large holdings or estates, before being subdivided (slowly or immediately, wholly or partially) into fields. In counties like Dorset, Wiltshire and Hampshire, the impression being gained is of a continuous pattern of estates being laid out along common axes or boundaries, as if planned in one great act of regional land allocation (Fowler, 1983, pp. 94–11). Comparable estate boundaries in the south-west are known locally as reaves and have been interpreted as demarcating the property of extended family groups (Fleming, 1978, pp. 97–123). Although highly relevant to any discussion of the way that the relationship between society and space altered, it must also be acknowledged that this growing tendency to give boundaries a physical representation in the landscape occurs almost 2000 years after the pioneer spread of farming and at a time when egalitarian tribes were giving way to chiefdoms. In the context of Britain, therefore, it may be necessary to qualify any facile presumption that the development of farming led immediately to a radical change in society's concept of space. It certainly intensified its relationship with space and, for this reason, must have intensified feelings of territoriality but there are relatively few signs before the end of the third millenium BC, that communities wanted to close or demarcate space physically with artificial boundaries or to symbolise them with barrows and cairns, even though society was capable of laying out long-distance ditch or bank systems and had evolved barrow and cairn burials before then. What this seemingly slow transition to 'private' space may signify is that the adoption of farming was not in itself sufficient to effect a radical change in society's concept of space. The extent to which farming packed communities together, relatively speaking, also mattered. Only where or when farming localised groups and juxtaposed their constituent interests one against the other, can we expect to find feelings of territoriality being translated into something more concrete and specific.

With this in mind, it is instructive to turn to the evidence for continental Europe where there seems to have been a quicker transition to the conspicuous privatisation of space. In many parts of central Europe, for instance, it is 'now reasonably certain' that the first farming communities, or the Bandkeramik complex, 'did not practise slash and burn cultivation' but, from the outset, established systems of permanent cultivation (Dennell, 1983, p. 172). Indeed, some have questioned whether shifting cultivation was the pioneer form of cropping anywhere in Europe (Sherratt, 1981, p. 290). In contrast to the trend of reasoning in Britain, continental work has depicted the early stages of cultivation as involving 'the intensive cultivation of good quality soils' along the major river valleys (Sherrat 1981, pp. 291–2). Overall, population levels remained low throughout the neolithic period but the fact that it was localised, or 'huddled' onto fertile pockets of easily-worked soil, meant that a modern landscape of fields and hedge-rows developed very quickly, especially in those regions occupied by the Bandkeramik complex (Dennel, 1983, p. 172). Complementary to the permanent cultivation of soil was the equally permanent occupation of settlements. We may typify this perma-nence by referring to the accumulated layers that make up the tell settlements of the Balkans, but there is now just as much evidence for the neolithic settlements strung out across the north German plain, from Holland to Poland, being occupied for centuries rather than for a few years (Sherratt, 1981, p. 291; Dennell, 1983, p. 172). What also stands out from these settlements is their inner uniformity of style, function and material culture, a feature which suggests that the society which produced them was organised around 'egalitarian social relations' (Sherratt, 1982, p. 10; see also, Sherratt, 1981, p. 292).

Running through any discussion of whether the earliest farming communities also experienced a heightened sense of territoriality is the question of whether it involved a change in concept. For North and Thomas, this change in concept was an essential part of the shift from hunting and gathering to farming. 'The hunting sector', they reasoned, 'must be considered within the framework of a common property resource and the agricultural sector as exclusive communal property regulated so as to border upon private property in its influence on man's behaviour' (North and Thomas, 1977, p. 235). In so far as they are claiming that rights of possession in land became more intense and more efficient because its conditions of use were clarified and because those who had access to it were narrowed to a smaller, more defined group, then we can agree with them. However, we must take issue with the way in which they define the social context within which this change took place. Their picture of small communities whose modest numbers enabled them to reach amicable agreements over husbandry 'almost as effectively as if private property rights had been established' (ibid, p. 235) compares uncomfortably with our knowledge of 'tribal' tenures. Under 'tribal' systems of tenure, assuming there is such a species of tenure, rights in land were in the first instance devolved from individuals but they eventually appear vested in kinship groups or lineages (Sahlins, 1968, p. 76). There are good reasons why this should be so. Once society became dependent on farming, it also became dependent on securing access to land. Those who first settled land naturally had prior claim over those who came later. Since these rights of access were inherited, it follows that rights in land became ancestor-focused. Furthermore, those first established on land naturally exercised a prior claim over the seed, livestock and labour invested in the land prior to each harvest. In an attempt to draw out the underlying differences between hunter–gatherers on the one hand and agriculturalists on the other, Meillassoux contrasted their different ways of using land: the former used land as a subject of labour whilst the latter used it as an instrument of labour (Meillassoux, 1972, pp. 99–100). The invested labour that sustained each harvest was a further reason why one had the 'emergence of the "family" as a productive and cohesive unit and of "kinship" as an ideology: priority of the relations between people over the relation to things' (ibid, pp. 99–100). In fact, for writers like Leach, the corporate nature of lineage groups was largely based on the simple fact that they were holders of land (Leach, 1961, p. 11). Their prime *raison de'être* derived from this proprietary function.

Setting these ideas in the context of prehistoric Europe, the following sequence of development might tentatively be offered. With the emergence of farming, the landscape would have become progressively partitioned into estates or family holdings. At first, perhaps over the neolithic period, the surplus numbers of each generation may have split away from parent groups to colonise new land. After all, the fact that farming enabled communities to adjust to smaller territories would have created a gross surplus of land, though not necessarily of cultivable land. But even at this stage, families, probably legitimised their occupation by acknowledging their descent from the person who first occupied the area. Once this space-filling exercise had run its course, and pressure built up on what was already held as property, the emphasis would have shifted to internal group expansion and the formation of lineages. Thus, after being narrowed between groups, rights of access would then have been deepened within them as multi-generational groups of kin secured their access to land by recognising an ideology of common descent. As their loosely-conceived notions of territoriality hardened into property, rights in land and particularly rights over arable land, would have become more privatised in the sense of being more clarified or disaggregated between family groups, but, in time, more communalised within them. Of course, whilst property would have been vested in the lineage *in toto*, individual families would have held a share of the estate in which they would have enjoyed a 'usufructory privilege – including control of the manner of use of its share, and of disposition of the produce' (Sahlins, 1968, p. 76).

Tribal Landscapes: The Imprint of Social Order, Alliance Structures and Exchange Schemes

It has become commonplace for prehistorians concerned with social archaelogy to record that with the advent of settled agriculture, larger social groupings emerged. The side by side juxtaposition of family groups, now set in a fixed spatial relation to each other through their possession of fixed blocks of land, led slowly but surely to these larger social aggregations, Nor were they simply mechanical aggregations. Spatial proximity meant an increased density of communication so that in addition to their prime source of integration, or common descent, there developed a range of other pan-tribal sodalities: these could include a common language, exchange system, belief system, ritual and rules of residence. Internally, the building blocks out of which these emergent tribes were fashioned, their basic units of interaction, were the lineages. Their structural importance stemmed from their functional role as the social units around which property – and therefore by summation the whole tribal territory – was founded. Collectively, they formed a lineal tribe, that is, an assemblage of egalitarian or non-stratified kinship groups.

Evolutionists like Service have been quite categorical in declar-

ing that 'tribal society . . . has general characteristics as a level or
stage in evolution' (Service, 1971, p. 100). It consisted of 'an
association of a much larger number of kinship segments' compared with the bands which it replaced (ibid, p. 100). We can draw
an important classificatory distinction between, on the one hand,
those tribes whose common ancestry at a tribal level was presumed
rather than demonstrable and, on the other hand, those whose
intra-tribal bonding could be expressed in more exact genealogical
terms and whose component segments or lineages 'maintained a
set of varying relations to each other with respect to putative
genealogical distance' (ibid, p. 116). This ordering on the basis of a
lineage's genealogical distance from the ancestor-founder of the
tribe had no instrumental value, meaning that it was not used as a
rank order of lineages in terms of status, power and prestige. The
main interpretative problem when dealing with such tribal systems
concerns the overall balance between the dissipative forces introduced by the relative independence of the various kin-groups and
the integrative or associative forces injected by pan-tribal sodalities. The extent to which the various kin-groups stood apart was
seen by Sahlins as threatening to 'condemn tribalism to an analytic
death' (Sahlins, 1968, p. 15). The fact that real political unity only
occurred during times of strife or warfare (Service, 1971, p. 104)
led others to cast them as a secondary phenomenon (Fried, 1975,
p. 30), whilst even Service intimated that they held together
mechanically rather than organically (Service, 1971, p. 133). Yet
in spite of such scepticism, the idea of the tribe has been accepted
by a number of scholars, including Service and Sahlins, as forming
a distinct phase of social organisation and, therefore, as a valid
unit of analysis.

But although accepted by evolutionists, its validity as a distinct
stage of social organisation has been strongly challenged, especially in the writings of those prehistorians who have begun the
reinterpretation of European prehistory from a Marxist perspective. Their case has been eloquently and capably expressed in the
broad syntheses offered by Friedman and Rowlands (1977), Rowlands (1980) and Ekholm (1981). In so far as it affects the identifi-
cation of lineal or segmentary tribes, the essence of their argument
is as follows. To have any validity, the evolutionary phasing of
prehistoric society must be based on the processes at work within
society and not on the latter's static forms. We need to identify the

'structures of processes' that were dominant, rather than the forms or institutions that were dominant (Friedman and Rowlands, 1977, p. 267). Conceived in this way, the question that needs to be answered by any critical analysis becomes one of when did particular 'structures of processes' first begin to operate rather than when did they produce particular frameworks of form or institutions. Applying this to the problem of tribes, Friedman and Rowlands argue that since the processes which generated absolute ranking and social hierarchies were operating from the very moment when settled, agricultural communities first emerged in the landscape, then it must follow that the concept of ranked or hierarchical societies must have been immanent within the very first tribal societies. In this process of becoming, tribal society suffers the 'analytical death' which, ironically, Sahlins thought might result from the very opposite trend, or from disintegration as opposed to the integrative processes with which Friedman and Rowlands enshrouded the problem. The distinction between lineal or segmentary tribes and ranked societies is thereby removed and the two reduced to a single, coherent 'structure of processes'. These processes will be discussed at greater length in Chapter 4. Suffice it for the moment to say that Friedman and Rowlands consider those which generated ranking to be rooted in the competitive relations that developed between kin-groups over access to land and the control of tribal exchange schemes, and they see both as present from the very inception of tribal systems.

Such an argument might be countered by suggesting that the same basic processes could generate quite different forms if, during growth, some form of scalar adjustment was needed and that, as geographers, we need to take account of these different forms. However, a more convincing reply can be developed by correlating tribes and ranked societies not only with different forms but also, with different processes. Such a reply makes use of the ethnographic evidence that shows how the egalitarian structure of lineal and segmentary tribes was conceptually based and how their exchange system, the basis for tribal integration, was articulated around the reciprocal exchange of equivalencies (Mauss, 1954, p. 11; Sahlins, 1968, p. 9). In short, the egalitarian structure of early tribes cannot be explained away as a measure, a misleading measure, of their structural immaturity but was a goal towards which the system as whole worked. Once such lineal and segmentary tribes are seen as existing, however temporarily, in a condition of homeostasis, as having their own system-maintaining checks and balances, then it follows that any shift toward ranking and unequal exchange had first to transform these underlying principles and processes of social order. The transition involved cannot be treated as a smooth process of adjustment, but must have involved systemic change and discontinuity.

The definition of early tribal formations presented at the outset of this section provided three broad problem-areas, namely, their social organisation and how their social relations were developed through marriage alliances and through exchange schemes generally. A discussion of each of these issues in the context of European prehistory has emerged over recent years.

Digging Up Tribes

Taking the social organisation of early tribes first, a number of studies are now available which link the first farming communities with egalitarian or segmentary tribal groups. Needless to say, Renfrew's work on the social context of megalithic tombs has been an important direction-pointer for such work. Addressing a study area perched on the edge of the European neolithic, or that of Orkney, he has argued that the peasant communities who erected tombs like Midhowe and Quanterness were small, egalitarian family groups. His case rests on the fact that the various sites display no obvious signs of ranking or wealth accumulation. Instead, they appear to replicate each other. As one would expect from a lineal or segmentary tribe, there is but one basic module of spatial order which is repeated, from one site to another. Renfrew's detailed comments on Rousay are especially informative. If these tombs had been the lavish burial monuments of chiefly families, one would reasonably have expected an island like Rousay to have had only one such site. In actual fact, it boasts fourteen surviving tombs, each one seemingly positioned beside its own share of arable land. The impression given is one of small, look-a-like communities, duplicated across the island (Renfrew, 1976, pp. 146–51).

Each territory must surely have been occupied by an extended family or lineage, all its inhabitants tracing their descent, or that of their spouse, back to a common ancestor. Modern ethno-graphic parallels suggest a tribal organisation and it is possible that each Orcadian island supported a single tribe or segments of a tribe (Renfrew, 1976, p. 151).

Elsewhere, in a further exploration of this same problem, he depicted megalithic tombs as boundary markers for 'segmentary tribes' (Renfrew, 1984, pp. 80–7). His use of the term segmentary here was meant to imply a tribe divided into clearly defined, loosely-coupled segments rather than one in which each family knew its exact genealogical relation to other members of the tribe. Proof of whether particular tribes were lineal or segmentary in a strict sense is really beyond recovery for prehistoric Europe.

A more explicitly spatial analysis of early tribal organisation is provided by Darvill's work on Ireland. His study makes use of two kinds of sites: court cairns dating from the early neolithic era and passage graves dating from the late neolithic era. On the basis of their distribution, Darvill argued that court cairns were associated with a segmentary tribal society and passage graves with an heir-archically-organised society. His comments on the type of society that built passage graves will be dealt with in Chapter 4. For the present, it is only his thoughts on the social context of court cairns that are relevant. These, he proposed, were not used primarily as burial sites but as local foci for rituals. They are distributed widely but evenly over the north of Ireland. Given their average nearest-neighbour distance of 4.5 km, Darvill reckoned that each local community or family group must have possessed such a site. Since there are no indications of personal accumulation or of site-ranking, he was drawn to the conclusion that their social context consisted of 'local segmentary groups' which 'seem to cover the landscape in a series of equivalent groups' (Darvill, 1979, p. 314). He favoured the term 'segmentary group' because whilst their material culture can be described as homogeneous, local variations in the design of cairns betokened 'a personalized or localized interpretation and adaptation of a more general idea' (Darvill, 1979, p. 314).

Outside Britain and Ireland, comparable tribal structures have been noted for a number of areas. Renfrew, for instance, prefaced his thoughts on the emergence of civilisation in the Aegean with what, at this stage in his thinking, were some tentative thoughts on earlier or neolithic tribal formations. Amongst the village groups which had taken shape by then, there was no evidence of social differentiation. These village groups 'may have been linked to form segmentary tribes' but this, he felt, was speculative. However, assuming some form of pan-tribal sodality to bind the various segments and settlements together 'seemed a plausible way of explaining the homogeneity seen within a given culture' (Renfrew, 1972, pp. 365–6). The apparent uniformity of local cultural patterns in neolithic Europe has been interpreted by others as diagnostic of egalitarian if not segmentary tribes (Sherratt, 1982, p. 10). However, others remain less convinced. There is little support, for example, in Randsborg's study of neolithic Denmark. The extent of geographical variation in the design of megaliths, their grave goods and artefacts like mace-heads and flint halberds left him sceptical about applying a tribal concept to his data (Randsborg, 1975, 106). On balance, he felt that geographical divisions explained the local patterning of his data far more effectively than any supposed tribal divisions (Randsborg, 1975, p. 106). Socio-political patterning, though, is not always discernible from material culture, especially where cultural hybridisation had occurred between adjacent tribal groups (Hodder, 1978, pp. 199–269). Randsborg's work can be set beside a more recent discussion by Kristiansen. He envisaged a progressive build-up of population during the opening centuries of the Danish neolithic era, 4100–3800 BC, with 'small family groups' practising slash-and-burn cultivation. By 3400–3200 BC, continuing population growth had led *pari passu* to a more intensive pattern of settlement and cultivation. With this intensification, the 'settlement system stabilized and a complex territorial organization developed that was sustained by elaborate ritual and exchange' on a communal basis (Kristiansen, 1982, p. 258). Kristiansen concluded that social ranking also emerged during this phase, with society becoming organised around big-men and local petty chiefs. His scheme concedes no special place for egalitarian tribes largely because, like Friedman and Rowlands, he saw societal integration beyond the 'small family groups' of the early neolithic era as proceeding fairly quickly and, from the very outset, as a process energised by the sway that increasingly dominant and avaricious individuals exercised over land, exchange and people. In other words, tribal formation is seen by him as a process of increasing heirarchisation as much as of integration, the one always being latent in the other.

Marriage Alliance and the Geographical Facts of Life

Fundamental to the relations that necessarily existed between kin-groups were their schemes of marital alliance and descent reckoning. These pose interesting but far from soluble problems. The most intractable centres on whether we can legitimately impose some form of evolutionary trend on this dimension of tribal society (cf. White, 1975, pp. 46–7), or whether the occurrence of particular schemes has no direction of development written into it. Broadly speaking, discussion of early European schemes of alliance and descent reckoning have pushed the problem back as far as the proto-Indo-European stage of cultural development. Translated into absolute chronology, this would roughly mean the mid to late Bronze Age. By this point at least, there is some consensus that European tribal society was fashioned around kinship groups that were patrilineal in terms of descent reckoning, patrilocal in terms of residence rules and whose schemes of marital alliance were of a generalised rather than elementary type. By generalised marriage alliance is meant that kin-groups contracted fresh alliances with each successive generation rather than maintained a stable, prescriptive alliance with the same group or groups, generation after generation. This supposed Indo-European pattern of descent reckoning and marital alliance will be commented on more fully later. For the discussion in hand, what needs to be considered is the thorny question of whether such patterns can be extended back unmodified into the pre-Indo-European period or whether – for neolithic farming communities – we need to think out the problem afresh.

In his seminal study of elementary structures of kinship, Lévi-Strauss firmly rejected any case for their former existence in early Europe. There is, he declared, 'no need for us to reconstruct some archaic state in which Indo-European society practised cross-cousin marriage, or even recognized a division into exogamous moieties' (Lévi-Strauss, 1969, p. 472). Reviewing the purely linguistic evidence, Friedrich agreed (Friedrich, 1966, p. 29). His data, though, was entirely drawn from the mainstream of Indo-European linguistic tradition, a context in which the smothering of older forms would have been more complete. If we wish to detect traces of older, residual forms, a more flexible approach is required. It has become an axiom of European cultural history to seek evidence for its most archaic traits along its western periphery rather than in its core. More to the point, it has already been argued that in areas like Atlantic Europe, Indo-European traditions were fused with, rather than had displaced, older pre-Indo-European forms. This model of cultural absorption rather than displacement in the peripheral areas of the European West has gained strength since its first statement by Fox over fifty years ago (Fox, 1932). It is, for example, a theme in Evans's survey of Irish cultural history, the input of Celtic or Iron Age culture being diluted and that of pre-Celtic, but especially neolithic influences being dilated (Evans, 1973, p. 45). It is against this sort of background that we should evaluate speculations on whether some of the earliest Irish tribes had prescriptive forms of marriage alliance (Macalister, 1921, pp. 244–5). Likewise, it is in relation to the pre-Indo-European component in their cultural make-up that we should evaluate suggestions that the Picts may have operated an elementary form of marriage scheme, with lineages or tribal groups being paired and bound together in permanent alliance (Jackson, 1971, p. 140). In his *Elementary Structures*, Lévi-Strauss noted that the Welsh law codes, a corpus of legal tradition first redācted in the tenth century AD, gave 'gift by kindred' as one of the ways in which marriage could be contracted (Lévi-Strauss, 1969, p. 475). Naturally, such gifts by kindred could be symptomatic of a generalised scheme of marriage alliance. Lévi-Strauss himself interpreted it in this sense. That there existed an earlier stratum of custom based on a more elementary scheme of marriage though, cannot be dismissed. One of the mythical stories making up the collection known as *The Mabinogion* tells the story of a figure called Peredur. Wandering through a valley, he came across a flock of black sheep on one side of the valley and a flock of white sheep on the other. When a black sheep called, a white sheep came and became all black. When a white sheep called, then a black sheep came and became all white. In between them, stood a tree, half in leaf and half in flames. The story is clearly didactic. It is not unreasonable to hazard the suggestion that encoded within it is a marriage alliance scheme between two kin-groups. The relationship described, in fact, is exactly what we might expect from a patrilateral scheme of marriage alliance. Under this sort of scheme, an alternating flow of women takes place between two opposed kin-groups, with one group providing women for the other in one generation and the other group reciprocating in the following generation. The imagery of the tree is a stock symbol for the ever-present renewal and decay of life within each generation, a cycle sustained by marriage. In effect, the tree is like a metronome, timing the rhythm of life itself. Such scraps offer no basis for a positive conclusion but they should make us hesitate before discounting the existence of elementary marriage alliance at some stage in the European past.

Similar caution needs to be exercised before any blanket acceptance of patrilineal schemes of descent reckoning among pre-Indo-European cultures. It is now reliably established that the Picts of eastern Scotland were organised on a matrilineal basis (Jackson, 1971, p. 140; Boyle, 1977, pp. 1–10). A case has also be made out for seeing the pre-Celtic tribes of Ireland as being organised on a matrilineal basis (Macalister, 1921, pp. 241–5). Standard definitions of tribal formations do, in fact, accommodate both patrilineal and matrilineal systems of descent, so no special case is being pleaded here. One possible explanation for this extra adaptation is to see the earliest forms of arable husbandry as based on hoes or digging sticks and as a largely female activity. In these circumstances, some cultures may have sought to avoid the drift of property and skills by adjusting to matrilineal forms of descent and matrilocal forms of residence (Sherratt, 1981, p. 297).

Given the possibility that matrilineal systems of descent existed alongside patrilineal systems, we cannot tacitly assume that residence rules were invariably patrilocal, with wives moving to their husband's settlement. The possibility of uxorilocal, with the husband moving to the wife's settlement, has to be admitted. To place this in a more specific context, Jackson thought that the Picts may initially have had uxorilocal rules over residence (Jackson, 1971, p. 140). Obviously each of these schemes would have imprinted its own character on the settlement geography of tribal space. We should also note here the possibility of settlement geography being influenced by tribal schemes of marriage alliance. As noted in respect of hunter–gatherers, elementary schemes tended to have the effect of dividing or pairing groups into symbolically-opposed sections or moieties. Presuming that elementary schemes survived after the conversion to farming economies, we can assume that early farming communities also preserved some semblance of this dual organisation. The difference between them is that early tribal systems were settled cultivators not mobile hunter–gatherers. What served as a system of absolute order in a world of relative

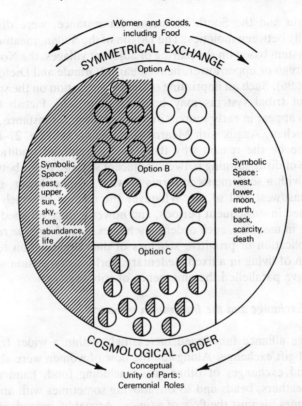

FIGURE 3.1 *Egalitarian Tribes and the Symmetry of Symbolic Space*

NOTE Dual organisation was also a feature of hunter–gatherers. What was distinctive about tribes and what this diagram tries to show is that once we are dealing with a sedentary system of dual organisation, then it could be mapped into space in a stable and far-reaching way.

space now became a system of absolute order in a world of absolute space. The ongoing use of dual organisation became a basis for the spatial ordination of society, a symbolic overlay on its spatial order. Three possible arrangements exist. Groups paired through marriage alliance could live in distinct but symbolically paired districts, or they could live in symbolically paired settlements that were set side by side or they could live in symbolically opposed spaces within a single settlement (see Figure 3.1). The literature on dual organisation vouches for each of these solutions to the symbolic ordination of tribal society in space. Villages in

Indonesia and the South Moluccas, for instance, were divided internally between moieties. The Dogon of the Sudan, meanwhile, had a system based on the pairing of adjacent villages, the Nommo and Yurugu or upper/lower, heaven/earth (Griaule and Dieterlen, 1954, p. 96). Such an imprinting of dual organisation on the spatial order of tribal systems may be the reason why Pictish tribal districts appear in early sources in a paired form, for instance, Mar with Buchan, Angus with Mearns (Dodgshon, 1981, p. 27–8). It may also be the reason why there is a widespread tradition in Europe of distinguishing between adjacent settlements or between spaces within settlements in terms of what is upper/lower, great/ little, east/west and so on. Whatever the context in which they were used in subsequent periods, and however impoverished they became in meaning, such ordering schemes may *ab origine* reflect the application of primitive schemes of dual organisation to the problem of living in a fixed, sedentary world, a conversion which must have parallelled the emergence of tribal systems.

Tribal Exchange and the Integration of Space

Marriage alliance functioned increasingly within a wider framework of gift exchange. Alongside the flow of women were also to be found exchanges of other gifts, including food, hand axes, flints, feathers, beads and so on, moving sometimes with and, at other times, against the flow of women. Arguably, indeed, essential to the whole notion of exchange amongst egalitarian tribes, these exchange schemes would still have been structured on the basis of reciprocity, reinforcing the equivalence and symmetry between those involved (Mauss, 1966, p. 11; Polanyi, 1968, pp. 9–12). In 1965, Clark depicted the spread of neolithic hand axes away from their production centres in terms of a gift cycle involving a chain of reciprocal exchanges (Clark, 1965, pp. 1–28). But although Renfrew has recently defined the sort of artefact distribution we can expect from reciprocal exchange (Renfrew, 1975, pp. 42–8), European case studies remain few.

Viewed from a geographical perspective, the greatly reduced range of spatial mobility which accompanied the shift into farming meant that the range of resources (both food and artefact, functional and ornamental) to which communities had access was correspondingly reduced. In this context, primitive exchange provided a means by which early tribal formations could offset the material impoverishment that came with sedentarism. With this in mind, we can expect the spread and intensification of farming to have injected primitive exchange with a still greater sense of purpose, with increased factor mobility being used to make good the decline in human spatial mobility (cf. Sahlins, 1974, p. 228). At the same time, we need to bear in mind that whilst farming offered a higher form of energy capture, it was narrower, more precarious form of resource exploitation. The material and social support afforded by exchange networks served as an insurance against risk, enabling abundance in one habitat to be set against scarcity in another (Gall and Saxe, 1978, p. 259). To adapt a phrase of Sahlins, the tribal economy was forced beyond itself, compelled by its increasing localisation to set itself in a wider network of relationships (cf. Sahlins, 1974, p. 140). Given the enlarged role which primitive exchange now had to play, we can freely concur with Friedman *et al.* in their view that:

this external exchange, which tempts us to signal the importance of the larger regional system, is not simply a fortuitous juxtaposition of local societies. From the point of view of reproduction, the local society only rarely has at its disposal all the means necessary for the maintenance of a given social form of existence. While earlier tribal societies may have been more locally autonomous, this certainly did not remain the case for long (Friedman and Rowlands, 1977, p. 270).

In time, the outcome of these developments was that tribes came to exist at both a local and supralocal level (Kristiansen, 1982, pp. 240–81) each as necessary as the other. We have the paradox of an increasing localisation of relationships at one level producing a supralocal network of relationships at another.

The Day the World Stood Still

The earlier discussion of marriage-alliance schemes touched on the question of how early tribal formations used their concept of symbolic order to orientate themselves in space. This question has wider implications which I propose to take up at greater length here. Broadly speaking, the relationship between the symbolic order of early tribal formations and their spatial order can be seen in terms of two interrelated themes.

On the one hand, the cosmologies and cosmographies that had governed the thought and behaviour of hunter–gatherer bands, with their ordering of social relations and processes in space, were now imposed on a world of experience that was static and localised and, as a result, more intensely felt. Their *axis mundi* was positioned and raised for the last time in a world that had, literally, been brought to a standstill. Tied to a specific locality and to permanently laid-out settlements, society now had far greater scope for ordering man-made space in accord with some heavenly prototype. This earthly reconstruction of human settlement in the image of some heavenly prototype has been most fully explored in relation to the sacred centres – the *axis mundi* – around which the early civilisations were pivoted, with their temples, sanctuaries, shrines, palaces and cities being laid out in replica of a heavenly paradigm (Eliade, 1954, pp. 12–17; Wright, 1965, pp. 667–79; Wheatley, 1969, pp. 3–40). But far from being instituted at this point, or interpreted as a form of cosmography specifically tied to urban genesis, this absolute accordance between what lay above and what society created below has its roots in the earliest human cosmologies. The first farmers would certainly have laid out their settlements after this fashion. We can expect them to have lived entirely within the conceptual framework provided by their symbolic order, interpreting and ordering their world through it (Needham, 1969, xxxvi), and we cannot hope fully to grasp the one without first comprehending the other.

On the other hand, we must not exclude all possibility of change. Just as the emergence of settled farming communities must have replaced a generalised relationship between society and space with a more localised and focused relationship so also must their concern for the abundance of many species have been replaced by a deep concern for the abundance of a few and a heightened concern for the concept of fertility and plenty. Symbols of fertility now abound, including carved visibly-pregnant fertility goddesses. The idea of a great fertility goddess may, as Gimbutas believes, have originated back in the upper palaeolithic period, but her symbolic powers must have been far more keenly sought by a society that witnessed the whole cycle of growth from seeding or birth through to harvest. For Gimbutas, the great goddess was 'the primary Goddess of the Old Pantheon'.

She creates from her own substance a concept of creation quite different from the Indo-European Earth Mother, who as the impalpable sacred earth-spirit is not herself a creative principle: only through the interaction of the male sky-god does she become pregnant (Gimbutas, 1982, p. 196).

There is another sense in which symbolic order might have changed with the advent of settled, farming communities. A whole new range of ideas, practices and activities based on crop and livestock husbandry now came into being, not to speak of the crafts (such as pottery-making) which now began to develop. We need to consider how these new practices and ideas were absorbed into the conceptualised world of early farmers. Bourdieu's notion of the habitus provides us with some clues on what we might expect. The habitus consisted of 'the durably installed generative principle of regulated improvisations' (Bourdieu, 1977, p. 78). Exemplifying his ideas with reference to the Kabyle of north Africa, Bourdieu maintained that 'understanding ritual practice is not a question of decoding the internal logic of symbolism but of restoring its practical necessity by relating it to the real conditions of its genesis' (Bourdieu, p. 114). If I understand Bourdieu correctly here, he is saying that ritual practice was forged through a combination of a 'durably installed generative principle' and everyday practical activities like ploughing or harvesting. In the case of the Kabyle, this 'generative principle' involved the structuring of the world through simple binary oppositions, each treated as homologous with each other, so that we find all elements of their universe (east/west, sun/moon), aspects of their social existence (male/female, life/death) plus an array of ordinary everday activities (hoeing/ploughing/harvesting, etc.) structured in a similar homologous fashion. It is not suggested that Bourdieu's stimulating reconstruction of Kabyle symbolic order can be shipped across the Mediterranean, lock, stock and barrel, or for that matter, transported back in time, but given the possibility that the 'durably installed generative principle' on either side of the Mediterranean bears some comparison, it may offer some clues for us. Expressed in the most general of terms, we might expect the symbolic order of early European tribal formations, with their supposedly-like emphasis on dual organisation, to have been extended and enriched by the incorporated of a whole range of new activities which began to develop from the late mesolithic/early neolithic onwards. Bearing in mind that we are dealing with 'durably installed generative principles', peasant cultures of more recent times do in fact show different dimensions of experience (for instance, human life cycle and that of plants and animals) being ritually linked through simple homologues, with, for example, the act of spring ploughing, of preparing the soil for fertilisation, being seen as akin to the breaking of the maidenhead and the last sheaf to be harvested being seen as the old maid.

Is There a Tribal System of Spatial Order?

A number of strands can be teased out of the foregoing discussion and woven into a spatial order of early tribal formations. The first is that with the shift from hunting and gathering to farming, human spatial organisation became characterised by a greater localisation of activity in place of the vast-areal spread of earlier systems and by permanently-occupied camps in place of temporary, seasonal camps. Relatively speaking, spatial order now became structured around points and localities in place of vast distended ranges, and around daily patterns of movements in place of annual or seasonal migrations. More cautiously, it can also be said that spatial order now started to become as much about the patterning of structures as about the patterning of processes. In effect, the almost wholly processual character of earlier spatial order now acquired a material structure; it became wrapped around with a sort of spatial carapace, one invested with labour in the form of cultivated fields, boundary markers, more substantial dwellings, etc. It is as if a powerful river-flow, on being checked, began to deposit a sedimentary load in forms and patterns that mirrored the now slower movements of its interacting currents.

Once society had adjusted to a wholly sedentary system, its social organisation became restructured into larger, more complex aggregations. Strong-conflicting viewpoints have to be confronted here. The view I have upheld takes a stubbornly geographical perspective. Spatial propinquity bred social propinquity, or rather –

given the progressive hiving-off or fissioning of lineages – maintained social propinquity. The greater density of communication now possible bred a larger unit of sodality, the tribe. In addition, the localisation of human activity induced a more active articulation of social relations, which, in time, became drawn upon to offset the diverse resource-mix which had been lost by localisation. In short, increased social interaction and social integration was used to compensate for reduced spatial mobility.

The symbolic order of early tribal formations contributed to their spatial order in two ways. First, it offered a grand, archetypal design for the ordering of their human landscape. Needless to add, as the human use of space became more intensive and the opportunites for man-made space broadened, the prospects for employing their symbolic order to arrange as opposed to merely interpreting space would have been enhanced. Second, embedded within the cosmology of early tribal formations – a direct inheritance from early band systems – were deep-rooted classificatory structures. These classificatory structures were part of Bourdieu's generative principles and, as with the bands that preceded them, were used to arrange the symbolic order of early tribal society into a series of simple binary oppositions, one that interlocked their social, natural and spatial orders together. With the spread of farming, this whole gamut of binary oppositions and orientations could now be set down in the landscape on a permanent plan, a plan that divided the landscape into a mosaic of affective space or regions. The whole travelling circus of symbolic orientations, alignments and oppositions now had a permanent theatre – the local community and its evolving farmscape.

4
Hierarchies in Society and Space: Reflections on their Orogenesis

The first emergence of ranked and stratified societies, the replacement of homogeneity with hierarchy, marks one of the great systemic changes in the history of mankind. By a ranked society is meant one which displays differences of absolute status and power between individuals and groups. By a stratified society is meant one which displays differences between individuals or groups in terms of their accessibility to resources and their accumulation of wealth. The appearance of such hierarchically stretched societies clearly signals important changes in the nature of both social and economic ralations. Accompanying these changes were far-reaching adjustments in the organisation of society. For Renfrew, the prehistorian can read this organisational development from visible changes in spatial organisation: the one embodying the impact of the other on landscape. As a transformation of spatial order, the shift towards ranking and stratification in society led to the emergence of dominant centres within systems of spatial order that had hitherto been organised around homogeneous, egalitarian and structurally-equivalent spaces. Renfrew was especially anxious to highlight this reorientation,

> for it is the existence of the centre, and of the central person who generally goes with it and actually does much of the co-ordinating, which establishes the asymmetry which is surely the crucial element of ranked societies, distinguishing them from the essentially symmetrical mechanical solidarity of egalitarian ones (Renfrew, 1982, p. 3).

By humanising these emergent centres, pivoting their control on individuals, he is reminding us that the emergence of spatial 'inhomogeneity' as he has tagged it (Renfrew, 1977, p. 98) is the story of how these individuals imposed a new instrumentality of meaning onto the landscape.

In exploring this problem further, I propose to begin with a brief survey of early forms of ranking and stratification and the role played by 'big-men' and tribal chiefs. The second section will consider some of the case-studies now available which have tried to establish when and where early early forms of social ranking and stratification, the first chiefdoms, developed. This is very much a case of inferring the growth of hierarchical order from changes in the spatial organisation of society. There are major problems to be confronted here. Archaeological data can tell us whether ranking or stratification of a sort existed, but it does not enable us to establish precisely how the hierarchies involved were structured or configured. The essentially speculative nature, the crudity even, of attempts to do so is the prime reason why social archaeology has been received with such scepticism by some. On a slightly different tack, we must also acknowledge from the very outset how the interpretation of archaeological data is greatly complicated by the fact that early systems of ranking and stratification – like later versions – were not stable. We need to have in mind Sahlins and Service's distinction between General and Specific Evolution. We can talk of a continuously evolving system of hierarchy at a General Level, but, at a Specific Level, the precise patterning and configuration of hierarchies were subject to considerable flux, with particular systems of ranking and stratification taking shape then collapsing (Rowlands; 1980, p. 47; Ekholm, 1981, pp. 249–56; Friedman, 1982, p. 182). In sharing this problem with the prehistorian, the geographer must pay close attention to the way in which these cycles of development and collapse were organised in space. New hierarchies emerged out of the periphery of older, declining systems, producing a constant tension between the core of such systems and their periphery (Ekholm, 1981, p. 243). The third section will ask why systems of ranking and stratification emerged and why they were 'fragile creations which tend to collapse in the slightest of breezes' (Ekholm, p. 259). Two broad groups of causative factors will be explored: one based on the competition which developed between individuals or families over access to land and the other on the control which individuals or families sought to exercise over intra- and inter-tribal exchange. But although distinguished for the purpose of discussion and illustration, these two sets of causative factors are not mutually exclusive. We can identify vital cross connections: this interrelationship needs to be drawn out if we are to appreciate what Rowlands described as 'the corporate basis of elite status' (Rowlands, 1980, p. 20). The fourth section will examine the way in which society's concept of symbolic order continued to influence spatial order. The discussion will concentrate on how the focus of political and economic power at particular centres became legitimised through cosmology and ritual. The tributary organisation of space around such centres became the right order of things, an expression of their moral no less than their spatial order.

The Social Topography of Chiefdoms

The earliest ranked or stratified societies were chiefdoms. These developed out of lineal or segmented tribes. Their formation involved the integration of the various lineages or segments into an absolute hierarchy of rank and power under the control of a big-man or chief. In the process, tribal structures became centralised and politicised around 'a permanent central agency of co-ordination' (Service, 1971, p. 134). The change constituted a systemic or qualitative change, a quantum leap in societal organisation and complexity, one that added a control function to societal integration (Service, 1971, pp. 132–4; Renfrew, 1977, pp. 95–112; Peebles and Kus , 1977, p. 427). It was a transformation that produced not simply a greater or more renowned chief but 'a system of chieftainship' (Sahlins, 1968, p. 26). Compared with the purely mechanical integration of earlier tribal formations, chiefdoms acquired an organic unity. Because they were no longer equal in rank or status, lineages were no longer the interchangeable building blocks of egalitarian tribes (Peebles and Kus, 1977, p. 427). With time, these rank differences were emphasised as chiefdoms became integrated into still more complex systems of greater and lesser chiefdoms. 'The tribal plan was purely segmental', wrote Sahlins when drawing out their differences, 'the chiefdom pyramidal' (Sahlins, 1974, p. 228). Moreover, the different parts of the pyramid became functionally interdependent. We can, in fact, correlate the rise of chiefdoms with the appearance of economic – especially craft – specialisation.

Within each chiefdom, lineage groups were meticulously graded according to their genealogical distance from the ancestor-founder of the chiefdom, the chief himself being regarded as the closest living descendant. This cascade of absolute rank from the chief downwards provided the system with 'a hierarchy of major and minor authorities holding forth over major and minor sub-divisions of the tribe' (Sahlins, 1968, p. 26). We can translate it into a geographically-contoured hierarchy for geographical distance from the core of the chiefdom tended to correspond with genealogical distance (Service, 1968, pp. 157–8), the hierarchy of kinship relations serving to bind 'the hinterland hamlets with the strategic heights' (Sahlins, 1968, p. 47). Yet despite their finely-graded system of social ranking, and the implications which this had for the social ranking of settlement, the spatial structure of chiefdoms can be seen as overlain by a simple but sharp dichotomy between the chiefly centre and other settlements. The whole system appears two-tiered, with the chief's settlement being set apart from the rest of the tribal community through its pivotal position at the centre of the chiefdom's political, economic and religious life (see Figure 4.1). The sacredness of the chiefly centre helped to make it a deeply-felt spatial dichotomy, and served to remind everyone that it was a societal system organised around a single, dominant node. Only as lesser chiefdoms were absorbed by greater chiefdoms so as to form systems of chiefdoms would this simple two-tier organisation have been modified into something more elaborate, with the dominance and centricity of local chiefly centres being supplemented by the greater dominance and centricity of regional chiefdoms.

The focus of activities around chiefly figures or dominant centres is most clearly apparent in the context of tribal exchange. Chiefs assumed the role of 'tribal banker', supervising the exchange system on behalf of the tribe at large. Sahlins' portrayed this change as 'a centralization of reciprocities' (Sahlins, 1974, p. 134). For Polanyi, it marked the formation of his redistributive systems, one powered by the centrical flow of goods into and out of dominant political centres (Polanyi, 1968, p. 149). However, having assumed a supervisory control over exchange, chiefs 'break into it, pressur-ize it and divert new-found surpluses to a collective economy' (Sahlins, 1968, p. 24). This creation of a public or collective economy that extended beyond the ordinary domestic mode of production is a pivotal point in Sahlins's discussion of the tribal

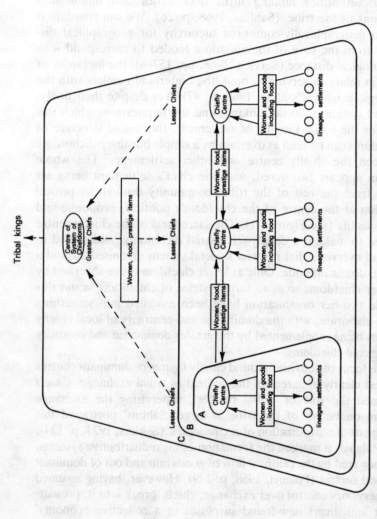

FIGURE 4.1 *Early Hierarchies and the Beginning of Nodality*

NOTE The development of early hierarchies can be seen as passing through three phases. The first (A) involved the emergence of chiefs over a tribe and the creation of a chiefly centre. The second (B) involved the creation of symmetrical relations between chiefs. The third (C) saw the emergence of a system of chiefdoms, with one chief being ranked higher than others.

economy. The extension of chiefly control over exchange helped to overcome the limitations of the domestic mode of production. It replaced the restraint of the latter with a new liberality. Giving out part of what they received was one of the ways in which chiefs pushed out the social boundaries of their authority. But in creating 'a coherent good beyond the conception of and capacity of the society's domestic group' (Sahlins, 1974, p. 140) chiefs extracted a premium. Not only was more now extracted for exchange but more significantly, the giving and receiving of gifts acquired an instrumental value. What was given to the chief became tribute whereas what was given out by him became pure gift. The entire system of gift and counter-gift, presentation and counter-presentation, was thus used to reinforce the now-superior status of the chief. Initially at least, the ordinary tribesman was not without some benefit from this fundamental change. Although they refrain from seeing redistribution as an essential characteristic of chief-doms, Peebles and Kus do note that the organisational cost of chiefs in terms of the extra energy which they extracted from ordinary tribesman was more than balanced by the gains made to the system at large through better information-processing and greater adaptability (Peebles and Kus, 1977, p. 430).

From a structural point of view, the emergence of big-men and chiefs added more than just a new layer of expectation and appropriation to exchange relations. It fostered new kinds of relationship and new kinds of exchange. In addition to the ongoing flows between lineages in respect of bride-price payments and the like, there now emerged a new vertical movement of items be-tween chiefs and those beneath them, with tribute, corvée, debts, etc., moving upwards, and redistributed surplus moving down-wards. There also developed a material exchange between chiefs: this, in theory, represented inter-tribal exchange adapted to the chief's purpose (Friedman, 1975, especially pp. 175 and 179–80). These different axes or directions of exchange formed different spheres of exchange, each with its own bundle of items and values. The exchange network that bound chiefs and tribesmen was usu-ally based on food, though other basic materials like wool or leather or even processed materials like cloth could be involved. Gathered in volume, such produce and goods enabled the chief to display his superior status through lavish feasts, to sustain his household and to maintain individuals (such as bards) or whole communities of craftsmen whose products were essential to the maintenance of his rank. Flows in the reverse direction, down the slope of rank, enabled chiefs to use redistributed food as a levelling mechanism or as a buffer against crop failure and in the process to strengthen the dependence of groups on his support. The exchange flows between chiefs tended to comprise prestige items, like weapons, beads, feathers, ornate tunics and so on. Such items usually figured large in the ritual roles and sumptuary dress adopted by big-men and chiefs. Naturally, their exclusive control over the exchange of such items helped to reinforce their status. Clearly, laden with social, political and religious functions, as well as the more obviously economic ones, exchange remained something embedded in society.

By their very nature, most of the aforementioned points have a direct bearing on the spatial order of chiefdoms. They provide some of the principles behind its processes and structure. Any doubts over whether the emergence of chiefdoms formed a substantive change in spatial order are dispelled by the way in which anthropologists and prehistorians have tackled the problem. Contribution after contribution has not only set the problem firmly within a spatial context by emphasising such intrinsically spatial themes as asymmetry, redistribution, inter-regional exchange, economic and environmental specialisation and the importance of a territorial base to chiefdoms, but have also drawn out the way in which this spatial component mattered to the way they functioned. Admittedly, some prehistorians (for example, Bradley, 1980, p. 57) have recently voiced some misgivings over those approaches which treat the problem solely in terms of its spatial structure. Their misgivings though, are not founded on a rejection of the relevance of spatial structure, but on the need to enliven such static forms by introducing the social relations which overlay them, social relations which – as some recent studies have argued (Friedman and Rowlands, 1977, p. 270; Rowlands, 1980, pp. 37– 41) – have considerable meaning for spatial structure: the two sides complementing each other. 'By considering societies in terms of forms of reproduction we are brought to a re-evaluation of space as well as of time' (Friedman and Rowlands, 1977, p. 269).

The Spatial Context of Early Social Hierarchies

The first signs of social ranking and stratification, and therefore of spatial nodality, started to appear in Europe during the late fourth and early third millenium BC. Pride of place in any review of this problem must be accorded to Renfrew's studies of the Aegean and also of Wessex.

In the Aegean, the locus of change was centred initially on Crete. From around the seventh millenium BC until about 3000 BC, Cretan society was organised around small egalitarian communities. Their spatial order can be construed in terms of what I have defined as an early tribal formation, with small, modular, seemingly equivalent units tied together across settlements by pan-tribal sodalities. Societal change began to occur around 3000 BC, at the outset of the Minoan period. Archaeologically, we can detect this change through the appearance and elaboration of metal ornaments and weapons and through the construction of megalithic tombs. Altogether, the impression is of a new dynamic at work, broadening and articulating the social and economic system of the island. Renfrew reappraised the origin of this profound change, seeing it as 'home-grown' rather than something which diffused from the Near East and linking it to the processes which, in time, generated social ranking and stratification and transforming the spatial symmetry of the neolithic period into the marked asymmetry or nodality of the Middle Minoan period, 2000 BC. This new asymmetrical system of order is symbolised by the flowering of the great palace centres like Knossos and Phaistos. Each palace functioned as the centre of what Renfrew calls a principality, a unit which was 'effectively organized economically, but otherwise not differing so strikingly from chiefdoms' (Renfrew, 1972, p. 369). That palaces articulated local systems of society and economy is affirmed by the decipherment of linear-B tablets from Knossos. Their purpose was to record the vast quantities of sheep and textiles being handled by the palace's bureaucracy. The changing character of the seals provided Renfrew with a still-deeper point of interpretation. The seals of the Early Minoan period were elaborate in design and rich in their variety. Each of the different type of seals probably represented the personal seal of a family or its elder and was presumably intended to signify the goods which they fed into the island's network of gift exchange. By the Middle Minoan period and the age of the palace cultures, however, the quality of seals had fallen away noticeably. Renfrew correlated this change with the emergence of a centralised system, based on palace centres. He argued:

> The greater simplicity of a palace-based redistribution where most consignments were either to or from the palace can be contrasted with the earlier, more complex situation where a much greater number of people, including local village chiefs, were recipients (Renfrew, 1972, p. 389).

To sum up, then, the Minoan palace culture appears as a strongly-centralised, hierarchical society, perhaps developing out of a system of local petty chiefs that flourished during the Early Minoan period. The asymmetry which now dominated the organisation of the island's society and economy – with wealth and power focused on powerful territorial chieftains – was replicated in the spatial organisation of each principality, with palaces acting as dominant nodes around which flows of wealth, power and patronage were structured (Renfrew, 1972, pp. 362–403; Renfrew, 1976, pp. 211–37). By 1600 BC, a similar asymmetrical and hierarchical system of societal and spatial order had emerged on the Greek mainland as the palace culture of Mycenaean Greece took shape (Renfrew, 1976, p. 216).

Attuned to the problem of social ranking and stratification, Renfrew next turned his attention to neolithic and Bronze-Age Wessex. Towards the close of the neolithic period the tribal groups who had flourished in the area show signs of being organised around elite ceremonial centres, or the henge sites (that is, Stonehenge, Woodhenge and Avebury). Renfrew proposed that these henge sites functioned as the focal points of 'group-centred chiefdoms' (Renfrew, 1979, p. 307). The crux of his case rests on the supposition that a socially-exclusive priesthood appears to have been involved. Wessex society would have depended on this priesthood for the mediation of its more vital ritual practices. In suggesting that social hierarchy in southern England first manifested itself through the emergence of an élite, socially-segregated priesthood, Renfrew is not pleading for an exceptional development here, for many aspiring chiefly lineages legitimised their position by claiming a special 'hot-line' with the gods. By the second millenium BC, the data bearing on local ranking and stratification becomes easier to decode. During the early Bronze Age, Wessex saw the florescence of a culture which stands out in the archaeological record as possibly England's first 'consumer' culture – the Wessex culture. To judge from their grave goods, they bore all the hallmarks of personal affluence and wealth, with an impressive array of bronze weaponry and other status 'titles' like faience beads as well as no shortage of drinking bowls and the hardware for feasting. Set among more impoverished sites, those of the Wessex culture are notably prominent. Renfrew convincingly depicts them as a society based on 'individual-centred chiefdoms' (Renfrew, 1979, p. 307). Other contributors to this debate have made them out to be pastoralists, for – in the context of the Bronze Age – it was much easier to store and accumulate wealth in the form of cattle than grain (Fleming, 1973, pp. 580–1); grain could be stored socially, via the prestations and counterprestations of their exchange system, but not physically, at least not for any great length of time (Halstead, 1981, p. 192).

Building on the problematic identified by Renfrew, a number of other studies have now appeared which likewise address themselves to the question of social ranking and stratification in Bronze-Age England. Ellison, for instance, has surveyed Middle Bronze-Age Wessex in order to test whether social differentiation was an ongoing feature of society. Her conclusions serve as a fine demonstration of how archaeological material is now being arranged beside what we can call the predicted spatial component of standard anthropological models. She talks of 'recurring modular units by the Middle Bronze Age' occupied by 'an extended familial unit'. Although, like other writers, she favours a patrilineal, patrilocal system of descent and residence, she keeps the door open for other possibilities. On the basis of grave goods, she accepts that unambiguous evidence for ascribed ranking (that is, ranking at birth) is not available, but 'the existence of prestige items which were produced by full-time specialists and distributed across the exchange networks of other classes of metal and ceramics strongly suggest the existence of high-ranking individuals' (Ellison, 1981, pp. 432–3). In terms of spatial structure, she confirms the existence of an evident settlement hierarchy. Whilst these settlements had the capacity to be self-sufficient as regards subsistence, the analysis of pottery and metal-work pointed to 'a complex network of interlocking productive activities on a local level' whose distribution added up to 'a complex system of small-scale interlocking exchange networks' (Ellison, 1981, p. 434). Her study highlights features of spatial order that simply would not have been evident prior to the late neolithic/early Bronze Age – hierarchy, asymmetry and functional integration.

Elsewhere, the transformation of spatial order wrought by this emergent hierarchical structuring of society is well-captured by Darvill's comparison of Irish court cairns and passage graves. The former date from the neolithic era and were reviewed briefly in Chapter 3. The latter were constructed during the Bronze Age and differed from court cairns in a number of ways. Apart from being funereal as well as ritual sites, when compared with court cairns, passage graves appear more evenly spread over northern Ireland. The fact that their design was more standardised and that they served larger territories, with an average nearest-neighbour distance of 10.4 km (as compared with 4.5 km for court cairns) encouraged Darvill to suggest that society had probably become more integrated by the Bronze Age. On the basis of their size and clustering, he further proposed that a hierarchical order was in evidence, with a number of cemetery clusters standing out from the general distribution of graves. These cemetery clusters were broadly aligned along an east–west line but to the south of the main weight of distribution. Setting his ideas within a patently diffusionist framework, he saw the cemetery clusters as signifying the primary centres of settlement and control, with communities to the north having tributary relationships to them (Darvill, 1979, pp. 311–27).

One or two recent studies of this problem have moved beyond the study of the single situation or society and have striven to establish the point that the hierarchical structuring of society was not a smooth irreversible process. From the late neolithic onwards, we are faced with veritable cycles of social integration succeeded by disintegration, the emergence of powerful chiefdoms and elaborate social hierarchies being followed sooner or later by their disintegration. It is doubtful whether ranking or stratification, once present, ever disappeared totally, but their degree of development apparently concertinaed between structural and spatial extremes. The idea of such a cycle, for instance, is implicit in Bradley's reassessment of Late Bronze-Age Wessex. Building on recent radiocarbon datings which reveal that, far from being a supposedly Late Bronze-Age growth, the Deverel–Rimbury culture was broadly contemporaneous with the Wessex culture of the Middle Bronze Age, he constructed a new perspective in which the Wessex culture formed the chiefly element in a society whose basic peasant stock was represented by the Deverel – Rimbury culture, the latter having long been thought of as capable farmers and responsible for intensifying husbandry and laying out the extensive field complexes that are so much a feature of Middle Bronze-Age Wessex. The productivity of the Deverel–Rimbury farm economy was complemented, and possibly explained, by the firm control which the Wessex élite appeared to exercise over exchange, especially over status goods like bronze weapons, and over rituals. Bradley sees this two-tiered hierarchy, though, as collapsing towards the Late Bronze Age. Control over circulation in southern England, and especially over bronze goods, shifted to the adjacent middle and lower Thames valley, where there are signs that the core of a new system of ranking and stratification developed. The Wessex area, meanwhile, adjusted initially to a less-hierarchical system, one in which local production systems and local exchange networks came more to the fore and in which the power of territorial chiefs waned in favour of local big-men. Soon after, however, Bradley sees a recovery of integration taking place. He roots this new hierarchy in competition for land and its output. The absence of obvious ritual centres and the paucity of prestige items by the close of the Bronze Age suggested to him that control over ritual and inter-regional exchange now mattered less in the determination of this new social hierarchy (Bradley, 1980, pp. 57–79; see also Bradley, 1984, pp. 68–127).

An even more elaborately calibrated cycle of growth and decay has been proposed by Kristiansen in a study of how tribal systems developed over the neolithic and Bronze Age in northern Europer, 4000–500 BC. His comments draw a great deal on the experience of north-west Zealand which he regards as a microcosm of northern Europe on account of its ecological variety. Viewed in terms of the relationship between society and the environment, the period 4000–500 BC saw a gradual shift from a dispersed pattern of farming settlement to a more concentrated pattern, first in the interior and then on the coast. Predictably, this intensifying pattern of settlement was first apparent on the better, heavier soils, before spreading to the lighter, less productive soils. Kristiansen matches such changes with broad shifts in the nature of societal organisation.

Commencing in the neolithic, he interpreted the construction of large, communally-used ritual sites, like long barrows, and the production of specialised items like polished stone axes as signs of a society that was becoming more integrated and interdependent through the practice of shared rituals and beliefs and through a developing exchange system. At this stage, though, he offers little evidence for hierarchy. By the middle neolithic period, the building of numerous megaliths and, more especially, the engineering of causewayed camps for 'inter-clan activities' tokened what he terms 'a specific pattern of territorial chiefdom organization' (Kristiansen, 1982, p. 259). Personally, I would hesitate to see his 'dispersed pattern of extended families in a forest environment who based their existence on extensive slash-and-burn agriculture' and the supposed 'seasonal function of communal and territorial central places' as a basis for talking about chiefdoms: the latter could just as easily have been used by egalitarian tribes drawn together by shared or pan-tribal beliefs and rituals (compare Renfrew, 1976, pp. 250–3). Whatever the case, these integrated systems of societal organisation appear to have collapsed into more localised systems by the late neolithic era 3200–2300 BC. Territorial centres like causewayed camps were no longer used. Items that had sustained elaborate networks of inter-regional exchange (for example, pottery, amber) became scarce. New exchange patterns, such as those based on battle axes, give the impression of more localised system of production and circulation. For Kristiansen, these changes marked a new phase, one based on more localised hierarchies, perhaps with local big-men taking over from territorial chiefs as system-managers. During the late neolithic era, 2300–1900 BC, and the Bronze Age, 1900–500 BC, the pendulum swung yet again. A vigorous colonisation of more marginal soils got under way, with mixed farming systems being developed around grain, sheep and cattle. New crafts flourished, and inter-regional exchange enjoyed a resurgence with prestige items circulating freely amongst élite groups. Social ranking and stratification were projected upwards into more elaborate and more extensive hierarchies, an extension which can be correlated with emergent differences in the rank status of settlements. This heightened state of social integration and organisation, though, lasted only until the late Bronze Age, when the whole trend reversed yet again. Social hierarchies collapsed downwards and inwards, as more localised and flattened systems of societal order reasserted themselves (Kristiansen, 1982, pp. 248–63). This hummocky movement of societal organisation would not have been atypical of Europe generally. If we place Bradley's discussion of southern England during the Bronze Age alongside Cunliffe's survey of the area during the first millenium BC, we find a similar long-term flux (Cunliffe, 1976, pp. 343–57).

Somewhat surprisingly, few of the case studies now available on prehistoric chiefdoms make an issue of whether they integrated not just more people and more space, but also, more varied environments. This is a significant lacuna in the debate for it has been argued by anthropologists that chiefdoms commonly lay astride a variety of different habitats, and used the complementary implicit in this resource-mix to achieve higher levels of energy output and greater system stability. One illustration of this complementarity in a prehistoric context is Clarke's exemplary work on Glastonbury lake village in Somerset, an Iron-Age settlement. Sited on the edge of the Somerset Levels, Glastonbury's immediate hinterland was a risk-laden environment subject to seasonal flooding. It could only have been occupied on a secure basis if the risks inherent in the site could be spread through the security offered by a wider network of social relations. With this in mind, and given the likely source of some of the material culture found at the site (for instance, pottery, querns, spinning whorls, etc.), Clarke posited a link between Glastonbury and the larger settlement of Maesbury, a hillfort situated 16 km away on the Mendips. Maesbury was the centre to which Glastonbury 'owed its political allegiance and thus its customary tribute' (Clarke, 1972, pp. 854). Without this tributary or client relationship to Maesbury, and the redistributive flows between them, he argues, Glastonbury could not have been occupied on a permanent basis.

Discussions of early chiefdoms are mostly based on prehistoric data. Here and there amongst the literature, however, are examples from later contexts. Thompson, for example, has published a valuable survey of early German tribes which shows how the egalitarian tribes, or *pagi*, of the first century BC, with their rule of elders, gave way by the end of the first century AD to a more noticeably hierarchical system, with the more acquisitive and dominant individuals acquiring conspicuously more wealth through their manipulation of tribal exchange and a retinue of warriors and followers (Thompson, 1965, especially pp. 1–71). For comparison, discussion of early Anglo-Saxon tribes in England has gone some way towards establishing their political identity and locality (Davies and Vierck, 1974, pp. 223–93). But whilst it is probably true to say that it is 'groups and associations of people that form the raw material of early Anglo-Saxon political development' rather than fixed, administrative districts (Davies and Vierck, 1974, pp. 224 and 228), it had already started to become a society led by kings and lords (Davies and Vierck, 1974, p. 225; Binchy, 1970, p. 4) though it is debatable whether the concept of tribal kings as propounded by Binchy is really different in substance from a strong tribal chieftain. We are, however, in a position to document late surviving chiefdoms in Scotland and Ireland. In both cases, examples survived down to the end of the medieval period and in Scotland, even beyond. Taking those of Scotland first, each of the lineages or *sliochden* that made up the chiefdom were ranked according to their genealogical distance from the ancestor founder of the chiefdom. In some case, this ranking could involve an elaborate ordering of lineages within clans and clans within chiefdoms, the whole pyramid of relations forming what anthropologists call a conical clan (Macpherson, 1966, pp. 1–43; Fox, 1976, pp. 95–121). Just as having access to land established the viability of the chiefdom *in toto*, so also, did one's position in this hierarchy of kinship relations establish an individual's right of access to land. The old Highland saying that a clan without land was a broken clan and a man without a clan was a broken man neatly encapsulates these ground-rules of chiefdom existence. By the sixteenth century AD, when detailed documentation becomes available, the vast bulk of landholders were tenants holding land from their clan chief. The widespread payment of rent in kind (including grain, sheep, poultry, cloth and such like) can be couched as basic flows within a scheme of redistributive exchange (Dodgshon, 1986b). In origin, they were probably personal payments of tribute that had slowly taken on the meaning of land rent. What is not in doubt is that when we see such payments being gathered in by chiefs during the sixteenth and seventeenth centuries, their scale was considered to be the measure of the chief. Martin Martin, for instance, wrote of one clan chief being 'reckon'd a Great Man here, in regard of the Perequisites due to him; such as a particular share of all the Lands Corn, Butter, Cheese, Fish, etc' (Martin, 1716, pp. 98–9). Some of this food was used to sustain the chief's retinue, including genealogists, pipers, craftsmen and fighting men and some was used to redistribute in times of stress, thereby helping to strengthen the bond of mutual dependence between the chief and his clansmen. The larger chiefdoms usually had a central storehouse, the *girnal* house, to accommodate the food which was gathered in, just like Bronze-Age Cretan chiefs or latter-day Hawaiian chiefs. The Macdonald of the Isles, for instance, had his *girnal* house on a small island in Loch Finlaggan (Islay). Alongside it stood the castle and meeting-house where the chiefs who were tributary to the Lordship of the Isles met. For all its apparent isolation, these small islands in Loch Finlaggan formed the symbolic centre for a vast, sprawling chiefdom whose hierarchical, asymmetrical structure differed little from the stereotyped chiefdom defined at the outset of this chapter.

Irish chiefdoms can be dissected in even greater detail. The earliest glimpses of Irish tribal structure take us back to the fifth and sixth centuries AD. At this point, totemic tribes were still present. Alongside them were tribes organised on the *mocu* or *maccu* principle, that is, by common descent (MacNeill, 1907, pp. 42–7). Initially, such tribes appear as independent clusters of loosely-linked kin-groups. By the seventh century though, 'no *tuath* [= tribe] exists in spendid isolation: all are linked together in a network of alliances and hegemonies' (Byrne, 1971, p. 133). Just how complex and hierarchical the system had become is demonstrated by the fact that early Irish tracts distinguish between a chief or king of a *tuath* (a *rí*), a superior king (a *ruiri*) who held the kingship over two or three different tribes and a king of superior kings (a *rí ruirech*) (Binchy, 1970, p. 31). Consistent with current thinking by prehistorians, Byrne does not see the trend towards tribes and space being integrated into ever larger polities as a sustained process. Reversals occurred, during which tribal confederacies dissolved. Speaking very generally, he envisages a provincial hierarchy taking shape during the tail-end of the Iron Age, followed by a possible collapse back into a system of numerous, independent tribes during the fourth, fifth and sixth centuries AD, a condition of fragmentation which he labels as the 'pre-Celtic polity'. This, in turn, was followed by a restoration of the trend towards integration on a provincial scale by the seventh century (Byrne, 1971, p. 135). Not everyone would accept this phasing of tribal integration, some opting for a more progressive drift (Binchy, 1970, p. 6).

The evidence for these early Irish chiefdoms documents the important role played by intra- and inter-tribal exchange. In fact, the Irish law codes draw a careful distinction between *focad* and *frithfocad*, which Binchy translates as gift and counter- or retaliatory gift (Binchy, 1975, pp. 23–30). The operation of such a gift-cycle is recorded in the *Lebor na Cert* or *Book of Rights*, a document dating from the mid-eleventh century. Its information is presented in the form of two poems. One expands on the 'stipend received by the provincial King [of Leinster] from the King of Ireland and the stipend paid by him to the tribal kings or chiefs of the province [Leinster], the other on the tributes he receives from the tribe' (Dillon, 1962, p. x). Specified are not only flows of basic items (such as grain, sheep, gulls' eggs, etc.) and prestige items (such as cattle, horses, swords, shields, spears, tunics, helmets, saddles, bracelets, chess sets) but also slaves and women: the latter are variously described as 'strong', 'swarthy', 'graceful', 'women of high spirit', 'women from over the Great Sea', 'women with large families' and 'women whom he [King of Leinster] had not dishonoured' (Dillon, 1962). One can discern in these payments of stipend and tribute the roots of an early Irish exchange system with its flows and counter-flows of women, everyday material needs and prestige goods.

The close similarity between these early Irish chiefdoms and anthropological stereotypes is further underlined by an extract from *The Annals of Connacht*. Bemoaning the death in 1562 AD of Brian son of Eogan son of Tigernan son of Tadc son of Tigernan Mor O'Ruairc, it eulogised over him as

the man who most compelled the neighbouring territories to yield him rents and tributes, who offered the best hospitality and the greatest gifts to musicians and entertainers and men of war . . . who had the greatest number of Irish gentlemen and nobles in receipt of payment and wages from him, and who acquired the most charter-land and sword-land on every side. This was the man who bought more wine than any other in

Ireland, and drank it without stay or stint . . . who possessed
the most gold and silver and wealth, horns and cups and goblets,
arms and armour and ordinance, flocks and herds and goodly
cattle; for, as the proverb says, he who scatters, gathers (Freeman, 1944, p. 739).

Embodied in this extract are all the attributes that one would
expect of a chief. Its stress on his superior rank, his vast territorial
holding, his accumulation and displays of wealth, his feasting and
liberality, and last, but not least, his control over an extensive
redistributive system can all be transposed into spatial order, a
spatial order that organised large areas into a coherent hierarchy
of social and economic relationships and pivoted them around a
single, dominant node.

Hierarchies and Nodalities: Why?

The question of why the first social hierarchies emerged, and with
them, the first central places, has provoked much debate over the
last decade. The explanations offered are varied but the more
important can be divided into two broad groups: first, those which
stress the growing competition over access to land and, second,
those which stress the growing competition over who controlled
tribal exchange (Renfrew, 1982, pp. 5–6).

Could Spatial Intensification Produce Social Hierarchisation?

Explanations invoking change in the balance between society and
space are long-standing. All aspects of the relationship have been
drawn into the debate. Some interpretations, for instance, present
the emergence of social hierarchy or ranking as a problem of
ethnology or human behaviour. The introduction of farming, with
its more intense 'captive' relationship between society and space,
is seen as leading inexorably to territorial competition, conflict and
dominance-hierarchies (Reynolds, 1973, p. 472). Others have
instated population growth as the key variable. In a popular
version, the biological success of particular cultures is seen as
creating a Malthusian problem of too many people and too little
land: the expansion of their surplus into the territory of adjacent

but weaker tribes is seen as producing a simple hierarchy out of the unequal relationship between victor and vanquished. In another version, the growth of a managerial element, or control hierarchy, within vigorously-growing populations is seen as a home-based solution to the problem of growing pressure on resources. By reorganising or being reorganised into simple hierarchies under the leadership of big-men and chiefs, such societies gained from better information processing (a function of greater integration and a more structured network of communication) and greater adaptability (through functional differentiation and resource complementarity). Admittedly, this higher level of energy-capture and systemic stability came at a price, the symmetry and equivalence with which earlier relations were infused being replaced by asymmetry and inequality.

Insight into one of the mechanisms by which competition for land led to social hierarchy is provided by Meillassoux's thinking on tribal societies in West Africa. As the possibilities for colonising fresh land became diminished, then inheritance took on a stronger, more acute meaning as the prime procedure by which individuals gained access to land and livelihood. Because fathers naturally preceded sons, it follows that the latter were always in debt to the former and to their more distant forebears not just for their foothold on the land, but also, for their share of the whole family complex of skills, seed, stock and equipment. In a situation of growing land scarcity, it is easy to comprehend how the land and livelihood secured through one's membership of a descent-group could lead to a simple, but vital, plane of differentiation within groups. Fathers asserted prior claims over sons, elders over the young and those closer to the distant founder-ancestor of the tribe over those who, genealogically-speaking, were more removed. Age-sets and a relative ranking of kin groups could easily arise out of this situation, prompted by little more than a principle of 'first come, first served'. Under still more pressure, its conversion into a dominance-hierarchy would seem straightforward.

What makes changes in the broad relationship between society and land such an attractive avenue of enquiry is the fact that the rise of social hierarchies, especially over the Bronze Age, can be correlated with far-reaching developments in farming and the intensity with which space was occupied. The case for seeing these two trends as formatively linked has been most emphatically stated by Sherratt. His argument is structured around his concept of 'the secondary products revolution'. Key strands in this concept were first outlined in a paper on European societal change that was published in 1973. A fuller, more refined version appeared in 1981 (Sherratt 1981, pp. 261–305). The cornerstone of his argument is that over the late neolithic era and early Bronze Age, there occurred a series of interrelated developments which had the effect of integrating arable and stock farming within a single system of husbandry: these innovations included the use of animals for draught purposes, with ploughs and animal traction taking over from hand-tools like the hoe and digging-stick, and the introduction of carts; the development of crafts based on animal products like wool and leather; and lastly, the utilisation of animal food-products like butter and chesse. Sherratt is in no doubt that the motor behind the 'secondary products revolution' was sustained population growth and territorial expansion. Whereas – under his interpretation – the earliest phases of farming had been largely confined to localised valley sites, this new phase saw population pushed out onto more marginal environments. In his own words, 'settlements broke out of the tight constraints which had previously produced a highly linear pattern . . . immediately related to water courses and spread to a wider range of often dryer and less fertile soils' (Sherratt, 1981, pp. 292–3). In contrast to the intensive cultivation of fertile pockets that had characterised the earliest phases of farming, this new phase involved more extensive systems of husbandry based on both crop and stock. The large areas of forest cleared by this wave of colonisation provided ample pasture and a broader basis to the farm economy (cf. Jones, 1981, pp. 11–13). Significantly, it is at this point in time that we find large planned field-complexes being laid out in areas like Wessex or on the heathlands of Jutland. Overall, Sherratt sees his 'secondary products revolution' as having its greatest impact in central and northern Europe.

We could be forgiven for thinking that any extension and intensification of land use must have released any pent-up pressure on resources, without the need for tieing it to new forms of societal order. Sherratt, however, pursues a different line of argument. Because the 'secondary products revolution' generated major alterations in the allocation of subsistence roles between the sexes, with men becoming more involved and dominant in farm activity, it created new social structures and patterns of organization, and by giving new importance to the transmission of land, it necessitated new mechanisms of inheritance (Sherratt, 1981, p. 297).

The new mechanisms of inheritance which he had in mind were prompted by Goody's distinction between homogeneous devolution – a system common in Africa and associated with hoe cultivation and the organisation of property around lineages – and divergent devolution – a system prevalent in historic Europe and associated with plough cultivation, family groups and the successive splitting and recombination of holdings through inheritance and marriage (Goody, 1976, pp. 9–22). Somewhat speculatively, he concluded that divergent devolution had established itself in Europe by the second millenium BC, following the spread of plough cultivation and the re-symbolisation of farmland as a wholly male title. For Sherratt, it was their spread in combination with other ingredients of the 'secondary products revolution' that precipitated the shift towards a more differentiated and hierarchical society. Precisely when the different parts of Europe experienced this shift depended on when the different local societies (having exhausted the possibilities of colonising marginal land) began to compete more aggressively both within themselves and between each other for a finite supply of land. Sherratt believes such conditions were reached in the Near East and Mediterranean by the start of the Bronze Age, but that in what he terms 'inland' Europe, they did not appear until about 1000 BC, or during the late Bronze Age.

Did Society 'Exchange' Homogeneity For Hierarchy?

Inspired by the concern of Marxist anthropologists for relations of production and by the concern of the American substantivist school of anthropology for the way the economic relations of the tribe were embedded in social relations, there has emerged a wide-ranging debate over the past decade on how exchange relations provided a ready-wired system of communication and interaction through which social relations could be revalued and subjected to wholly new ulterior demands earthed in the production of food and goods. In so far as the upsurgence of social hierarchies was a change in the nature of social relations, it was to be expected that a closer scrutiny of exchange relations should prove a fertile source of ideas on why such social orogenies occurred, especially when we bear in mind the manifold functions discharged by exchange relations.

In theory, exchange could engender social differentiation and ranking through a simple transformation, with established systems of reciprocal exchange breaking down and being replaced by one of asymmetrical, unequal exchange. Given the values encoded within the material flows and counter-flows of exchange, such a disruption, if established on a permanent basis, would have necessitated a revaluation of the social relations involved. Of course, some fluctuations in the budgeting of exchange flows must have been present even under reciprocal schemes. But so long as the maintenance of exchange equivalencies and symmetry was a system goal, then negative feedback mechanisms would have acted to preserve such values. The critical moment was when such fluctuations reached a scale or degree of deviation at which they threatened the entire ideological construction of the system, its inbuilt instrumentality of meanings one which matched unequal exchange with unequal relations. Disruptions of this sort could follow major natural disasters. Those lineages who faired better may have played the part of a relief agency, funding the materials essential to the maintenance of the exchange system at large. Alternatively, growing pressure on land may have affected the problem by reducing the ability of some kin-groups to meet the obligations placed on them by their exchange relations, causing them to become debtors or, worse still, a dependent or client group. Having an insufficient supply of land with which to uphold their status seems to have been one of the means by which kin-groups in early Ireland sank into inferior, client status (Charles-Edwards, 1972, pp. 9–10). Yet another possible line of development was for tribal groups to appreciate the benefits of having a co-ordinator of exchange, a 'tribal banker', someone who could supervise the collection and transfer of gifts both within the tribe and beyond.

Whichever route is followed, the vital juncture was not when some fortunate individual began simply to act as tribal banker, but when the principles of reciprocity which had hitherto sustained the tribal gift-cycle was replaced by principles which overlay the centrical movement of gifts to and from big-men with notions of unequal exchange. The honorary position of the tribal banker was from this moment transformed into a position of rank superiority. His control over exchange not only tightened but was infused with new values. What flowed in to his store-house was tribute. What was re-distributed was pure gift. His control over exchange became the king-post of his superior rank and status. 'He began as a redistributor because of prestige achieved as a contributor or some other role but eventually he holds status because he is the redistributor' (Service, 1971, p. 139).

Once established, the position of big-men was reinforced through greater and greater centralisation of roles. Not only was gift-exchange mediated through him, but marriage-alliances were negotiated through him, with his position as a wife-giver placing him above those who were ranked as wife-receiver. There also took place a deliberate mystification and ritualisation of his position. Reconceived as the senior lineage of the tribe, his superiority was conceptualised through descent. He became the direct descendant of the founder-ancestor of the tribe, of the eponymous person who first secured the territorial claims of the tribe: their affinity of kin being confused absolutely with their affinity in space. As the direct descendant of the tribe's ancestor-founder, the would-be chief naturally became the person best able to receive the offerings and prestations traditionally given to the tribe's ancestors. He assumed a central position in the tribe's ritual behaviour, even being accorded semi-divine status. This ritualistic dimension to chiefly powers has been drawn out in an increasing number of discussions. It has generally been correlated with the collective construction of large ritual monuments (such as henge monuments, palaces, etc.), the ritualistic decoration of personal items, and with conspicuously higher levels of personal consumption. As the various kin-groups and tribes were integrated into larger, more structured systems under powerful territorial chiefs, still higher levels of exchange appeared, based on flows of exotic, prestige items (such as bronze weaponry, faience beads, obsidium) and circulated via more extended networks of inter-regional and even intercontinental trade. Needless to say, beyond the reach of ordinary tribesmen, these prestige items added to the chief's displays of superiority. To summarise these trends, then, would-be chiefs carefully threaded the radial strands of a complex tribal web around them and, at the same time, slowly overlaid established local systems of exchange with high-order systems based on the long-distance movement of prestige goods.

Implicit in this deepening and broadening of control by big-men and chiefs was the increasing use made of exchange systems as a means by which social relations could be used – for the first time – to accumulate benefits around some individuals more than others. One of the themes given particular stress by Sahlins is that the spiralling demands which chiefs imposed on exchange systems drove the domestic mode of production still further beyond its own immediate needs. If constructed around its own limited require-ments, the domestic mode of production would have been geared solely to the production of livelihood with no incentive to go beyond this point (Sahlins, 1974, p. 86). Of course, in order to insure against bad times, it needed the security that came from having a regular and reciprocal exchange of gifts with other groups. Social relations then, were already invested with a surplus of sorts. With the formation of chiefdoms, the domestic mode of produc-tion moved into realm of even greater security, but only by being pressurised to produce livelihood plus a still greater surplus. The entire enveloping system of hierarchical relations that now grew up around the domestic mode of production was sustained by the extraction and appropriation of this enlarged surplus. But what had previously been part of intergroup relations, and judged as equivalent, was now not only centralised but personalised around a chiefly figure. In time, it became an acknowledgement of the latter's chiefly status. Meillassoux's comment that 'prestation be-came tribute to a lord' (Meillassoux, 1972, p. 101) discloses exactly what was afoot here.

Latterly, Marxist anthropologists have seized on this emergent network of social relations in order to draw out their paramount role in shaping the direction of societal change. Without the flows that moved between them at an intra- and interregional or local and supralocal level, tribal systems would not have been able to reproduce themselves as societal forms. In direct contrast to those who see the ecological base of chiefdoms as paramount, scholars like Friedman, Rowlands and Ekholm assert that 'the kind of phenomenon which concerns us here is a social one' (Friedman and Rowlands, 1977, p. 270). The external relations being articulated through exchange schemes are instated as necessary for the internal reproduction of the tribal system. For Friedman *et al*, recognition of this outer skein of relations forces us to establish two levels of perspective: one focused on the individual tribe and the other on the congeries of interrelated chiefdoms and lesser tribes, cores and peripheries, in which they were embedded. Ekholm talks about each level 'having a certain kind of totality' (Ekholm, 1981, p. 246) but clearly feels that the ultimate explanation of changing tribal formations must be sought at the wider, supralocal level, with the external relations of tribes being the key to internal change (Ekholm 1981, pp. 246–7).

As exchange systems have come to occupy a more central place in discussions of early social change, so have more analyses of their functioning within the context of hierarchical societies and chiefdoms been published. An early essay on the problem is provided by Renfrew's work on the Aegean. Distinguishing the rise of 'urbanization' from that of 'civilization', he saw the growth of towns or proto-urban centres in the Aegean area during the early Bronze Age – with their 'stone-built houses, fortifications, a flourishing metal technology, some evidence of social stratification and several new indications of wealth' (Renfrew, 1979, p. 35) – as caused principally by 'a sudden and marked increase in trade' (ibid, p. 35) and not by any local change in population or agricultural efficiency. The introduction of metallurgy acted as a powerful stimulus to trading activity, providing it with material that had great value, utility and, when converted into weapons or ornaments, considerable prestige. When he first penned these thoughts in 1969, Renfrew couched his ideas in terms of a purely economic model of trade. In subsequent discussions, he coupled his ideas more closely with anthropological concepts of exchange, drawing out its social and political functions as opposed to its narrower economic role (Renfrew, 1975, pp. 3–59). But overall, whilst he appreciated and placed great stress on the interconnectedness of trade with other spheres of what he calls the 'culture process', such as social stratification and craft specialisation, he did not try to distinguish cause from effect but construed the different variables involved as a complex circle of interactions.

Particularly fruitful studies of the formative influence that exchange systems may have played in the 'reproduction of given social forms' have been published by Rowlands using data for Bronze- and Iron-Age Europe. Like Friedman and Ekholm, he starts with the assumption that whilst we can talk of local units of social order (that is, the lineage, tribe, etc.) we need to recognise the fundamental role played by wider interregional systems of exchange in which these local systems were enmeshed. Tribal societies reproduced themselves only within the wider framework of their exchange networks and cannot be treated as socially isolated. This calls for a macro- as well as micro-scaled approach to exchange. It is an approach that Rowlands has pursued himself. Writing in 1973, he argued that Bronze-Age Europe must have been occupied by myriad kin-groups and tribes, and an equally impressive number of alliances and hegemonies. Around these kin-groups and tribes, he envisages two levels of exchange: dense local networks of exchange based on functional goods and long-distance networks involving flows of prestige goods. Addressing himself to the high-order exchange of prestige goods, he depicted large segments of European space and society being integrated via three vast, semi-continental circuits or rings: the Mediterranean, central Europe and Atlantic Europe. The character of these three networks was further explored in a subsequent paper in which he talked confidently of a Mediterranean economy, a central European urnfield complex and an Atlantic economy (Rowlands, 1980, pp. 15–55). Essential to his argument is the way these circuits were structured. Taking the Atlantic economy as an example, this had taken shape by the late Bronze age, about the ninth century BC. Its heartland comprised the tribes and chiefdoms of south-east England and north-west France. These were probably organised into a series of local hegemonies that were linked, one with another, through the high-level exchange of prestige goods. Rowlands believed their core status is also attested by the local production of high-quality metalwork using bronze traded from as far afield as central Europe or Ireland. Beyond this core of chiefdoms would have stretched a periphery of lesser chiefdoms and tribes. Included within this periphery were groups as distant as Wales and Ireland on one side of the Channel and the Netherlands and the Loire on the other. These would have been linked to groups in the core through the high-level movement of prestige goods between élite groups. In some cases, the exchanges between core and peripheral tribes may have involved an element of political tutelage.

Thus, like Bradley, Rowlands thought it possible that the Downland area of Wessex may have become subordinate to more powerful chiefdoms located in the Thames valley by the late Bronze Age, with the former supplying livestock and livestock products in return for bronze metalwork (Rowlands, 1980, p. 38). Indeed, at one point, he speculated on whether this contrast had wider implications, with elite groups in lowland, riverine areas actively seeking new alliances with peripheral groups and establishing a complementary interchange of desirable goods, such as livestock for metalwork (Rowlands, 1980, 35).

At a still higher level of exchange, Rowlands even felt there was a case for seeing his three semi-continental networks of exchange as having some interchange with each other. Drawing an explicit analogy with the ideas of Wallerstein, he introduced the possibility of a continental-wide geographical division of exchange roles, with the Atlantic economy supplying items like lead, tin and gold to central Europe and receiving, by return, items like copper and salt (Rowlands, 1980, 41). In a joint paper with Friedman, the suggestion is even made that both the Atlantic regional economy and that of the central European urnfield complex may have functioned as peripheral regions to the more vigorous exchange economy of the Mediterranean, with the latter and the central European urnfield complex both actively expanding their network of alliances along their northern and north-western periphery (Friedman and Rowlands, 1977, p. 271). It may be that further work will redraw Friedman and Rowland's bold picture of Bronze-Age Europe's trading account, at least in terms of its details, but the central proposition of their argument is likely to prove more durable, and that is, that we are already dealing with a complex hierarchy of interregional and intercontinental exchange by the second millenium BC, with dense local systems of exchange being overlaid – socially and geographically – by the long-distance exchange of prestige goods between élite groups, albeit on a limited scale.

Despite their differences over what promoted social ranking and stratification, there are interesting parallels to be drawn betwen Friedman and Rowland's ideas on exchange and those offered by Sherratt. The latter developed his case in the context of the Great Hungarian Plain, an area in which communities show signs of ranking by the fifth millenium BC. Consistent with his thinking on social hierarchies, Sherratt saw the development of exchange as arising out of the material basis of production, not the other way around. The interaction between population, technology and environmental resources are seen by him as providing the base-conditions for any change in the nature of exchange. This change, when it took place, followed a simple plan. With the 'secondary products revolution' and the establishment of new communities in forest and marginal environments, an extended range of products became available for exchange, including livestock and timber-based products. These fresh inputs probably served to invigorate exchange systems, sustaining dense local flows between the long-established riverine communities and the younger communities that now inhabited forest and marginal upland areas. Sherratt sees control over these new intercommunity and interregional exchange flows as resting in the hands of big-men. In time though, supplies of fresh land would have dried up. Continued population growth would have pressurised resources. Out of the more aggressive struggle for land, social hierarchies would have been projected upwards and big-men would have been supplanted by more powerful territorial chiefs. But at the same time, Sherratt sees the complementarity between regions declining as valley-based communities also adopted mixed farming systems. Items of exchange based on new goods like metal may have emerged. As a prestige good, trade in bronze formed part of a more rarified system of exchange between élite groups. Although this sequence of development, with the exchange of functional gifts being supplemented by an exchange of prestige items, was conceived in the context of the Great Hungarian Plain, Sherratt pleaded its wider relevance, the only major difference between the various parts of Europe being one of chronology, with 'peripheral' areas like southern England not experiencing the growth of exclusive channels of exchange between élite groups until the Late Bronze age (Sherratt, 1982, pp. 22–4).

The Geographical Underpinnings of Social Hierarchy

Both the interpretations of social hierarchy already reviewed and illustrated incorporate a strong spatial component. Moreover, this component is treated as an intrinsic part of the processes at work. Of course, this may be because geographical differences in wealth and consumption form an obvious way of verifying the existence of social hierarchy through archaeological data. The geographical lobby, though, is not so easily dismissed. Thus, speaking broadly, Sherratt stresses the changing relationship between society and space in terms of gross population densities, the way society responded to the 'secondary products revolution' and the way in which the penetration of new environments boosted exchange systems. Taken out of this geographical context, his thoughts on the initial rise of hierarchies and on the emergence of 'salient' ranking would both lose their force of argument.

Writing jointly (Friedman and Rowlands, 1977, pp. 201–76) and individually (Rowlands, 1980, pp. 46–8; Friedman, 1982, pp. 175–96), Friedman and Rowlands are equally concerned with drawing out the spatial dimension of early social hierarchies, indeed, of all hierarchies. Part of the 'structure' implicit in their 'structure of processes' is that conferred by the structuring of social relations in space. Moreover, the tendency for continuous change which they build into their model, the process of always becoming, likewise has an explicitly geographical structure to it. Thus, élite groups are seen as establishing core areas within which they sought constantly to monopolise wealth and prestige goods by securing absolute control over exchange, centralising the circulation of all commodities and blocking their transfer to other groups. Driven by an inner competitiveness between families and kin-groups, they are seen as having an inbuilt tendency to expand socially and geographically. As more and more people and more and more space were integrated, the superstructure of core groups rose commensurately. But in order to supply the ever-expanding appetite of élite groups resident in the core, peripheral areas eventually acquired emergent growth centres of their own through which local exchange systems could be harnessed to the needs of the wider system. Around these peripheral centres, there now emerged new élites with ambitions of their own, ambitions that conflicted with their politically- and genealogically-marginal position within the system as a whole. Fractured by such conflicts, the system tended, in time, towards disintegration. The tendency of chief-doms to grow and then fission is, in fact, a feature of their character (Cohen, 1978, p. 35). Thus, the Atlantic regional economy described earlier had dissembled into 'a more isolated and fragmented social landscape by the end of the 6th Century [BC]' (Rowlands, 1980, p. 46), only to be followed soon after by yet another cycle of development in which new élites and new core areas become prominent (Cunliffe, 1979, pp. 343–57). For Friedman and Rowlands, then, establishing the nature of historically-framed hierarchies is only a first stage of analysis. We should go on to identify the cycles of centralisation and decentralisation through which such hierarchies developed in space and the conflicts that ensued between core and peripheral areas. Above all, we should understand how the interplay of centralising and decentralising processes effected 'regular shifts in political location in time and space' (Rowlands, 1980, p. 47).

In trying to resolve these differences of interpretation, it is tempting for the geographer, impressed by their regard for space, to highlight what they have in common and to argue that, in essence, they have been mixed from the same palette of ideas. Rowlands, for instance, fully appreciates how man–land relations sustained social relations. 'Relations of circulation and exchange cannot be separated from the production of surpluses needed for such transactions' (Rowlands, 1980, 46). Likewise, Sherratt concedes a vital role for exchange in his view of the problem. In effect, what we are presented with is a circle of interrelated causative factors, with the different protagonists in the debate simply disagreeing over which factor was the *primum movens*, over the point at which the stimulus to growth was injected into the system and, therefore, the point at which we should slice into the problem. But modelling the problem in this way would still only give us a partial coverage of the issues involved. It would tell us nothing, for instance, about the discontinuities which have characterised the history of social hierarchies.

These discontinuities have geographical underpinnings. This has been well brought out by Rowlands and Ekholm. Eschewing the idea of a 'stages' approach to cultural evolution (that is, one based on bands, tribes, chiefdoms and states) they seek instead to reconstitute the problem in terms of a core–periphery system. Through their centralisation of wealth, power and status, dominant or élite groups established themselves as the social and geographical core of vast extended networks of alliance and exchange, evolving into highly complex territorial chiefdoms – or civilisations as Ekholm prefers to see them – with the degree of hierarchy manifest at the core being directly correlated with the overall extent of the system. These core groups and regions are seen as surrounded by a periphery in which social hierarchy is more subdued or totally absent, a world of lesser chiefdoms, lineal tribes and even residual bands, all tied by a complex web of direct and indirect exchange and alliance to the needs of the core. Although Rowlands and Ekholm write of an ongoing or lineal development of core–periphery systems at a general level, with society *in toto* always being organised into core–periphery systems and with even an evolutionary trend to the way in which they were organised, they see the history of specific examples as characterised by discontinuity. What was core and what was periphery was continually being redefined. This ultimate tendency for cores to pass through cycles of formation and disintegration and for new cores to arise out of peripheral areas can be understood only through a clearer appreciation of the processes at work within core–periphery structures and, in particular, through an understanding of the conflict that was latent in core–periphery relationships. As the overall system expanded, Rowlands and Ekholm postulate the growth of a competitive and potentially destabilising relationship between, on the one hand, the established élites of the core and, on the other hand, the emergent élites of peripheral areas who were called into being as the local agents through which the people and resources of peripheral areas were drawn into the wider system of alliance and exchange. For a whole variety of reasons, they see the balance of competitive advantage shifting towards one or more of these peripheral groups. Thus, the eventual disintegration of core areas is matched, indeed, inextricably bound up with, the emergence of a new core out of what had hitherto been a peripheral area.

There is a close comparison to be made here with the thinking of Sahlins and Service on cultural evolution. Their ideas on the phylogenetic and local discontinuity of progress would lead us to expect successive systems of chiefdoms, the locus of each system being displaced from one society to another and one space to another as the map of chiefly power was constantly drawn and redrawn. They would see the reason for this leap-frogging movement of 'progress', with the mantle of 'advanced forms' moving from one culture to another, one locality to another, as tied up with their Law of Evolutionary Potential which states that the more a culture becomes adapted to the prevailing social, cultural, technical and environmental circumstances of its existence, then the more it tends towards stability and ossification, whereas the more generalised or undeveloped a culture, then the more chance it has of responding to new opportunities of development.

I have dwelt on these ideas at some length because I feel that they contain a fundamental point for the geographer. Far from being a mere stage for events, the geographical underpinnings of societal change, including the pioneer rise of social hierarchies and their innate flux, may form an intrinsic part of the processes involved. Whether we see this geographical dimension as the lesson of the periphery, the local discontinuity of progress or the privilege of historic backwardness, it must form a central theme in any long-term history of spatial systems and will be taken up again in later sections.

Were the First Central Places Divinely Inspired?

Once individuals began to assume absolute superiority over a tribe, it was inevitable that they would seek to substantiate their position in every way. Given that the most powerful forces at work within tribal society were those commanded by their deities, it was only logical that big-men and later, chiefs should invoke the support of deities for their position. Their assumption of divine support can be arranged along a continuum. At one end, stood those who bolstered their position with the fiction that since the founders of the tribe were the offspring of the gods and since they were the closest in genealogical terms to these founders, they were *ipso facto* the people best able to mediate between the tribe and its gods. The chief stood as an intermediary, the senior priest or functionary in any tribal ritual. Quite a number of early European chiefdoms have, in fact, been interpreted as involving a strong priestly element. There has been a tendency, though, to see this priestly element as a role distinct from any chiefly lineage rather than confounded with it (see, for example, Renfrew, 1976, pp. 173 and 260; Burgess, 1980, p. 166). But as a cautionary note, we should keep in mind Hocart's conclusion, based on a wide review of primitive kingship, that the 'earliest known religion is a belief in the divinity of kings' (Hocart, 1941, p. 1), a divinity which surely would have prefigured in the spiritual assumptions of chiefs. At the other end of the continuum, were those chiefs whose status had been enhanced to that of being gods on earth. These were the divine kings, powerful hereditary chiefs who had elevated themselves spiritually above the tribe. From being the representatives of God on earth, the more powerful now became worshipped and received sacrifices as gods (Hocart, 1941, especially p. 9–11).

This assumption of divine status by chiefs and tribal kings led to a profound recontouring of tribal cosmography. Just as chiefs had assumed a central role in the organisation of society and economy, so also, did they now assume a more central position in the ritualistic observance of tribal cosmology. This does not mean that the ordinary tribesman ceased to be a participator in tribal rituals. Every family would still have had a repertoire of rituals whose practice ensured the continued abundance of crops and stock, the renewal of life from one year to the next. However, over and above this ongoing tradition, a new panoply of ritual practice was raised over the tribe, one pivoted around chiefs and élite groups. These too, would have been designed to ensure the annual renewal of life and the established order of things, but with the extra purpose of legitimating and substantiating élite power, they would naturally have carried a greater, more intense meaning. They established the place and moment at which the power of the gods was visited on the earth and harnessed to the needs of society. Hints of this hierarchy of ritual practice, with major communal rituals being used to 'earth' the power of mythological deities and local family-based rituals being used to distribute their symbolism over a wider area, were to survive long afterwards (see, for example, Brown, 1973, pp. 128–9).

The extent to which the power of élites became imbued with sacro-religious authority and meaning is more visibly demonstrated by the way in which centres of ritual practice took on a more elaborate and lavish appearance. Through their command of tribute, corvée and slave labour, they were able to initiate the construction of monuments that were patently meant to impress. We find the small, localised mortuary sites of the early Neolithic giving way over the late Neolithic and Bronze Age to centres whose scale of construction and exclusiveness marks them out as regional centres. In the Middle and Far East, the emergence of these large-scale religious centres, with their clustering of royal palaces, temples, shrines and ceremonial platforms, have been interpreted by some geographers as providing the nuclei of proto-urban centres (Wheatley, 1969). In relating what I have to say here to the 'origins of urbanism' debate, it is important to make it clear that the inception of symbolic centres was not in itself a novelty. What was new and significant was the subversion of their purpose by élite groups, the new lavishness and scale of the one being fused with the image and status of the other. At a more modest level, comparable concentrations of ceremonial activity – all in a Bronze-Age context – have been noted for the north German plain (Sherratt, 1981, pp. 192–3), for southern Britain (Burgess, 1980, pp. 174–5), Ireland (Darvill, 1979, pp. 321–5), and the Aegean (Willetts, 1962, p. 302). In the case of the Aegean, the focus of ritual shifted from local clan chiefs during the neolithic period to the priest-kings, palaces and temples which emerged within the proto-urban centres of the Minoan period (Willetts, 1962, p. 302).

Just as their genealogical seniority and centralisation of exchange conferred a nodality on tribal chiefs, so also did their assumption of sacro-religious authority add to this nodality. Indeed, all three dimensions were seen as indistinguishable and mutually supportive. With this in mind, it is easy to see how the enlarged meaning and presence which chiefs imposed on the symbolic centre of the tribe had the effect of transforming tribal space in a topological sense. The more élite groups and chiefs assumed sacro-religious authority as a prop to their position and, above all, the more the latter assumed divine status and became the embodiment of the gods on earth, then the more the territory of the symbolic centre became sacred space, more akin to the world above than the world around. Eliade appreciated the geographical significance of this change, seeing the plan of the symbolic centre as

being a 'sacred space', consecrated by a hierophany, or ritually constructed, and not a profane, homogeneous, geometrical space . . . What we have here is sacred mythic geography, the only kind effectually real, as opposed to profane geography, the latter being 'objective' and, as it were, abstract and non-essential (Eliade, 1958, p. 39).

Thus, the contrast maintained by earlier cosmographies between what lay above and what lay below was transposed – to the infinite advantage of chiefs and tribal kings – into a contrast between the sacred space of the tribe's ceremonial centre and the profane world that lay around it.

So long as there existed a symbolism of the centre, then we can speak of continuous strands in the nature of primitive and archaic cosmography. Admittedly, its precise representation did alter with time. What for hunter–gatherers may have been a simple sacred pole, a portable *axis mundi*, re-erected at each base camp or perhaps, a series of sacred trees scattered strategically across their annual territory became, with the emergence of tribes, a fixed ceremonial centre and, with the emergence of élites, a centre invested with all the munificence and labour that only chiefs and tribal kings could muster. Nevertheless, some themes persisted. The elaborate ritual centres that emerged in the Middle and Far East preserved the notion of an *axis mundi*, a conceptual pivot for the world above, below and around. Likewise, the great heathen temple at Uppsala, at which both Odin and Freyr reputedly worshipped, was associated with a symbolic ash tree, a tree which had special meaning in Scandinavian cosmology as the tree of life and which, as an *axis mundi* around which all things were developed, almost certainly originated in an older tradition of cosmology (Branston, 1955, pp. 76 and 79; Davidson, 1964, pp. 190–6). This whole question of how cosmologies changed over prehistory, though, is a thoroughly contentious problem. Taken at face value, the archaeological evidence suggests that abrupt changes can be expected. In Britain, for instance, the abandonment of the megalithic tradition of stone circles and alignments by the late Bronze Age suggests a radical change in belief no less than in societal order, a change which Burgess highlighted by distinguishing the 'Age of Stonehenge' from the subsequent 'Age of Hillforts' (Burgess, 1980, p. 354). By comparison, the analysis of myths suggests that the cosmologies of later prehistory may have been more resilient and adaptable. A major theme in such work is the way an interest in a Sky Mother is joined by a Sky Father, a Lunar Goddess with a Sun-God. It is a broadening of the primitive pantheon which can be read from figurative representations of primitive deities, with the very pregnant figurines of the neolithic being joined by the orbs and discs of Iron-Age sun-gods. Preserved myths sometimes capture their relationship in terms of a struggle. Early Irish myths surrounding the festival of Lughnasa, for example, tell how the male god, Lugh, struggled with an older fertility goddess, or Crom Dubh, who was responsible for bringing wheat into Ireland for the first time. It was a struggle enacted yearly through ritual (MacNeill, 1962, pp. 409–10). In Crete, cults based around fertility goddesses prevailed over the neolithic and Early Bronze or Minoan period, but by the end of the Minoan period, had conceded ground to cults whose primary deities were male (Willetts, 1962, pp. 70 and 79). One interpretation put forward for this change is that it reflects adjustments in the sexual division of labour within farming, with the hoe-based systems of the neolithic and Early Bronze Age drawing largely on female labour and the plough-based systems that came in with the Late Bronze Age shifting the burden more to men. For other scholars, the change signifies a political change, a means whereby a new élite sought to justify its power. Discussing the traditions that surrounded the festival of Lughnasa, MacNeill saw them as depicting a struggle between matriarchical and patriarchical cultures seen through a drama of rival gods (MacNeill, 1962, p. 412). Indeed, embodied in some versions is the notion that Lugh was 'a newcomer who enters the domain of an established lord and gets possession of the lord's wealth, his bull or his corn, or wins a woman of the lord's household' (MacNeill, 1962, 409)

Clearly implicit in some discussions is the possibility that the conflict between gods did not lead to the replacement of one with another, but merely established positions of inferiority and superiority. The re-enactment of their struggle through ritual served simply to re-establish their relative positions. The fact that male and female gods survived side by side and were even incorporated into common rituals may be indicative of this political meaning. Such an interpretation would help to explain why older cults and shrines survived in a diminished form, giving cosmologies of the later prehistoric period a cumulative or composite appearance with fertility goddesses of the neolithic still flourishing alongside male gods of the Bronze and Iron Ages. From a geographical point of view, the elevation of male gods to a position that rivalled or excelled that of older female goddesses introduces the possibility that cardinal features in the human landscape may be classified by gender. The practice of linking deities to particular features of the landscape meant that by the end of the Iron Age, there was both a feminine (for example, the Rivers Severn, Shannon and Boyne) and a masculine (for example, Cader Idris) side to landscape.

How Did Primitive Classificatory Schemes Cope With Hierarchy?

The structure of society and space around dominant élites begs the question of how primitive classificatory schemes coped with these new conditions. Two contrary lines of development would seem relevant. On the one hand, the broadening range of human activities over the Bronze Age, particularly the skills and crafts (such as ploughing, cheese-making, weaving, metal-working, wheel-making and boat-building) which formed part of the secondary products revolution, provided extra scope for the application of classificatory schemes. An initial response may well have been to organise their practice through simple classificatory oppositions, establishing simple structural homologues between them, so that the unfolding activities of the community became rich in allusion and metaphor. If this was the case, then the classificatory order of such communities would, like Vivaldi's many concerti, have appeared to be composed of a single dominant theme, around which they produced many variations.

On the other hand, there is the question of whether the growing organisational complexity of society acted as a solvent, overburdening classificatory schemes with too many relationships and too many categories. On the face of it, the build-up of hierarchy and societal integration over the Bronze and Iron Ages, including the many reversals, must have worked in this direction. To some extent, even binary schemes of classification could cope with an increasingly complex social order by simply fissioning into quarters or eighths or by interposing a mid-category (Durkheim and Mauss, 1969, pp. 10 and 48; Tuan, 1974, p. 17). A fine illustration of how an essentially primitive scheme of classification could be restructured into a more complex form, with people, places and attributes being assigned to more than two categories is provided by early Irish cosmographies (Rees and Rees, 1961, pp. 118–39). In the long term, though, we must expect complexity to have worked against the Procrustean simplicity of primitive classificatory order, providing it with problems with which it could not cope without more radical adjustment. The question is, how soon did this take place? In one of the few attempts to consider symbolic classification in an evolutionary perspective, Needham has related the problem to the changing nature of kinship structures. So long as society maintained a prescriptive system of marriage alliance, then we can also expect it to have maintained a conceptual relationship between itself and its scheme of symbolic classification at all times. With the shift to more generalised schemes of marriage alliance, we can expect such a relationship to have narrowed and to have held only for ceremonial purposes. Finally, with the advent of open, cognatic schemes, we can expect the relationship to have dissolved away entirely (Needham, 1969, p. xxxvii). If we take this scheme as a working hypothesis, it would enable us to see the problem, albeit rather crudely, through the more familiar perspective of prevailing kinship structures. Apart from a carefully argued but doubtful suggestion by Rowlands to the effect that, from the Bronze Age onwards, European society was organised on a cognatic basis and that household units had taken over as the building blocks of society, the balance of opinion favours the view that kinship structures over the Bronze and Iron Ages were predominantly based on lineages that were patrilineal in terms of their descent and patrilocal in terms of their residence rules (Friedrich, 1966, p. 29; Charles-Edwards, 1972, p. 17; Clarke, 1972, pp. 845–8; Meinhard, 1975, p. 4) though pockets of matrilinearity were still to be found in a number of areas down to the end of the Iron Age (see, for example, Thompson, 1965, p. 17).

Charles-Edwards's work is especially instructive. Drawing on the linguistic evidence for Celtic kinship, he depicts early Irish and Welsh kinship structures, or the structures which they brought with them from the continent during the first millenium BC, as based on agnatic groups of kinsmen linked together across four generations (Charles-Edwards, 1972, p. 17). He sees these patrilineal groups as having patrilocal rules of residence, citing the contempt which in early Wales was reserved for men who went to live with their wife's kindred and who, thereby, 'followed the buttocks of a woman across a boundary' (Charles-Edwards, 1971, pp. 115–16). Setting his ideas in a wider context, he thought 'that the society of early Germanic and Celtic Europe was relatively uniform' in terms of its kinship structures (Charles-Edwards, 1972, p. 19; though on Germanic Europe, see also, Thompson, 1965, p. 17). In northern and north-west Europe at least, there are indications that these patrilineal and patrilocal systems did not finally break down until the complex political shifts which accompanied the transition from prehistory to history. Applying Needham's thoughts on the changing context of symbolic classification, this would suggest that many sections of European society may have maintained – at the very least – a ceremonial relationship between their societal order and their symbolic scheme of classification until the end of the Iron Age. Given the stress placed earlier on the many cultures which had binary schemes of symbolic classification, it is worth adding that even generalised schemes of marriage exchange could sustain a scheme of dual classification. That such schemes of dual classification continued to be used amongst some cultures is borne out by the evidence which has survived for the dual classification of tribes and kinship groups in early medieval Ireland and Scotland (Dodgshon, 1986a).

The Birth of Spatial Hierarchy?

In spite of the diversity of situations in which social hierarchies developed and the wide variety of forms which they assumed, there are broad principles which we can abstract about their spatial order, principles which justify the separation of early hierarchies and chiefdoms as a phase *sui generis* in the history of spatial order.

As early tribal formations underwent the social orogenesis that produced, first, community big-men, and then, tribal chiefs, the structure of tribal space altered from being a homogeneous, undifferentiated plane, to being a surface undulated by social hierarchy. In short, landscape acquired nodality (Renfrew, 1977, pp. 100 and 104–5; Beardsley *et al*, 1962, pp. 386–8). Admittedly, conceptually-constructed centres in the form of an *axis mundi* had existed previously and pan-tribal sodalities had sometimes produced fairly conspicuous meeting places (for instance, causewayed-camps), but the centres which arose around big-men and chiefs were different in both their appearances and the processes that sustained them. Dominant élites not only personalised the meaning of these centres, they polarised them. Social relations became orientated towards them, with genealogical distance becoming a first principle of absolute rank. The tendency for distance from the centre to correlate with genealogical distance meant that social relations moved down-slope from these centres. The same kinship ties which integrated the constituent clans, lineages and septs of the chiefdom also integrated the territory which they occupied, the identity of the latter being mediated through the former. It is as if the kinship distances and declivities implicit in the term conical clan were mapped three-dimensionally into the landscape.

Whereas earlier tribal exchange networks had been built up through local, equivalent flows between tribal communities, these new centres of élite power not only acted as a gate through which all exchange flows now passed, but they also effected a change in the meaning of exchange. They interwove the various strands of intercommunity exchange into a single regional system of exchange: they extended tributary exchange links outwards so as to tap the exchange flows of the petty chiefdoms, lineal tribes and client groups that lived around the periphery of the chiefdom: and, at a higher level, they projected long-distance links to the centres of other major chiefdoms. Supported by these new and more actively-articulated exchange links, and by their propensity for collecting in more than they redistributed, the organising centres of chiefdoms became distinguished by their high levels of personal consumption and display, the visible symbol of the polarity which had now emerged in social, economic and spatial relations.

Once élites extracted surpluses via their control over exchange, then a public economy took shape under the managerial direction of chiefs. Specialist craftsmen were called into being. Through redistribution the specialist products of one community could be set against the products of another. The diversity which had marked the economy of earlier communities could, in theory, be narrowed into a more specialised mix of products, provided chiefs buffered them against the increased risks. Even if the allocation of specialist roles which chiefdoms permitted remained an unrealised potential, it does not detract from the significance of this point. However modestly developed, functional complementarity signalled the emergence of a more complex society and not just a more hierarchical one, a society dependent on the control mechanism exercised by chiefs. Once this point is reached, local segments of space and the society which they supported can no longer be regarded as entire unto themselves, but were integrated through exchange into wider systems of space, or into what some have called 'supralocal' space.

Although exchange relations had their own *raison d'être*, they were further legitimised through the role of big-men and chiefs as religious leaders, either as priests or, in some cases, as divine kings. The control which they exercised over labour and resources, combined with their sacro-religious authority, led to the construction of more elaborate ritual centres, replete with palaces, temples, shrines, sanctuaries and the like. Nodality became a sacred fact of geography. Indeed, so crucial was the sacro-religious authority of chiefs, that where local sanctuaries and shrines abound, we can assume that social and political authority was equally diffused.

At a wider, more abstract level, the establishment of social hierarchies and the marked polarity which they imposed on the ordering of space led to the formation of core–periphery systems. That such systems were present in Europe by the Bronze Age has been emphatically demonstrated by Friedman, Rowlands and Ekholm. Instead of seeing early social hierarchies as local, self-contained pockets of cultural advancement, surrounded by vast areas of cultural retardation, they prefer to see such social and spatial contrasts as integrated into core–periphery systems through their participation in a common exchange system, the various flows and obligations acting like sinews to help to bind the different limbs and parts together. What Wallerstein has argued for sixteenth- and seventeenth-century Europe is seen as operative – albeit with appropriate scale adjustments – as early as the Bronze Age. Rowlands and Ekholm construed the problem at two levels. At a specific level or when dealing with individual examples, we are presented with a pattern of continuous flux, with cores taking shape, thriving, then collapsing. At a higher or general level, though, core–periphery systems had a continuous history in the sense that core–periphery structures were always present somewhere not just throughout later prehistory but also, throughout the historic period (see especially Ekholm, 1981, pp. 258–9). Far from being born in the sixteenth- and seventeenth-centuries AD, core–periphery structures had deep-rooted antecedents. As Ekholm phrased it, 'while there is no geographical continuity in the distribution of centres and peripheries over time, there is a structural continuity between the systems of different epochs' (Ekholm, 1981, p. 251).

Friedman *et al* see their formulation of societal change in terms of core–periphery systems as a direct and irrefutable challenge to a 'stages' approach. My disagreements with them on this point are specific rather than general. First, we cannot ignore the fact that core–periphery systems only emerged as structural forms with the rise of social hierarchies over the late Neolithic and Bronze Age. In other words, it is an organisational form that, in the first instance, had to evolve: the only satisfactory framework for this evolution is that of a 'stage' approach, with bands giving way to lineal tribes and lineal tribes to simple hierarchies and the latter to the elaborate territorial chiefdoms which signal the birth of core–periphery structures. To argue that social hierarchy and the processes that underpinned core–periphery structures were immanent within the earliest tribes (and even, for some, bands) – thereby establishing the total universality of core–periphery systems in processual if not structural terms – is an unconvincing way of circumventing this dilemma. Second, we must be wary of freezing the historical movement of the past by establishing too inflexible and monolithic a view of core–periphery systems. It has always been a prime criticism of a 'stages' approach to cultural evolution that it ran out of ideas with the early states, condensing almost 2000 years of subsequent history into a single stage. To note the establishment of core–periphery systems by the Bronze Age and to insist on their continuity thereafter, albeit at a General Level, invites the same criticism. To be fair, both Rowlands and Ekholm acknowledge that core–periphery systems evolve at a General Level but they do not specify precisely how. This is a crucial gap in their discussion. The notion of a core–periphery system can be broad in scope and loose in meaning, so much so that to assert their necessary existence for social reproduction at all times does not exclude the possibility of a 'stages' approach, but simply redefines the boundary conditions within which such 'stages' must be sought. To put this more directly, once social hierarchies emerged, our problem becomes one of seeking to understand how the simple core–periphery structures into which they were initially organised subsequently developed into larger, more elaborate forms. As I will try to show, these larger, more elaborate structures required changes in the basis of societal integration as a precondition of their stable development. In other words, the forms produced on the ground give meaning to the structure of processes that underpinned them, the scalar growth and elaboration of the former being dependent on qualitative changes in the latter. It is in this sense, that we can talk of core–periphery systems providing the boundary conditions within which we can seek out the subsequent 'stages' of societal organisation.

5
A Geography of Regulated Space: The Rise of State-systems

There is a profound difference between what Sahlins described as the establishment of territoriality in society and the establishment of society in a territory (Sahlins, 1968, p. 5). The shift from early social hierarchies to early states involved precisely this change, at least when viewed through spatial order. The idea of space organised through kinship and, therefore, of a space identified through the kin-groups who occupied it gave way to a society organised, first and foremost, within a defined framework of territory, a territory whose physical definition of the state transcended any constitutive meaning given to it by ties of kin, etc. Instead of space being organised through society, it was now – at this level of organisation – a case of society being organised through space. Chiefs, or kings and emperors as they now became, no longer ruled over tribes or kinsmen but over a territory and its people. Formally fixed and bounded territories, not the ties of kinship, now marked the limits of their power.

The rise of early states generally involved a change in the scale of societal organisation. This is because they were invariably fashioned out of a hierarchy of chiefdoms with an aspiring dominant chief exerting his superiority over lesser chiefs and becoming their over- or high-king. Organisationally, it has been characterised as a shift from a simple two-tier system to one involving three or more levels, with the local or regional centres which flourished under chiefdoms now being overshadowed by still higher levels of organisation (Peebles and Kus, 1977, p. 427; Trigger, 1978, p. 20), though such a shift would have been initiated with the rise of systems of chiefdoms, with lesser chiefdoms functioning within greater chiefdoms. As still larger and more complex systems, the formation of early states brought new problems of integration and administration. The European solution discussed here was based on feudalism, but it has to be noted that some anthropologists see European feudalism as atypical in the context of early state systems generally. Yet much depends on precisely which aspects of its character we chose to emphasise. If we take a broad organisational view of European feudal states and compare it with organisational views of early states generally (Claessen and Skalnik, 1978, pp. 3–29; Cohen, 1978, pp. 31–75), we will find that there is a great deal of overlap. Both, for instance, appear as centralised systems, with ultimate power emanating from a dominant centre. Both involved a clearer differentiation of administrative roles (that is, the military, the church and the judiciary), each with its own nascent bureaucracy, and of a new and more clearly-defined set of sub-systems though there is an important qualification to this latter point that we must make in regard to feudal societies (see p. 166). Inextricably bound up with this differentiation of roles and sub-systems were changes in the basis of social integration. Although kinship ties continued to define particular interest groups, they no longer served to integrate society as a whole. Instead, the fabric of society became woven with a warp and weft of a wholly different character. Viewed horizontally, society acquired a net-work of defined sub-systems that were functionally segmented in a spatial sense but not in the sense of each being burdened with distinct and specialised roles. At the same time, if we look at the way it was structured vertically, we find it organised into stratified groups that were differentiated from each other by their unequal access to wealth and resources. Adam's sweeping generalisation that with the rise of the state:

> older, vertically oriented, solidary forms of organisation were replaced by more functionally specialised, authoritarian, and all-encompassing horizontal ones that were better adapted to the administrative requirements of large and complex societies (Adams, 1966, p. 120)

is just as readily applicable to the feudal states of Europe as to the Mexican and Mesopotamian systems around which he developed his ideas. Finally, stereotyped views of the early state no less than those of the feudal state stress the role which service to the king and major officers of state played in structuring dominant relationships.

There is, however, a crucial point of difference between European feudal systems and early state systems elsewhere. It can be introduced through some thoughts of Cohen. In a comparison between chiefdoms and early states, Cohen argued 'that chiefdoms have a tendency to fission as part of their normal political and demographic process, to break up and form similar units' (Cohen, 1978, p. 35) whereas the state was a system that managed to overcome this tendency to fission (Cohen, 1978, p. 35). Of the essence to this distinction is the fact that with the larger, more elaborate chiefdoms, that is, with systems of chiefdoms, 'each nodal point in the structure of the polity is the exact replica of that at the centre' (Cohen, 1978, pp. 35–6), so that each has a capacity to be free-standing if and when fission occurs. Indeed, the very fact that the lesser chiefdoms which invariably existed within the body politic of larger chiefdoms preserved their organisational self-sufficiency had the effect of lowering the threshold of fission. With states, though, the various sub-systems were redefined so as to be less complete in themselves and, therefore, more dependent on each other: they became less complete not only because they acquired more specialised 'lean-to' economies, but also, because vital managerial functions (including the enactment of law and the determination of external policy) were hived off and relocated at the higher level of the state. It is in this respect that feudal states differed from broader definitions of the early state. Although having an internal differentiation of role and function, the lordships which emerged as the building blocks of the feudal state still tended to replicate the roles and functions of the royal centre above them. Set one beside the other, their functional specialisation was minimal so that we can hardly describe them as forming a strongly differentiated or integrated system. Moreover, much of the power which early feudal kings hived off local chiefs in order to create the feudal state·was devolved downwards again as a device of government. The whole style of feudalism, with kings conceding not just land but powers of lordship to their major vassals meant that the latter could behave, within their fiefs, like little kings. As a result, the early feudal states were beset with almost the same fissiparous tendencies as chiefdoms, with lordships exercising their capacity to stand alone.

These forces of disintegration within the very heart of the feudal system were brilliantly portrayed by Elias in a book dealing with

French, German and English feudalism and which has considerable interest for the geographer. He saw early feudalism as a
system in which the forces of disintegration could easily prevail
over the forces of integration. As soon as central rulers 'showed the
slightest sign of weakness, the local ruler or his descendants sought
to demonstrate their right and ability to rule the district entrusted
to them, and their independence of the central authority' (Elias,
1982, pp. 16–17). A prime example of this fissiparous tendency
within the feudal state is the western Frankish kingdom which, by
the end of the twelfth century had collapsed into a multitude of
near-independent lordships. Only with the establishment of more
centralised, absolute monarchs were these centrifugal tendencies
eventually overcome and the integrity of the feudal state stabilised. Interestingly, Elias sees this more-securely-integrated state
as developing from greater interregional specialisation and interaction, a process to which he refers as a growing 'interdependence
and interweaving of human activities' (Elias, 1982, p. 25). Informed by these thoughts of Cohen and Elias, we are in a better
position to assess the true relationship between feudal states on
the one hand and the early state as a general concept on the other.
Far from being an aberration the early feudal state was simply an
immature state system, one which preserved an important structural feature of the chiefdoms that preceded it. Only with the later
emergence of Elias's secondary or 'absolute' state does the feudal
state catch up with our definitions of the early state.

Resolving the lineage of the feudal state does not answer all the
difficulties surrounding it. A further problem in establishing the
feudal state as the organisational successor to European chiefdoms
and tribal kingships is that it makes the gross error of ignoring the
presence and significance of growths like the Roman Empire.
Carneiro has pointed out that with many hundreds of chiefdoms
and tribal kingships still flourishing to the north of the Roman
Empire, the question of what we should regard as typical and what
as exceptional is an open one (Carneiro, 1978, pp. 205–6 and
211–12). What such growths serve to underline is that there was
nothing inevitable about the societal forms that succeeded chiefdoms and tribal kingships, though I would agree with Jones when
he says that the variegated environments of Europe were neither
conducive nor supportive of vast exploitive empires to the same
extent as the riverine basins of the Near and Far East (Jones, 1981,

pp. 9–11) and with those who believe that the concept of the Roman Empire was defeated as much by the friction of distance and the problems of accessibility as by the Barbarian hordes.

Turning to the organisation of the European feudal state, the ultimate successor to chiefdoms everywhere, there can be no doubting the far-reaching implications which it had for spatial order. It affected spatial order in various ways. To start with, it replaced kinship with lordship, the hierarchy of one with the hierarchy of the other and the territoriality of the one with the defined territorial base of the other. At a grass-roots level, the spread of feudal ideas meant that social élites now assumed full or increasing control over production as well as exchange. Land, the material basis of all production, now passed to the king as the ultimate superior. Under feudalism, possession of it became a right held of the king rather than something inherited through membership of a descent-group. In the process, social relations became increasingly shaped by the conditions on which land was held either from the king directly or through the pyramid of lesser lords arrayed beneath him. As a result, space became something interposed between king and vassal, lord and peasant, part of the means by which their relationships were structured and regulated.

The control now extended over the productive forces of society by kings and ruling élites was not a substitute for their control over exchange, but a supplement to it, a sort of backward take-over. Control over exchange continued but with critical modifications. Initially, the different spheres of exchange – local and inter-regional – 'followed different paths of development. As society slowly became more organised on a feudal basis, the tribute payments that made up local or intraregional exchange networks were transformed into rent, the basis on which land was held rather than the social act of paying tribute to one's chief. Interregional and long-distance exchange, though, evolved very differently. Its organisation passed more and more into the hands of specialised groups, or merchants. But far from being free agents, their activities were closely regulated by the rulers whose domains they served. In the hands of these merchants, what we can label as the diplomatic function of trade faded before a new trading function, a willingness to barter for gain. Eventually, these two strands of exchange – the local and the international – were spliced together with the emergence of market centres. The idea of exchange taking place at a formally-designated centre of trade encapsulates the regulated basis of the feudal state and the new values which it fostered. We shall see how this revaluation so threatened traditional values of exchange that, at first, it was kept on the periphery of the new states. Only at a later, secondary, stage do we find trading markets being established within rather than on the edge of society.

From what has been said, the rise of early states clearly confronts us with three broad problems. First, there is the question of how the notion of the state affected the definition and structuring of space. Second, there is the question of how the early states coped with the problem of managing larger, more extensive systems of space and society, a problem which, in Europe at least, directs us to a consideration of feudalism's geographical basis. And last, there is the problem of how the emergence of states transformed the problem of exchange.

Early States as a Revolution in Spatial Order

For the geographer, the most important distinction between chiefdoms and early feudal states stemmed from the way in which they constituted themselves as polities in space. The integration of chiefdoms depended, first and foremost, on the integration of kinship groups. The smaller, simpler chiefdoms may have maintained an ideology of kinship, a belief that everyone was linked by a vast web of kinship. In the larger, more complex chiefdoms, those involving hierarchies of greater or lesser chiefs, kinship sodality was extended by alliance. Bound together by kinship or by a combination of kinship and alliance, the geographical limits of such chiefdoms were its social limits. As such, its territory could be inflated or deflated in lung-like fashion by the life breath squeezed in or out of it by the politicking and warring of tribes.

By comparison, the territorial basis of early states was conceived in terms of quite different principles. Marx talked of early tribes being constituted in terms of either kinship or locality: 'kinship tribes historically preceded locality tribes, and are almost everywhere displaced by them'. With early state systems, this simple trend of development was advanced further. Any claim to polities having a unity of kinship, whether real or fictitious, whole or partial, faded. Instead, we are faced with greatly enlarged polities

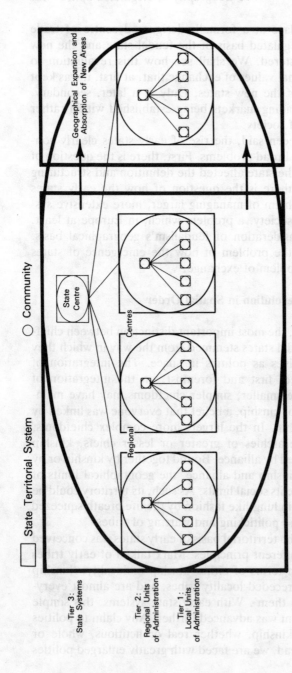

FIGURE 5.1 *Early States and the Political Integration of Space*

NOTE With the formation and territorialisation of state systems, we enter a phase in which the political definition of space transcends community at all levels.

that defined themselves, first and foremost, in purely spatial terms, or rather as the area ruled over by a particular dynasty. The question of what the state comprised in social terms was reduced to a secondary consideration, a matter of whoever lived within the territorial bounds of the state (see Figure 5.1). In this simple but profound change, we are confronted with one of the decisive revolutions in human spatial order, yet one sorely neglected by geographers.

The change being discussed here was a change in concept. After all, earlier polities had established bounds, even constructing boundaries where natural features did not lend themselves to the purpose. The domain of kings now became physically constituted before it was socially constituted, or, to put it another way, they ruled over people through their rule over territory, not over territory through their rule over people. It was a change to be expected when the sheer number of kin-groups exploded the myth of common descent and when the customary law which regulated behaviour between kin-groups – the blood-feud – became enveloped by a law emanating from kings. This is an aspect which Binchy brought into sharp focus with his study of Celtic and Anglo-Saxon kingship. Using the examples of Ireland and Wales, he described how chiefs and tribal kings came to be ruled over by 'high' or 'superior' kings. He saw this as a transition which affected Indo-European kingship generally, but maintained that it was most legible in Ireland where chiefs and tribal kings were still inhabiting the political landscape over the fifth to eight centuries AD. The rapidly developing authority of superior kings is read from the way in which they became, first, an arbitrator in disputes between kin-groups, a source of judgement, and then, a source of law itself. Binchy sees this as a process whereby private law becomes enveloped and transcended by a public law (Binchy, 1970, p. 12). In these circumstances, we can hardly be surprised that such kings established a domain of rule, a defined territory within which their rule held sway, and that, a part of the same process, they should each establish themselves as a *dominus terrae*, the person from whom all land was held.

Establishing the primacy of territory over kinship was one of the ways in which the rulers of early states coped with the scale problems of their new polities. As larger and socially more-heterogeneous systems, establishing a continuity in space was far easier than establishing a fictional unity on kinship grounds. But this was not their only response to the scalar problems posed by states. Equally vital was their adoption of or adjustment to a more complex societal order, a complexity which we can measure through greater hierarchisation and differentiation. This too, had its geographical dimension. Logically so, for the scale problem posed by early states was a question of how rulers could project their authority over the provinces or periphery of the state, out beyond the immediate seat of power. The problem of coping with the greater scale of early states was as much about how authority was structured in space as about how the state, *in toto*, was defined. Considered globally, the internal structuring of early states reveals a variety of response. Taking a European view, what distinguished feudalism as a response was its greater emphasis on the geographical rather than functional differentiation of sub-systems. Different tiers of the system and the different sub-systems of each tier were carefully defined in spatial terms and, to this extent, we can describe them as functionally distinct, but it does not follow that each tier and each sub-system had roles that made them distinct, one from another. It was a hallmark of the early feudal state that whilst the manors and lordships into which each tier was divided were integrated upwards through a hierarchy of service and obligation, each preserved a high-degree of self-sufficiency. This is most apparent in respect of the major lordships which appear as microcosms of the state, replicating the functions of the state but at a lower scale. The precise workings of such a system, especially the means by which it integrated space, will be explored more fully in Chapter 6. Of more immediate interest is the fact that in order to function, feudalism led to the territorialisation of lordship at both a regional and local level.

In a sense, feudalism presents us with a paradox. Although ostensibly a relationship between lord and vassal, or lord and peasant, such relationships had first to be enframed within a hierarchy of geographical space, simply because the extension of feudal jurisdictions, obligations and burdens in space was the dimension through which they were structured and proportioned. Despite its dependence on the superiority of one man over another, feudalism could only function when such social relationships were set within a geographical framework. The new hierarchy of social order which it created around the king had no meaning except as a hierarchy of control over a hierarchy of spaces, their inhabitants and resources: the one delimited the other. Just as the state *in toto* involved a rule over people through their signification in space, so also do we find the state being structured internally in a like manner, with the relationship between lord and vassal or lord and peasant being subsumed within a defined framework of spatial order. What we are witnessing is the feudal construction of space, one which replaced land as part of the patrimony of kin with land as part of the patronage of kings. Whereas the drama of chiefdoms was one in which the parts died with the actors, because they played themselves, the drama of states was a play in which parts and actors became distinguishable, the one having a life beyond the other. To put my point more directly, under feudalism, kings and lords created an abstract political concept of space, one capable of distinguishing space from the people who lived in it, people who, hitherto, had charged it with a purely social identity.

The Birth of States: A Midwife's Report

Before exploring the process of state-formation through particular case-studies, it will help if we familiarise ourselves with the debate over why state systems developed. As with other decisive changes in societal organisation, it is a debate which, latterly, has shifted from a concern with simple, monocausal explanations to more complex interpretations, from simple stimulus–response models to systems of interacting variables that were given a forward movement by the incorporation of positive feedback. Broadly speaking, explanations can be grouped under two headings: those based on conflict and those based on alliance.

Those based on conflict construe the problem in terms of either conquest, with stronger tribes absorbing weaker ones, or class conflict, with élite groups using the institutional structure of the state to secure their overriding claim to wealth and resources. Neither offers a wholly satisfying explanation. Although strong tribes do subjugate weaker ones, it was not a factor in the formation of any of the so-called primary states, or those which marked the emergence of state systems *de novo* (Service, 1978, p. 31). The class conflict model is naturally a Marxist-inspired approach. It too, has its weaknesses. The prime weakness is that inequality arose, in the first instance, from differences in kinship ranking and sacro-religious power and were only transformed into a system of stratified ranking or a class structure through the state and not vice-versa (Service, 1978, p. 32). Even amongst those who accept that unequal access to wealth was inevitable from the moment when society became dependent on agriculture, there are some who regard class conflict as having no creative role when it comes to state formation: such conflict arises out of the state rather than before it (Cohen, 1978, pp. 51–2).

Explanations based on alliance or on factors which served to integrate society have a stronger appeal if only because most early state systems appear to have originated in this way, with a cluster of advanced regional chiefdoms undergoing the shift into state-hood simultaneously and, in many cases, becoming ultimately fused into a single, large state. Renfrew has put this in the form of a descriptive model of state-formation. Instructed by the state systems which lay at the hearts of Mesopotamian, Mycenaean and Etruscan civilisations, he has proposed that early states were based on a cluster of territorial units which he labelled as early state modules (ESM). Each ESM was around 1500 sq.km in size. Typically, the genesis of states involved a honeycomb of around 10 ESMs, though he concedes that as many as 20 ESMs could be involved. Structurally, each module is seen as organised around a dominant central place: these central places are seen as being within a day's journey from all parts of their modular setting and within 40–50 km of each other.

Renfrew's stress on the accessibility of these central places, both within and between early state modules, is tied to his thesis that the prime integrative forces behind state-formation were trade-based. Despite their modular structure, early state systems display a uniformity of material culture and a high-degree of spatial interaction, both within and between ESMs (Renfrew, 1975, p. 12). Renfrew does not ascribe this high degree of interaction and integration simply to proximity. The growth of farm production and craft specialisation are seen promoting a more active network of exchange. With this quickening of trade activity came a pressing need to regulate trade on a system-wide basis, that is, throughout the whole network of ESMs. Out of this trading process as Renfrew calls it, slowly came intermodular agreements, co-operation and political alliance. In short, the whole system of ESMs was impelled towards statehood and even unity by the intensity of trading interaction and association (Renfrew, 1975, p. 44). Amongst other writers, Elias offered an identical view, with the political space of early states being defined by the unfolding pattern of trade and spatial interaction between tribal groups (Elias, 1982, p. 25).

For others, the integration of chiefdoms came about when society appreciated the benefits to be gained by having a still higher managerial level of organisation. Interpretations of this type can be subdivided into those which root the adjustment in specific problems and those which see it as a response to the general pressures acting on society. Typical of the former is the hydraulic theory of early civilisation. This supposes that the birth of civilisations or state-systems like those of Mesopotamia was preceded by a climatic phase of increasing aridity. To survive, society was forced to establish large-scale irrigation schemes. Out of the co-operation and managerial adjustments required, there arose pristine state systems. Explanations which link state-formation to a wider range of pressures can be illustrated by Wright's work. Constructing the problem in organisational terms, Wright places great stress on understanding how changes in the flow of information and energy may have induced state-formation. Any intensification in the flow of information and energy generates a need for more decision-makers: the more decision-makers, then the greater the need for a hierarchy of decision-makers. These adjustments towards a more elaborate system of organisation though, were more likely to be made when the normal running of the system was threatened by the sheer burdens of the task involved. Drawing upon his work on Mesopotamia, he suggests that threats to the system from a single direction were probably insufficient to produce the emergence of specialised administrators and that it is only when the flow of information became too burdensome in a number of different spheres – thereby threatening system-collapse – that we can expect the creation of a hierarchy of decision-makers to emerge and with them, the nascent state (Wright, 1978, p. 65). Wright's approach demonstrates the difficulty of disentangling individual causal factors from each other. By the very nature of his argument, he admits the likelihood that a range of critical variables were involved (Wright, 1978, 52).

Running through many reviews of this problem is the basic

assumption that in order to explain state formation, we must concentrate on why it involved a quantum leap in both the scale of societal systems and their organisational complexity. Logically, this means that explanations have tended to revolve around situations which inflate the operating scale of key variables (that is, trade, defence, communal works, class conflict). Some lay down very specific geographical or environmental conditions in the belief that where key variables are bounded or prescribed in the way they operated in space, then their effect must have been supercharged. This line of approach is most clearly articulated in the work of Carneiro, with its stress on the critical role which the social or geographical circumscription of growth played in state-formation (Carneiro, 1970, pp. 733–8). We can, of course, take the build-up of population as a surrogate measure for the super-charged growth of other key variables (that is, trade, production). The sort of factors which might circumscribe population include the localised distribution of fertile soils or the hemming-in of territories by mountain ranges or inhospitable zones. There is a direct comparison to be made here with the work of Pounds and Ball on early European states. Without exception, their core areas were based on localised pockets of highly-fertile riverine soils. What is more, these core areas display far higher levels of popula-tion and farm production and a more intense development of feudal relationships than the peripheral areas which encircled them (Pounds and Ball, 1964, pp. 24–40). For Carneiro, this circumscription of population growth triggered off the organisa-tional changes which we label as state-formation. Clearly, if we accept his ideas, it would introduce a geographical component into the discussion. In fact, few would dispute this. What matters is that we proportion its significance correctly, for as Cohen has said, 'the understanding of state formation is not to be found solely in the wind, the rain and the location' (Cohen, 1978, p. 39).

Arguably, what we learn from the geographical context of state formation is not the importance of environmental factors *per se*, but the importance of seeing how the different socio-cultural variables were structured, and interacted, in space. The import-ance of seeing how particular variables interacted in space per-meates a number of discussions. It is, for instance, an underlying factor in Cohen's valuable reformulation of the problem. To recapitulate on the main thrust of what he has to say, chiefdoms had a tendency to expand, but the organisational implications of sustained expansion were avoided by a policy of strategically fissioning when further growth could not be accommodated without a radical restructuring of the system's organisation. State-formation came about when the forces working for the greater integration of society eventually prevailed over those which worked towards its continual disintegration. We can phrase this another way by seeing states as systems which, by their higher level of organisation, were able to internalise growth problems which, once they had reached a certain pitch, were continually being externalised under chiefdoms. In short, they redefined the boundary between what was inclusive and what was exclusive. Taken in this sense, Cohen's ideas are not incompatible with Carneiro's notion of states being born where population was socially or geographically circumscribed. For once circumscribed in its growth, society was forced both to internalise its growth problems and to adopt systems of organisation that could cope with larger, more densely-settled populations. At this stage, the mechanisms invoked by Wright probably became significant, with the rapidly evolving circuitry of social, economic, political and religious interactions creating a need for more decision-makers and, eventually, for a more elaborate hierarchy of decision-makers. This may seem a too-mechanical rendering of state formation when compared with the class-conflict model of Childe *et al*, but it does offer a closer fit to what we now know about the way that the so-called primary states were formed.

A geographical perspective also helps to draw out the role played by new forms of communication. Just as the demographic size and geographical spread of these emergent states made certain forms of organisational change advantageous, so also must there have been pressure for new ways of storing and transmitting information. Earlier systems relied on the capacity of the human memory to store data and on word-of-mouth for its transmission. The complexity of the interactions that emerged with the early states, coupled with their greater extension in space, exposed the limitations of such media. Just as larger systems functioned more effectively if their formation was accompanied by organisational changes that emphasised their systemic coherence, so also were there gains to be made from having a form of communication that could cope with the lags and limitations that now emerged in the flow of information, one that enabled data to be stored and transmitted in larger quantities and over greater spans of time and space. Seen in this way, the association of early states with the development of writing is easy to comprehend. Commentators on the effects of writing have, in fact, stressed the crucial role which it played in allowing societies to extend themselves over space and time (see, for example, Goody and Watt, 1962–3, pp. 311–19).

The earliest writing was based on pictograms and originated in Mesopotamia about 3200–2800 BC (Hawkins, 1979, pp. 113–14). As its use became more established, elaborate logographic and syllabographic systems were developed, systems that needed thousands of characters to convey anything like the full range of human expression. By the start of the first millenium BC, the first alphabetic system had appeared in Greece. Because it involved only a small number of characters, an alphabetic system made writing a far easier skill to acquire. Broadly speaking, such changes in the character or technology of writing, together with shifts in its use, are best interpreted as responses to specific organisational needs of society rather than chance innovations. This was an idea pursued by Innis when speaking of the switch from parchment to paper as a medium of writing, a switch which occured in western Europe over the Middle Ages. He saw the early use of a durable but easily worked medium like parchment as occurring in states in which religion had a central role and in which time, through the keeping of annals, had a crucial, ideological significance. Its replacement by paper from the twelfth century onwards was seen by Innis as reflecting the needs of state systems in which political power was being centralised and in which the extension of control over space had become the dominant objective (Innis, 1972, pp. 7, 140 and 170). That writing helped to foster a real sense of history, of time past, and that it helped to maintain social interactions over greater areas of space cannot be questioned. To arrange these effects into successional forms, though, is less acceptable. Yet, this caveat made, Innis's argument does make it clear that state-integration – be it through time or space – depended on the kind of data storage and handling that writing provided. Case studies of how writing spread make this point even more emphatically. Clanchy's work on England, for instance, shows that whilst early clerical scribes did compile annals, the storage of information in society at large was still based on the human memory and its transmission by word of mouth until the end of the eleventh century. As in other parts of Western Europe, the transition to written records occurred over the twelfth and thirteenth centuries (Clanchy, 1979, p. 5). Their expanding use to record property transfers and enactments of court involved a spread outwards from the main centres of feudal power and a filtering-down from the affairs of the major territorial lords. By the end of the thirteenth century, even property transactions between the peasantry were being recorded by charter (Clanchy, 1979, pp. 31 and 38). In the space of two centuries, the English kings were provided with an elemental system of information storage and transmission based on the written word that was to be essential if the state as a whole was to be managed as a single, coherent system.

European States: From Communities of Kin to Communities of Place

Documentation of the shift from communities organised around kin groups and chiefdoms to communities organised within state systems, each carefully emplaced within a hierarchy of politically-defined spaces, varies greatly across Europe. The fact that writing was part of the revolution in communication which accompanied state-formation tends only to cast the problem in illuminated darkness rather than a revealing light. However, despite the problems of data, it is a well-studied theme and, reassuringly for the geographer, those scholars who have contributed to it have appreciated its significance for the history of human landscape. The following review of case-studies will include examples drawn from the Mediterranean world (the Aegean and Etruria), Celtic areas (Wales and Ireland) and from amongst the early states of north-west Europe (England and Denmark).

The Mediterranean World: Greece

The emergence of the Greek city-state, or the *polis*, must take pride of place in any discussion of early European state-systems. Towards the close of the second millenium BC, the Mycenaean world collapsed. By the ninth century BC, its culture and institutions had disappeared completely as living forms. Symptomatic of this collapse was a drastic depopulation of the countryside (Snodgrass, 1980, pp. 15–18 and 21). Society regressed, becoming organised around 'primitive' tribal systems in which kinship sodalities (locally clans, phatries and tribes) provided the main source of societal integration. By any standards, it was a dramatic reversal of societal organisation, one illustrative of the discontinuous nature of societal evolution at the local level. Yet by the eighth century BC, population had started to renew itself. With this rapid recovery came far-reaching social changes. Inevitably, the rapid expansion of population has been seen as a prime causative factor behind this societal change, a factor which by itself called for a 'tighter and more complex social organization' (Snodgrass, 1980, pp. 22–5). At the heart of this change to a more elaborate societal system was the Greek city-state. Although any connection between the two must have been blurred and tenous, the city-states arose in the self-same areas which had previously been occupied by the Mycenaean palace-culture, or eastern Greece and the islands. The central and western areas of the mainland experienced a less dramatic leap forward in terms of societal order. There, social organisation took the form of the *ethnos*, polities which had some of the formal structure of states but which were still ruled by tribal assemblies and ordered through kinship groupings (Snodgrass, 1980, pp. 42–3) though an alternative interpretation is that they were simply states without an urban focus (Ehrenberg, 1969, p. 22).

The character of the *polis* can be phrased in organisational terms. In size, they ranged from around 1000 sq. km for the more typical to over 2500 sq. km for the larger (such as Athena, Sparta). This size and, indeed, their sheer number has been linked to environment, an environment in which the interface between land and sea dominated and which broke society up into small localised pockets of development (Ehrenberg, 1969, p. 6; see also Elias, 1982, pp. 55–7). When the Greek city-states expanded territorially, it was not at the expense of their hinterlands so much as overseas, with colonies like Paestum, Metapontino and Syracuse being founded in southern Italy and others along the north African coast or in the Levant. At the centre of the *polis* stood the urban centre. To the modern mind, these would appear relatively modest centres of urbanism, with few having populations of over 10 000 (Starr, 1977, p. 104). Another vital feature of their character is the lack of any sharp town–country dichotomy. The two spheres of the state were distinguished neither politically nor socially (Ehrenberg, 1969, p. 28; Finley, 1973, pp. 124–5; Snodgrass, 1980, p. 31). As a society based squarely on the possession of land (Ehrenberg, 1969, p. 28; Starr, 1977, p. 173), such a distinction would have been inconceivable. In Plato's Republic, each of its 5040 citizens was to have a farm, divided so that one part was 'near the centre of the State, one near the boundary' (Saunders, 1970, p. 216). Plato was clearly conscious of how core–periphery relationships could adversely affect the integrity of the state. Together, the emergence of urban centres and the act of political unification which it symbolised constituted a process of synoceism. This was a process which began during the eighth and ninth centuries BC. In some instances, it consisted of the slow, gradual fusion of various scattered villages (=*demos*). In others, the city was created to a plan, replete with government buildings, temples, *agora*, etc. (Snodgrass, 1980, p. 34). The spiritual focus for the site and a justification for its location was invariably provided by a cult centre, for the organisation of each city state was suffused with a religious ideology (Ehrenberg, 1969, p. 74; Snodgrass, 1980, p. 64).

The Greek city-state hardly qualified as a state-system on account of its size. Its eligibility as a state-system rests on how it organized itself as a polity. 'The regional connections of kinsfolk and clans were decisively destroyed' (Ehrenberg, 1969, p. 29) and replaced by what even Aristotle in his day could see as a community of place, one bonded through ties of locality not blood (Sinclair, 1962, pp. 101–6). The rule of the *polis* lay not with a tribal assembly but with those who lived within its bounds. It was, as Ehrenberg proclaimed, 'the state of its citizens' (Ehrenberg, 1969, p. 47). At first, old and new forms of franchise commingled in the affairs of administration, but the formative history of the *polis* was the transposition of the latter at the expense of the former. As a community based on locality, its bounds were fixed. It was no longer a case of territorial limits being defined through the community, but of the community being defined through territory. Their relations were inverted, with territory now transcending the community.

A feature of the Greek city-state, as well as of those modelled on it elsewhere in the Mediterranean, and one which distinguished it from the state-systems of central and northern Europe, was its constitution. Part of this distinction derived from the fact that kingship played no part in the process of synoceism. Aristotle talked about kingship giving way to aristocracy and then to polity, though he also saw each as having a deviant form, namely tyranny, oligarchy and democracy. He also perceived links between them. Kingship and aristocracy differed by degrees, the former being a sovereignty of the individual and the latter of the few. Likewise, the difference between oligarchy and democracy was a matter of degree: both qualified citizens through wealth but one enfranchised the few and the other, the many (Sinclair, 1962, pp. 113–7). What stands out from Aristotle' writings on government is the range of possible forms already present by the fourth century BC. Of course, even where democracy established itself, it did not mean rule by all the state's inhabitants but only those accorded the status of citizens. At the same time, distinctions can be drawn between full and lesser citizens, whilst beyond lay a grading of serfs and slaves who performed the labour of the farm and household (Ehrenberg, 1969, pp. 38–43; Finley, 1973, pp. 62–94; Starr, 1977, pp. 90–2).

Although internally structured into complex systems of administration, with what Aristotle termed 'a proper differentiation of offices of government' (Sinclair, 1962, p. 249), the Greek city-states were less predisposed to fuse themselves into a larger, grander state. Indeed, their character offers a healthy challenge to conventional theories of state-formation. It is almost as if their organisational form had run ahead of system needs. We can explain the particularism and localism of Greek city-states by reference to the facts of geography and the importance of maritime communication, but we cannot explain their organisation as states. Even the fact that once formed, city-states showed little real interest in a wider system of unity (Andrewes, 1971, p. 81) poses interesting questions. Those pan-Hellenic institutions that did develop were limited in scope and meaning. Religious cults or amphictyonies provided a loose form of integration, such as with the Delphic amphictyony which survived until the fourth century BC. During the fourth century BC, the rise to power of Philip of Macedon and his son, Alexander, imposed a unity of sorts on the Greek city-states, conjoining them with a vast empire that stretched across the eastern Mediterranean area and Asia Minor. Their political achievement though, was to produce a system of states rather than a single, unified state (Ehrenberg, 1969, p. 138). Even within Greece, Alexander opted to work through the city-states system, binding them into the League of Corinth, a forced rather than natural alliance under his command. The divisions and warring that followed his death produced a number of military alliances in search of a common peace. The Achaean League, for instance, expanded from its original core in a northern and isolated part of Peloponnesus to command allegiance throughout the Peloponnesus by the third century BC, but eventually collapsed from within. The Aetolian League was a military confederacy that flourished over the second half of the third century BC, being eclipsed when defeated by the Romans in 167 BC. The incorporation of the Aegean area into the Roman Empire during the second century BC provided yet again the prospect of a political order that transcended the city-state. The Roman practice of basing colonial administration around city-states, though, prolonged their political meaning. But by this stage, Greece had become a marginal system of states, set within the periphery of the Roman Empire and 'flattened' into 'a quiet provincialism' (Andrewes, 1971, p. 81).

Peninsula Italy

The city-states that developed in Italy during the second half of the first millenium BC in peninsular Italy had many features in common with their Greek counterparts. So much so, that it is impossible not to see them as part of a Mediterranean-wide adjustment in political order, or as what one writer termed a 'political mimetic process' (Pallottino, 1975, p. 131). The Etruscan city-states afforded one of the examples used by Renfrew to illustrate his notion of ESMs. Over the sixth and fifth centuries BC, the tribal monarchies that held sway along the western side of peninsular Italy between the Tiber and the Arno 'gave way to oligarchic states with temporary collegiates and elective magistracies: the process is at times paralleled and followed by a seizure of power on the part of individuals (tyrannies) or by solutions of a democratic nature' (Pallottino, 1975, p. 131). As in the Aegean, political transformation was accompanied by urbanisation, with newly-formed cities (for example, Tarquinii, Caere) replacing earlier patterns of village development (Grant, 1980, pp. 20–33). Again, religion had an instrumental role in structuring city space. Their discipline, or the rules which governed the relationship between society and the gods provided them with a celestial model of how space should be divided and oriented. City space were arranged so as to reproduce exactly the lineaments of their celestial model, with the main axes of the one (or the *cardo* and *decumanus*) becoming the main axes of the other (Pallottino, 1975, pp. 144–5). Despite their cultural affiliations and a growing degree of spatial interaction between them, the twelve states into which Etruria became divided never moved towards any form of political integration, though an inconclusive case has been made out for a period of Tarquinian hegemony. Apart from the exchange networks that ran between major city-centres and beyond, redistributing the agricultural produce and metals which Etruria produced in some abundance, the only formal connections between the various city states were religious. The sacred site at Voltumna near Volsinni appears to have been the focus for a cult comparable to the Greek amphictyonies, with annual ceremonies involving all the different city-states.

The growth of Rome affords an outstanding specimen of the transition from a tribal order to a city-state, with a process of synoceism being followed by its upgrading into a centre for a system of states, or the Roman Empire. Tradition has it that the Rome was forged out of the political amalgamation of seven villages set on the Palatine Hills. This synoceism can be dated to the eighth century BC, or more or less contemporary with the emerging urban centres of the Etruscan states to the north. Tradition also has it that Romulus laid out Roma Quadrata (=squared Rome) in a deliberate act of planning, ceremonially ploughing out a furrow to mark the city's outer limits and dividing the space enclosed into a grid of streets. Beyond the city stretched the Acer Romanus, or the Ager Romanus Antiquus as it became known, the territory over which the new city-state exercised its sovereignty. With the establishment of Rome itself and the territorialisation of its bounds came changes in administration. By 509 BC, the Etruscan king who hitherto ruled the district was expelled and replaced by an oligarchy of local aristocratic families or *gens*. These were organised into clans that bore names like Fabius or Vornelius. The plebeian element that existed beneath this aristocratic crust did eventually secure its own assembly. By 287 BC, though, these distinctions were put aside with the creation of a democratic system of government. In theory, this signalled the ascendency of locality over kinship as the community of administration. In practice, though, affairs of state were still controlled via élite families drawn from both the aristocratic and plebeian sections of the city.

Overall, the transition from a tribal society to a state-system was a long-drawn-out process. Traces of kinship structures survived well into the era of republican Rome. The senate, for example, probably began as an advisory body of clan elders and probably preserved some of its original character before being eventually democratised (Ogilvie, 1965, p. 55). Continuing traces of these tribal antecedents were apparent through the tribal structuring of city space. Initially, or when Romulus supposedly cast Roma Quadrata into form, the emergent state was seen as consisting of three tribes. As the new state flourished, extra tribes were formed and incorporated. But in character, such tribes were naturally token, artificial creations (Ogilvie, 1965, 80), an attempt to harness newly assimilated or created communities to the spirit of the state's pioneer foundation. Relevant debate has also surrounded the origin of the city's curiate system. Literally defined, the term *curia* meant 'a fellowship of men', all of equal status and with ethnic if not kinship ties (Palmer, 1970, p. 75; Ogilvie, 1965, pp. 51–2). Its derived form, or *curiae*, has been interpreted as denoting an ethnic district within the early city, a sort of hybrid between a community founded on kinship and one founded on locality, or between what had been and what was to be.

By 266 BC, Rome's domination of peninsular Italy was complete, having systematically taken control of Latium, Etruria and Umbria before projecting its authority southwards into Campania, Lucania and Bruttium. As with Alexandra's Greece, though, conquest did not mean instant unification, but unlike Hellenist Greece, the special achievement of Republican Rome was that it did ultimately, or during the time of Augustus (31 BC–14 AD), create a politically unified Italy, a scale of city-state which 'was something quite new in the world' (Dudley, 1975, p. 35). The Roman confederation was bound by various means. Some areas were administered through city-states, with Rome taking over an established system or speeding up the local process of synoceism by creating a new urban focus or *municipia*. Still other areas were ruled simply as territories. Some communities became citizens of Rome, others were merely its allies. Invariably land was confiscated by Rome and used to endow estates for Roman citizens or to found new communities of *coloni* from Rome or Latium. In effect, tribal space was slowly torn asunder, and replaced by communities that were defined politically or through an imposed spatial order, one unaffected by its precise social content. The interdependence between these new local communities and Rome gave rise to a new mentality, one in which 'it was accepted that a man might have two loyalties – to his own *patria* and to Rome' (Dudley, 1975, p. 36).

Early Celtic States: Ireland

The progress of Ireland towards a state-system provides us with a different trajectory of development, though one not untypical of north-west Europe generally. Here was no city-state system condensing around proto-urban nuclei but an upward integration of tribal and exclusively rural kingships.

Back in the sixth and seventh centuries AD, the Irish countryside was fragmented into a complex array of what Irish historians have termed tribal kingships, possibly as many as eighty to one hundred in number. Each tribe had its own king or *rí*. These kings were not simply symbolic or religious leaders, but political leaders, ruling over their people or *tuatha* (Binchy, 1970, pp. 2–5). This pattern of tribal kingship has been seen as common to all Indo-European society by the late Iron Age (Binchy, 1970, 7). By the Dark Ages, the communities ruled over by Irish tribal kings, or their *tuatha*, had generally lost their integrity of kinship, though not necessarily their presumption of common descent: thus, genealogies for early medieval Leinster claimed that fifteen of the seventeen tribes who formed the Laigin or the people of Leinster descended from Setna Sithbacc, the son of the mythical king, Labraid Loingsech, who led the Laigin from Gaul to Ireland (Smyth, 1982, pp. 13–14). Such genealogies were of course fabrications, designed to strengthen local alliances by forging an affinity of kin. But by the early medieval period, Irish tribes were already compounded of different tribal groups. They had become tribes of locality, unified through the rule of a king.

What we see over the period between the seventh and tenth centuries is the transformation of this tribal landscape into a state-system, 'the spectacle of a tribal society being transformed by the introduction of a dynastic polity to a state wherein territorial lordship replaces hegemony over tribes as a political principle' (Byrne, 1971, p. 162). It was a prolonged rather than a hasty transformation. At its core, was the upward integration of kingship. Tribal kings became clients of over-kings and the latter of provincial kings or *rí ruirech*, their territories or domains being slowly immersed in a wider and wider system of administration, as what started out as a ceremonial ordering of kings hardened into a hierarchy of political power. It is impossible to say when provincial kingship first blossomed. There are clues suggesting that it represented a very early (possibly late Iron Age) ordering of dynasties if not tribes. What is clearer is that the various provincial kingships, the so-called 'fifths' of Ireland, had taken on an active political meaning by the eighth century. Nor was this their final form of integration. Above the fifths, or from within their ranks, there emerged two more-dominant dynasties, one based on Tara and the other on Cashel, each asserting its authority over one half of Ireland (Binchy, 1970, p. 32). As more and more space was integrated through kingship, the character of the latter slowly changed. Instead of being all things rolled into one – chief priest, war-leader, law-giver and controller of tribal exchange – kings began to delegate their different roles (Binchy, 1970, p. 15). The redaction of the Irish law codes is proof of how royal power was being disaggregated into different spheres of bureaucratic interest, though, as Binchy points out. Irish law was still private during the early medieval period, a matter between kin-groups, with no royal prerogative or veto. The idea of a king's justice was yet to come (Binchy, 1970, 15).

Ensuring that this transformation of political order was also a transformation of spatial order was the progressive territorialisation of the new emergent state. The tribal kingships which preceded the state were socially defined. Although their boundaries made use of the stable features of their natural environment – its rivers, mountain belts, woods and bogs (Smyth, 1982, p. 10) – the limits of kingship were still a social concept. Tribes were set within a territory, but the latter was still defined through the former and was not yet something which transcended the social concept of the tribe. Under such conditions, 'people rather than district was the concept uppermost in men's minds when they spoke of the *tuath*' (Byrne, 1971, p. 162). The new order of things created a fixed territorial division of space, imposing territorial units that were politically contrived rather than implied incidentally through the structuring of social space. In time, these new unitary orderings of landscape became based on lordships, areas of privilege held of the king in return for loyalty and service.

We must not hurry this conversion from a landscape structured through kinship to one delineated by the hand of an increasingly centralised administration. The will of centralised monarchy replaced the independence of tribal kings by degrees. Quite a number of tribal territories took on a new life as lordships within the new political landscape of the state, a sort of new wine in old bottles. This re-evaluation of tribal space was especially common after the Anglo-Norman invasion of 1169. For all their political ambition and appetite for land, the Anglo-Normans can hardly be said to have hastened the shift towards an integrated state. Large areas to the north and west remained in the hands of Gaelic kings and chiefs. Even in the east, where Anglo-Norman landholders were implanted in significant numbers, areas of Gaelic kingship persisted. Smyth has surveyed this problem in the context of Leinster, an area where Gaelic tribes and kingship survived 'due solely to the protection afforded by that very hostile landscape to which Gaelic kings proved capable of adapting' (Smyth, 1982, p. 109). The contrast which Smyth has drawn between the domain of the Anglo-Normans and of the Angevin and Plantagenet kings on the one hand and the older, tribal order of Gaelic kings is one between two landscapes, each with its own principles of spatial order (Smyth, 1982, pp. 101–17). Although increasingly penetrated by feudal ideas, these late-surviving Gaelic kingships and chiefdoms provide us with a richly-documented view of what a kin-based system of spatial order was like. A sixteenth-century survey of the great MacCarthy Mor chiefdom in the south-west, for instance, shows very clearly how the different branches and septs fitted together, jig-saw like, to form a vast coherent territory bound together through kinship and space. Examples of how genealogy was mapped into landscape at a finer level abound. A study of Gaelic landownership in Co. Monaghan during the period 1591–1640, just when such property was being confiscated by the

English Crown, provides us with a well-researched example. The different levels of landholding – the barony, *ballybetagh* and *tate* – still being identified as the closed, territorial space of particular families or their client groups (Duffy, 1981, pp. 1–26). Generally speaking, though, the trend was from a landscape of tribal space to one of feudal space: the world of chiefs, clans and septs giving way to lordships held of the crown and to a hierarchy of administrative units through which responsibilities derived from the crown and dues owed to it could be scaled.

Wales

The rise of the state-system in Wales over the period from about the eighth to the tenth century enable us to bring extra themes into the discussion. During the centuries which followed the Roman evacuation in the fourth century, the political landscape of Wales re-emerged as a series of tribal kingships. A strongly-rooted tradition, one with some truth in it, relates how, after the Roman withdrawal, a British king called Cunedda, from southern Scotland, helped to defend Wales from attacks by the Irish. After his death, parts of west and north-west Wales became divided up among his sons, each of whom established a tribal kingship, for example, Ceredigion, Merionydd. In time, local kingships of this sort became grouped into still larger polities, such as Dyfed, Gwynedd. By the seventh century, the number of kingships in Wales as a whole had already shrunk to only seven. The prospect of a single, united kingdom embracing the whole of Wales was first brought into view by Rhodri Mawr during the late ninth century. From his base in north-west Wales, or Gwynedd, Rhodri Mawr extended his kingship southwards into Powys and Seisywllg. Although his death in 878 AD saw a temporary reversal of this trend towards integration, his grandson, Hywel Dda, sought to re-establish it, and managed during his lifetime to unite the whole of west and north Wales. There can be no doubt that by this point, or by the early tenth century, Wales had reached the stage of being an incipient state-system. Binchy has, in fact, drawn attention to the way in which Welsh kings like Hywel Dda had moved away from the concept of tribal kingship and now appeared as rulers who used their authority to apply the law and who stood as *domini terrae*. Hywel Dda especially, modelled the innovatory features of his rule on the example of Anglo-Saxon kings (Binchy, 1970, p. 23).

The progression from tribal kingship to state-system can be monitored through the changing consciousness over who was a kinsmen, a member of the same tribe. The root or early meaning of the Welsh term *alltud* was 'a man from another *bro*', that is, from another kingdom or *tud*, as opposed to a *cymro* which referred to someone from the same kingdom or tribe. By the time the Welsh law codes were redacted during the tenth century, however, the term *cymro* denoted a Welshman whilst *alltud* had come to denote a stranger from outside Wales, that is, an Englishman. Charles-Edwards sees in this expanded consciousness about who constituted a fellow-kinsmen, the slow replacement of the old *tud* – *ab origine* a tribal grouping – by over-kingdoms like Gwynedd and Powys. Subsequently, these over-kingdoms were themselves replaced by a Welsh state or Wales 'as a legal and political unit' (Charles-Edwards, 1971, pp. 116–17). Needless to add, once this expansion of consciousness began, the idea of polities being bound through kinship was effectively shattered, and the mould of Welsh spatial order as a series of tribal spaces was irrevocably broken: though kinship continued to have some impact on the development of landscape through the survival of a kin-based tenure called *gwely* tenure until the fourteenth and even fifteenth centuries.

A particularly valuable aspect of the evidence for early state-formation in Wales is the light which it sheds on how the new state was structured. As elsewhere, state-formation involved the creation of a hierarchy of administrative spaces. Wales's history over the medieval period left it with traces of two hierarchies of administrative order, one bequeathed to it from the era of Welsh independence and the other by the Norman settlement. The conquest of eastern and southern Wales by the Normans during the late eleventh century led to the immediate Normanisation of these areas, with patterns of Welsh lordship and administration being replaced by Norman patterns. However, this precedent was not followed when the north-west of Wales was eventually subjugated by the English Crown during the thirteenth century, with Welsh administrative forms being simply taken over by the English Crown. This left the countryside divided between the Welshry, or those areas where Welsh forms of administration survived, and the Englishry, or those areas where English forms of administration held sway. If we consider the areas of the Welshry, we find a hierarchy of administrative order that consisted of townships, *commotes*, and *cantrefs*. The exact origin of this system is shrouded in some doubt, but there are reasons for believing that just as Hywel Dda was responsible for having the Welsh law-codes redacted, so also was he responsible for devising the scheme of administrative order into which west and north-west Wales appears divided during the latter part of the medieval period. We have to imagine a sort of dark-age Redcliffe-Maud commission under Hywel Dda's direction reducing the old tribal divisions of the kingdom to a new imposed order, one which set aside notions of tribal space and established communities of locality. If such an act of planned reorganisation did take place, it would be typical of the revolution in spatial order which underpinned the rise of state-system. However, we need to tread warily. In many cases, the apparently new administrative districts created were based directly on older, pre-existing social territories, the one ghosting through the layout of the other. The fact that many of these administrative units, at both the level of the *commote* and the *cantref*, bore toponyms based on personal names is simple proof of this (Richards, 1965, pp. 205–12). Of equal interest is the device employed by the originators of the scheme to distinguish between pairs of units. This is most apparent amongst *commotes*, large multi-township units. Most of them appear paired, sharing a common toponym but distinguished from each other by prefixes like *Is/Uwch* (meaning above/below, upper/lower) (Richards, 1964–5, pp. 9–18). Although these simple oppositions have been taken literally and attributed to the underlying geography of particular *commotes*, with one being seen as upland and the other as lowland, or to the fact that one was north of the *commote's caput* or headquarter settlement and the other below or south of it, their meaning is far more likely to have been purely symbolic, a carry-over from earlier schemes of dual classification. Less easy to answer is whether the use of dual classificatory schemes in this context reflects its continued use as a generative principle, a principle called upon whenever the need arose to partition space, or whether it was an attempt to take a dual classification of tribal order – even one used only for ceremonial purposes – and to reproduce it in a fixed territorial form. We have no way of deciding between these possible answers. However, the very use of dual classificatory schemes to order administrative space does reinforce the point that the conversion of tribal space into feudal space was essentially a change in concept. There was no reason why earlier patterns of spatial order, or tribal divisions, should not have survived albeit in a now reified form. What mattered was the change in the way they were bounded, a change which eventually if not immediately replaced communities of kinship with communities of locality.

Anglo-Saxon England

Although many standard texts discuss the making of the English state, most deal with the problem in a somewhat aspatial way, concentrating on the dynastic and legal aspects of the problem. Few construe it as a geographical problem, or as a problem of how different regions and spaces were integrated and how, once joined, they were internally divided for the purposes of communicating the king's will to all his newly-integrated domain and, by return, the collection of tribute or the raising of an army. Those who have thought it out geographically, though, leave no doubt that we are dealing with the same sort of transformation in spatial order that we have already noted elsewhere.

A glimpse of the tribal structure of early Anglo-Saxon England is afforded by the tribal hidage, an assessment compiled during the period 650–825 AD, and probably during the years approximately 670–90 AD, for the purposes of collecting tribute (Loyn, 1962, pp. 306–9; Davies and Vierck, 1974, p. 225). The assessment is organised according to tribes: these, not territories, formed 'the axis of early social institutions' and 'the raw material of early political development' (Davies and Vierck, 1974, p. 224). The tribes depicted were constituted as kingdoms, dependent tribes and small independent kin-groups. The kingship involved was kingship over people, tribal kingship (Kirby, 1967, p. 163). But not all the groups listed in the tribal hidage were constituted as kingdoms. Some were minor peripheral groups, perhaps tied by alliance but not yet absorbed by their more powerful neighbours (Davies and Vierck, 1974, p. 240). Some were named after the sort of environment in which they lived, such as the Pecsaetan or Peak dwellers, the Wilsaetan or settlers on the River Wye and the

Merscwara or marshmen. Others took their identity from an eponymous ancestor, such as Haestingas or Sumursaetan. Davies describes these as 'existing, conceptually, apart from their territory' (Davies and Vierck, 1974, p. 240), by which she means they were constituted socially not territorially. Yet others are arranged into geographically-opposed groups, such as East and West Wixna. Needless to add, these could well be symbolic groupings. Even by the time the tribal hidage was compiled, we can still regard some of these tribes as 'fluid groups who inhabit an elastic area with a fluctuating band of territory between them' (Davies and Vierck, 1974, p. 228). Frontiers in the sense of permanently fixed lines were 'largely irrelevant', instead, use was made of 'broad belts of no-man's land' (Davies and Vierck, 1974, p. 279).

As societies, these early Anglo-Saxon kingdoms and tribes were organised around what Jolliffe called the concept of folk-right. A person's folk-right was 'a complex of privileges, status and obligations coming to him with his father's blood and his material inheritance of land and goods' (Jolliffe, 1954, p. 5). However, whilst the persistence of the blood-feud can be vouched for in early Anglo-Saxon England, the holding of land by kin-groups cannot. Indeed, it has been suggested that the joint holding of land by kin-groups died out even before the Anglo-Saxons came to England.

By the time the tribal hidage was compiled (about the late seventh century) the various kingdoms and tribes, and the smaller *provinciae*, *regiones* and *maego*, were already being slowly fused into a single state-system. In 600 AD, it has been calculated that the number of kingdoms was down to twelve, though this estimate excludes the fairly numerous lesser tribes and chiefdoms which still peopled the landscape and to which the listing of the tribal hidage bears witness. By the end of the seventh century, the political formation of the country had simplified itself further into the seven major kingdoms of the Heptarchy. As in Ireland, kingship was now graded, with kings or *regnavit* and over-kings or *imperavit*. The latter were the Bretwaldas or rulers of Britain or at least, *reges anglorum*. Supremacy amongst the kingdoms of the Heptarchy shifted between dynasties. During the seventh century, it lay with the Northumbrian kings. During the eighth, it lay with the Mercian kings. By the early ninth century, it was the turn of the Wessex kings. By this point, the number of kingships had been reduced to only four, namely, those of Northumbria, Mercia, East Anglia and Wessex. The Danish invasion soon extinguished the sovereignty of Northumbria, Mercia and East Anglia. When Wessex reversed this tide of Danish expansion and established its superiority over the Scandinavian areas of England during the reign of Edward the Elder, England was brought to the point of unity. But not until the accession of Edgar in 959 AD was this unity finally secured.

As the English state took shape, it became not just a larger, more centralised polity, but a more organised one. In becoming more organised, it became 'a territorial state' (Jolliffe, 1954, p. 5). 'In all facets of government', declared Loyn, 'the English realm was divided into geographical units held responsible for duties exercised in an earlier age by kindreds' (Loyn, 1962, p. 302). This territorialisation occurred at all levels: the village, hundred, shire and monarchy (Loyn, 1962, p. 314). The territorialisation of the village will be dealt with in the next chapter. The creation of the hundredal system and the shire can be dealt with here for they encapsulate the way in which the machinery of government was territorialised, given a geographical framework of reference that transcended people, as the needs of the state expanded. Quite a number of discussions note the link between the scale of the system and its organisational needs. The first level of administrative order to be cast into fixed territories appears to have been that of the shire or *scir*. These had emerged in Wessex by the time of Ine, that is, during the late seventh and early eighth century. Those of Mercia appeared later, either during the ninth century (Chadwick, 1905, p. 202) or tenth century (Loyn, 1974, p. 2). Some shires manifestly mirror earlier social groupings. The Wilsaetan, for instance, became Wiltshire, whilst the Sumursaetan became Somerset-shire (Loyn, 1962, p. 225; Kirby, 1967, pp. 175–6). Initially, the shires were the primary units of administration, facilitating the exercise of justice, the levying and collection of tribute and the raising of the *fyrd*. The earliest *fyrd* were the responsibility of *ealdermen*, one of whose principal tasks was to assemble and lead the *fyrd* in battle (John, 1966, p. 142). A similar territorialisation affected the hundred. Its establishment as an administrative unit of fixed bounds appears to be 'a product of the greater England of Edward the Elder and his successors' (Loyn, 1974, p. 13; see also, Chadwick, 1905, p. 248). However, to say that it was given a fixed, territorial form at this point does not rule out the possibility that it had antecedents which stretch back deep into Anglo-Saxon history and that what we mean by its origin is simply the mapping of an institution which had previously operated in a purely social or tribal dimension. Like the larger shire that encompassed it, the hundred may have existed in a quite different form before it was set down in the landscape as a fixed territorial unit, perhaps originating as a folk grouping (Kirby, 1967, p. 178) or as a set of rights and responsibilities pivoted around such a grouping (John, 1966, p. 143). Whatever the answer, we are still left with something new, a territorial unit of administration that contributed materially to the replacement of communities of kin, the folk, with communities of locality and one whose tidy assessment as 100 hides, if not their tidy disposition on the ground, has rightly been seen as betraying the 'authoritarian nature of the new kingdom of England' (Loyn, 1974, p. 2). A similar debate surrounds the wapentake, a territorial unit to be found in areas of Danish settlement and burdened with a similar range of functions. Indeed, as long ago as 1905, Chadwick thought that the territorialisation of the wapentake may have inspired the fixing of the hundred within set geographical limits. The most important function for the hundred, as for the wapentake, was as a territorial basis for the judicial system. Its court met regularly on a four-weekly basis, and became the court through which the ordinary person related to public law. Although some writers see the hundred court as an institution established during the reign of Edward the Elder and whose functions evolved thereafter, there is an equally strong case for seeing it as a direct successor to the folk-moots of the early Anglo-Saxon period (Jolliffe, 1954, 11). What cannot be disputed is that the territorialisation of the hundred and the wapentake occurred at a time when the law was increasingly associated with the power of the king and when private law was being encompassed by public law (Loyn, 1974, p. 4).

Apart from stressing their possible connections with the folk divisions of the early Anglo-Saxon period, commentaries on the development of the shire and hundred have highlighted one other feature of interest to the geographer. Both originated as fixed territorial units in Wessex. Bearing out this role of Wessex as a hearth area for administrative reforms is the fact that both the shire and hundredal systems of Wessex appear as natural or evolved units with a variety of shapes and sizes. Yet when we examine their structure elsewhere, they appear more planned and artificial, with a noticeable uniformity of size and layout (Loyn, 1974, p. 2). The impression given is that the unitary subdivision of the new state had a different kind of gestation in its core area of Wessex when compared with other areas. Needless to add, this has a direct bearing on the question of whether such units were shaped around earlier social groupings or whether they were purely artificial creations.

One final point to be noted about the administrative structure of the English state is that whilst social groupings were suppressed at the expense of geographically-framed relationships, we must not conclude that, henceforth, spatial relations were impersonal. As the kin or folk basis of Anglo-Saxon society receded, a new set of relations took their place. These new relations were based on lordship. The whole course of Anglo-Saxon history is marked by 'lordship by service ... gaining ground on the idea of lordship by blood' (Loyn, 1962, pp. 213 and 360). Kinship was eroded not simply by the territorialisation of the state, but by the assertion of a new kind of lordship, namely, feudal lordship (Jolliffe, 1954, pp. 13–14). Territorialisation then, does not imply the de-socialisation of spatial structure, though Jolliffe was anxious to stress that feudal lordship did not advance in exact step with the retreat of folk-right (Jolliffe, 1954, pp. 4–5). Nevertheless, the broad trend was towards a balance of relationships succintly expressed by the Anglo-Saxon Chronicle: 'No kin is dearer to a man than his lord'.

The Danish State

The base conditions for the formation of the Danish state were similar to those of English state. Its pre-state organisation was based on tribal kingships. Although there is ample evidence for the persistence of the blood-feud into the Viking period, there is little positive evidence for the joint possession of land by kin-groups (Sawyer, 1982, pp. 44–6; Jensen, 1982, p. 272). In character, it was still a rural society controlled from ceremonial centres like Jelling. Its early urban centres, such as Hedeby, were based on external trade rather than political activity. The decisive phase for the formation of the Danish state was initiated during the ninth and tenth centuries by a process of dynastic and spatial integration that spread out from Fyn, the first large area to be unified under a single king. The incorporation of peripheral areas was achieved by 'an advancing system of royal vassalage and new holds on land' (Randsborg, 1980, p. 33). As this integration proceeded, the centre of gravity of the new state shifted westwards to Jutland, with Jelling become instated as its centre of royal power. With the physical growth of the new state came fresh problems of organisation. Direct evidence for these administrative changes is lacking, but some inferences can be made from later material on how the new state may have been territorialised. Thirteenth-century surveys show Jutland as subdivided into fourteen large shire-like units called *syssels*. These are further subdivided into units equivalent in scale and character to the English hundred and called *herreds*. Elsewhere in Denmark, the *syssel* is absent, administration being based solely on the *herred* (Sorensen, 1978, p.134; Sawyer, 1982, p. 56). No exact dating can be offered for the inception of these units. One familiar possibility is that the *syssels* were formerly units of tribal kingship. With the emergence of the Danish state, they were adopted as the basis of Danish royal administration (Sawyer, 1982, p. 56). According to Sorensen, when Danish kingship became united under the Jelling dynasty during the tenth century, 'a need arose for a new centrally directed administrative division of the kingdom', for a still finer scale of administration: the outcome was the *herred*, a unit found in both Jutland and Fyn (Sorensen, 1978, p. 141).

Conclusion

The broad thrust of what I have tried to say in this chapter has been to emphasise the geographical revolution wrought by state-formation. Put simply and directly, communities of kin were replaced by communities of place. Everywhere, the kinship basis of earlier tribal landscapes disintegrated or dissolved, supplanted by a new political landscape in which societies and communities were constituted through politically-defined territories, through the locality in which they were set. It was, as quite a number of historians have said, a process whereby the state became territorialised. However, we must be careful to specify what exactly is meant by this territorialisation of the state. Tribal societies too, were bounded, divided off one from another by boundaries, natural or otherwise. The novelty in the way early states territorialised themselves stemmed from the fresh concepts which they imputed to spatial order. The way in which states organised themselves in space was one of the ways, but a very crucial way, in which they objectified themselves, removing themselves beyond the realm of consanguity. The more elaborate the organisation of the state, the more elaborate was its hierarchy of administrative order. The state strove to organise society through space, not vice versa, so that spatial structure became accessory to the needs of the state. Admittedly, the precise structure of the administrative order devised for the new state was, in many cases, fashioned around the territoriality manifest in the social geography of earlier tribes and kin-groups. To this/extent, they continued to have meaning in space long afterwards, especially at a local level. However, the whole force of state organisation was to assert the importance of its concept of spatial order. In time, the patterns of lordship enframed by this new concept of spatial order would have overwhelmed the cohesiveness or integrity of any kinship grouping in space. Slowly but surely then, we move from a world of fellow-kinsmen to one of fellow-countrymen, from communities organised through family and lineage to communities organised around lordship and locality.

We can discern at least two ways in which this change in the conceptual meaning of spatial order came about in Europe. In the Graeco-Roman world, tribal kingship played no part, the change being associated with, and distinguished by, the process of synoceism. By contrast, elsewhere in Europe, we are dealing with a process of societal change that was bound up with the advancing interests of tribal kings. What these two lines of development have in common though, is the fact that in neither case did the process of state-formation occur as a geographically isolated process: early state modules, to use Renfrew's term, were invariably part of a system of proto-states. Precisely how this broader socio-political environment affected the formation of states must remain an open question. But speaking very generally, there can be no doubt that proto-states within these systems of states interacted with each other positively, through exchange, shared religious cults, dynastic and military alliances and political agreements, and negatively, through competition for the same resources of land and through military struggles. The drift of recent discussion has been to see this wider network of relations and conflicts as crucial, a source of pressures and inducements for internal change. Although a case might be made out for seeing one sphere of inducement (such as trade) or pressure (for instance, circumscribed population growth) as a sort of leading edge, most contributors to the debate have stressed that we cannot treat causative factors in a singular fashion, but must relate them to a series of interlocking variables. No less pertinent to the geographer's interests is the question of why some systems of early states, like Etruria, remained as such – a collection of states – and why others, like those of England, matured into larger, single states. Arguably, once states interacted, then rulers would have jostled for the coveted position of the most superior ruler. As with the formation of primary states, the integration of early state-systems to form a larger single state was probably a matter of when integrative forces eventually prevailed over those which worked to preserve the separate identity of states. Arguably, where the appetite of early rulers forged ahead of the wider integrative forces which worked to bind the interests of states together, such as happened in the Empires of Alexander or Rome, it produced an integrated system of quite a different character.

6
Regulated Space and the Feudal State

As a subject, geography has experienced a phase of intense intellectual colonisation over recent years. Yet despite its greatly expanded horizons, many of its practitioners would still look upon feudalism as being *terra incognito*. This neglect is surprising, for medievalists like Maitland and Stenton talked freely about 'feudal geography'. They had in mind the way in which basic units of feudalism, like the knight's fee and manor, were disposed across the countryside. Seen as a straightforward exercise in mapping, such a reconstruction certainly lies within the compass of the geographer. Geographers, though, have hardly responded to this task. With the notable exception of Glanville Jones's work on multiple estates (Jones, 1976, pp. 15–40), the most laudable attempts at mapping the pattern of lordship have been by historians. If we examine what is still the most significant piece of work by any historical geographer – Darby's *Domesday Geographies* – we find that the most important single obstacle which he struggled to overcome was the reconstitution of *vills* as geographical units, the units which the Domesday Commissioners had perversely torn apart in order to present their data on a feudal basis, that is, per tenant-in-chief. The feudal dimension is seen as standing in the way of a geographical perspective. Of course, the geography which Darby *et al.* have produced is of immense value, a veritable datum line for any work on the history of the medieval landscape, but it does illustrate the point that feudalism has not been the first priority of the historical geographer, and certainly, there is no hint of feudalism creating its own geography of space to the extent that we can speak of a feudal landscape *sui generis*, one whose principles of spatial order set it apart from earlier or later landscapes. The purposes of this chapter will be to argue the case for such a landscape. Its emphasis will not be on how the medieval landscape was fashioned by the woodman's axe or the farmer's plough, but on how the principles behind feudalism helped to shape a recognisable pattern of spatial order, one which reinforced the territorial state within which it was set.

The debate over feudalism's meaning has not been a harmonious affair. Working through its now extensive literature is like ascending the staircase of some academic tower of Babel, so numerous and divergent are the ideas being voiced. There is some measure of unanimity about it having to do with the relations between king and those under him, that it involved the hierarchical ordering of these relations through different grades of lordship and that it involved the holding of land in return for service of one sort or another. However, beyond this broad generic definition, disharmony breaks out. At one extreme are those scholars who have argued for a narrow, specialised definition, construing it solely in terms of knight's service, or the holding of land – the knight's fee – in return for the service of a knight. At the other extreme are those who have framed its meaning in the broadest possible terms, making it a catch-all for everything medieval or appropriative. Amidst all this welter of opinion, we need to pursue two major themes. First, we need to consider the way in which feudalism was used to bind early states together. To this end, I intend to examine the nature of lordship and military feudalism as devices of government, or as the means by which kings wove a web of authority and dependence that reached out to all corners of their realm. Second, we must also examine the way in which feudalism reached down to the ordinary peasant through the institutional framework of the manor and its demand for labour services and food rents.

Feudalism as a Study in Spatial Integration

Constitutional historians have always placed stress on the primacy of lordship to any definition of feudalism. For Maitland, the concept of seigneurial authority and justice embodied in the idea of lordship was 'a deep seated cause of many effects, a principle which once introduced is capable of transfiguring a nation' (Maitland, 1897, p. 258). Whether definitions rest their case on knightly service and vassal homage or labour service and servile homage, the one fact which made it all possible, as Maitland makes clear, is seigneurial authority and justice. In an attempt to point up the differences between what he saw as the contrast between the early and late Anglo-Saxon periods in England, between what he described as the primitive or kin-based societies of the former and the advanced state-based polities of the latter, Jolliffe talked of lordship being present in the early medieval period but described it as a passive form, a matter of blood or status and implying no authority over others, whereas later lordship was imbued with concepts of *hlaford* (=bread-giver) and *mundbora* (=protector and warrantor) (Jolliffe, 1954, pp. 13–14). Put in the simplest of terms, we need to envisage a progressive switch between two systems of reference. By the seventh century, and possibly earlier, men with ambitions detached themselves from their kin and became members of the king's household or members of a nobleman's retinue. In a word, they became *gesiths*. They became 'a man of another man' (Bloch, 1962, vol. 1, p. 145). Their social realignment involved an act of submission, or homage, and, in time, an act of fealty or an oath of loyalty to their new lord. We can see this shift of allegiance taking place in England (Jolliffe, 1954, p. 14; John, 1966, p. 118) and in other parts of western Europe (Bloch, 1962, vol. 1, pp. 157 and 163; Fleckenstein, 1978, pp. 5–6). The early stages of the process in Germany have been well-described by Thompson. Talking about the period from the first century AD onwards, he depicts a society in which tribal 'big-men' each gathered a retinue or *comitatus* around them, retinues whose affiliations cut sharply across older ties of kinship. Disdaining the labour of the fields, these retinues survived on booty and the fighting equipment given to them by their leader. As the power of the latter broadened into lordship, and as kinship structures lost their exclusive command over the army and justice, there slowly emerged 'some of the organs of the State, though in an embryonic form' (Thompson, 1965, pp. 48–71; see also Fleckenstein, 1978, pp. 5–6).

A critical moment in the development of feudal society was when, instead of providing their vassals with maintenance at court and with fighting equipment, kings began to grant land, the means by which they could support themselves. For Elias, this change was bound up with the growth and enlargement of states. The success of particular dynasties, or courts, like the Carolingians, in unifying large areas into a single state-system is seen as creating a world of opportunity. New territories had to be controlled, bound to the will of the king (Elias, 1982, pp. 64–5). In some areas, this process of state expansion and consolidation involved native or local kings simply acknowledging state-kings as their superior and holding their territory thereafter as a *fief de reprise* (Bloch, 1962, vol. 1, p. 173). However, there were other areas where local rulers were displaced by the advancing overtures of state kings. Fine examples of these twin processes of continuity and discontinuity are provided by Barrow's discussion of how the incipient Scottish state was finally gathered into a unified kingship over the twelfth and thirteenth centuries (Barrow, 1980, pp. 157–8). The new land acquired by kings became land in his gift, land to invest in return for service. 'In repeated waves,' said Elias 'the kings, strengthened by conquests, send their trusted friends, relations and servants into the country as their envoys . . . ' (Elias, 1982, p. 17). A framework of lordship was established, tieing the relationship between lord and vassal to a territorial framework and, in the process, projecting the king's authority out over his expanding realm. This was how he coped with the spatial implications of a state-system. But no matter how novel the practice of kings granting land to their vassals may seem, such grants drew some of their meaning from a concept of exchange that was of far greater antiquity. The loyalty and obedience which vassals owed to their lord could not match the latter's gift of land. Maitland remarked that the 'king's most absolute gift left something owing and continuously owing to him' (Maitland, 1897, p. 317). His point is put even more precisely by Charles-Edwards. The contrast between 'the completed gift of land and the incomplete gift of service' buttressed the lord's authority over his vassal by leaving the latter 'always in debt to his lord' (Charles-Edwards, 1976, p. 183).

By the time local kingships were absorbed by more vigorously growing state-systems, we can expect the former to have already developed some form of lordship in the manner that Thompson described for early Germanic tribes. The umbrella of lordship now held over such groups by the kings of greater states clearly involved a development of lordship at a different level but may not be a *de novo* development of the concept. We can see this problem in the context of England. Some scholars have talked of the Anglo-Saxon settlement as consisting of lords and their dependents (Aston, 1958, p. 83) and of early Anglo-Saxon society being permeated from top to bottom with the powers of lordship, a lordship exercised as much by the nobility as by kings (John, 1966, pp. 133 and 142). Others, however, see it as a much later affair. This dilemma of deciding when lordship actually appears on the scene is further clouded by the not unrelated problem of calibrating how lordship developed as a concept. We need to know, for instance, when kings began to grant rights of jurisdiction and rights to the profits of jurisdiction, both essential props to any scheme of controlling the provinces at a distance. In England, these two rights were known as *sake* and *soke*. Such grants were being made by Cnut's reign, though Maitland felt there was a case for extending them back to the seventh century (Maitland, 1897, p. 282). He saw the practice of devolving jurisdiction to the great landholders as one of the more critical steps by which the territorial lord 'begins to stand between free men and the state' (Maitland, 1897, p. 289). Broadening the scope of this devolved lordship further was the notion of immunity from burdens on land. For Maitland, implicit in grants of jurisdiction was immunity from all secular service except the *trinada necessitas*, that is, army service, bridge bote and burh bote (Maitland, 1897, pp. 270–4). The great landholders gained the right to collect tribute and food rents previously rendered to the king, the king's *feorm* becoming the lord's *gafol* (Maitland, 1897, p. 324, Jolliffe, 1954, p. 20). John has discussed the same trend in relation to the problem of bookright and book-land. This was a tenurial institution that appeared in a number of early English states but, as Bede informs us, was especially widespread in Northumbria. It involved royal grants of land to noblemen that empowered them to intercept the dues or *feorm* which had hitherto been yielded to the king and for them to choose their own heirs. Altogether, John sees book-land as a prime means by which superiority was formally granted by the king (John, 1966, p. 99; see also, John, 1960, p. 11). Once established, book-land gave the nobility a means of securing an hereditary control over their estates, albeit under the lordship of the king. Paradoxically, such a freedom, if gained in the right circumstances could re-establish the ideology of kinship. Speaking of northern France, where the aristocracy, about 900 AD, 'won their autonomy from the great territorial princes and began henceforth to bestow freely their honour, now completely integrated with their patrimony, upon their eldest sons', Duby claims that it had the effect of creating a new awareness of genealogy, of their place within a descent group, to the extent that it competed with and even displaced the horizontal ties of alliance, especially those to their king or local ruler (Duby, 1977, p. 147; see also, pp. 59–80 and 134–8). Such a rupturing of the ties between king and vassal, though, must be seen in relation to the special circumstances that prevailed in tenth-century France.

The idea that feudalism was a device of government is a well-established theme, in which feudalism is seen as a means of controlling the large extended polities that emerged over the period from the sixth to the tenth centuries when, to use Binchy's words, 'Great Kings' replaced older systems of tribal kings (Binchy, 1970, p. 6). As a structuring of power around kings, however, feudalism contained this paradox. On the one hand, it represented a greater concentration of power in the person of the king – power over men, over land, over justice and so on. When fully matured, kings ruled over all men and all land without exception. Customary rights based on kinship and the idea of an alternative source of right, were suppressed before the absolute authority of the crown, though we can find areas, like Germany, where this happened later rather than sooner (Thompson, 1928, pp. 296–7)). On the other hand, the concentration of power and property had its counter-movement, with the king granting estates and powers of lordship to his vassals. This give-and-take served a purpose. As the early states came into being, and as their social and physical scale increased, they posed totally new problems of administration and organisation. The territorialisation of the state was one facet of their solution but, on its own, it did not ensure success. 'The principal difficulty' faced by the newly-centralised Carolingian state, wrote Bloch, 'was to reach individual subjects, in order to exact services and to impose the necessary conditions' (Bloch, 1962, vol. 1, p. 157). The problem common to all early states and feudal monarchs was 'getting one's will carried out at a distance, of administrating the provinces' (Brown, 1973, p. 52). The larger the state, the larger the problem. In theory, a range of possibilities were open to feudal monarchs, ranging from regional self-government under appointed governers to a bureaucratic net-work of salaried officials. The choice of feudalism must have appeared attractive because it grafted the problem on to a 'firmly established network of protective relationships' (Bloch, 1962, vol. 1, p. 157). It not only constructed a system of government around the absolute authority of the king, but it also took the relations of lordship developed within royal courts between the king and his retinue and projected them into a set of relations set down firmly in space, with the relationship between lord and vassal being anchored to specific blocks of land. Wherever we look in Europe over the ninth, tenth and eleventh centuries, we find feudal relations between kings and noblemen being actively used to govern the new states, to reach out to the provinces. Feudal lordship became to the newly-enlarged states like the metal tyre to the felloe, the means of holding its parts together. The roads along which it rolled, though, like all medieval roads, were uneven and deeply rutted. Not infrequently, the spokes of the wheel came adrift.

This shaky, faltering history was almost inevitable, for – by its very nature – feudalism created a peculiar form of geographical tension, a tension which was acutely perceived by Elias. Once ensconced in their provincial niches, the king's vassals would have sought to secure the effective independence of their region. This meant broadening their position from one in which they possessed land to one in which they also possessed rights of jurisdiction, so that they became territorial lords rather than mere controllers of big estates. To this end, we find the king's vassals securing – albeit in the king's name – rights of jurisdiction, the right to the profits of jurisdiction, the right to collect food-rents formerly paid to the king and, above all, the right to the hereditary possesion of their estates and privileges. In practice, the extent to which provincial lords were able to slip the lead and to function as if they had no superior varied greatly in time and space. For Elias, their variation depended on changes in the balance between centrifugal and centripetal forces at work within the very structure of feudalism. The predominance of one or the other depended on mechanisms of supply and demand. Where or when states were under threat or expanding, central authority tended to be strong, a source of much-needed protection and much-sought-after land. During times of stability though, central authority became enfeebled simply because its roles as a protector and as a provider of land was diminished. In such circumstances, we can expect provincial lords to assert their independence (Elias, 1982, pp. 16–17). Elias illustrated his point by drawing a detailed comparison between western and eastern examples of the Frankish kingdoms which emerged after the collapse of the Carolingian Empire, or the area ruled over by the House of Francia, the 'embryo of what was to become France' (Elias, 1982, p. 22) and the hub of what was to become the German *Imperium Romanum*. With the break-up of the Carolingian Empire, each portion followed its own path of development. In Francia, rule passed to a cluster of petty king-ships and lordships, with superiority amongst them eventually being established by the House of Francia, a dynasty based around the Ile de France. Its position, however, was rarely more than token and by the time Hugh Capet was installed as king in 987 AD, we find the area dissembling into a dense network of small, *bannum* lordships that functioned independently of the Capetian kings. In a process that has been seized upon by many writers on feudalism as the illustration *par excellence* of the fissiparous tend-encies of feudalism, each petty lord built himself a castle and exercised his jurisdictions and privileges as if he had no superior (Elias, 1982, p. 23). In marked contrast, the century or so follow-ing the collapse of the Carolingian Empire, saw the eastern Frankish area enter a period of sustained expansion and military struggles, factors which 'constantly restored the preponderance of the cen-tralizing royal function' (Elias, 1982, p. 23). But even here, we eventually find a reverse movement. From the twelfth century onwards, said Elias, 'the social centre of gravity moves ever more clearly and inevitably towards the territorial rulers of Germany too' (Elias, 1982, p. 25). The system of local *castellany* or *burgbe-zirk* founded from the late twelfth century onwards were sympto-matic of this devolvement of power, providing a territorial basis for the exercise of jurisdictions now more confidently assumed by territorial princes and the local lords who now flourished beneath them. An especially critical moment in this drift away from cen-tralised authority came in the thirteenth century when the territory of the Hohenstaufen princes, the acknowledged core of any Ger-man state-to-be, collapsed into a mass of petty lordships. It was 'a territorial failure' (Barraclough, 1938, p. 135; see also Thompson, 1928, pp. 296–7 and 321).

At a higher, more abstract plane of reasoning, Elias sees early feudal states as experiencing a long-term shift in the balance between disintegrative and integrative forces. The creation of territorial lordships over the ninth, tenth and eleventh centuries turned feudal states into what, potentially, were very fragile affairs, easily fractured along the lines of cleavage which such lordships necessarily introduced into them. Although chronologies varied from system to system, Elias sees this phase of potential and, for some systems, actual disintegration, being replaced by a phase of more positive integration, a phase culminating by the end of the medieval period in the rise of absolute monarchs, who saw territorial lordship as a challenge rather than an aid to their rule of the state. Elias explains this change by a two-pronged argument that has important geographical implications. Growing state-systems, each jostling for space, created a world of new opportunity for territorial lords. From Charlemagne onwards, the king's vassals acquired land and jurisdiction in return for fealty and service. Within a few generations though, the positions opened up by this systemic adjustment, were filled and 'a system with open opportunities becomes a system with closed opportunities' (Elias, 1982, p. 59). Thereafter, we are dealing with societies beset with internal conflict, as individuals competed for a finite number of opportunities. If we presume that provincial lords began on equal terms, 'untempered by pre-existing monopolies', we can expect some to be more successful and others to be less so, so that 'as a result, fewer and fewer will control more and more opportunities' (Elias, 1982, p.106). Out of this sifting and sorting process, emerged the larger and more centralised systems which prevailed in Europe by the sixteenth century. Elias' stress on this closure of opportunities is an insight of the utmost importance. However, we need to modify it slightly. We need to see it as a closure of opportunities within feudalism. As will be explained at greater length in Chapter 8, European society still had scope for internal growth, a growth whose inbuilt opportunities for change were used to redirect 'the civilising process'. Elias's second line of argument highlights the role played by the growth of population and trade from at least the eleventh century onwards. Here is very much a geographer's creed. Regions are seen as becoming intertwined with each other through their greater social and economic interaction. Aided by improvements in land transport, he sees people and goods moving more freely within and between regions. In the process, states became more systemically fused, with a growing differentiation of roles and interdependence at a state level. In short, the task of integrating the feudal state ceased to be a purely political process and broadened to become as much a socio-economic process (Elias, 1982, p. 27).

As a means of integrating both society and space, lordship was buttressed by military feudalism. Indeed, some concentrate their definition of feudalism on the existence of a specialised class of warriors, or knights, each bound to the service of his king or lord through vassalage. Quite apart from their training in horseman-ship and combat, knight's service involved a ceremony of investi-ture and, thereafter, ties of fealty and homage to the king. Having a class of knights at his command enabled the feudal king or lord to defend his realm. The more important tenants in chief, the great earls and barons, invariably held their fiefs in return for an agreed number of warriors. In turn, they enfeoffed lesser landholders on their estate, obliging them to provide the services of a knight. In this way, the military obligations placed on the major lordships were scaled down virtually to a community level. In all parts of the countryside were to be found major territorial landholders whose position depended on serving the king as a knight, either directly or through military service for one of his great vassals. There was no fixed link between the number of knights provided and the size of estate granted; nevertheless, even a generalised link was suf-ficient to ensure that strategically located in all areas were land-holders whose possession of land, whose maintenance, was fused with the defence of the realm and the king's superiority over them.

Equating feudalism exclusively with knight's service obviously imposes a precise but restricted meaning on it. In fact, one or two scholars have squeezed the concept still further. In a carefully argued essay, Brown has tried to confine its primary meaning to the social tie between the king and those invested as knights, with the knight's fee having only a secondary meaning. He acknowl-edged that possession of an estate was needed to support a knight but considered that such land-grants were accessory to its essential meaning as a tie founded on vassalage and military service. In effect, this would be to reject the whole notion of a feudal society, except in so far as it applied to those who actually controlled society. This is what Brown intended when he wrote of feudalism being 'an upper class affair' (Brown, 1973, p. 23). It also lies behind his suggestion that feudalism was not a system of social order. Those issues which have a bearing on its meaning as a system of social order, like lordship and serfdom, are seen by him as unrelated to a feudalism based on knightly service. Military feudalism was something pragmatic not conceptual, a reaction designed to cope with the unsettled conditions that accompanied the rapid expansion of state-systems and their incorporation of quite disparate regions and societies. But without denying the value of discussing knight's service for its own sake, to centre feudalism's meaning entirely on it hardly helps the wider debate. In a sense, it makes the mistake of seeing the problem in terms of labels rather than meanings. By this I mean that to exclude other aspects of feudalism from consideration in a search for a more exact meaning of the term *sensu stricto*, does not remove the problems we face in discussing aspects like lordship or serfdom as associated devices of government. One is almost tempted to say that if feudalism cannot be used as a generic term to capture the interrelated dimensions of the feudal state, then a new term would need to be devised.

Knight's fees could be created directly by kings or by enfeoffment from one of the great provincial lordships: they could be held for the service of a single knight or for a handful of knights. Their significance for the integration of states stems from the fact that their creation was generally accompanied, either immediately or subsequently, by a grant of powers of jurisdiction. The nature and extent of these powers varied greatly, but their effect was to turn many a small estate-holder into a petty lord or seigneur. In other words, the creation of knight's fees became the means by which the administrative structure of the feudal state was elaborated below the level of the great territorial lordships. We can see it as a more local form of lordship, the bottom rung in an extending ladder of authority, one that reached down to, but stopped short of, the great mass of men, an ultimate act by kings and great nobles to project their authority downwards over the people and provinces, attuning it on a more local scale. Of course in other circumstances, we can see it as a dissembling of royal authority downwards. For those with an interest in systemic change, there is a temptation to see the widespread creation of petty lordships and seigneuries based on relatively small estates and owing relatively modest amounts of military service as a later development. Once provincial lordships were established, the next logical step was for provincial lords to create a lower grade of administration by granting estates and a share of their powers of jurisdiction to vassals in return for military service, replicating through subinfeudation or rear vassalage the same terms of relationship which they had with the king. There is some support for this progressive elaboration of lordship through smaller and smaller units of space. Writing of northern France, Duby has depicted the development of lordship in terms of a simple cascade. It began when counts secured their 'autonomy' from the great territorial princes or kings around 900 AD. By about 1000 AD, it was the turn of 'the masters of castles to gain their independence and to appropriate the castles which they had commanded in the name of another' (Duby, 1977, p. 147). Finally, by about 1030 AD, 'concessions of fiefs multiplied amongst the lesser aristocracy and feudal tenure assumed a more obviously hereditary character' (Duby, 1977, p. 147). We can see the same process of lordship being territorialised at a more localised scale in Germany from the twelfth century onwards (Thompson, 1928, pp. 296–7 and 301). It is important to appreciate that the devolution of such lordship could involve different dimensions of change: the levying of a specific amount of military service, the acquisition of an estate, grants of immunities from royal dues and tributes and grants of jurisdiction, each with their own chronology of development. In a sense, the debate over feudal origins is a debate over when these different aspects of the problem came together. This is certainly the case in England. We have already seen how the nature of lordship was developed over the Anglo-Saxon period, albeit more quickly for some writers than for others. But once book-right was introduced and the great estate-holders not only acquired the hereditary right to their estates but also, the right to alienate land, we find them investing their own vassals with land. Through the process of sub-infeudation, it led to the creation of lesser lordships within greater lordships and a territorial hierarchy of lordship. The question of how military service fitted in with such tenures is no less problematical. Scholars like John see Anglo-Saxon society as permeated throughout by the bonds of lordship and vassalage so that it is difficult to imagine members of the king's retinue being granted land, especially loan-land, without the obligation of military service (John, 1966, pp. 139–42). Others attribute their development to the knight's fees introduced by the Normans during the years immediately following their arrival (Stenton, 1932, p. 121). As yet we cannot resolve this disagreement, support still being offered for both positions (see, for example, Dyer, 1980, pp.

42–3). But no matter how we interpret their precise trajectory of development, the outcome of these trends was the same. By the end of the eleventh century, England had become divided into a dense pattern of knight's fees, some held directly from the Crown and others subinfeudated from one or other of the great territorial lords. More importantly, through the institution of the manor, each enjoyed some rights of jurisdiction, including the right to hold a court. In effect, through the spread of knight's fees and subinfeudation, the exercise of lordship – or at least the exercise of jurisdictional rights – had spread downwards. We see the process clearly in Davies's description of the Marcher Lordships of Wales during the twelfth and thirteenth centuries. He talks of powerful Marcher Lords 'mortgaging' their power by creating a numerous pattern of knight's fees. So far did this trend progress in areas like Gower, that what began as 'an act of seigneurial largesse' led to knights establishing their own jurisdiction over the peasantry – 'a victory of vassals over lordship, of subinfeudation over dominium' (Davies, 1978, pp. 99–100).

The Bottom Line: Lords and Peasants

For the great mass of society, feudalism was not about the exercise of lordship but about the burden of lordship; not about military service and vassalage, but about labour services, feudal dues, and servitude. At this level, or at the level of the ordinary peasant, it was a system of exploitation and appropriation.

At the root of feudalism as a system of exploitation and expropriation was the dependence of peasants on lord. These ties of dependence ranged from outright slavery, through varying degrees of serfdom and unfreedom, to being one simply of jurisdiction by a lord over a peasant. Establishing exactly where particular groups stood on this scale demands data of a full and precise character. For many countries in western and northern Europe, such data is lacking until well after early states had emerged. This is a critical gap for some have argued that we need a deep-rooted perspective if we are to understand the full history of unfreedom. We can see this in relation to England. Old assumptions of a free peasantry sinking slowly into unfreedom over the eleventh, twelfth and thirteenth centuries are no longer tenable. Separate claims have been made for the existence of substantial numbers of unfree peasants during the late prehistoric period (Jones, 1976, pp. 15–40), during the Roman period and during the Anglo-Saxon period (Aston, 1958, pp. 59–83; John, 1966, pp. 140–2). Needless to say, if we assume that a strong lordship was already exercised over the peasantry throughout the Anglo-Saxon period, then it greatly affects how we interpret its apparent development over the medieval period.

To set down my own view, we cannot divorce the question of medieval feudalism from the sort of society which it replaced. The anthropological concept of tribal chiefdoms and kingships is quite clear on what we can expect to find. Through their sacro-religious authority and through their control over tribal exchange, tribal chiefs and kings enjoyed a superiority over the tribe. The food renders which they gathered in had the instrumental value of tribute, a public recognition of their superiority and special powers. We can hardly exempt from this generalisation the Germanic and Celtic tribes that flourished in western Europe after the collapse of the Roman Empire. Once we accept this as our baseline, then the history of social relations over the early medieval period becomes a history of how these long-established superior/inferior relationships were exploited more fully, rather than how they were incepted as something novel in the history of society.

A series of interlocking changes was crucial in bringing about this transformation, changes precipitated by the emergence and subsequent enlargement of state-systems. Some have already been mentioned, notably the replacement of folk armies like the Anglo-Saxon *fyrd* with a retinue of warriors with quite different ties and the increasing role of kings as arbitrators of customary law and, increasingly, as someone who issued laws of a wholly new kind, or public law. The prime factor that determined how lords came to exercise a more exacting superiority over the ordinary peasant, was the emergence of lords as holders of very large estates. At a time when the more successful kings added dramatically to the territories over which they ruled, there was, as Elias has reminded us, ample opportunity for members of the royal court or retinue to acquire estates as a reward, to live on the fruits of their own estate rather than at the table of their king. This relocation of royal vassals from a courtly life to a provincial life was under way by the ninth century. The dramatic fall in population which is slowly being documented for sixth- and seventh-century Europe may also have played a part in creating a situation in which kings had land to invest in return for service (Elias, 1982, p. 65). In the first instance, this would have served to expand the number of vassals directly dependent on the king (cf. Charles-Edwards, 1972, pp. 9–10). In the second instance, it enabled such tenants-in-chief to recreate further tiers of dependent relations below themselves. Of interest here, are those based on vassalage and servitude as opposed to those based on vassalage and homage, that is, the relations which they established with the peasantry as opposed to those which they established with petty lords and knights. Just as grants of land from the king to his vassals placed the latter in the permanent debt of the former, so also must tenures between lord and peasant, or between *gesiths* and *ceorls*, to use the language of the mid-Saxon period, have placed the latter in debt to the former. However, for *ceorls*, what seems to have been crucial was the lord's grant of a home: this is what tied him to his lord and the soil. 'It is the acceptance of a home', maintained Charles-Edwards, 'which lies at the root of villeinage' (Charles-Edwards, 1976, p. 186).

No less vital would have been the pre-existing ties between peasants, even free peasants, and their tribal king as regards the food, goods and corvée rendered as tribute and the hospitality which such rulers had right to expect from their people, all ties widely documented amongst chiefdoms and tribal kingships. At the outset, such tribute would have been used to service the royal court and its retinue. With the granting of estates to the king's vassals, it must have seemed a logical step to allow them to collect and to keep the renders previously given as food renders or tribute to the king, the more especially now that the enhanced scale of polities placed the quantities involved beyond even the lavish consumption levels of royal courts and because polities were now too extensive to allow such tributes to be reasonably consumed even by travelling courts. Though kings could still draw vast quantities of food from the estates which they maintained in their own hand, they effectively relinquished their interest in food renders when they gave grants of land and lordship to their vassals. In the hands of provincial lords, the payment of food renders became a condition of tenure, a payment for the rent of land. The consequences of this subtle change were far-reaching. Lords succeeded in fusing the payment of food renders as a mark of their superiority with the holding of land from them. In the process, renders ostensibly levied on the person now became anchored in the soil, the one as a payment for the other. As in other spheres, the state was territorialising its interests. When we study Carolingian polyptyches or *censiers*, says Doehaerd, we are faced with services that have 'been transferred from the person on to the land which they held by heredity, so that the services became, so to speak, rooted in the land' (Doehaerd, 1978, p. 182). In a later context, Davies has made a comparable point in respect of the Welsh March. At the outset of their lordship, the Marcher Lords were little different in character from the Welsh Lords whom they replaced. They were lords of men, gathering in vast quantities of food renders. By the thirteenth century, though, a revaluation was in progress. They had become *rentiers*, or landlords, concerned with rent rather than tribute (Davies, 1978, p. 115).

As lords asserted a more exacting superiority over the peasantry, the latter would have been slowly drawn into a feudal system of exploitation. What began as a higher control over exchange had been slowly extended so as to become a control over the very means of production. A managerial hierarchy that had previously had only partial control now had the means of fully controlling the system. The institutional framework through which this social and economic subjugation of the peasantry became organised was the manor or seigneury. Although areal exceptions can be found, there was an impressive uniformity about the way in which the great estates in most arable areas of western Europe, both lay and ecclesiastical, became organised on a manorial or seigneural basis (Slicher Van Bath, 1963, p. 46; Duby, 1968, pp. 47–53). Structurally, the manor was divided into two sectors. One consisted of the demesne, *la réserve*, the part which the lord kept in his own hands for his own use. The remainder of the occupied land was tenant-land, leased or farmed out to tenants. In addition to seigneurial exactions like entry fines, heriot, leyrite, etc., tenants paid for their holdings with payments in kind and/or labour service, *ad opera*, that consisted of so-many boon days on the lord's demesne. Some of these exactions were old-established ties given a new meaning and a new focus. Others were fresh impositions born out of the more exacting and defined superiority of the medieval period, a period when the greatly inflated superiority of state-kings was brought, via devolved lordship, to the very door of the

2 The European Past

peasant. What had been a relationship based on obligation became one of coercion. The legal instrument of this coercion was the seigneurial or manorial court. Through it, lords were able to enlarge and redirect the corvée which peasants had previously owed for the maintenance of royal courts and public works onto their demesne. Through it, the lord imposed the restrictions on peasant mobility and established the close relationship between the personal status of peasants, their service commitments and their tenure of land that were essential to the operation of a demesne system. In short, it was the seigneurial court that determined local custom, the institutionalised conditions on which land was to be held.

The origin of manorial systems like those just defined has been variously interpreted. In England, for example, opinion ranges from an 'origin with the Saxons' view to an 'origin with the Normans' view. The interpretation upheld here is that their development occurred generally throughout western Europe between the eight and eleventh centuries, and that they can be seen as part of the organisational adjustment to the formation of state-systems. Taking up this second point, a critical factor in their evolution was the progressive morcellation of estates and jurisdictions discussed earlier. The fact that this process started sooner in France and Italy and proceeded further in prime arable areas has a direct bearing on when and where we find the so-called classical manor. However, we must avoid the mistake of believing that as soon as estates and jurisdictions were reduced to the scale of the local farming community, then manors sprang into existence. There is growing evidence from countries like England and Denmark to show that a dramatic revolution in the organisation of settlement occurred over the ninth and tenth centuries, with patterns of dispersed settlement being gathered into nucleated settlements. As Hodges has observed, (Hodges, 1982, p. 140), such a change could be tied up with manorialisation, signal proof of the lordship now being exercised over the peasantry and a logical step to take at a moment when peasant holdings were being territorialised, that is, being given an assessment on the ground that matched the services owed for its tenure. Such a change would also have established the social foundations of the manor, creating the closed relationship with a farming community which typifies the classical manor. However, the fact that manorialisation was grafted onto an ongoing process whereby estates and jurisdictions were being devolved downwards must make us cautious over how we link manor and community. During the early stages of manorialisation, the continued break-up of estates and jurisdictions through subinfeudation or straightforward inheritance may have threatened the link (see for example, Lennard, 1959, p. 22; Aston, 1958, p. 77). Manors too, could be fissioned, after all, this is what subinfeudation was all about, but what happened to the farming community? Some will have been fissioned with the manor, forming new settlements (Dodgshon, 1980, pp. 108–19), but as in parts of England (especially eastern England), the village may have retained its physical integrity, becoming divided internally between more than one manor. Maitland talks about a manorial system which, even by 1086, appears to have been 'forced upon the village, but fits it very badly' (Maitland, 1897, p. 85). The point which I am trying to make here is that to talk of a 'perfect' manor as something fashioned around the farming community is to underplay the wider forces that affected its development. The continued working-out of these forces, even after manorialisation, will have created some of the structural variety that makes it so difficult to generalise about the manor, whether in England (Postan, 1966, p. 571) or western Europe generally (Duby, 1968, pp. 47–53).

The character of the manorial or seigneurial economy showed important variations over time. The prime source of variation was in the balance between demesne and tenant land. In theory, the two were co-variable in the sense that the amount of demesne determined the amount of tenant land. In fact, working on the Carolingian polyptyches, Coleman has proposed a veritable ecology of relationships, with not only the amount of demesne and tenant land, but also, the number of people, labour-bearing tenements and ingenuile tenements and the respective amounts of labour services, payments in kind and cash all being interrelated (E. R. Coleman, 1977, pp. 688–9 and 701). Over time, though, the lord's interest in demesne farming varied so that the whole system of balances within the seigneury were progressively recalibrated. We can chart the extent of this variation through two regional examples: Italy and England. The emergence of the great Italian seigneuries dates from the late eight century, perhaps through a bargain 'struck between the labour-hungry rich and the growing number of land-hungry poor?' (Herlihy, 1959, p. 62). These demesne-based economies, however, flourished only for a limited period. By the end of the ninth century, as political conditions in the peninsula became more unsettled and trade more risk-laden, demesne production contracted sharply as seigneurs 'disinvested' from the land (Herlihy, 1959, p. 65). By 1000 AD, though, we find signs of a recovery and a resurgence of dependent tenures. Demesne-cultivation and labour-services never regained their earlier importance. Instead, land became held more for cash rents and for payments in kind. The growth of cash rents, although slow, pressurised the peasant economy into becoming more commercial, more market-oriented, selling their produce to raise the cash needed for the rent dues. This broad change between the eighth and ninth centuries on the one hand and the period beginning in the eleventh century on the other has been observed not just in Italy, but also elsewhere in Western Europe (Herlihy, 1959, p. 68). It is a change which continental historians have entitled *la revolution censive*.

Turning to England, manorialism was developed more strongly in the south and east than in the north and west and more strongly on larger, older estates than on those formed after the Norman Conquest. In addition, we find broad secular swings in the importance of demesne-cultivation and labour-service. Initially, demesne served to maintain the lord's household. Even in the eleventh century, some of the larger physically-scattered estates, the lord's household followed an annual circuit around the estate, consuming the produce of its demesne (Greenway, 1972, p. xliv). In a backward glance at conditions in 1066, *Domesday Book* shows that royal manors, easily the most extensive in England at this time, yielded to the king a portion of their produce that was called the farm of one night or night's farm, notionally, the amount of food needed to sustain the royal court for a single day (Stafford, 1980, pp. 491–502). Geared to the sustenance of the lord's household, the manorial economy would have approximated to the natural or self-sufficient economy that some have seen as constituting the essence of its meaning (Kosminsky, 1955, p. 15). But already, with the growth of towns over the tenth, eleventh and twelfth centuries, demesne was presented with a new outlet. A new elasticity of demand began to govern the scale of demesne production, with output ebbing and flowing in accord with market conditions. Broadly speaking, demesne-farming was at a peak

during the eleventh and early twelfth centuries, then contracted
during the mid-twelfth century, recovered during the late twelfth
century only to contract as pressure of land became acute from
about 1300 onwards (Hilton, 1969, pp. 15–16; Postan, 1973, pp.
252–4; Harvey, 1974 pp. 353–4). The extent to which lords
squeezed tenants for labour-service obviously fluctuated in step
with this phasing of demesne production. Demands were especially burdensome during the tenth and eleventh centuries, when
labour was scare but demesnes large. Although reimposed after
the contraction of the mid-twelfth century, labour-service was now
increasingly supplemented by hired labour (Hatcher, 1981, p. 35;
see also, Postan, 1973, p. 257). Alongside these broad changes in
the manorial economy were changes in the status of tenants. The
ordinary tenant of *Domesday Book* – *villani* – slowly sank into
unfreedom or serfdom. By the time of common law villeinage, or
during the mid-thirteenth century, approximately 60 per cent of
the English peasantry were classed as unfree, unable to seek action
in the courts against their lord (Hilton, 1969, p. 16; Hilton, 1975b,
pp. 127–8; Hatcher,1981, p. 37), though it could be argued that
restraints on the behaviour and mobility of villeins imposed on
them a *de facto* unfreedom by the eleventh century even if their
legal status before the law was one of freedom (Hatcher, 1981,
p. 32).

Was There a Specifically Feudal Landscape?

The ulterior purpose of this chapter has been to argue that feudalism created its own landscape *sui generis*. The notion of feudalism
as a distinct system of spatial order depends not simply on feudal
relations, on kings establishing themselves as lords of all men and
as the crowning apex of an elaborate social hierarchy, but equally,
on the feudal monarch as *dominus terrae*. From these central
concepts evolved a whole range of ideas concerning the organisation not just of society, but also, of those aspects which we would
regard as its spatial order. It is my contention that feudalism was as
much about spatial relations as about social relations. The complex
grid of feudal relations – with their co-ordinates of lordship and
vassalage, freedom and unfreedom, military service and labour
service – overlay a purely geographical grid onto which it had been
purposefully projected. To put this another way, the feudal

relations developed between king and vassal, lord and serf, were not abstract aspatial relations, but were firmly anchored to specific territories and specific spaces: the latter being the quantum basis for the calculation of the other. If we had to find a word to convey the principles of this new spatial order, it would be the word regulated. Under feudalism, spatial order became socially regulated. Far from being an unintended side-effect, I would see this structuring of relations in space as part of the very essence of feudalism. It was the means by which the king's rule was projected out over the provinces.

We can explore this theme of regulated space at two levels. At a macro-scale, we can examine how feudalism was used to achieve spatial integration at the level of the state. To reiterate a point made at the outset of the previous chapter, we need to consider how state administration and the establishment of feudal lordship became an exercise in the territorial structuring of society as opposed to earlier systems based on the social structuring of territory. At a micro-scale, we need to examine how the relations between lord and peasant were similarly set within a regulated framework of spatial order, one that mapped them into a chequerboard of spaces and meanings.

From a political point of view, early medieval Europe contained systems that ranged in size and complexity from the small city-states of the Mediterranean to the Empires of Rome and Charlemagne. Such extremes of spatial organisation posed different problems of integration. By virtue of its small scale, the city-state posed the least problems. Yet for this very reason, it did not pioneer the sorts of organisational structures that were demanded of larger state-systems. Indeed, once their institutional character was fixed, the more successful found it difficult to cope with territorial growth (Griffeth and Thomas, 1981, p. 195). Pivoted around a single node, and with many of its inhabitants having property in both town and country, its integration was greatly facilitated by the fact that there was no conflict of interest between these two spheres. Nor did its scale or the distance from its centre to its periphery pose any threat to its unity. In so far as city and hinterland formed a coherent activity system, there was a logical basis for the city-state as a political system. However, whilst it constituted itself first and foremost, or in aggregate, as the inhabitants of a particular territory rather than as members of a common descent-group, nevertheless, kin groups were present as a consti-tuitive element. Not only do we find these kin-groups inhabiting the early Sumerian city-states, but they were also present during the early growth of Italian city-states, with particular districts of the state's urban focus being occupied by particular kin-groups or extended families. Hughes's study of twelfth-century Genoa prob-ably provides the best illustration of how kinship could continue to organise space within the territory of the city-state, with most of the noble families colonising particular sectors of the city and even establishing their own separate spheres of economic activity (Hughes, 1975, pp. 4–5 and 9). Whilst Genoa provides the most celebrated illustration of these kin-groups, we must not overlook that the fact that it was a feature of other city-states, both prehis-toric (Griffeth and Thomas, 1981, p. 191) and historic (Griffeth and Thomas, 1981, p. 191; Heers, 1977, p. 248).

The early European empires present quite different problems. Arguably, they are just not numerous enough to enable us to construct a general type. Each must be seen as individual, at least as regards the manner in which it integrated space and sustained its authority over vast distances. Eisenstadt's analysis of empires world-wide offers a whole series of relevant insights about how they were organised, but surprisingly, he does not deal explicitly with how they coped with the problems of governing extensive areas of space (Eisenstadt, 1963). Indeed, the size-component tends to be taken for granted, so that it is not always clear how his 'bureaucratic empires' differ organisationally from states of a lesser scale (see, for example, Eisenstadt, 1963, p. 21). One is left to surmise that their geographical growth stemmed from the way in which the centralised power of rulers depended on their control over what Eisenstadt calls 'free-floating resources'. In effect, he appears to see them as systems experiencing a form of runaway growth, with the 'free-floating resources' offered by new areas funding an increase in the power-base of rulers and giving them the capacity to mount a search for still more resources, so that power and colonisation fed on each other (Eisenstadt, 1963, especially pp. 314–16). Exactly how they mapped their power into landscape is not specified. We need only to consider the vast areas over which the rules of Alexander the Great, the Roman empire and Charlemagne were spread to appreciate that this could pose organisational problems of considerable magnitude, problems made all the acute by the practical difficulties that surrounded the flow of information. Some have argued that their ineffective solution to these problems was the reason why such empires failed to survive in this form. Each had its own system of administration, some based on the force of personalities and others around the carefully-defined power of appointed officers. Thus, at its maximum extent, the Roman empire had some provinces under the control of the *princeps* and others under the senate: the former, most of which were on the frontiers of the Empire, were ruled locally by a procurator and the latter, by proconsuls. By its sheer scale, degree of integration, organisational complexity and rule through bureaucracies and democracies as opposed to tribal hierarchies, the Roman empire has always proved a headache to 'successional' interpretations of societal organisation. Even if we concede wholly to the recent emphasis on how much may have survived in terms of political patterns and settlement structures our conclusion must still be that its collapse left European society less organised and less integrated,: though even the most hard-headed Germanist must admit that subsequent feudal states everywhere were influenced by Roman ideas. Elias's broad conclusion that systems of societal organisation based on military conquest tend to produce structures of integration rather than processes of integration may be one way of absorbing it into a wider concept of societal change. Alternatively, we can draw on another of his ideas and see the weakness of the Roman empire as arising from its singularity. Later feudal states constituted a whole universe of systems, one in which the strong was continually being filtered out from the weak. The Roman empire, like all empires, lacked this sort of proven adaptability.

In comparison with its Roman predecessor, the Carolingian empire rested on the strength of its kings and the obedience of its nobles. The 'Empire was not a territory', wrote Boussard, 'it was a power' (Boussard, 1968, p. 39). The practice amongst the Frankish kings of dividing their kingdoms between their sons or designated heirs posed a continuing threat to the territorial integrity of their domains. They viewed their kingdoms as 'little different from private property' and 'divided them as desire and, often, necessity dictated' (Wood, 1966, p. 1). What kings struggled to unite tended to disassemble at their death. Even Charlemagne's 'imperial mirage' (Ganshof, 1971) was divided among his three sons at his death in 814 AD. Integration was a temporary alliance, with states welded through the authority of a single king rather than through an ongoing constitutional arrangement. To reiterate Cohen's point, state organisation was one which overcame the fissiparous tendencies of chiefdoms or tribal kingships. The making of the feudal state, therefore, involved the abandonment of partible kingship and the acceptance of a narrower dynastic succession, ensuring that only one son inherited the kingship. Arguably, such a step was a *sine qua non* of the feudal state if we are to see it as being qualitatively different from earlier systems of societal organisation.

So long as early states remained located in their core-areas, or the areas of high productivity and high population defined for us by Pounds and Ball (Pounds and Ball, 1964, pp. 24–40), then they would have faced few problems of either political or spatial integration. Problems arose only when power was projected beyond the confines of these core areas. Jones has talked of the high cost of assimilation and amalgamation once early states confronted the task of incorporating different cultures and different environments. Such costs, he argued favoured a consolidation within like-regions and between like-cultures as a first stage (Jones, 1981, pp. 106–7). As regional states with a maximum of internal homogeneity, they could survive without a great deal of organisational, change. However, once the power of the polity was projected beyond these stable core areas, new organisational adjustments will have been called forth. In the context of early European states, feudalism was the solution which they adopted in dealing with this problem of integrating larger, more heterogenous territories. It achieved this greater integration of space through the concept of feudal vassalage, granting individuals jurisdiction over vast territorial lordships in return for fealty, homage and military service. To be more exact, the concept of vassalage probably developed during the very earliest stages of state-formation, when kings gathered around themselves a retinue of fighting men whose loyalty and service were given in return for protection and maintenance. With the enlargement of the more successful state-systems and the emergence of polities that could no longer be securely ruled from a single centre, kings transformed the notion of vassalage as a purely social relation into one in which it became a socio-spatial relationship, with vassals of the king being granted both land and lordship in return for fealty and military service.

Relations of court became relations of space, as service and lordship became structured and tokened through space. The expanding polity was carved up into large territorial lordships that were granted to favoured members of the king's retinue. In some cases, though, we must allow for a degree of continuity. Rulers of former tribal kingships might be re-employed, becoming vassals of the state-king and holding their former kingdom as a lordship. In theory, the partitioning of the feudal state occurred at two levels and, possibly, in two stages. The first involved the creation of the major territorial lordships: these are represented in England by the shires, and later by the great territorial baronies like the Palatinate Earldoms and Marcher Lordships and in northern France and Germany by the duchies and principalities. The second stage involved the creation of smaller, finer units of lordship, carrying the authority and military obligations of the king down to a local level: these were the knights' fees, bannal lordships and castellanies. Although attractive as an idea, we must not assume that this territorialisation of lordship within the feudal state worked itself out at a broad territorial level and then, only then, at a local level. Much depended on how and when expanding states absorbed smaller ones. When the Mercian state absorbed the smaller kingdom of Hwicce, the latter may not have had a well-developed system of territorial lordship, but we can hardly say this of the far-larger kingdom of Mercia when it became absorbed into the incipient state of England. In short, when we come to talk about the territorialisation of the larger, mature state-systems like England, we cannot assume that their rulers were acting on some *tabula rasa*. The new areas which they absorbed may already have been partitioned into a network of feudal lordships.

By their very nature, the early feudal states were precariously structured organisations, so much so, that we are forced to class them as immature state systems. Having assumed absolute power over all men and all land, their monarchs could only sustain power by conceding it, sharing out land and lordship amongst their vassals on a territorial basis. It worked so long as nobles continued to accept that their lordship descended from the king, that it was an emanation of the king's greater lordship. But sharing out land and lordship inevitably created lines of potential weakness running through the state. As Elias has pointed out, the conflicting forces within the feudal state had to be carefully balanced if these centrifugal tendencies were not to outweigh the centripetal designs of their kings (Elias, 1982, pp. 15–30). Some feudal kings were better at this balancing act than others. In England and Wales, for instance, lordships never lost their dependence on the king even though some, like the Marcher Lordships, wielded a great deal of power, not least because 'lordship and honour were geographically coterminous' and provided lords with 'a monopoly of fealty within its boundaries' (Davies, 1978, p. 78). Nevertheless, even in England, there was a constant drift of power downwards, from kings to the great territorial barons and from the latter to the petty lords and knights. In France, it was a different story. The balance of power shifted so far in the direction of provincial lordships that it undermined the integrity of the state. The process of fragmentation began when kingship over the west Frankish area became divided during the ninth century and the various provinces assumed greater power for themselves. By the tenth century, these provinces had emerged as independent duchies and principalities, like Aquitaine, Normandy and Burgundy, with the reality of Frankish kingship reduced to the northern nucleus of Nuestria. The process of disintegration was still not complete. Over the eleventh century, even unitary control over the duchies and principalities disintegrated, power being refocused on powerful local lordships, the so-called bannal lordships.

The feudal landscape appears no less regulated when we focus down on the world of the ordinary peasant. Once the peasantry held land of a lord in return for labour services, payments in kind and other feudal dues, then there arose the need for lords to scale the amount of land held by the peasantry against the services and dues which they rendered. In practice, feudalised communities throughout western Europe acquired an assessment based on a fixed number of land measures. Some of these land-measures were based on tax assessments, the *iugatio*, and others on the amount of land which a plough-team could cope with in a year, or the amount of land needed to support a family. Despite their widely differing backgrounds, these land assessments all had the same meaning under feudalism, proportioning the amount of land held by the *vill* or *villa* to the amount of services, renders and dues which it owed to its lord.

There are strong reasons for believing that feudal services and renders were *ab origine* burdens on the person. Their extension to land, an extension which imbued them with the character of land rent, was a secondary stage of development. For the geographer, this conversion has enormous significance. It signals the penetration of lordship into the relationship between the peasant and his holding and, as such, an intensification of the relationship between society and space. From this point onwards, feudal relations could shape relations within the territory of the *vill* or *villa*. At this moment, peasant holdings ceased to be allodial. They became subject to a new definition, a definition that imposed a new categorical order on the landscape, granting to each peasant family a measure of land for a measure of service, renders and dues. For the peasantry, feudal space was bounded space. It was no longer a world of boundless or unlimited opportunities to be colonised when need arose. For each and all, it was a world delimited by the land assessment imposed on the settlement. In effect, the landscape became divided into a chequerboard on which occupation was legitimised in some spaces but not others. Within the former, arable rights in land were assiduously regulated through the relations of lord and peasant. Outside these assessed areas, that is, over the surrounding waste, peasant communities had certain use-rights, such as rights of common grazing, turbary, wood for fuel, etc., but not the right to extend their arable land since this would breach their assessment and, in the process, the conditions on which they held land. New arable or newly-assessed land could only be created by the king or lord since, during the heyday of feudalism, it meant extending the feudal concept of land tenure, apportioning blocks of assessed land in return for a fixed levy of services, renders and dues. Clearly, feudalism restructured the farming landscape on its own terms. In reducing peasant tenures to dependent tenures, in feudalising them, it also territorialised them by taking the ties between lord and peasant and setting them down in an explicitly spatial framework. The distinction imposed on the landscape between what was assessed and what was non-assessed land, or between what was arable land and what was waste, became symbolic of the distinction between what lay within and what lay without the defined relations between lord and peasant.

7
Regulated Space and the Rise of Markets

Through a series of books and papers, Karl Polanyi argued strongly and eloquently for seeing early state-formation as associated with a profound change in the character of exchange. Prior to the appearance of states, exchange was embedded within society. By that, he meant that exchange was not separately organised as an economic process, with its own free-standing institutions and mechanisms, but was accessory to other spheres. In a work published posthumously, he talked about exchange being 'instituted in terms of kinship and made to serve not just economic ends, but also, political and religious ends' (Polanyi, 1977, p. 61). Amongst primitive and archaic societies, it was the interweave of kinship relations that 'formalized the situations out of which organized economic activities spring' (Polanyi, 1977, p. 55; see also, Polanyi, 1968, especially pp. 7–23). The exchange relations built around such economic activities involved status transactions, meaning that they served to establish the symmetry or asymmetry of social relationships, that is, the reciprocal flow of gifts between tribes or the flows between a tribe and its chief or ruling theocracy. In effect, exchange had an instrumental meaning that went far beyond any purely economic meaning. With the emergence of early states, there emerged alongside these status transactions a new form of integration based on trade, transactions that referred 'not so much to the status of men as to the importance of goods' (Polanyi, 1977, p. 58).

Ports of Trade and Early Markets: Polanyi's Case

The growth of economic transactions was not a natural development, a straightforward extension of the processes already operating within society. It introduced a new form of gain through trade

193

which, if unchecked, threatened traditional values of intra- and inter-tribal exchange. It completely overturned the equivalencies that underpinned symmetrical schemes and created alternative bases of wealth that vied with established centres of redistributive exchange. For these reasons, it was a form of trade that was not allowed to grow in an uninhibited way but, from the very outset, was subject to the close control of state-rulers. Put simply, they sought both to constrain and to marginalise it. Polanyi outlined a number of ways in which rulers might regulate this purely economic trade. In many early states, it was allowed to develop alongside customary exchange schemes only under the strict legislative control of the state itself. It formed what Polanyi described as state-administered trade. In its most extreme form, a form upon which Polanyi elaborated in the context of Mesopotamia and the Near East, administered trade was managed by traders, merchants and *tamkarum* who were actually employed by the state. Private venturers and would-be entrepreneurs simply had no place in such a system. The kinds of goods traded between states were regulated by treaty and their value carefully controlled through an accepted scale of equivalencies. The state also ensured that these new economic transactions affected only external not internal trade. A contrast tended to emerge between the economic transactions of external trade and the continuing organisation of internal exchange around established systems of reciprocity and redistribution. One of the devices used by early state-rulers to externalise such economic transactions was by confining them to a strictly demarcated, politically neutral site on the edge of the state-system, usually at a break-point between the land and sea, beside a major river or at the point of contact between two major ecosystems (Polanyi, 1968, p. 239; Humpreys, 1969, p. 192). Polanyi labelled these sites as ports of trade and saw them as "a universal institution of overseas trade" (Polanyi, 1968, p. 239), though others have tagged them as 'gateway communities'; they offered protection to foreign traders; facilities of anchorage and warehousing; lawful arbitrators; agreements over goods to be traded; and agreements over the amount of different goods in each sorting (Polanyi, 1977, p. 95).

Just as important as the state's control over the location of such trade and the type of goods involved were its attempts to regulate the conditions of trade in respect of prices. In theory, we might expect ports of trade to have been places of gainful trade, or trade in which one party sought to gain at the expense of another. After all, as sites peripheral to the state, this is where negative reciprocity, the notion of gaining something for nothing, was at its strongest (Sahlins, 1974, p. 199). In fact, early states probably regarded this spirit of selfish gain as a 'peril of solidarity' (Polanyi, 1977, p. 58) or at least a threat to the monopolistic control of wealth by its élite groups. They had good reason, therefore, for keeping such trade not just on the geographical periphery of the state, where trading complementaries were maximised, but also, on the social and economic margins of the state. To have allowed the scarcity value of commodities to determine their exchange rate would have encouraged new concentrations of wealth outside the control of existing élites and would have allowed production to become organised in response to new imperatives as market demand was fed back into the economy. The state's reaction was to ensure that such trade remained an accessory to the state by making sure that ports of trade were neither free nor price-fixing markets. As we shall see, it licensed traders and taxed their activities, thereby creating a new source of wealth for itself. It established equivalencies for the exchange of basic goods and, through the protection which the state alone could offer, ensured that élite groups continued to have a monopoly over prestige goods, prestige goods that now began to move as much through the efforts of traders as through the ongoing operation of traditional exchange mechanisms. So tightly administered was this new type of exchange, that we even find traders being employed by the state as its agents. Such regulation meant that for all their novelty and potential, the activities of ports of trade were kept at arm's length from society – something that went on around rather than within it.

Polanyi saw ports of trade as a first stage of change. As a second stage, he saw market-based systems of trade becoming geographically internalised by the state but – and this was of cardinal importance to his argument – no less regulated. He used the *agora* of the Greek city-state as an illustration of his argument. In origin, the *agora* was a public meeting-place which took on the functions of a market-place (Starr, 1977, p. 101). In direct contrast to the marginal position of ports of trade, the *agora* stood firmly within the core of the *polis*. It also differed from the former in the character of its business. Whereas ports of trade were primarily engaged in external, long-distance trade, and dealt more (though not exclusively) with high-value goods, the *agora* dealt more with the sort of produce that served everyday needs, 'a feeding place for the population' (Polanyi, 1977, p. 126). But although enlivened by countless transactions involving small quantities of staple goods, with – to use Polanyi's terminology – a true demand crowd and a true supply crowd, he did not consider these early Greek markets as price-fixing markets. Their motive or organising force was the principle of householding, or balancing the surpluses and deficits of the domestic economy. Economic transactions, trade for gain beyond the labour value of commodities plus a modest profit for the trader, were alien to their ethos. Aristotle, for instance, insisted on 'the unnaturalness of commercial gain' (Finley, 1970, 18). Polanyi himself made much use of Heriod's *Work and Days* to argue that the rise of Greek markets was seen as a threat to the commonality of interests and welfare that had prevailed under earlier tribal systems of exchange. In response, prices were fixed in accordance with what was considered a just price and not in relation to prevailing levels of supply and demand, a price that enabled the necessities of life to be exchange for each other. Polanyi called this 'non-market trade' because the *agora* lacked any mechanism by which it could fix prices in keeping with the ebb and flow of supply and demand, but had to operate through agreed equivalencies between different commodities.

This exact regulation of market conditions lasted until the fourth century BC. At this point, we can detect the first signs of prices starting to fluctuate with market forces. It was a change clearly evident in the Athenian grain market. By the 320s AD, the eastern Mediterranean faced a grain shortage. With its growing population, Athens suffered the effects of this shortage more acutely than most city-states. It solved its problems by drawing more grain from its hinterland and importing grain via its port of trade or emporium at Pireaus. These two sources, though, had different price levels: the problem for the Athenian state was how to prevent the lower of the two (imported grain) from disrupting the supply of the higher (local grain). The policy which it adopted involved interposing an institutional buffer between them so that the two price-levels were only partially linked (Polanyi, 1977, pp. 234–5). At the same time, the strict determination of grain prices was relaxed: thereafter, they were allowed to move within set limits. By the

time Cleomenes had assumed command over Egypt and the Aegean, the continuing shortage of grain called forth a further
institutional response. Cleomenes created a base for his agents on
Rhodes, together with warehousing facilities. The duty of these
agents was to establish forward links with each of the city-states
and to move grain to those with the highest prevailing prices.
Thus, the whole area became a single integrated grain-market,
with supply and demand being matched if not balanced through a
state-administered system of agents based on Rhodes (Polanyi,
1977, pp. 238–51). But even at this point, Polanyi refrains from
seeing it as a totally unfettered market, describing it as a price-
fixing market hemmed in by strict administrative controls (Polanyi, 1977, p. 248). It did not, for example, affect production
decisions, at least not in Polanyi's view. Its effects, therefore, were
restricted. Indeed, before its full significance was realised, the
Roman Conquest of the eastern Mediterranean had created a
different pattern of trade. Like the Greeks, the Romans relied
heavily on a maritime network of grain supply. To ship grain from
one end of the Mediterranean to the other only added 16 per cent
to its market price, a level of opportunity cost that land transport
simply could not match (Rickman, 1980, pp. 14 and 120). In a
direct comparison with the nature of earlier Greek trade, Rickman
has also noted the role played by governments agents in the
organisation of Roman trade. However, whilst he concedes that
they interfered directly in trade, he rejects any suggestion that
they were the main agents of trade. The Roman grain trade, he
argued, cannot be seen as 'state-run', private enterprise being 'the
backbone of the whole business' (Rickman, 1980, pp. 27–8). Of
course, to say that the grain trade was in the hands of independent
rather than government agents does not rule out the fact that such
agents had to work within a set framework of customs and values,
one which the authorities applied stringently.

Polanyi's discussion of both ports of trade and his discussion of
early regulated markets forms part of a wider analysis in which he
maintained that market-dominated societies – that is, societies
whose organisation was determined through the market-place –
were a much later phenomenon. Furthermore, the inception of
trade for gain did not necessarily coincide with the establishment
of market-centres, nor did the latter see the growth of price-fixing
or free markets. These three elements of a market-based society –

market centres, trade for gain, and price-fixing mechanisms – could exist apart. For Polanyi, their early history is the history of their separate origins. We find trade before we find market-centres and we find market-centres long before they had the ability to integrate society by regulating prices in accordance with levels of supply and demand and, through this self-regulation of prices, the power to influence production decisions and the allocation of resources. Although Polanyi spent the latter part of his life documenting situations in which his ideas held firm, his general interpretation of trade in archaic and early state societies has not been without its critics. His work on Greece was criticised for underplaying the role of price fluctuations as opposed to fixed prices (Humphreys, 1969, p. 186), though his *Livelihood of Man* went some way towards answering this particular criticism by its deeper analysis and clearer chronology of change. Latterly, though, a strong attack has been mounted on his ideas regarding the state-administered trade of the Near Eastern states. Polanyi saw these areas as providing the archetypal examples of state-administered trade, a trade organised around paid state-officials and carefully confined to specially-designated quays or *karums* on the edge of the main ports, with no sign of markets in the accepted sense of the term. However, recent work has castigated his conclusions as a false reading of the evidence. Not only are there signs of market-places now being discovered in the towns of Old Babylon, but also, there are strong reasons for believing that a substantial private sector existed amongst its merchant class, a private sector that operated without state interference (Gledhill and Larsen, 1982, pp. 203–8; Silver, 1983, pp. 815 and 822–3). There are also indications that market prices fluctuated by the second millenium BC, that such fluctuations could be quite sharp, that they moved in response to scarcities and supply problems and that they moved independently of any state-promulgated price (Farber, 1978, pp. 1–51; Silver, 1983, p. 823). In the most recent riposte, Silver has directly challenged Polanyi's most basic assumptions by inferring that state systems like those of Assyria and Babylon already had free markets in produce, land and labour by the second millenium BC, and suggesting that production decisions were already being based on price movements (Silver, 1983, pp. 807–10), conclusions that would admit the possibility of von Thünen landscapes within the very earliest states. Such was their precociousness that he sees

them as experiencing a pioneering revolution in commercial technique, with 'besides credit, banking houses, and negotiability, the
commercial loan market widened by resorting to suretyship or
third-party guarantee of payment' (Silver, 1983, pp. 803–4), all
this almost 3000 years before the first Italian medieval banking-
house!

Ports of Trade and Regulated Markets: the European Dimension

Over recent years, a vigorous debate has also emerged on the
applicability of Polanyi's ideas to western Europe. On balance, his
basic insights into the social embeddedness of the earliest economic transactions, into ports of trade, into the state-regulation of
early trade and into the absence of free or price-fixing markets
have much to teach us about the period from the late prehistoric to
the end of the medieval period.

The most disputed aspect of this broad problem has been the
nature of trade over the late prehistoric period. Unfortunately, the
evidence tends to be ambiguous, to permit different interpretations. Detailed reconstructions of regional pottery styles, for instance, have been credibly interpreted as manifesting tribal-
exchange structures and as the market areas produced by the
trade in pottery around production centres. Naturally, coinage
has been seized on as offering instructive clues. Coins of Greek
origin spread into southern Gaul by the fourth century BC, mainly
by way of long-distance trade networks. By the first century BC,
low-value coins were in circulation, both in Gaul and southern
Britain (Collis, 1971, pp. 97–100). The distribution of this low-
value bronze coinage is weighted around the large *oppida* and
around early ports of trade like Hengistbury Head (Dorset).
Coinage around the latter discloses a marked distance-decay as
one moves away from it, gold and silver coinage becoming more
common at greater distances from the site. This concentration of
low-value coinage around Hengistbury Head has been taken by
some as denoting a monetised economy, the site acting as a
cross-over junction between long-distance and regional trading
patterns (Collis, 1971, p. 102). As a counter-argument to this
suggestion, it has been pointed out that to accept a wholly monetised economy around centres like Hengistbury Head, around the
first century BC, would be to make such economies as advanced as

the economies of the eastern Mediterranean. Stressing the continued embeddedness of the economy within 'the ritual of social relations', Hodder has offered two alternative explanations for the weighted distribution of bronze coinage around major trading centres in southern Britain and Gaul, seeing it as a reflection of either the use of such coinage as payment for tribute or, its use as a local standard to aid intra-tribal exchange at fixed rates (Hodder, 1979, pp. 190–1).

Similar problems arise when dealing with the impact of the Romans on the exchange patterns of areas like Britain. Their occupation collapsed or seriously modified tribal exchange systems, especially long-distance exchange networks, replacing them with their own system. Long-distance flows, though never on the same scale as from other parts of the empire, became something channelled through the Roman hierarchy of military command. Local or regional flows, meanwhile, became organised around a network of market centres which the Romans either took over from local tribes or established for themselves. The increase in market trade, however, does not mean that local economies became wholly concerned with supplying markets. Hodder has convincingly argued that the Roman economy in areas like southern Britain continued to be embedded within social and political processes until the second and third centuries AD. Only at this date do we find the appearance of large quantities of low-value coins and local pottery distributions breaking out of old tribal divisions (Hodder, 1979, p. 192), and even these changes could be accounted for by the dramatic inflation of prices, debasement of coinage and a shift away from cash transactions that was occurring throughout the empire by the third century AD.

The major difficulty with this sort of analysis is that whilst the evidence for coinage is relatively abundant, there is little on prices. Even if we refocus the problem at the wider, more general level of the empire at large – a reasonable alternative given that the modest flows between its core and peripheral areas qualified it as 'a vast common market', at least by the second century AD (Jones, 1964, vol. 2, p. 824; see also Hopkins, 1980, p. 112) – data on price movements is still relatively sparse. Admittedly, there can be no doubting the impact of Rome's demand on prices. Its food and land prices were notoriously higher than in surrounding towns (Duncan-Jones, 1974, p. 345; Hopkins, 1980, p. 119). Half the annual rent of a 'dark abode' in the capital, it was said, would buy the freehold of a fine house and garden in the countryside (Duncan-Jones, 1974, p. 345), and there are signs that speculators' were demolishing small properties so as to replace them with greater, rent-enhanced properties, 'a most vicious kind of 'speculation' declared the Senate in the reign of Claudius (Lewis and Reinhold, 1966, p. 211), though there is no sign of land uses within Rome being differentiated according to their ability to pay for preferred locations (Ramage, 1983, pp. 88–9; see also, Raper, 1977, pp. 206–17). Rome's ability to pressurise prices upwards is understandable given that we are dealing with a city that had an estimated population of over one million (Ramage, 1983, p. 64). Other large cities of the time, especially in the Eastern Empire, such as Constantinople, had a similar effect. Arguably, what their impact on prices illustrate is that where supplies of both habitable land and food were prescribed by the constraints of transport, and where the concentration of population was considerable (after all, Europe did not see cities of over one million inhabitants again until the eighteenth century!) the sheer scale of demand could thwart any statutory attempt to regulate prices within socially-determined norms.

It is generally agreed that the Roman empire saw the gradual development of a monetised economy, with its expansion, especially its expansion westwards, being accompanied by a dramatic growth of both local and interregional trade, of market centres and of coinage (Hopkins, 1980, p. 112). For Hopkins, a critical factor behind this commercial revolution was the imposition of taxes in money and the effect which this had on local economies, economies which had hitherto been of a primitive, non-commercial character. He proposes a threefold division of the Empire into a core (Rome and Italy), an inner ring (including southern Gaul, Spain, North Africa and Asia Minor) and an outer ring of frontier provinces (including Britain) (Hopkins, 1980, p. 101). He reasoned that faced with a tax burden computed in money, the inner ring needed to export to the consumption centres of the core goods to the value of their tax burden, the one being their only means of raising the other. The outer ring differed from the inner ring in so far as the presence of large standing armies provided it with a means of raising money locally, without the need to export goods out of the region to the same degree. But in case we see this 'tax-stimulated trade' as Hopkins calls it as a means whereby the entire labour and produce of peasants and artisans became commodities of the market place, we should keep another of his propositions in mind. 'The Roman state', he argues, 'was supported by many millions of small contributions' (Hopkins, 1980, pp. 116–20). Its tax levels were low. It generated a great deal of revenue simply because its tax burden was spread over so many people. The surplus extracted as tax from the average peasant or artisan amounted to only a small portion of his total labour. When, over the third century AD, the decline of trade and rapid price inflation caused a shift from taxes in money to taxes in kind, the economy of the ordinary peasant and artisan was relatively untouched by such events (Hopkins, 1980, pp. 16–20). Far from being a society deeply penetrated and organised by market forces, then, the Roman Empire 'constituted a thin veneer of sophistication' (Hopkins, 1980, p. 104) that touched the vast majority of its inhabitants only lightly.

With the collapse of the Roman Empire and the gradual emergence of state-systems in western Europe, the political context of trade altered fundamentally. The market system which had evolved over the Roman period fell into disuse. The base conditions for the development of medieval trade owed very little to its Roman antecedents. In fact, what we witness during the early medieval period is a marked lull in interregional trade and exchange. By the eighth century, though, there are signs of a resurgence. It was a resurgence in which traditional exchange schemes still played some part. However, the main foci of growth were ports of trade and emporia. As institutional forms of trade, these probably appeared for the first time during the late Iron Age. A number of writers have commented on the exchange networks that grew up between the tribes of southern Britain and those of northern Gaul towards the end of the Iron Age, an exchange network eventually foreclosed by the Romans. Many of the larger *oppida* on both sides of the Channel were located on the border between tribal groups or in locations which served as a point of intertribal exchange. Hengistbury Head was such a site. Sited on the Dorset coast between two tribal territories and facing the Channel, it has all the hallmarks of a port of trade. Defined but not defended by a low bank and ditch, its excavation has shown that it traded over a wide area of southern Britain and northern Gaul, gathering and distributing tin, copper, lead, silver, pottery, slate, amphorae and wine, and that a wide range of raw materials was processed or worked at Hengistbury itself (Cunliffe, 1978, pp. 63–81). There are also clear indications that it was the centre of a monetised economy, not least because it minted coins(Collis, 1971, pp. 100–2). Like other ports of trade, its activity fell away with the Roman occupation.

During the immediate post-Roman period, trading activity is thought to have declined throughout Europe. The waning power of Rome and the Barbarian invasions disrupted patterns of trade, lowered consumption levels and made the activities of merchants far more risk-laden. But as Pirenne long ago pointed out, there was continuity where it mattered, with the trading networks that criss-crossed the Mediterranean, drawing the wealth of the Near East and North Africa into the trading circuits of Europe, manifesting what he saw as a 'vigorous continuity' (Pirenne, 1925, p. 14). When the Germanic tribes pushed south to the Mediterranean their objective was 'not to destroy the Roman Empire but to occupy and enjoy it' (Pirenne, 1925, p. 5). As long as this Mediterranean trade continued, then, there was still the possibility that long-distance trading circuits worked their way across the rest of Europe, for the Mediterranean had always been a generator of such traffic. Pirenne appreciated this (Pirenne 1925, p. 12), but he underestimated the extent to which these northern offshoots of Mediterranean trade were able to renew themselves quickly once German tribal kingships had supplanted Roman provinces. Over the sixth, seventh and eighth centuries, there emerged over north-west and northern Europe, a wide-flung network of ports of trade and emporia, through which, the reinvigorated flows of a long-distance trade began to move. The character of these early market centres as emporia, a fact often signified by the place-name element *wik*, was first identified by Polanyi(Polanyi, 1968, pp. 244–6). In a more recent analysis of the problem, Hodges has distinguished between four types according to their function or position. The first consisted of those which handled traffic between the Carolingian Empire and Scandinavia and which were mainly located in Frisia, such as Dorestad and Hedeby. The second were those established under the authority of a regional or tribal king to handle the external trade of the state. These were fairly widespread and included such examples as Hamwik, or Southampton in southern

England, Kaupang in Norway and Birka in Sweden. The third type is represented by the inland trading sites, of which Verdun in northern France is the most obvious example. The fourth type represented those ports of trade based on an estuary or fjord, with traders dealing with local chieftains from their boats (Hodges, 1978a, pp. 97–101; Hodges, 1982, pp. 47–86). The essential feature about all these ports of trade is that they were located on the geographical periphery of new or emergent state-systems. Like Hamwik on the edge of the expanding state of Wessex, a short but significant distance from the political centre of Winchester, they were kept at a distance from the social and economic core of the state. They were the key nodes in a carefully supervised upper circuit of trade, a means by which the king and nobility of such states provisioned themselves with luxury goods and symbols of status.

It was Pirenne's great thesis that the real discontinuity in the history of European trade came over the eighth and ninth centuries AD when the expansion of the Islamic Empire across and along the Mediterranean sealed European trade off from a route-way that had been a virtual lifeline. After living off the fruits of the East, thanks to the easy passage of the Mediterranean, European élites were now forced to live off their own resources (Pirenne, 1925, p. 17). For Pirenne, here was the reason why European society turned in on itself, adopting the enclosed, self-sufficient economy of the manor. However, we can find a different reading of events by looking at Hodges's work. As the superstructure of long-distance trade in Europe collapsed after the Moorish take-over of the Mediterranean, Hodges sees the rulers and élites of the secondary states of north-west Europe as turning to internal 'competitive' markets based on local trade as a means of continuing their political and economic advancement. These differed from ports of trade by being based on local trade and located, unequivocably, within the geographical, social and economic heartland of the new states. A concept of exchange fastidiously maintained as something external to society is thus internalised. The creation of this new kind of market centre began during the ninth century when kings like Charlemagne and Alfred of Wessex laid out large numbers. By the tenth century, many of the new states of north-west Europe possessed a basic network of these inland market centres, all sustained by local trade (Hodges, 1982, pp. 162–84).

Hodges's basic assumption that a broad shift occurred over the ninth and tenth centuries from a system of trade that was long-distance, external and peripheral to a system of internal markets sustained by local trade is given support by other writers (Sawyer, 1977, p. 154). Interestingly, Elias thought that a significant difference between the city-states of the late prehistoric and the states which took shape over the medieval period was that whereas the former were small littoral formations, the latter included large areas of inland space: they were, he surmised, a type of polity that required improvements in the facilities of overland transport (that is, road improvement, better harnesses, waggons, and policing) as a precondition of their integration through trade (Elias, 1982, 55–7). In a study of road improvements, Lopez stressed the gains made over the latter part of the medieval period, but especially during the thirteenth and fourteenth centuries, with locally-sponsored schemes giving way to state-sponsored schemes by the late fourteenth century(Lopez, 1956, pp. 25–8). We can measure some of this improvement by comparing the costs given for trans-porting wheat overland in the Diocletian Edict of 301 AD with figures derived for fifteenth- and sixteenth-century England: the former were one and a half to three times the latter (Duncan-Jones, 1974, p. 368). As Elias reasoned, the high cost of overland transport in classical times was sufficient to isolate inland areas when it came to the movement of staples, making their 'scarcities irremediable' and their populations vulnerable (Jones, 1964, vol. 2, p. 844; Rickman, 1980, p. 120). The interior states of the medieval period had to overcome this friction of inland movement. Their success as polities and their integration through trade being, for Elias, indistinguishable. Hodges, too, sees these problems as associated, with the growth of internal trade being one of a number of systematically-linked changes that were set in train over the ninth century, changes that included the maturation of state-systems, the rise of feudal institutions (including the manor), and the growth of a hierarchy of market centres whose concerted action produced 'the greatest socio-economic change of the me-dieval period' (Hodges, 1982, p. 162; see also, Hodges, 1978b, pp. 442–6). The difference between Pirenne and Hodges is that the latter sees the growth of urban centres as a response to the collapse of Mediterannean trade rather than as something delayed or inhibited by it and as a function of local rather than long-distance trade, a local trade sustained by a manorial economy that marketed the surplus produce of seigneurial demesnes almost from its very foundation.

Looking more closely at the pattern of English markets, Hodges discerned a three-tier system. The highest tier was made up of what he terms solar markets, or those which performed major political or administrative functions as well as servicing whole districts in terms of their economic needs; these included long-standing urban centres like London, York and Winchester. A second tier composed of what he calls first-phase burhs like Chichester and Wareham. Burhs were planned, fortified towns – the earliest dating from the age of Alfred's Wessex – whose excavation has revealed that they also had servicing functions. Finally, there also existed a crowded lower tier of small market centres whose creation dates from the reign of Athelstan onwards (Hodges, 1978b, pp. 443–4; Hodges, 1982, pp. 167–8). Hodges's perspective was confined to the ninth and tenth centuries. If we extend the perspective forwards, we can see that the creation of market centres by kings and lords was ongoing. Some were integral to the many boroughs that developed over the twelfth, thirteenth and fourteenth centuries. Many others, though, had no status other than as a small market centre. Just as Hodges argued for those that began to appear over the tenth century, Britnell has suggested that many of those established over the twelfth and thirteenth centuries manifest the upwelling of local trade, an 'increase in local purchases by small households' (Britnell, 1981, p. 218; see also, Hilton, 1982b, pp. 5–6). Reading through his discussion, one gains the impression of a pattern of market provision that left no opportunity untapped, one which reached down to the level of the humblest household. Indeed, if we accept Bracton's suggestion that, ideally, the length of a person's journey to market should be no more than 6 2/3rds mile, then many areas were over-provided with marketing outlets. Their cheek-by-jowl jostling of each other is a reminder that their creation owed as much to the attempt by kings and rulers to regulate trade, as to the needs of an economy that was moving slowly towards greater social and spatial interaction. We can match these conclusions at a wider European level. The number of market centres began to increase noticeably over the ninth and tenth centuries (Lopez and Raymond, 1955, pp. 50–1; Doeheard, 1978, p. 182) though the process did not reach a peak until the thirteenth and fourteenth centuries (Pounds, 1974, pp. 100–1). As in England, their numerous creation in areas like Italy and southern France as early as the ninth century was 'not because interregional or international trade was then picking up, but because each market catered almost exclusively to the needs of its surrounding area' (Lopez and Raymond, 1955, p. 51).

Yet whilst we can endorse the significance which writers like Hodges attached to this early appearance of local trade, we must not ignore the growth of trade at other scales. A central assumption in Polanyi's discussion of medieval trade was that it developed initially at two quite different levels: local and international. What was lacking was trade at a national level, or interregional trade. With the proviso that the scale of many early state-systems must have meant that much national trade was, in effect, local or regional trade, this stands as a fair summary of how the enlarged trading activity of the medieval period developed. One serviced the basic subsistence needs of local communities whilst the other provided élites with prestige goods, goods whose value owed as much to the distance across which they were brought as to any scarcity at source. All that scholars like Hodges and Britnell have done is to demonstrate that a vigorous lower circuit of trade had begun to emerge before the resurgence of an upper long-distance circuit in the tenth century, thereby inverting older chronologies. There is a logical basis for this sequence of trade development, for the higher needs of élite groups presupposes they had accumulated wealth through locally extracted surpluses. Almost from the very start, it seems, the natural economy of the manor was prised open by the opportunities of the market-place.

Understandably, long-distance trade faced more problems of organisation than did local trade. So long as it served royal courts or the like, then it was not only tied to predictable markets but also it invariably operated under the protective wing of royal authority. However, once such trade began to re-expand from about the tenth century onwards, and once it became market- rather than court-oriented, new problems arose. There were obvious practical difficulties in assembling and distributing small quantities of high value goods on a continental scale. It was to solve this logistical problem that long-distance trade became associated with the development of fairs. These first began to emerge during the tenth century. By the twelfth century, they had secured a major role for themselves. Those held at Troyes, Provins, Lagny and Bar-Sur-Aube in Champagne were, collectively, the most important. By the thirteenth century, they handled so much of the overland traffic that had built up between north-west Europe and the towns of northern Italy, not least in Flemish cloth, that they have been cast as centres of 'the world economy of the Middle Ages' (Verlinden, 1963, p. 126). The timing of the various fairs was synchronised so as to form a single system or 'connected cycle' (Van Der Wee, 1963, p. 310), providing merchants with an all-year round opportunity for trade and a means whereby they could greatly lower their search and information costs. They neutralised what Van Der Wee called the 'psychosis of insecurity' which inevitably followed from 'the immobility of the primitive economy'. By concentrating merchants and goods in certain places and periods, he wrote, 'they created confidence in people and products and prevented a disturbance of the price mechanism' (Van Der Wee, 1963, p. 31; see also, North and Thomas, 1973, pp. 54–5).

Were Medieval Markets Embedded in Society?

Although Hodges described the inland markets that flourished from the ninth century onwards as competitive markets, the extent to which they were competitive needs careful statement. Admittedly, they appear to have been graded, some having higher functions and larger trading catchments than others. There is also ample proof that their trading activities were monetised almost from the outset. The Anglo-Saxon kingdoms of England first minted coins during the late seventh century. Of greater significance though, was the sharp increase in the quantity of low-value coinage that occurred during the late tenth century, just when the impact of an expanding system of inland markets would have been felt (Sawyer, 1977, p. 154; Hodges, 1978b, p. 446). However, it is doubtful whether we can speak of free markets in the purest sense at this stage. Until the fourteenth century at the earliest, even the largest centres would not have had the institutional freedom whereby they could organise the space within or without their bounds according to those uses that yielded the highest rents or returns. They were still regulated or fettered markets. Postan's comment to the effect that early towns were islands of freedom in a sea of unfreedom captures the personal status of burgesses and traders relative to the plight of the ordinary unfree peasant, *adscripti glebae* (Postan, 1972, p. 212). We must not overlook the stark fact that early boroughs and *villae mercatores* were still dependent institutions, licensed by kings and lords. Conceived within the feudal system, they were necessarily regulated as to their location and size, just as they were regulated in terms of the privileges and freedoms which they enjoyed and the tolls and customs which they owed in return. Would-be traders and merchants were hemmed in by a complex scaffolding of rules and regulations. To relate this to Polanyi's concept of early market trade, they were still very much an instrument of state-administered trade. In truth, we can expect little else in a feudalised society in which all freedoms, including the right of trade, were held ultimately of the king (Hilton, 1982a, pp. 7–13).

Their regulation stemmed in large measure from the way in which early trade had grown up on the margins of the state as a form of transaction that was quite different in spirit from earlier tribal systems of exchange. An extension of court-directed exchange and concerned primarily with exotic, prestige goods, such trade could be expected to be carefully administered by early state rulers. The prescribed nature of ports of trade and emporia symbolises the tight control which early state rulers exercised around market trade (Sawyer, 1977, p. 152; Hodges, 1982, pp. 52–6). Not only were their resident merchants largely alien to the state, but so also, were their customs of trade. They looked to kings for protection no less than for the right to trade. If to this we add the fact that they 'injected the element of a profit motive into a society so organised as to exclude it from aspects of its daily life' (Grierson, 1959, p. 127), then it can hardly surprise us if kings not only licensed their activity but also taxed it through a variety of tolls, customs, rents and fines. *Mercatores* not only serviced the royal court and noble households by ensuring a supply of luxury goods, they also helped to fund them. An eighth-century edict issued by the royal court at Pavia in Lombard warned that any merchant found wandering the kingdom 'without a written permit of the king or without authorization of his judge . . . he shall pay his *wergild*' (Lopez and Raymond, 1955, p. 38). Later edicts show that such *mercatores* were required to pay duty on their goods as they entered the kingdom, and that they were required to enter via recognised custom posts. Anglo-Saxon merchants were exempt from such customs but only because they were required to make regular direct payments to both court and treasury of silver, greyhounds, shields and swords (Lopez and Raymond, 1955, pp. 56–7), precisely the sort of goods that might have flowed between chiefs or tribal kings in an earlier age.

When kings came to establish market systems within their kingdoms, to admit into the sphere of local exchange the same organisation and motives that had previously been confined to external trade, they would already have appreciated how such markets could be made a source of profit. Thus, despite the sharp contrast which some writers have drawn between internal and external trade – or between local and international trade – they were linked in so far as one could be substituted for the other. When the opportunities and profits of external trade declined, internal trade opened up new prospects (Hodges, 1982, pp. 162–84). It was the idea of local markets as a source of new profit that probably encouraged kings like Charlemagne and Alfred. Pirenne's concern to see trade as a solvent of feudalism and, therefore, as something incompatible with it, is questionable for this very reason. So long as early trade was seen as a privilege held of the king and so long as it yielded feudal rent in return for this privilege, then the two concepts – trade and feudalism – had much to gain from each other (Hibbert, 1953, p. 17; Hilton, 1982a, p. 5). On the continental mainland, royal control over markets was established soon after the collapse of Roman Imperial authority. In England, the process was slower. Anglo-Saxon kings can certainly be seen trying to control the rising tides of trade (see especially Hodges, 1982, pp. 151–61). The extension of royal tolls from ships to waggons between the eighth and late ninth centuries, for instance, was probably intended to secure royal authority over local trade (Sawyer, 1977, p. 153). There were even attempts to force trade into the newly-created system of licensed markets, most notably the attempt by Edward the Elder to confine all transactions of over 20 pence (20*d*) to official market centres. However, there is some doubt over the effectiveness of such legislation. Writers like Loyn and Britnell feel that it had no lasting effect (Loyn, 1971, p. 122; Britnell, 1978, p. 187). Indeed, speaking more generally, Britnell sees royal authority as exercising no monopoly over the licensing of trade or markets prior to the

Norman Conquest. In the first place, not all Anglo-Saxon trade was confined to markets. Some still took the form of intertribal gift-exchange (Grierson, 1959, pp. 37–9; Sawyer, 1977, pp. 149–50). Britnell also allows for a substantial amount of informal exchange between peasants. This is linked to his further suggestion that when we see markets being created over the late Anglo-Saxon period, they were responding to the growing volume of trade. They did not, in themselves, create trade. In the second place, he argues that not all markets were licensed by the king. This is linked with his work on English hundredal markets. On the continent, early markets were invariably located at hundredal centres. There were good reasons for this. Not only were hundredal centres, or the equivalents, a local focus for royal power, but, as Phythian-Adams has conjectured, when royal courts ceased to shift on a circuit basis, the disposal of any food renders that were gathered in to such centres must have been a strong inducement for the establishment of a local market (Phythian-Adams, 1977, pp. 33–9). By way of a qualification to this, Britnell has shown that early markets in England were not located exclusively at hundredal centres, and that, as a consequence, there are no grounds for seeing those that were as 'vestiges of some regalian monopoly of marketing institutions' (Britnell, 1978, p. 189). We can only speculate on how these non-regalian markets may have originated. Some were possibly of great antiquity, perhaps evolving out of tribal assemblies and seasonal gatherings (Sawyer, 1977, p. 145). Their existence means that we cannot assume that Anglo-Saxon kings necessarily exercised an absolute monopoly over markets. On the other hand, it would be misleading not to see the legislation of the late Saxon period and the creation of new markets by license from the king as shifting the conditions of internal trade slowly towards such a monopoly.

Putting aside the question of how quickly or slowly it developed, the regalian monopoly over trade and markets in western Europe reached its zenith by the tenth and eleventh centuries. If we take this point as a baseline and consider how the regulation of trade and markets developed thereafter, we are faced with various dimensions of change. First, there were changes in the way control over them was structured or instituted, with the direct and immediate control of kings giving way to a greater say by urban communities, or by those who managed the day-to-day business of trade and markets. Second, there were wide-ranging changes in the actual nature of regulation, with the simple licensed/unlicensed mechanisms of the early states giving way to a much wider range of specific regulations and with regulations intruding into whole new areas of practice. Third, there were changes in the way in which trade and markets were organised, with the unspecialised nature of early markets and *mercatores* giving way to a more complex differentiation and hierarchisation of function. Patently, these changes were interrelated, as cause no less than as effect. As the volume of trade and the number of markets increased over the Middle Ages, 900–1350, we can expect their organisation as an interacting system to have become more complex. Not only would the flows and nodes of the system have become organised hierarchically but so also would the management functions concerned with the system's regulation. In short, the idea of trade and markets being regulated by royal officials – as if they were part of the royal household economy (Elias, 1982, p. 109) – would no longer suffice. The centralisation of control that came with its absolute monopolisation was no longer feasible once the scale of trade and number of market centres began to increase markedly from the ninth century onwards. A hierarchy of control functions became almost a *sine qua non* of system growth, with more decision-making capacity and more role differentiation being required at a more localised level. Clearly, this is a system-view of events; one that relates the elaboration of trading organisation to the growing volume of trading activity.

Taking each of these different dimensions of change in turn, the regalian monopoly over trade and markets began to yield or to devolve control in favour of local urban communities during the eleventh and twelfth centuries. It was a process that affected all parts of western Europe at more or less the same time (Reynolds, 1977, p. 91). However, the relatively synchronised way in which the downward movement of control functions occurred throughout western Europe must not deceive us into thinking that there was a uniformity about the process. As Reynolds makes clear, it worked in different ways and with greatly divergent effects. In one form, it resulted in the centralised control over trade and markets being replaced entirely by more localised systems which, though increasingly interlocked through the activity of trade and market operations, were nevertheless independent and self-governing as bases of interaction. This is best exemplified by what happened in Italy over the eleventh and twelfth centuries. There, the breakdown of regalian control over trade and markets was inextricably bound up with the collapse of Carolingian kingship. As local bishops and nobles sought to fill the resultant power vacuum by seizing control, political authority became focused on a series of urban communities. By the eleventh century, these urban communities had emerged as the dominant force behind a new territorial structuring of the political landscape. The first of the Italian city-states to emerge were Pisa and Lucca, both of which had established themselves as free communes by 1086. Others, like Florence, Siena and Venice, soon followed, each assuming complete control not only over its own affairs but also over those of its surounding hinterland or *contado*. Dominated politically by communities that relied totally on trade and marketing for their continued growth and survival, the Italian city-state proved a natural custodian of the idea that such activities should be regulated.

Comparable developments took place in north Germany. With the inability of Imperial authority to sustain a strong centralised state, the political landscape fractured into a series of loosely-coupled regional lordships in which real or effective power was wielded by princes, nobles and bishops. Again, this shift of power towards the regions worked to the advantage of urban communities and their commercial interests. Although they never acquired the formal independence of their Italian counterparts or the political control which the latter had over their *contado*, nevertheless, they did secure considerable freedom over their own affairs. The first signs of this freedom became manifest by the twelfth century when old-established towns like Cologne and newly-founded towns like Lubeck gained the freedom to govern themselves (Dollinger, 1970, pp. xviii, 14 and 20–1). The founding of Lubeck (around 1159) and the fairly rapid concession of privileges to it (confirmed by 1188) was especially significant. The merchants who dominated its ruling council became the prime movers in a much wider league or community of merchants. At first, it embraced merchants only from Wendish towns like Lubeck itself, Kiel, Wismar, Rostock and Hamburg. By the fourteenth century, it had transformed itself into a league or Hanse of towns, the Hanseatic League. In addition, the number and distribution of member-towns expanded dramatically. At its height, the League welded together the mercantile interests of almost 200 towns. Most lay along the main east–west trade-route that ran via the Baltic between Novgorod, Lubeck, Hamburg, Bruges and London, or along one of its many feeder routes. The corporate strength of the League gave it considerable power to act in its own narrow commercial interest. In fact, so powerful did it become, so unfettered in the control which it exercised over its own economic affairs, that it even negotiated directly with foreign kings over its terms and conditions of trade, succeeding at one point in acquiring a monopoly of trade between England and Norway at the expense of Norwegian traders!

Urban communities in England and northern France also gained privileges and freedoms, but it was a concessionary process that worked within rather than outside the power of kings and nobles. This can be illustrated by looking at what happened in England. By the end of the eleventh century, English kings had established their supreme right to license markets and to levy customs and tolls on the trade of goods. In fact, we can see many instances of this right being exercised over the eleventh, twelfth and thirteenth centuries, usually through the creation of boroughs. Yet no sooner had kings secured their command over the creation of markets and the taxing of their activities, than they began to devolve control. By the thirteenth century, the great territorial barons can also be found enjoying the profits that accrued from the licensing of markets. Whether licensed by the king or nobles, these markets existed in two forms. Many were settlements or sites that had simply been given the right to hold a weekly market, for which tolls or customs were paid. Others, however, were incorporated as part of the privileges of a borough. By the time we see them being established over the eleventh and twelfth centuries, boroughs had something of an omnibus character. At the heart of this character was the notion of burgage tenure. Charter references to such tenures first occur during the reign of Henry I, though there are reasons for believing that it may have taken shape by the tenth century. In a sense, they did for the borough what customary tenures did for the countryside, providing the personal burdens and privileges of the borough with a defined and fixed spatial framework. The basis of this spatial framework was the burgage tenement. All boroughs, whether based on old established or newly-founded towns, possessed a grid of burgage plots as the basis of their layout, each tenement carefully proportioned and disposed according to standard measures (Slater, 1981, pp. 211–16). To partake of the full privileges of the borough, to qualify as a burgess, a person needed to hold a burgage tenement. At the outset, the foremost privilege of a burgess was the right not only to practise a craft, and to trade from an open shop, but also, the right to trade at the borough's weekly market and at its yearly or bi-yearly fairs without paying the customary toll due to the king or the borough's superior. In return, burgesses paid a cash rent for their tenure, the total sum thus raised by the borough being its *farm* or *firma*. Already by the eleventh century, the larger boroughs had achieved a sufficient degree of solidarity and separateness to enable them to bargain with the king over their privileges and freedoms. As well as securing more privileges in the form of exemptions and monopolies, boroughs began to gain greater control over their affairs. A crucial step in this direction was taken when they acquired the '*farm* of the borough' or the privilege of collecting their own *firma* on behalf of the king. Previously, this task had been performed by reeves, officers appointed by the king and responsible to him not to the borough. Boroughs which assumed this responsibility in place of reeves were effectively empowered with a greater authority over their day-to-day affairs and the appointment of its key officers. In effect, some of the control functions over marketing had moved down the hierarchy of state administration and had been reconstituted as a series of local sub-systems. But in seeing this downward drift as a trend towards the *liber burgi* or free borough, it does not follow that it produced either fully autonomous communities or markets that were free in the sense that they allowed the interplay of supply and demand to determine prices and the allocation of resources. They were free only in so far as they could now govern their day-to-day affairs without undue interference.

At the same time as urban communities assumed a greater controlling interest over their trading and marketing affairs, the range of regulations governing such activities was both deepened and broadened. In short, more immediate control led to a closer, more fastidious control, a trend consistent with the overall expansion of trade and markets under conditions of regulation. It was a case of a greatly enlarged system of regulated activity being subjected to more checks and constraints. Two spheres of regulation can be identified, one concerned with the way urban communities secured privileges of trade outside their town walls and the other with the way they established conditions of trade within their walls.

We have already noted how the burgesses of English boroughs acquired exemptions from the tolls levied on trade within their market. Exemptions of this sort were sought by urban communities throughout western Europe over the eleventh and twelfth centuries. In practice, they were privileges that worked to the advantage of specific communities and to the even greater advantage of specific groups within those communities. As Pirenne wryly observed, they saw their 'freedoms' as monopolies, something which was enhanced by not being shared (Pirenne, 1925, p. 221). Town-dwellers invariably benefited more than country-dwellers, at least in so far as the former avoided any tolls payable on the movement of goods into the town. Such a sweeping generalisation though, glosses the pecking order that developed between towns and within towns. Some of the more powerful urban communities established a complete monopoly of trade within a specified hinterland. This was the case with Italian cities like Florence and Siena, as also with the head boroughs of some Scottish shires like Perth or Lanark (Ballard, 1913, p lxxi and 210). In some cases, it could be a more circumscribed privilege. Tradesmen in the counties of Derby and Nottingham, for instance, were restricted from selling their goods on Fridays and Saturdays in any other market except that at Nottingham (Ballard, 1913, p. lxvii). The implementation of a staple policy could provide towns with a comparable form of monopoly. Through such a policy, towns were able to force merchants trading along a particular route or in a particular trade to visit specific markets and to offer their goods for open sale. A town like Cracow, for instance, could insist on merchants travelling between Hungary and the Baltic offering their wares for sale in its market-place. Like more exclusive monopolies over trade, the operation of staple policies had the effect of distorting the 'natural' flow of goods, so much so, that the line taken by foreign merchants passing through an area 'could be the longest distance between two points as long as that line passed through one's own town' (Hibbert, 1963, p. 163; see also, Gras, 1926, p. 90). Another type of privilege enjoyed by the more successful urban communities was the freedom to trade in other markets without paying their tolls. This was the sort of privilege which the Hanseatic League obtained for itself in many other trading centres (Dollinger, 1970, p. 187). In Britain, 'politically' high-ranking boroughs enjoyed the freedom of other markets too. The merchants of York enjoyed exemptions from tolls and customs throughout England and throughout Normandy, Anjou, Aquitaine and Poitou (Ballard, 1913, p. lxix).

For most towns, the control which they increasingly assumed over their own affairs during the eleventh, twelfth and thirteenth centuries gave them greater scope for regulating trade within their own walls. Altogether, we can discern six areas of possible control. First, there were regulations governing the payment of tolls or customs by those entering the town with goods to sell and, in many instances, on the sale of such goods within the official marketplace (see for example, Unwin, 1981). In some cases, a simple hierarchy of privileges developed, with freemen, gild-members or burgesses having fewer toll burdens than other townsmen, and townsmen having fewer burdens than outsiders or foreigners (see, for example, Reed, 1981, p. 120). One arrangement was for the open market to be 'the province of the non-freeman, the shop that of the freeman, and neither was to trespass on the other's preserve' (Palliser, 1972, p. 102). Second, there could be regulations ensuring that goods or produce were brought to open market. Forestalling or illicit trading, especially in vital products (that is, food, staple raw materials) was especially frowned upon (see, for example, Thrupp, 1948, pp. 92–7). Third, there were regulations against the ingrossing of goods, as also against the formation of cartels amongst dealers. Civic authorities were especially vigilant over the hoarding of agricultural produce. Fourth, there were regulations over the quality of products or produce sold in the town, or at least in its official markets and open shops (Unwin, 1981, pp. 239–40). Fifth, there developed a wide range of regulations governing the conditions of trade, including strict regulations over apprenticeships, hours of work, wages and quality of materials used. Regulations of this sort were usually formulated through a town's gild system (see for example, Rörig, 1967, p. 151; Palliser, 1972, p. 96). Sixth and last, there were invariably strict controls over prices, especially those of agricultural produce (De Roover, 1958, p. 425). The question of price regulation in a medieval context is a contentious one. It is a question that takes us to the very heart of our problem for it asks what, in the absence of self-regulating or price-fixing markets, determined the values of exchange? There is a great deal of support to suggest that most urban communities employed notions of a 'just price'. There is, however, disagreement amongst modern scholars over what this meant. Was it an attempt to establish an equivalence as regards the labour value of goods, so that when marketed, each person's product was sufficient to provide them with their basic needs, an attempt to establish a social rather than a purely market value for labour. This is an attractive interpretation, but it has its critics. As an alternative, it has been argued that if its meaning is considered in relation to the way the concept was actually used in a medieval context, then it simply meant the prevailing market price (De Roover, 1958, p. 421). Far from leading us round in circles, this is a reasonable supposition. In the context of medieval markets, the market price was one reached under open, supervised conditions, that is, in a situation where the quality of goods, their true measure and the general price of things had all been reasonably considered in the determination of prices (cf. De Roover, 1958, p. 437). More important, it was in the official markets that supervision worked most effectively to prevent speculative dealings and *'excessif wynnyng'* (Thrupp, 1948, pp. 92–7). Inevitably, larger towns, having the larger, more complex systems of trade and marketing, needed more elaborate systems of regulation. Their greater size involved more than simply greater problems of supervision and enforcement. Their larger, more complex systems of trade brought with it a more complex organisation of trade and marketing, so that the whole question of their regulation was supplemented by a still finer, more specialised level of need.

If, from all the welter of trading activities that sustained the medieval town we are forced to select those that were subjected to closer regulation than others, they would unquestionably be those concerned with its provisioning. All medieval towns were concerned to ensure both that food supplies were sufficient and that they were cheap. The larger the town, the larger the problem. The problem with agricultural produce was that annual supplies could fluctuate widely, modulated by the gratuitous impact of good and bad seasons. To compound the problem, medieval markets tended to be insular, circumscribed affairs. The surpluses of one region were not easily moved to offset the deficits of another. Products like grain could be moved relatively cheaply by water, but had to be drawn up a very steep cost-gradient when moved over land. Only where river networks provided a high degree of interconnectedness, as between Flemish towns (Van Der Wee, 1963, p. 23), do we find medieval grain-markets coalescing into systems that embraced a large regional cluster of towns. Otherwise, most medieval grain-markets were localised structures, sometimes made more so by the restrictions imposed on the interregional movement of grain whenever scarcity threatened (Miller, 1963, p. 324). An analysis of English grain-markets during the medieval period concluded that – even when large areas of northern England and Wales are excluded from the calculation – as many as fifteen separate regional systems existed, each behaving differently from its neighbours (Gras, 1926, p. 47). They behaved differently of course, because they functioned separately. In such circumstances, we must expect the amplitude of local price fluctuations to have been all the greater, simply because each market was unable to trade away its deficits and surpluses (Postan, 1972, p. 227). There was nothing that urban communities could do to prevent this endemic fluctuation in food prices. However, most were able to dampen their movement and to control the profits made out of them. It was their role in moderating prices, as opposed to determining them, that caused Thrupp to declare that medieval prices 'at least of victuals – were a question of law' (Thrupp, 1933, p. 260). Sooner or later, most gained the power to institute such law in the context of their own markets. Admittedly, many were simply re-enacting legislation on prices and profits that had previously existed at a state level. To cite a case in point, the Carolingian kings instituted legislation dealing with grain and bread prices as early as the tenth century. When urban communities became more responsible for their own affairs over the eleventh, twelfth and thirteenth centuries, and began to introduce ordinances that regulated the marketing of food, they were merely reconstituting this earlier state legislation at a lower level of operation. However, there was this change. Enacted by urban communities that flexed an increasing freedom over their intra-urban affairs, the ordinances which they passed were charged with their self-interest.

Having a political authority no less than a trading influence that could be projected out over their surrounding hinterland, the leading Tuscan towns provide us with an extreme example of how urban communities could regulate the marketing of agricultural produce in the interests of the town-dweller. All of them operated a policy of ensuring a regular supply of cheap food for those within their walls (Herlihy, 1958, p. xi; Herlihy, 1967, p. 58; Bowsky, 1981, p. 209). As well as forcing produce into their markets (Herlihy, 1967, p. 156) they passed a wide range of regulations over the quality and price of produce (Herlihy, 1958, p. 69; Herlihy, 1967, p. 124; Bowsky, 1981, p. 208). Many even established municipal mills and grain-stores in an effort to moderate the extremes of the trade. All in all, restrictions on trade in grain were particularly tight. They 'characteristically exercised a strict supervision over the wheat market and rigorously intervened to prevent excessive price fluctuations in the years of scarcity' (Herlihy, 1967, p. 124). Elsewhere, he has provided a detailed study of how the Pisan authorities 'pegged down' grain prices, so much so, that local farmers actually shifted out of grain production (Herlihy, 1958, pp. 109–17). For Herlihy, their deliberate capping of grain prices had the effect of using the rural sector to subsidise the urban sector at a time when the needs of the latter were growing rapidly.

By comparison, a city like London wielded a more prescribed power over its food supply. It could control what went on within its own bounds, but its ability to force trade into its markets in the first place depended on the somewhat geographically-limited trading privileges granted to it by the king and on its willingness to pay more than rival markets. An analysis of late medieval prices in southern England suggests that whilst it did offer farmers in its hinterland a better market for their produce than other nearby markets, nevertheless, prices were higher in other more distant market areas (Rogers, 1866, p. 407; Gras, 1926, pp. 43–4). Like other towns, London followed a cheap food policy. There was a limit to how far it was prepared to bid up for its food. It exercised stringent controls over the marketing of agricultural produce once it had moved within its bounds (Gras, 1926, pp. 66–8). Any form of forestalling or engrossing was severely punished. In the victualling trades if not in others, middlemen were viewed with suspicion, a source of price inflation. In fact, even in the fourteenth century, when it was a thriving city of over 100 000 people, it sought to keep the marketing process as simple as possible by encouraging the farmer and smallholder to sell their produce direct to the consumer. To facilitate this face-to-face contact between producer and consumer, special areas of the city were designated as open markets where all comers might sell their produce (Thrupp, 1933, p. 278). It has also been suggested that the short-lived London Act of 1363, which compelled retail merchants to deal in one type of commodity only was expressly designed to limit the influence of middlemen (Thrupp, 1933, pp. 260–1). The price of a staple product like bread posed particular problems for its marketing unavoidably involved a compound relationship between farmers, millers, bakers and consumer, a relationship with ample opportunity for speculative dealing. There were two forms of control operating here. The marketing of grain was kept rigorously open. In addition, the price of bread, like that of ale, was fixed by assize, its value being strictly related to prevailing prices of grain and to its quality. Clearly, this had the effect of allowing its price to move in relation to the prevailing market-price of grain, but avoided any excessive profit by millers or bakers. This was a country-wide procedure, not one confined to London (Webb, 1904, pp. 200–1). In a town like London, though, it was a form of regulation that was assiduously supervised. Even if not actually fixed by assize, other food prices were regularly scrutinised. A whole battery of wardens patrolled open shops and markets, ensuring that the price of produce was reasonable for the quality and quantity involved.

The Changing Organisation of Medieval Trade

Inextricably linked to the increasing regulation of trade were changes in its organisation. The development of commerce, wrote Previté-Orton when discussing Italian trade, moved from the simple to the complex and what began as the simple-cell structures of the early twelfth century became 'the multiple-celled community' of the mid-thirteenth century and later (Previté-Orton, 1926, p. 235). Initially, or at the start of what Lopez has called the 'commercial revolution 950–1350', trade would have been organised around two distinct groups of traders, one responsible for local and the other for long-distance trade. Quite apart from their different spheres of interest, these two groups would have differed in so far as the merchants who controlled long-distance trade were usually foreigners and confined to a designated part of the town or even quartered outside it (Doehaerd, 1978, pp. 58–9). In the practical day-to-day affairs of the town, these differences continued to matter. Yet the fact remains that as merchants and traders emerged as the dominant force behind the growth of towns, they became organised into a single undifferentiated action-group, the gild or Hanse of merchants. When, over the eleventh and twelfth centuries, urban communities bargained for greater autonomy and privilege, it was these gilds and Hanses that forced the issue. Their leading role at this point is thrown into sharp relief by the fact that they were the first institution or agency through which the self-interest of town could be expressed. In England, membership of the borough's merchants gilds appears implicit in the earliest grants of burgage tenure. When we speak about the privileges which towns secured for themselves over the eleventh, twelfth and thirteenth centuries, they are privileges as seen through the eyes of its merchant gilds. They were privileges designed to maximise their profits at the expense of 'foreigners' (Lopez, 1976, p. 126). To this end, they sought privileges that gave them exemptions from tolls, not just in their own market but in those of other towns, and trading monopolies over as wide an area as practicable. In short, space and spatial interaction became inclined to their gross advantage, a function not of natural hinterlands and market attraction but of political will.

Starting in the thirteenth century, a further change in the organisation of trade began to establish itself firmly, involving the development of craft gilds. These had first appeared in the larger centres back in the twelfth centres (Postan, 1972, p. 215). However, over the thirteenth, fourteenth and fifteenth centuries, their number proliferated rapidly. Generally speaking, their growth went further in the larger industrial centres, simply because their volume of trade called forth greater specialisation (Thrupp, 1933, p. 292; Postan, 1972, p. 215). In towns like Florence and Venice, the number of separate gilds grew to over fifty. In effect, it was a logical elaboration of trade organisation, one that added a still lower level of role specialisation. In some cases, it was a development that went through stages. One might have the emergence of a gild of smiths as a first stage and then, as the volume of trade grew still further or the significance of one section grew, a second stage of disaggregation into more specialised gilds for goldsmiths, silversmiths, locksmiths, lorimers and so on. As the number of gilds increased and the differentiation of trades became more acute over the fourteenth and fifteenth centuries, there arose a greater likelihood that they would be ranked in terms of status, as with the crude distinction that emerged in London between the so-called livery and yeomen companies. In character, the craft gilds differed from merchant gilds in that they placed great emphasis on equality between members (Lopez, 1976, p. 126). As well as surrounding themselves with trading monopolies, they imposed uniform conditions of work on their members, binding them to the same hours of work, terms of apprenticeship, quality of materials and standards of workmanship. It was the detail which they brought to the management of trade over the fourteenth and fifteenth centuries that made the economy of the late medieval town such a 'highly regulated' affair (Hibbert, 1963, p. 181). They 'regulated growth without stopping it' as Lopez put it (Lopez, 1976, p. 126). Others have been less charitable in their judgement and have seen the growing conservatism and maladaptation of the urban economy over the closing centuries of the medieval period as threatening it with extinction.

Did Medieval Markets Organise Space?

Of the essence to what I have tried to argue is the fact that medieval markets were politically and socially prescribed institutions. Seen thus, we can hardly instate them as having an unrestrained allocative function, one that caused the use of space to be reassigned to the highest bidder. Its potential role as an allocative device was over-ridden by social or political mechanisms. Places of trade, conditions of employment, quality of goods, spheres of market influence and prices were all regulated to a greater or lesser degree. What is more, significant areas of the economy lay beyond the influence of markets, either because production was for use rather than for exchange or because the value of things was set through custom rather than in the marketplace.

The idea of an expanding system of markets firmly embedded within society, as opposed to one that was self-regulating, was a central proposition in Polanyi's argument. Since he wrote, the general drift of work has been to emphasise the extent to which markets were kept busy by local as well as by long-distance trade and, at the same time, to endorse his suggestion that European medieval markets – if not those of the Middle East – operated within socially defined rather than self-determined parameters. Critics of his work have not always appreciated these aspects of his argument. Macfarlane's treatment of it is a case in point. Discussing Polanyi's work in the context of England, he sees him as arguing for 'a non-market peasant society' before the eighteenth century (Macfarlane, 1978, p. 199). To be fair, Polanyi could not have anticipated the extent to which recent work would uncover signs of the ordinary peasant going to market as early as the twelfth and thirteenth centuries. However, his stress on trade being as much local as long-distance makes it abundantly clear that he did not see the ordinary peasant as tied to the soil for 365 days of the year, living out his life and needs through the natural economy of the manor. The crux of what he had to say about early markets though is that their business was checked and restrained by social or political mechanisms. By ignoring Polanyi's stress on regulated trade, Macfarlane weakens his own argument. We cannot dispute the fact that peasants were marketing small amounts of produce as early as the thirteenth and fourteenth centuries or that 'most "objects" from labour to rights in all types of property were marketable and had a price', (Macfarlane, 1978, p. 152), but it surely does not follow *ipso facto* that they were traded through 'free' markets as Macfarlane asserts (Macfarlane, 1978, p. 152). The only support which he actually offers for this claim is the knowledge that the market in peasant land which had emerged by the thirteenth century involved well-to-do tenants, and not just those living on the margins of subsistence. In other words, the motives behind some dealings in peasant land could only have been personal gain and not just the procurement of livelihood. This is a reasonable point. Seen solely as individuals acting in their own interests – which after all, is the express intent of Macfarlane's book – many a medieval peasant, no less than medieval traders, must surely have harboured the inner hope that his transactions would favour him and that by some strange alchemy of trade, the product of his labour would be turned to gold. The individual, though, worked within the framework of market legislation and custom. It is this, not the motives of individual tradesman, that determined whether we can speak of free markets. Macfarlane makes no mention of market regulation. As a consequence, his attempt to use Polanyi's work as a foil for his own line of argument is unconvincing.

If we accept that medieval markets were held in check by a variety of socially-contrived constraints, then what effect did they have on spatial order? We can decompose this question into two parts. What part did market forces play in ordering space within the medieval town and what part did it play in ordering space without?

Intra-Urban Space

In regard to the first of these questions, there can be no doubt that urban land was being taken to market within the larger towns before the end of the medieval period. Indeed, there are signs that land values in a town like Milan were responsive to demand as early as the tenth century! (Wickham, 1981, p. 83). However, despite this early appearance of a price-responsive market in urban land, we are a long way from a truly free market. Any influence exerted by this wedge of 'free' market forces has to be seen within an interplay of factors, some working against it and others with it.

A potential restraint on how quickly such forces developed and advanced within towns derived from whether urban space was initially conceived within a fixed tenurial framework. Work on the phase of rapid urban growth between the ninth and early fourteenth centuries has drawn a clear distinction between those towns whose growth was a natural extension of an old-established core and those whose growth involved an element of planning. This element of planning could involve the imposition of a new ground-plan over an old site, the creation of a new *suburbium* for an old town, perhaps around a new focus such as a marketplace, or the *de novo* creation of an entirely new town, often in the shadow of a castle or stronghold (Carter, 1983, pp. 37–50). This distinction is acutely relevant to the long-term formation of a free market in urban land because it highlights the different relationships that could exist between urban growth and the feudal state, relationships that displayed a differing receptiveness to such a market. Faced with an old-established town that had survived as a community through the Dark Ages and through the general decline of urban life, early state rulers or would-be lords clearly had fewer options over how they exploited such towns. The idea of imposing a standard tenement over their layout was out of the question.

Many such towns were, in fact, characterised by a densely packed cluster of streets and buildings. The choice instead, was restricted to the imposition of tolls on marketing, the exercise and profits of justice and the levying of personal dues. In other words, there were limitations on how far feudal authority could territorialise the obligations which it imposed on such urban centres, making them a matter of geography as well as of society.

By contrast, where urban growth involved the laying our of a new town, or even just a new *suburbium*, it invariably meant the creation of a standard tenement as the basic building-block of the town's layout. As in the countryside, a person's rights no less than his obligations became set within a territorial framework. As lots of standard size, each bearing an equal portion of the town's burdens and freedoms, these tenements were understandably re-silient to easy change. In helping to frame the institutional charac-ter of the town, they inevitably became instated as a conservative factor in the town's organisation. Their rent became a customary value, one that expressed the equivalence of rights and burdens between their occupiers. One could not have a free market in land until the meaning and rigidities of such a system had been thor-oughly penetrated and undermined. In the context of a growing town, this could produce an incoherent land value surface, with some tenements still bearing the rents that were levied on them at the foundation of the town or *suburbium*, others of a similar age having improved rents and other, more recently-created ten-ements also bearing what – at their point of foundation – were more economic rents. In this sort of situation, tenements in similar locations could bear widely-differing land rents (see, for example, Hilton, 1967, p. 332). To complicate matters, older customary rents were not necessarily removed by a simple process of replace-ment and betterment. In some instances, they were undermined by an elaborate chain of subletting. Outwardly, they remained fixed – in some cases, for what was literally hundreds of years – but this outward stability masks an active market in subletting, with sub-tenants paying a more economic price, at least in relation to the level of demand that prevailed at the point of subletting. Of course, the fact that they ultimately adjusted to market forces in this cumbersome way simply underlines their rigidity in the face of market demand. The precise rate at which customary land values decayed also depended on the social context in which they were set. On the continent, not only were customary urban rents quickly challenged by market pressure, but one also had the early emergence of a *rentier* class, or individuals who not only accumulated a portfolio of urban properties but saw it as an investment and who, therefore, had a vested interest in the forward movement of rents (Pounds, 1974, p. 276). By comparison, we do not find a *rentier* class emerging in English towns until the sixteenth century (Hoskins, 1964, p. 77; Platt, 1976, p. 181). Indeed, it is generally recognised that the whole landholding structure of English towns militated against a truly active or efficient land market until the sixteenth century. A great deal of property was held by institutional landlords like the crown and the church whose responsiveness to market forces during much of the medieval period was restrained, the church especially, being looked upon as 'notoriously soft landlords' (Platt, 1976, p. 182). Revealingly, the redistribution of church lands which followed the dissolution of the abbeys and the greater willingness of the crown to convert lettings into sales was sufficient to inject a new dynamic into the property market of some English towns (Hoskins, 1964, p. 104; Platt, 1976, p. 181). However, we must not overstate the problems of supply. English towns experienced a marked economic depression over the fifteenth and sixteenth centuries, with tenements in some towns becoming derelict. Clearly in such circumstances, the problem was one of demand not supply.

Various factors were capable of advancing or retarding the pressure on urban land values. One was the extent to which tenements contained scope for internal expansion. The burghal tenements laid out in English boroughs were generously endowed with space. Those in the west Midlands, for instance, were generally about 60 by 200 feet in size and must have given such boroughs an open 'garden-city' appearance. Such a loose fit between needs and resources though, had a double meaning. It enabled growth to take place within the tenurially-defined space of the town. The splitting and tailing of tenements was rampant in the more successful boroughs by the thirteenth and fourteenth centuries (Williams, 1963, p. 17; Hilton, 1967, pp. 328–9). Such infilling meant the creation of tenures within tenures. We are presented with the paradox of an outer shell of fixed, customary rents but an inner, more yielding core of 'improved' rents. Whether we see this as advancing or retarding the growth of a freer land market would depend on whose interests we have uppermost in mind, those of the chief or sub-tenant. By comparison, many planned towns on the continent had significantly smaller tenements. German towns which acquired a planned element over the eleventh, twelfth and thirteenth centuries generally had tenements that were only half or even a quarter of the size of those to be found in English boroughs. Lubeck, for instance, had tenements of 25 by 100 feet (Dickinson, 1962, p. 385). Crowded together in this more neighbourly way, such tenements patently offered less scope for internal sub-division. Yet one could argue that scope of any sort was sufficient, for it attached an 'improved' value to old customary rents. More to the point, it brought forward the point at which new tenements were needed. These new tenements invariably carried 'improved' rents. Of course, not all medieval towns were organised around standard tenements. Some were based on small, irregular house plots. Towns of this nature appear closely settled as soon as we see them through early descriptions. A thirteenth-century description of Milan, for instance, emphasised its continuously built-up appearance and intense use of space (Lopez and Raymond, 1955, p. 61). The close-packing of properties was, in fact, a feature of Italian towns (see, for example, Wickham, 1981, pp. 82 and 84), one highlighted – rather than qualified – by the open, public *campi* that also feature strongly in their layout. Even the urban *palazzi* that began to appear over the twelfth and thirteenth centuries lacked elbow room, their generous consumption of space being invested in enclosed courtyards and building space rather than in distancing themselves from their neighbour. One passed, said Goldthwaite in a discussion of late medieval Florence, from the crowded, narrow streets of the town into the open and spacious courtyards around which the various *palazzi* were arranged (Goldthwaite, 1980, p. 102). Arguably, such a close use of urban space was bound to pressurise land values more quickly. The more limited opportunities for plot subdivision meant that access to particular locations was only through bidding up, whilst overall, the pressure for growth was fed more quickly to peripheral sites, where the creation of new building plots would have realised rents more consistent with prevailing values.

Urban land values could also be pressurised into market responsiveness by other forms of circumscription. Certain privileges of trade could be tied to specific tenements. More commonly, living anywhere within the walls of a town could confer economic advantages, as well as benefits of security, yet, by its very definition, the supply of intra-mural land was not instantly expandable as soon as demand warranted it. This was to be a particularly-relevant problem during the thirteenth and early fourteenth centuries when towns in many parts of Europe grew rapidly. Florence, for example, doubled its population over the thirteenth century, from about 50 000 to over 100 000. Work on a second town wall enclosing an area of 80 ha (hectares) had begun in 1172. By 1284, its insufficiencies were apparent and a second wall was begun, this time enclosing an area of 620 ha (Waley, 1978, pp. 15–17). Similar extensions of intra-mural space were occurring in other parts of Tuscany and Lombardy during the late twelfth and thirteenth centuries, usually in an effort to embrace suburban populations that had grown up outside their walls (Previté-Orton, 1926, p. 225; Wickham, 1981, p. 82). As at Florence though, the problem of having an insufficient supply of intra-mural space could be solved by forward planning. The town wall built at Cologne in 1106 embraced 118 ha. The replacement wall which the civic authorities were forced to construct in 1180 encircled 396 ha, enough to satisfy the needs of the town until the nineteenth century (Hodgett, 1972, p. 56). In complete contrast, the patrician groups who controlled Ypres during the thirteenth century saw their wall as a *cordon sanitaire* against the large artisan group that had grown up beyond it (Nicholas, 1971, p. 65). Conceived in such a variety of social contexts, town walls clearly had varying impacts on the supply of space within their bounds. Where their relocation was slow in responding to need, then congestion was almost invariably the outcome (Sjoberg, 1960, p. 92).

If we accept that the medieval towns had an active land market, then it raises the question of how it affected the use of space. Considered hypothetically, it could be argued that it need not have had any effect on space. Given that tenements and houses in many towns were set within a framework of customary values, it follows that signs of 'improved' rents is not in itself a sign that urban land values were subject to a bid-price mechanism. Ensnared in a system of customary values, any forward movement of ground rents may have served only to restore their link with prevailing market values. In other words, they may have still been seen as evaluating land in functional terms, as something to be used, rather than as a source of exchange value. If this was the case, then we cannot expect the values so set to distinguish between locations only between plot sizes. Vance's depiction of medieval towns as organised through use rather than exchange values would hold true, despite an active market in land (Vance, 1971, p. 102). However, once we find some locations being valued more than others, then it suggests that space was being organised through a bid-price mechanism and that space now had an exchange value. At first, any drift towards a competitive land-market may have been outweighed by the drag effect of any customary evaluation of land. Until an efficient land-market evolved, one in which land was regularly marketed, then it was possible that the value of land was more reflective of when it was taken to market rather than where it was located, even after the latter had become part of the resource being valued. In fact, to extend this line of reasoning, there is even a case for arguing that in those towns in which land values were frozen so to speak within a customary framework and where 'improved' rents, or rents that kept pace with prevailing market values were more easily established through the creation of new tenements or house sites, then there is a case for supposing that those medieval towns which grew out of a planned or customary core may have had a land-value surface which was the reverse of that which we might normally expect, with a periphery that was valued more highly than the core!

Despite these somewhat abstract qualifications, evidence for central locations being valued more highly than others is available for some, if not all, medieval towns. Easily the earliest such evidence is that showing that sites around the edge of Milan's central market and its adjacent mint were already arrented at a higher value than sites elsewhere (Wickham, 1981, p. 83). By the thirteenth century, other large towns had active land markets that rated central locations and main thoroughfares more highly than other sites (see, for example, Pounds, 1974, p. 277). One of the complaints made against the butchers of Siena in their long-running dispute with the ruling council of the town (the Nine or *Noveschi*) was that they had an unreasonable share of the 'better' sites. To date, the most detailed study of medieval urban land values by a geographer is Langton's analysis of Gloucester using a rental of 1455. It provides us with an unequivocal and graphic illustration of the higher regard placed on sites close to the centre and along the main thoroughfares of the city by the late medieval period (Langton, 1977, p. 267).

Writing about the pre-industrial city, Sjoberg argued that the forcing of city centre values was due to the fact that such locations were seen as the most 'prestigeful' and because this was 'where fullest advantage may be taken of the city's strategic facilities . . . tightly bunched for the convenience of the élite' (Sjoberg, 1960, p. 99). That such locations were prestigeful is beyond question. That they were meant to be in the mind of the town's inhabitants was also beyond doubt once increasingly self-conscious civic authorities began erecting municipal buildings (such as town halls, market halls) and laying out public squares and market-places. Whether such central locations were of enhanced value because they maximised accessibility and opportunity is much more dubious. Admittedly, Sjoberg is never quite clear whether his pre-industrial town is an exclusively early modern form or whether he meant it to include medieval forms. The problem is partly one of scale. No inhabitant in even the largest of medieval towns was more than a 15–20 minute walk from the centre. Furthermore, the servicing element of the medieval centre was not a point but a zone, one increasingly broadened by the segregation of specialised markets and public squares. In these circumstances, it would suppose a society acutely concerned with the optimisation of movement (and time) to assert that the centre was valued for its greater accessibility.

Distinguishing the prestige of a town-centre location from its purely economic benefits is not to be dismissed as a trivial point. It is significant because it distinguishes between a factor which only affected the centre and a factor which, if operating and well-tuned, had a capability for organising the entire town through a single, coherent scheme. If we discount the latter, at least before the emergence of extended towns during the early modern period, then what do we put in its place as the organising force behind urban spatial order? The answer is to look at the way society itself was organised, for the spatial order of medieval towns was simply a manifestation, albeit a substantive manifestation, of medieval social order. Once this is grasped, it means that there can be no static or equilibrium model of their social geography. Instead, we must expect the changing organisation of urban society between the tenth and fifteenth centuries – itself a response to the growing scale and complexity of towns – to have used space as a means by which such changes were structured: the shift from a relatively undifferentiated community to one that was, first, more differentiated and, second, more hierarchical, being impressed on the way such communities were arranged in space. At the outset, the only conspicuous form of differentiation would have been that conveyed by the dominant presence of a castle or perhaps, an important ecclesiastical centre like an abbey or priory. In the vast majority of cases, though, these pre-dated the town, the latter being planned out beside them. There may also have been an external community of merchants, invariably foreign merchants. In some instances, trades which had environmental side-effects, like butchery or tanning, may also have been loosely segregated. What would have been lacking is any overt differentiation rooted in social or economic causes. Subsequently, as such towns internalised the notion of trade, a development symbolised by the increasing number of new towns planned around market places or forums, and as merchants emerged as a distinct and dominant group, we can expect the first pressure for the social differentiation of space. The further decomposition of the urban community into a welter of craft gilds over the thirteenth, fourteenth and fifteenth centuries provided the basis for an even finer differentiation of space. The 'archetypal' medieval town is one structured around these distinct craft districts (see, for example, Sjoberg, 1960, pp. 100–1). In a society organised around craft gilds, this localisation obviously facilitated the flow of information and raw materials, but there is no reason to suppose that such clustering was economically constituted in the sense that it was part of some cost-minimising strategy. As Vance argued, the lives of the ordinary craftsmen, their norms and values of behaviour, were mediated through the institution of the gild, so that their localisation in space is more credibly seen as a symbolically-constituted expression of their socio-economic integrity or solidarity *vis-à-vis* the rest of the urban commmunity rather than as something seen in narrow cost-benefit terms. In time, though, the latent conflict of interest between the old-established patrician class and the newer craft gilds introduced an hierarchical element into spatial order, a broad distinction between rich and poor which was slowly to overwhelm the more elaborate division of the town into districts on a craft basis. How quickly this social distinction was set down in space depended on a variety of factors, each town having its own relaxation time or phasing of response. The early and sharply-accentuated divisions between 'fat' men and 'small' men in Florence did not dissuade the rich from building their *palazzi* evenly across the town rather than defensively-clustered in one rich sector, whilst rich and poor jostled each other for the same living space in the Old Town of Edinburgh until the late eighteenth century. In other towns though, there was a speedier translation of the growing social distance between classes into geographical distance. In Paris, for instance, the rich had already been decanted into territorially-discrete districts like Sainte-Oppotune, Saint-Jacques la Boucherie and Saint-Denis by the fourteenth century (Pounds, 1974, pp. 277–8). The ongoing tendency for medieval and early modern towns to dump their urban poor into extra-mural suburbs, as with towns like Ghent, Bruges and Ypres during the thirteenth century (Nicholas, 1971, p. 54) or Leicester in the fifteenth and sixteenth century (Hoskins, 1964, p. 92) albeit in suburbs that were eventually incorporated, helped the segregation of classes. Langton's study of sixteenth-century Newcastle offers us a perspective on a town caught in transition between these two phases of adjustment, with signs of both an ordering around gild districts and one based on class. (Langton, 1975, pp. 1–27).

The Hinterland of Medieval Towns: A Microcosm of Der Isolierte Staat?

The impact of medieval towns on the surrounding countryside can be seen as a complex interaction not just between levels of demand and supply, but equally, between those factors which worked to regulate trade and those which worked to deregulate it, and between those forces which served to insulate rural production from market forces and those which worked to harness it to the needs of the market-place.

We can begin to disentangle this web of contrary forces by asking what, on the supply side, affected the marketing of produce. Fluctuations in demesne output were obviously one source of variation, both geographical and temporal. Though part of this output was used to sustain the seigneurial household, the demesne economy, especially on the larger demesnes, soon shifted from a natural economy. Indeed, the excess production of the great demesnes 'underpinned the growth of trade' from the ninth century

onwards (Duby, 1968, p. 46). This growth of demesne production, however, was not sustained. In Italy, the great estates and
their demesnes were already being broken up and leased out by
the end of the ninth century. Although large estates recovered
some of their integrity after 1000 AD, labour service and demesnes never recovered their former importance (Herlihy, 1959,
pp. 66–8). Fluctuations in demesne cultivation were evident elsewhere. Areas like Lorraine, Burgundy and Bavaria shared in the
switch out of demesne-farming which was evident by the end of the
ninth century, but in these areas, it was only a temporary adjustment. In England, we know that demesnes were being leased out
over the twelfth century but taken back into the lord's own hands
from the 1180s onwards (Harvey, 1974, pp. 353–4). Taking a
general view, the final, irrevocable swing away from demesne-
farming in countries like England, France and the Low Countries
was under way by 1300 (Duby, 1968, p. 318). The leasing-out of
demesnes invariably meant a conversion of labour-service into
cash rents. Whether we are talking about the localised swing out
of demesne farming observable by the end of the ninth century or
the more general swing evident after 1300, we are dealing with *la
revolution censive* (Herlihy, 1959, p. 68). Whatever its timing, it
was a revolution that had a deep impact on urban food supplies.
The peasantry, not seigneurial lords, now bore direct responsibility for marketing their surplus produce. Where their labour-
services were commuted to cash rents, then we can assume that,
willingly or unwillingly, tenants were forced to market surplus
produce so as to raise the cash needed. Commutation, though, was
not the only source of change. Many new tenures created during
the vigorous land colonisation of the thirteenth and early fourteenth centuries were generally held for cash rents.

This intrusion of money into the peasant economy was not in
itself sufficient to make it market responsive. Strictly speaking, we
are dealing with two lines of development. Before we can talk of
farming being market-responsive, these two lines of development
had to converge and act in unison. Production had first to become
market-dependent. Most of the peasants drawn into marketing
between the tenth and fourteenth centuries were, in fact, involved
in only a marginal way. The essential objective of their farm
economy was still subsistence. Any tendency for their obligations
of service or their payments in kind to be commuted to cash

obviously forced them to broaden this strategy so as to satisfy their cash needs. Additionally, the farm economy of some peasants was incapable of providing all-round support. They had what Postan called 'imperfections' which could only be rectified by trade (Postan, 1972, p. 198). Such peasant households probably increased substantially over the thirteenth and early fourteenth centuries as colonisation took settlements into more marginal, livestock and woodland environments. The farm economies developed in these sorts of environments tended to be more specialised and for this reason, to be more market-dependent. Areas like the Weald and Chilterns, for instance, boasted specialised sheep, cattle, pig and fruit farming by the late thirteenth century, all servicing the growing appetite or material needs of nearby London.

Yet even where peasant producers marketed a high proportion of their produce, it does not automatically follow that such dependence equalled market responsiveness, with peasants adjusting their farming system in response to the run of prices. Market responsiveness needs to be seen as a different line of development, albeit one that slowly converged with market-dependence. We cannot ignore the fact that peasant producers set out to produce livelihood, not livelihood plus a surplus. So long as they traded in use rather than exchange values, then it would not matter whether their market involvement was marginal or substantial. Admittedly, any increase in market-dependence may have lowered the threshold at which peasant producers became interested in profit rather than simply livelihood, but this alone does not mean we can treat the two lines of development as one. We certainly cannot deny that profiteering did develop in some spheres or sectors of medieval farming. Arguably, interest in a profit beyond livelihood began amongst those landholders who can be seen accumulating large personal holdings of land even as early as the thirteenth century. By the late fourteenth and fifteenth centuries, after the decimations of the Great Plague had made land relatively more abundant, the idea that land was evenly distributed between members of the village community was a thing of the past. These more well-to-do landholders, or *kulaks*, clearly had an interest that went beyond mere livelihood. The sort of responsiveness we now find is symbolised by those farmers of Midland England who, at the expense of thriving communities of arable farmers, converted land into large grass farms for the production of sheep at a time when prices were swinging in favour of stock. Yet whilst conceding that commercial farming was establishing itself by the late medieval period, its significance must be kept in perspective. The economic horizon of most peasant producers was still concerned with subsistence rather than profit, with trading in use rather than exchange values. For these peasants, marketing was still about obtaining cash for feudal dues or with correcting the imperfections of their farm economy. It was more an exercise in maximising the opportunities afforded by their environment than in maximising the opportunities offered by the market-place. This is what Thirsk implied when, writing of sixteenth-century England, she described farming as still primarily organised around the natural physical divisions of the country rather than dominant markets, meaning that farmers were looking more to what they could most easily produce from a particular environment than to any production role allocated to it by urban markets (Thirsk, 1967, especially pp. 2–5). In short, it was a system of production that took more account of environmental suitability than of location, one more concerned with supply economics than demand economics.

Logically, any limitation on the amount of rural produce actually marketed would have led to supply areas being drawn at a larger, more extensive scale. Of course, in a medieval context, there were positive frictions against the unlimited expansion of supply areas in areal terms. Except where rivers or water-borne transport lowered opportunity costs, the feasibility of moving farm produce at an interregional level was greatly affected by transport costs. In a free market, these extra costs could be offset by higher market prices. To a limited extent, such price adjustment was part of the solution used to satisfy the dietary needs of growing populations. Both Florence and London reportedly had higher food prices than surrounding towns. Allowing prices to rise freely so as to draw in food from a wider supply area, though, was not acceptable to municipal authorities. Their vested interest was in having a food supply that was cheap as well as sufficient. Allowing any sort of price adjustment to cope with supply problems was likely to occur only where urban hinterlands were distinctly unproductive or where growth pushed demand out beyond their confines. Fourteenth-century Florence was certainly in the latter category. With over 200 000 inhabitants, it was exceptional for its age, both in relation to its *contado* and other towns. Not surprisingly, it drew only two-thirds of its grain-supply from its own surrounding *contado*. It made up the shortfall by importing grain from elsewhere, including cheap grain from as far away as Sicily. Once we grasp the acute difficulties which many medieval towns must have faced in reconciling their rapidly-expanding dietary needs with the extra penalties of cost that came with the expansion of supply areas, then we can understand why such towns had a vested interest in appropriating as much food as possible out of their immediate hinterland before looking further afield. To put this another way, medieval towns had a critical interest in forcing local peasant farmers to yield up a greater surplus and to do so via their markets.

To this end, we can expect the early interest in taxing trade to have been joined by an equally sharp interest in making sure that produce was brought to market. Whereas the former was prompted by the avarice of kings and seigneurs, the latter vented the developing interest of the urban community itself. As towns grew, the need to secure a food supply that was both cheap and sufficient must have grown apace. For most growing towns, this was a case of making sure that if farm produce was marketed, then it was marketed in their market-place and marketed openly. The larger, more rapidly-growing towns faced more acute problems over provisioning their populations. Sooner or later, as their supply areas were expanded, they would have faced the task of raising the volume of produce that was actually marketed from their immediate hinterland, simply because – other things being equal – the latter's opportunity costs would have been lower than for those supplies drawn at a distance. Naturally, much depended on the precise circumstances of a town. A city like Milan was reportedly able to live entirely on the harvest of its immediate hinterland. By comparison, Genoa received no corn whatsoever from its hinterland (Jones, 1966, p. 384). Such a contrast owed far more to differences in resource endowment than to any willingness or unwillingness of rural producers to market their surplus. In terms of the means by which towns could pressurise their hinterland, much also depended on the degree of political control which they wielded. The Italian city-states, the more powerful German towns and the *drie staden* of Flanders were better placed in this respect than towns elsewhere. Italian communes were able to take direct action, setting 'a prescribed amount of grain which had to be delivered by the different areas of the *contado*. This *impositio blave* was levied on all grain-producing territory, in proportion to the usual yield of the community in question' (Waley, 1978, pp. 61–2). Although having control over 240 villages in its surrounding hinterland, the German town of Lubeck actually purchased four-fifths of the rich, grain-producing island of Poel near Wismar in 1350, a manoeuvre solely designed to secure its grain supply (Rörig, 1967, p. 168). Individual landlords were capable of injecting a similar purpose. A feature of urban systems in countries like Italy, Germany and Flanders was the way in which successful urban merchants began buying up rural properties over the thirteenth and fourteenth centuries, thus creating a class of individuals who not only combined information on both production and consumption but who could also apprehend the market possibilities of linking the two. Their strategic awareness of market possibilities may be the reason why the extensive buying-up of rural estates by Tuscan merchants was linked chronologically with the gradual replacement of cash-rents with rent-payments in kind, using the *mezzadria* system, for it restored the landlord's direct control over a marketable surplus at the very moment when local urban markets were experiencing a phase of rapid growth. It may also be part of the reason why a tension between town and countryside developed over these crucial centuries.

Town–country relationships during the medieval period were also affected by the stilted way in which demand was fed into the equation. Contemporary markets were mostly licensed rather than spontaneous affairs, though latent demand obviously had some role in making out a case for the foundation in quite a number of examples. At the outset, the system of monopolies and trading dues that were attached to these licensed centres were designed to maximise the profit which kings and feudal lords derived from them. In other words, the whole concept of market area was something contrived, a matter of privilege, rather than a relationship worked out solely through the interaction of supply and demand. It was a fiscal device, a matter of one's political clout rather than impact of population size. The implications of this are clearly brought out by those studies which have mapped the potential trading areas of licensed market centres in various parts of England. Using Bracton's suggestion that a person should not have to travel more than $6\frac{2}{3}$ miles to market his goods as a yardstick, they have found that many areas had considerable over-provision, with a close packing of centres far beyond local needs. Such a situation could only have arisen in a world in which markets were an instrument of trade regulation rather than spontaneous outgrowth of trading activity. In such a world, market areas were bounded by political will not by the point at which distance-decay functions eventually gave out. More to the point, when medieval towns began to grow rapidly during the twelfth and thirteenth century, they had first to break through this Procrustean system of trading monopolies if their rapidly developing needs were to be met and if a more responsive relationship was to be established between supply and demand.

Given the way that the various influences which have been outlined could alter the relationship between town and country-side, there can be no case for supposing that modern and medieval towns differed in so far as the latter were surrounded by von Thünenesque landscapes similar to, but on smaller scale, than the former and that the latter had personal or isolated systems whereas the former involved complex hierarchical systems that ordered metropolitan, provincial, regional and local centres into a single system. This is not to imply that economic facts of life like distance as cost or levels of demand did not have a place, but so too did a range of other facts capable of either over-riding purely economic forces or disrupting their coherence. For these reasons, we cannot depict the landscape that stretched out from medieval towns in von Thunen terms. For practical reasons, we can expect a zone of intensive market-gardening under the walls and for historical reasons, we might expect there to have been a drift towards a rural landscape that was accessory to urban needs, one organised into production zones that were determined by the working-out of demand and rent–distance functions. In the regulated atmosphere of medieval markets, though, this drift towards a price-fixing market still had to overcome a battery of institutional rigidities before we can speak of a rural landscape forged in the market-place.

8
The Decline of Feudalism: A Study in the Nature of Geographical Change

It is of the essence to Sahlins and Service's distinction between General and Specific Evolution that the former is an abstract concept, compounded from the experience of cultures generally, whereas the latter, being the history of specific societies, is as much a record of decline and discontinuity as of growth. According to their principle of phylogenetic discontinuity, advance to the next higher stage of societal complexity is not sustained through the most advance society of the previous stage but works itself out through those next below it via a simple leap-frogging effect. Intertwined with this principle – its inevitable outcome – is their principle of geographical discontinuity. If the significant jumps in the evolution of societal complexity are not sustained through any one society or culture, then neither do they always occur in the same place. The baton of societal advancement as it were is passed from society to society and place to place. Not only is societal advancement uneven, but the map of what ranks as the most advanced forms and what is, relatively speaking, the least advanced is being continually redrawn. These suggestions bear comparison with the ideas of Friedman, Rowlands and Ekholm. For them, societal development always proceeded through core–periphery structures, at least once the first ranked societies or civilisations began to emerge from the late third millenium BC onwards. Although these core–periphery structures were always present at the level of General Evolution, their precise disposition was being constantly transformed. New cores developed in societies that had previously been peripheral and old cores 'slipped' back to peripherality.

There is no dispute with the ideas encapsulated in Sahlins and

240

Service's two evolutionary principles nor with the fully compatible 'real-world' thesis of Friedman, Rowlands and Ekholm that such patterns of development can be structured through core–periphery systems whose core- and peripheral areas were subject to relocation through time. Where appropriate, I have already drawn attention to structures and shifts of this kind. However, it is important to proportion the scale of these core–periphery systems correctly. For Friedman, Rowlands and Ekholm, they were, from the very beginning, global or world systems, that could embrace early states or civilisations, chiefdoms, tribes and even bands. Such a view denies the overall thrust of societal development as expounded here, because it eschews any significance for the organisational adjustments that I would read from the increasing scale of societal systems. I would not deny that exchanges did take place across system-bounds – between tribes, chiefdoms or early states and what lay around them – but I would reject the view that such societal forms depended on these extra-systemic links, so much so, that typologically, we cannot see them as independent forms. If we see the various societal forms as a problem of integrating larger and larger systems of people and space, then it would make a nonsense of our case if we also presumed that 'global systems' existed from the outset. As writers like Rappaport and Segraves have pointed out, organisation is – in the first instance – an adaptation to system scale. Changes in organisation can be seen as bound up with changes in system scale. Seen in this way, 'global systems' are an end-product of societal evolution not a beginning.

We can put this another way. Core–periphery structures – the dependence of local on supra-local space – developed within the boundary conditions laid down by the evolution of the various societal forms. In the first place, they only emerged as structures when ranked systems emerged. In the second place, they derived their significance from the fact that they functioned as co-ordinated or integrated systems. The very control functions that served to integrate them also served to delimit them. These control functions are not stable in time, but change from one phase to another. With each new scalar jump in societal organisation, new bases of integration also emerge. This qualitative change means that core–periphery structures do not just become larger. They are redefined, meaning that they are injected with new principles of co-ordination and integration. Indeed, I would contend that new scales of operation only emerge through these new principles. For this reason, we can expect the character of core–periphery systems to have evolved in step with the changing character of societal order, the one being the organisational imprint of the other. Thus, as simple chiefdoms evolved into systems of chiefdoms and chiefdoms into states, so also, can we expect core–periphery structures to have evolved into more complex and qualitatively different forms. With the larger state-systems, we have to envisage a nested hierarchy of control, an elaborate ordering of power around local, regional and national centres. Arguably, early feudal states form an exception to this structuring of societal order. For all their centralisation of ultimate power, the early feudal state in western Europe formed somewhat flattened, even questionable core–periphery structures if we take into account how actual power over people and resources was devolved. The emergence of core-periphery structures at a still higher, global level was a much later affair. Such a global system does not date from the mere appearance of long-distance exchange, a feature present by the third millenium BC, but from the point when society became embedded in the economy and when, as a consequence, there was able to develop an integration of space across a number of different polities, such that one can speak of specialised roles being allocated at a global level in the manner so brilliantly described by Wallerstein (Wallerstein, 1974). Even Wallerstein's dating of this point to the 'long' sixteenth century may be premature (Dodgshon, 1977, pp. 8–19).

I have explored the spatial dimensions of societal evolution at length because it provides us with the makings of an important geographical proposition. Seen in purely organisational terms, the reason why the leading edge of societal advancement was not sustained through the same society was because such societies were, almost by definition, the most adapted and organised when seen in relation to both their cultural and physical environment. As Sahlins and Service reasoned, sooner or later, this higher degree of adaptation was bound to displace the thrust of societal advancement into a new trajectory, for the simple reason that other less-well-adapted societies had greater potential for responding to the organisational possibilities created by new ideas, technology or environmental perturbations. With small-scale societal systems like bands or tribes, this displacement would have involved new bands or tribes taking up the baton of advancement towards greater complexity or increased organisation. With the advent of ranking and hierarchical societies, new levels of adjustment emerged. Not only could societal systems, whether chiefdoms or states, now leap-frog each other, but so could the increasing range of differentiated subsystems that flourished within them. To restate a point first made by Bateson, all evolving systems acquire subsystems that are potentially regenerative, subsystems that are capable of runaway growth unless positive feedbacks act to check their behaviour (Bateson, 1972, p. 511; Adams, 1975, p. 284). These checks have the effect of deflecting the pressure for change and adjustment into what Bateson called 'areas of unused freedom' (Bateson, 1972, pp. 511 and 285). For human society, these areas of unused freedom can take a variety of forms, but are most likely to involve the take-up of new processes, products or resources, or any combination of such opportunities. However based, we invariably find a spatial dimension to such change, with radical innovation being more easily achieved through an outward expansion into new areas of space or an upward extension into new areas of organisation for it is here that we always find the areas of greatest 'unused freedom'. In a sense, we are dealing with the freedom of the frontier, the greater scope for change that exists outside or beyond the existing order of things. As Turner put it when talking about his frontier thesis, a 'new environment is suddenly entered, freedom of opportunity is opened, the cake of custom is broken, and new activities, new lines of growth, new institutions and new ideas are brought into existence' (Turner, 1921, p. 205).

The assumption that radical change is more likely to occur with less adapted systems, or in areas where there is the greatest amount of 'unused freedom' within systems, clearly provides a geographical dimension to societal change. Paradoxically, previous attempts by geographers to discuss societal change, especially the transition from feudalism to capitalism, have tended to produce aspatial kinds of argument. A number seem content to reduce the mechanisms of such change to an internal revolutionary process, a child of conflict between the classes. Of course, there can be no quibble with their central assumption that conflict produces change. However, I would reject their insistence that it can stand as a sufficient explanation of all societal change. I would also reject the implicit notion that some form of disembodied class-conflict model is the best the geographer can offer, as if societal change occurs in space but is not of it. Incorporating an evolutionary perspective not only provides a more secure basis for understanding the different trajectories of change, including those rooted in conflict, but also enables the geographer to make a more genuinely helpful contribution to the wider debate on societal change.

As part of this contribution, I want to outline the following as a working hypothesis on the way that the geographer might approach societal change in the very long term. The significant jumps in societal evolution begin with the stresses and pressures that result from growth. In any customary or regulated society, sheer force of custom, institutional checks or consciously-contrived blocking mechanisms would have conspired to inhibit this growth from changing the way things were organised or done in the core-areas of society. In consequence, we can expect change of a radical or rapid nature, or any form of change that threatened the established order, to have been absorbed **more easily** at the margins of society, accreted to its social, economic and geographical margins in both a relative and absolute sense. New ideas, technologies and products were all more easily and, therefore, more likely to be innovated at the margins of society, simply because this is where 'areas of unused freedom' were maximised. Change in such areas carried with it less social cost and less disruption compared with change in the very centre of society. For Schon, it was more likely to be experimented with beyond the stable state because it posed less of a threat to established order (Schon, 1973). Certain forms of growth taking place within societal systems could also engender change. Thus, sustained growth could result in saturation: this was most likely to happen where the provision of particular services, goods or produce was defined by finite levels of demand. In such circumstances, the redirection of labour or resources was most likely to occur at the margins. Alternatively, sustained growth could extend society beyond the limits of prevailing organisation, creating a demand for new forms of relationship and integration: this scalar problem could be as relevant to a manorial system or medieval town as to a state system. Again, such adjustments were more likely to be made at the margins of existing systems. In the case of scalar growth, though, change is just as likely to have been directed upwards as outwards, generating higher levels of control and coordination. For these different reasons then, we can argue that any growth in the scale of societal systems ultimately brought with it the possibility of societal change.

Seen over time, such change would initially have involved the creation of new subsystems. These subsystems would have been distinguished in various ways. They could instate new levels of control. Alternatively, they could be low-order subsystems made up of communities organised in a different way, perhaps with a different type of status or tenure, a different level of living or a different economy. But whatever their prime basis of distinction, such subsystems invariably bore the added distinction of being functionally or locationally marginal to pre-existing systems, either in a relative or absolute sense. In effect, what is being asserted is the highly significant geographical fact that, viewed historically, society has shown an equal if not greater tendency to evolve or change through space than through itself, to change by evolution as much as through revolution.

Implicit in this suggestion is the further proposition that the growth of novel subsystems in this way could, potentially, effect a system-wide change. Put simply, they could grow so large or be so regenerative, that their needs and interests could outweigh those of older subsystems. This was always a possibility simply because newer subsystems were likely to be more adapted to prevailing opportunities and technologies. Only where older subsystems were able to exert strong controls or checks over newer subsystems, a common feature under command or regulated systems, was this 'biggest is best' thesis not likely to prevail as a matter of course. If subsystems produced system-wide change, then it was because at some point and in some way, the needs and interests of these newer subsystems were brought into conflict with those of older subsystems. Adams's concept of societal subsystems being identified, co-ordinated then centralised or integrated provides us with a possible staging of how this conflict of interest came about, but it tells us less about the precise processes involved. These depend on the institutional means by which subsystems are brought together. Prior to the spread of money, the integration of subsystems worked through an interweave of social, political, economic and religious factors, with social and religious factors being the more dominant in the case of tribes and chiefdoms but with political factors coming more to the fore with the formation of the early states. Any significant edge gained by one subsystem over another as regards energy capture was bound sooner or later to shift the fulcrum of power within the system as a whole. For reasons given earlier, this edge was always more likely to be discovered amongst the less adapted subsystems of the periphery. We can see this as providing a geographical context for a point made by Eisenstadt. Speaking about the source of change in historical bureaucratic societies, he referred to the dynamism injected by the 'constant tension and contradiction between the free-floating resources and flexible orientations, on the one hand, and the more traditional orientations and interests, on the other' (Eisenstadt, 1963, p. 317). With the florescence of markets and money, there emerged a still more powerful force for integration. Together, money and markets facilitated the easier interchangeability of goods and produce, thereby enabling a far more elaborate network of local and regional complementarities to emerge, and laying the foundation for a new phase of societal evolution through the enlarged potential which they created for spatial interaction (Elias, 1982, pp. 46–7). Money 'flows through virtually all barriers, increasing the coherence of the world system enormously' (Rappaport, 1977, p. 66).

New subsystems tended to find a niche in such a system as much by feeding into it new kinds of goods and produce as by making up for any shortfall in established items. This diversification of traded items was a cornerstone in Hirshler's argument concerning medieval trade. Accepting that true price competition was ruled out or suppressed by regulation, he countered it by arguing that other competitive instrumentalities were, nevertheless, available. Would-be producers, for instance, could exploit the 'areas of unused freedom' offered by forms or varieties of goods not covered by regulation, including newly-innovated goods not conceived of by such regulation: their break-in, therefore, was always more likely to be at the margins of the system (Hirshler, 1954, pp. 52–8). Arguably, this greater freedom for growth created by diversification was as much responsible for the phase of product innovation that can be dated to the fifteenth to seventeenth centuries as any expansion of market activity. The eventual emergence of price-fixing markets accelerated the process of integration, but with this change. Once subjected to the same market conditions, subsystems engaged in producing the same good were brought into direct competition. This was the age of process-innovation. Each new process-innovation brings about a change in production functions. Since they were more likely to be adopted in areas less adapted to established methods and processes, this sideways shift of production functions serves as a metaphor for the locational shifts that almost inevitably accompanied such changes. Under a capitalist free-market system, the constant search for revolutionary changes in production techniques, and therefore in profit advantage, will inevitably revolutionise the geography of production again and again. For some, change in such circumstances derives from conflict but whether we see it as a conflict borne out of an inner contradiction between class interests is surely of less immediate concern to the geographer than seeing it as a conflict between spatially distinct subsystems whose respective interests had been internalised within the same market system and set one against the other. In other words, it was change through accretion, through society reaching out beyond itself, that fostered conflict rather any contradictions inherent or immanent within the original undeveloped form of the system.

We can explore these ideas further by looking at the way that they compare with actual phases of societal change. The decline of feudalism over the late medieval and early modern periods provides us with the first such phase that can be documented in any detail. Four themes will be explored. First, the creation of more centralised states. Second, the extent to which feudalism in the European countryside changed through evolution as opposed to revolution. Third, the extent to which medieval towns and trade were similarly transformed; and fourth, to balance the broader perspective of these first two themes, I want to investigate the decay of feudalism at a more specific level by examining its decline in Britain, again drawing out a distinctly geographical perspective.

The Shift Towards Centralised States

It was noted in Chapter 4 that feudalism can be seen as intermediate between chiefdoms and mature states. With the various regional subsystems being territorialised within the politically-defined framework of a larger state-system but retaining a strongly segmented or autarkic character. The shift towards more mature forms of state organisation had begun by the twelfth century. It was a gradual metamorphosis that enveloped most parts of western Europe over the next three or four centuries, a move that began along 'the edges of the Old Holy Empire' (Rokkan, 1975, p. 576), culminating in the rise of highly centralised, nation-states during the sixteenth and seventeenth centuries. It was accomplished by kings and princes slowly clawing back the generalised power which they had earlier conceded to territorial lords, a concession that made feudal states prone to the same sort of fissiparous tendencies that had earlier plagued chiefdoms. Obviously, as kings assumed more and more control, new ways had to be found of handling the potentially greater flow of information that now passed through the royal court. The response, as with all centralised systems, was to institutionalise expanded bureaucracies to deal with the routine business of state. These professional bureaucracies became differentiated into distinct and relatively autonomous spheres of activity, each accorded their own goals and control functions. Those involving justice and finance were the first to emerge, the one symbolising the king's ultimate authority and the other providing it with a source of revenue by levying taxes and dues. As each sphere developed, it projected its activity out over the provinces through an increasing hierarchy of paid or unpaid crown officials, officials who symbolised the power of the centre.

The process of centralisation and with it, the slow emergence of differentiated bureaucracies as distinct and relatively autonomous subsystems, had begun in countries like England and France by the twelfth century (Strayer, 1970, pp. 40–1). Yet whilst it is correct to say that the process proceeded more quickly in England and France than in, say, Germany (Strayer, 1970, p. 48), the emergence of a coherent and differentiated system that reached out from the centre to all provinces and down to all communities was a prolonged affair, the outcome of numerous decisions over policy and procedure rather than something legislated into existence overnight. Quite apart from any decisions that established the separateness of particular spheres (such as justice, finance), there were the many problems of how the state at large could be brought under the direct sway of the various emergent ministries. The problem was not one of partitioning the state into fine-scale units of administration: that had been achieved during the early stages of state-formation. The problem now faced was one of establishing a more centralised and more direct control over local affairs through a network of royal officials and establishing a uniformity of custom and practice in matters of law, taxation and the like. The progressive adjustment towards more system-coherence was achieved more easily in England than in other parts of western Europe. Even when organised on a feudal basis, the king's power over the great territorial barons conferred some degree of coherence over the state as a whole. At the same time, forging a single, uniform system of law throughout the different regions of the system posed few problems. Nevertheless, creating a centralised state still needed time. It was not something that could be created overnight. Rightly, some have talked about an 'increase in governance' over the sixteenth and seventeenth centuries, with the penetration of local affairs by central government moving at a quicker pace (Wrightson and Levine, 1979, p. 10; Wrightson, 1982, pp. 222–3). This must not be allowed to conceal the fact that the process by which the affairs of an 'inward-looking periphery' were linked firmly and finally to the direct managerial control of an 'outward-looking core' has deeper roots and involved change in a range of different spheres (Smith, 1984, especially pp. 161–76).

The relatively greater ease with which the English state became centralised makes it somewhat atypical of European states at large. The French experience was nearer to the European norm. Viewed during the twelfth century, the Capetian monarchy had a nominal position as kings over the territory of the French state, but this was not a position that gave them any real authority. The independence of its numerous provincial lords and princes gave the French state little coherence or meaning. To centralise control over such a disordered system, the Capetian kings had to secure their power. It was not a sovereignty they could take for granted. Starting in the thirteenth century, they began to slowly expand their effective power beyond their hearth area, the Ile de France. Establishing centralised control over the whole of France proved a long, fitful affair. Every so often, the newly-welded structure collapsed back into its bits and pieces again, to be followed by an even stronger surge towards centralisation (Anderson, 1974, p. 86). Once direct royal control over the entire state had been stabilised, a position not reached until the end of the sixteenth century, there still remained the task of projecting that control out over the provinces through new organisational structures. This was largely an achievement of the seventeenth century. It was one that had to confront the strong sense of provincialism that existed in France. By the seventeenth century, the different provinces had their own local assemblies and some, like the Midi, were further insulated through their own legal custom and social institutions making their integration into a single system of government difficult. Strayer has described the means by which central government coped with such differences as ingenious, with existing institutions being allowed to survive but under the direction of officials appointed by the crown (Strayer, 1970, pp. 50–1). Aligning what Eisenstadt called the 'great' and 'little' traditions against each other (Eisenstadt, 1963, pp. 99–100) tended to create problems of conflict between core and periphery in all centralising states (see for example, Kiernan, 1980, p. 1). In France, the resultant conflict was considerable. In part, this was because of the practical difficulties of instituting a new, high-level system of management and projecting its control functions downwards so as to encompass provinces that had been effectively autonomous systems. The tendency for this fusion of the state into a more coherent, centrally-governed system to run ahead of its economic integration made it a purely political process, something that did not arise from the ordinary lives of people and communities. In part, it also sprang from the particular solution adopted by the state for projecting its power anew, with royal officials acquiring a supervisory role over existing institutions of administration in the provinces. As a solution, this led initially to a duplication of roles and demands, two systems within a single state (Anderson, 1974, p. 100). The hostility that emerged towards this intrusion of the centre into provincial life owed much to the greater burdens brought by this duplication. Instead of replacing local feudal dues and renders, the centralisation of the state merely added a new layer. Over the late sixteenth and especially over the seventeenth century, the expanded bureaucracy needed to run the state and the enlargement of France's standing army brought an upwardly-spiralling demand for tax, or *taille*, with more bureaucrats enabling more tax to be collected and a state army enforcing its authority (Anderson, 1974, p. 98: Wallerstein, 1974, p. 139).

The European Countryside and the Challenge of the Frontier

The history of European feudalism throughout the late medieval and early modern periods displays a curious but revealing paradox. On the one hand, peasantry in the various parts of western Europe found themselves progressively liberated from the burdens of serfdom, acquiring personal freedom, the commutation of work service and, in many areas, release from the feudal exactions (such as entry fines, merchet, etc.) that could so burden their capital resources. On the other hand, the peasantry of eastern Europe found themselves being slowly drawn into a more exacting 'second serfdom'. As Wallerstein demonstrated, we can only begin to interpret these divergent trends by linking the experience of individual estates and localities to the forces operating at a wider regional and, eventually, a continental level. They are hardly trends that can be explained by taking a closed or disembodied view of lord–peasant relationships as the starting-point, and establishing the priority of change in class relations over market relations, as Brenner would have us do (Brenner, 1977, pp. 30–75). The one is realised through the other not in a simple cause-and-effect sort of way but through a complex reciprocating relationship in which each can act as the cause of the other. In direct opposition to those geographers who have tried to uphold Brenner's stress on the causative and chronological priority of change in class relations, I would contend that it is precisely because class and market relations stand in reciprocal relationship to each other that we can speak of feudal decline having a meaningful geographical dimension. It is surely the lesson of Wallerstein for the geographer, as it is of other recent studies by non-geographers (such as Jones, 1981; see also, summary by Butlin, 1982, pp. 11–20). It is this geographical dimension on which I want to elaborate here.

So long as the manorial system is seen as a natural or self-sufficient economy, then the relationship between lord and peasant can be taken as self-contained, something explicable within its own terms. At the outset, or when early state rulers first began to invest lords and knights with an estate in the provinces, this sort of simple self-sufficiency probably did represent the prime objective of the manorial system. Such a system introduced the basic attributes of feudalism as an economic system, with its balance between the lord's demesne and service-bearing tenements and its checks on the personal liberty of peasants so that their labour could be secured. By the tenth century, the somewhat enclosed world of the early manor was already undergoing change. Demesne output became geared to the increasing number of local markets. In the short term, the prime effect of this change in the system's objectives was to release demesne production from the limited horizons of the lord's kitchen table or that of his retainers. No longer constrained by these purely domestic needs, individual systems of demesne could now expand in size, provided always that there was a corresponding increase in service-bearing tenements. Clearly, it was a change that signalled the emergence of extensive demesnes, including the 'federated grain factories' established by the great abbeys and secular lords. However, in becoming market-oriented, the seigneurial economy had undergone a change in its objectives. The quest for profit began to supplement and then outweigh subsistence as the system's prime aim. This revaluation of its objectives though, conferred on it greater flexibility of inputs and structure, meaning that seigneurial profit could be achieved in a number of different ways. In a sense this new-found flexibility which was essential for the manorial system now became subject to variables that were less easily controlled within the limits of what might be regarded as a stable system. In fact, in the long term, they were variables that were capable of runaway growth. It is for this reason that we can regard the early shift from self-sufficiency to market-involvement as possibly the most important single change in the history of the manorial system, for it introduced the seeds of its eventual transformation. Under certain market conditions, or when pushed into environments less suited for arable or more distant from centres of demand, the relative profitability of demesne-farming *vis-à-vis* other strategies of resource use could create pressure for change. We do not have to wait until the fourteenth century for these pressures for change to become apparent. However, there were strong institutional restraints inhibiting the seigneurial response to them. The efficacy of these restraints varied regionally across western Europe.

The rent revolution that began to seep through parts of Italy at the end of the tenth century provides an early example of a radical response, with labour-services and rents in kind being commuted to cash rents (Jones, 1954, p. 19). Viewed regionally, it was a change that had its local variants. In Genovese and Lucchesie, for instance, it removed manorialism entirely, whereas in Campania, it involved the use of freer, wage-based labour to work demesnes in place of customary labour services (Jones, 1966, p. 400). Given Italy's place on the periphery of the Carolingian Empire and the way in which – in the unsettled conditions that followed the disintegration of the Empire – the larger seigneuries were broken down and replaced by a new class of middling landholder concerned with efficiency and profits (Herlihy, 1958, pp. 23–41), it might be argued that it was better able to adapt to changing conditions than were areas more centrally placed within the Carolingian Empire. In a sense, the same 'generalisation' of power that enabled the early communes to emerge in the eleventh and twelfth centuries enabled the manorial system to be recast in a different form. When the success of the aforementioned communes altered market conditions yet again, landlords in areas like Tuscany turned not to a reinstatement of manorialism but to mezzadria, a leasehold system involving rent-payments in kind. As I pointed out earlier, the overlap of ownership between town and countryside provided both the necessary information and the means of communication by which this pressure for further change could be relayed quickly to the countryside. Interestingly, it was in the south, on the newly-defined periphery of the Italian city-states system, that we find signs of a regression into a more full-bodied feudalism. Their harsher, more extractive forms of labour exploitation enabled landlords to offset the cost of shipping grain from the Two Sicilies to towns like Florence. Out of these adjustments came a broad contrast which was to persist for a long time, with the north deriving its wealth from industry and trade but with the south remaining firmly tied to a wholly agrarian economy and, increasingly, a 'colonial dependence' on the north (Jones, 1966, p. 406).

Faced with the hardened crust of custom and an institutional organisation of their estates that inhibited a free response to changing market conditions, feudal lords turned to the one easy opportunity for change that lay open to them. If we survey the countryside of western Europe about 1100, the area embraced by feudal tenures, that is, arable land which had been incorporated into customary tenements and was held *ad opera*, would appear limited. Even on fertile low-lying valley ground, where feudalism thrived best, customary tenements did not form a continuously-occupied surface but were arranged into disconnected blocks, with abundant opportunities for colonisation in the interstices. Around ·and beyond these core-areas of feudalism, lay whole areas of forest, poorly-drained ground or hill pastures that were, as yet, hardly touched by settlement (Dodgshon, 1980, pp. 83–9). With the growth of towns, trade and population in the twelfth and thirteenth centuries and the pressures for change that were now brought to bear on demesne-farming, at least under certain market conditions, yet with the institutional framework of the manor investing the *status quo* with a certain degree of inertia, it was logical that landlords should direct these pressures for change toward the areas of 'unused freedom' that surrounded the assessed area of the manor or toward the larger regional pockets of waste that still characterised the west European landscape about 1100. Beyond the organised core of manorialised settlements, seigneurs had greater scope for changing the nature of lord–peasant relations so as to take account of changed market conditions or simply to take account of the different environments into which colonisation was now pushing.

Examples of feudal lords using colonisation to change the direction in which rural society was developing are available for many parts of Britain and will be discussed in the final section of this Chapter. Comparable examples abound for most other parts of western Europe during the great wave of colonisation that helped to fill out the countryside over the twelfth, thirteenth and early fourteenth centuries. Thompson's early review of colonisation in medieval Germany provides a sound starting-point. The whole theme of Thompson's discussion is that colonisation bred freedom. It operated at two levels. In the older settled areas of the south and east, there existed an internal frontier made up of the waste that surrounded settlements and the larger blocks of forest ground that covered upland massifs or the less fertile parts of the lower ground. As feudalism was consolidated and extended on the more fertile areas, Thompson envisaged a movement into the freer atmosphere of the forests by peasants anxious to avoid being drawn into the more exacting regime of the manor. As a result, whole areas of wilderness like the Black Forest, Odenwald, Upper Bavaria, the Harz Uplands, Westerwald and Thuringian Forest now yielded to the woodsman's axe as their recesses were pioneered (Thompson, 1928, p. 510). In fact, far from being an escape from the yoke of seigneurial authority, these inroads into remaining forests were largely sponsored by feudal lords. What was different was the fact that they instead of spawning new manors, the process led to the creation of rent-paying communities of free farmers (see, for example, Darby, 1956, p. 195; Pounds, 1974, p. 168).

At the same time that new communities of free farmers were being established in the forested areas of south and east Germany, a comparable process of colonisation was taking place along Germany's external frontier, north and east of the Elbe. Under the direction of powerful lords like Albrecht the Bear, whole new regions of opportunity in Holstein, Mecklenburg, Pomerania and Silesia were systematically colonised. The sheer scale of land involved here was matched by a high level of planning. Individual lords took responsibility for settling large areas of land. New villages were carefully laid out by locators. Tenants were attracted to them from the older settled areas by the offer of consolidated holdings and tenures that were held for cash or rents in kind but not for labour services and which involved none of the 'multitude of trivial and exasperating obligations' that so burdened peasants in old Germany (Thompson, 1928, p. 518). Thompson compares this great push beyond the Elbe with the American Frontier movement. It fostered a freer social environment, with fewer traditional rights to inhibit change and a simpler system of law and government (Thompson, 1928, p. 519). In a footnote, he alludes to suggestions that this greater freedom had a boomerang effect on the condition of peasants in the older settled areas of Germany, the freer conditions in the one contributing to the decline of manorialism in the other.

There is, however, a paradox to be noted, if not explained. The very areas of Germany which witnessed this shift away from manorialism, with communities of free-status peasants holding their land for cash or rents in kind, were the very areas which, along with adjacent areas of Poland, experienced a descent into the second serfdom during the sixteenth and seventeenth centuries. This was the age of the *gutsherrschaften*, a system under which the large estates that existed in these areas created extensive, grain-producing demesnes for themselves using labour-services exacted from the peasantry. Writing specifically of

Poland, Topolski has suggested that we need to see the long-term history of these areas as unfolding through a series of distinct phases during which the rural economy was activated by a different set of interests. Over the tenth and eleventh centuries, it was the state that dynamised the rural economy. Over the twelfth, thirteenth and early fourteenth centuries, when these areas were being subjected to extensive colonisation, it was dynamised by the major landowners who sponsored the great waves of colonisation that spread across east Germany and Poland. From the late fourteenth to the end of the fifteenth century, it was activated by peasants who found that having fixed rents at a time when prices were moving forward gave them more comfortable margins. Finally, during the sixteenth and seventeenth centuries, faced with an increasing decline of feudal income, land-owners recovered the initiative and succeeded in resetting the rural economy to their greater advantage, with the peasantry becoming tied legally and economically to the working of large demesnes, especially where access to major rivers like the Oder and Vistula enabled grain to be shipped out cheaply to the rising markets of west Europe (Topolski, 1981, pp. 377–80 but cf. Zytkowicz, 1972, p. 137). Topolski discounts any attempt to construe these changes in the narrow Brenner-like terms of a class conflict model. Class relations could be refracted, shifted to a different trajectory of development, when projected through the prism of market activity. He is also appreciative of the role that institutional rigidity could play in retarding any response to changes in market conditions. During the late fourteenth and fifteenth centuries, peasants were protected by the inertia built into their rent-contract, with its fixed payments in cash or kind. The tenurial relationship between lord and peasant though, was, as Thompson made clear, far simpler than in older, feudalised areas. Relative to the latter, it probably still offered greater possibilities for radical adaptation. I am talking here about adaptation in a very general sense. Invoking this 'privilege of historic backwardness' sort of model helps to explain why change occurred but it does not explain why this change involved a regressive development into serfdom and a system of demesne-production based on coerced labour. Considered hypothetically, land-owners could equally well have restored feudal incomes by other means. They could have pressurised existing rents by demanding more cash or more rents in kind. Why did they opt for demesne-production? Conceivably, the answer lies in Wallerstein's European world-system. The sixteenth and seventeenth centuries saw the first signs of a true world-system taking shape, one whose core was focused on the countries of north-western Europe. From being on the periphery of German society, the areas beyond the Elbe now found themselves located on the periphery of a much larger system, a nascent European world-system. Over and above the system of local or regional markets that flourished beyond the Elbe, many of which dated from the great wave of twelfth- and thirteenth-century colonisation, there now emerged a still higher level of activity, with the pulses of demand now being emitted from north-west Europe reaching out as far as eastern Europe. The provisioning of north-west Europe from grain-producing centres in eastern Europe though, faced this constraint: transport technology still made the movement of grain costly and prohibitive so that movement was only likely to occur along routes that had low opportunity costs. In fact, the first estates to establish large-scale demesne production on a feudal basis were those close to the major rivers that drained north to the Baltic, especially those giving access to Danzig (Peet, 1972, pp. 6–8). The forward movement of grain prices in Amsterdam, the organising centre for the European grain trade by the sixteenth and seventeenth centuries, was a further factor, since it enabled producers and traders to absorb higher costs. However, to reach the central point of what I am trying to argue, as market-prices on the one hand and production and marketing costs on the other drew closer, land-owners in eastern Europe may have seized on feudal production as the means by which the trend could be reversed simply because it offered significantly better margins than alternative responses. One estimate is that late-sixteenth-century grain prices in Danzig were only 53 per cent of those in Amsterdam (Kriedte, 1983, p. 27). Moreover, unlike reliance on the higher rents of free tenants engaged in capitalist farming, a feasible alternative, the adopted strategy of large-scale demesne farming offered significantly lower transaction costs, since it organised production and marketing on a 'co-operative' basis. In the early stages of developing a new pattern of marketing, one that called for a long-distance network of information, the lower transaction costs that accrued from large-scale demesne production would have been substantial.

A similar link between *l'âge des grands défrichements* and the spread of new relationships exists in France. Groups of free tenants, or *hospites*, paying rents in cash or kind but with no obligation to provide labour services for the lord's demesne were established as colonisation pushed into waste areas over the twelfth and thirteenth centuries. It was an adjustment of tenurial conditions through an expansion in space that we can see operating in many parts of northern France, including Normandy, Picardy, the Ile de France, Lorraine and Champagne (Koebner, 1966, pp. 72–3), in the Massif Central (Ganshof and Verhulst, 1966, p. 296) and in the Midi (Lyon, 1957–8, pp. 47–8). Taking a slightly different view of the same problem, Duby spoke of the way that areas of late colonisation (meaning that taking place between the twelfth and fourteenth centuries) were linked with enclosure, a symbol of the greater freedom of status and practice enjoyed by these new forest communities. It placed the entire holding in the privileged, independent position which, in old settled areas, was enjoyed only by the farmstead itself (Duby, 1968, pp. 84–5). Consistent with what is being argued here, Duby speculated on whether this was a change in direction thought out by seigneurs rather than a case of tenants trying to slip the yoke of service by absconding to the freedom of forest. The gist of his argument is that seigneurs, appreciating that these less-fertile areas were more suited to pastoral farming and that pastoral farming was becoming more profitable, adjusted tenures accordingly. Tenants were given freer tenures and consolidated holdings, but more importantly, seigneurs substituted tallage – an imposition which tied tenants and their families to their dwellings and to the cash dues with which the dwelling was burdened – in place of labour service, thereby adjusting feudal exactions to the new, dispersed economies evolved through colonisation (Duby, 1968, pp. 85–6).

A comprehensive review of how non-manorialised communities were established out of the 'unused freedom' offered by remaining areas of waste was published by Lyon. As well as noting just how widespread this association was in western Europe over the twelfth and thirteenth centuries, he provided a detailed cameo of how it developed in Flanders, especially in the extensive areas of coastal marsh that were reclaimed on either side of Dunkirk and in the poorly-drained land along rivers like the Zwin and Scheldt. Again, there are two themes to his discussion. On the one hand, there is the way in which this new land was used to create free communities that 'never knew seigniorialism' (Lyon, 1957–8, 57). On the other hand, there is his observation that this fringe of freedom 'wore down the seignorial system dominant in the interior of Flanders' forcing the early and rapid commutation of labour services (Lyon, 1957–8, p. 57). Lyon himself does say precisely how this reactive change by old manorialised areas took place. It could be that the batteries of freeholders that emerged around the settled edge of the Drie Staden were able to show more flexibility in producing for the urban markets that lay fairly near at hand and which formed some of the most rapidly growing towns in the whole of western Europe. Once such systems were brought within the same market area as the less flexible manorial systems, then the chances are that the weaker, less adaptable systems would have succumbed to the more adaptable. With their strengthening political control over their hinterlands and their concern for cheap food, towns like Bruges and Ghent would surely have encouraged this process, especially if it enabled them to replace fixed customary rents with cash rents, forcing tenants to adopt a more active marketing policy. In short, the sort of reactive change we might be dealing with may have been brought about simply by the reintegration of freer peripheral areas into the same regional system of market activity as older core areas, thereby setting old and new forms of societal order in competition.

Towns, Trade and Industry: Forward Sideways

Similar lines of reasoning can be followed in respect of trade and industry. When we survey their development over the late medieval and early modern periods, what stands out is the transient and cyclical nature of particular trading patterns. These patterns appear to move through a life-cycle. Initially, there is a phase of emergence and growth during which new centres of production and trade establish themselves. Their trend of growth is always towards greater elaboration. They acquire more organisation, meaning that roles become differentiated, specialised and hierarchical. Bound up with most new systems of trade are the take-up of new opportunities or innovations: new resources, products, production techniques, business techniques, trading organisations, transport technologies could all be involved, each helping to reinforce the others. It is this element of newness that confers trading advantage, for it enables systems which grow into change to achieve a high degree of adaptation to prevailing market opportunities.

The problem which such trading systems faced was that prevailing market conditions did not remain stationary. Systems of production and trade that adapted themselves closely to one set of market conditions found themselves poorly adapted, or maladapted, when those conditions eventually changed. The added problem for medieval systems of trade was that part of the trend towards increasing adaptation to specific market conditions involved the acquisition of defined privileges and monopolies over trade (see especially, Olson, 1982, pp. 40, 71–3 and 86). As with other spheres of feudal practice, these privileges and monopolies were place-specific: they were, in this sense, non-adaptive. Faced with change, late medieval towns at the centre of one trading system would have found themselves incapable of easy adaptation to new opportunities. Indeed, we can expect such established centres to be less and less competitive as market conditions moved further away from the base conditions which underpinned their initial success.

In these circumstances, a point or threshold would have been reached in which it would have been easier for peripheral centres and subsystems to respond to the challenge of new opportunities – to generate around them new systems that were geographically and organisationally distinct – than for established systems to adapt in response. It is not surprising, therefore, that alongside or overlapping with mature, highly organised systems, we find newly-emergent systems that were developing through new structures of practice and in new locations. As newly-emergent systems, they were relatively undeveloped and, in consequence, more capable of adapting themselves wholly to new conditions. Just as mature systems suffered from their over adaptation to conditions that were *passé*, so emergent systems gained from still having areas of unused freedom or organisational structures which were still capable of easy adaptation to the changing map of opportunities.

From a geographical point of view, the crux of what I am asserting is that the regular shifts which we can observe in the pattern and focus of early trade systems was not a random process. The tendency of trading systems to emerge as adaptations to specific sets of opportunity made them less able to respond to any radically new mapping or packaging of opportunities without radical internal change. For this reason it was easier – and therefore, always more likely – that radical changes of direction or adaptation would occur at the margins or in those areas which boasted a greater freedom to evolve organisationally. The resultant displacement of core areas which sooner or later occurs can thus be seen as an intrinsic part of the very process of societal change. I am not of course, suggesting that internal, revolutionary change played no significant part, but I am anxious to point up its insufficiency. Without question, late medieval and early modern towns were riven with conflict, notably between the patricians who increasingly controlled civic affairs and the ordinary craft or artisan gilds, and this conflict could engender change. Yet it is also undeniable that the focus of trading systems shifted in time and space, with previously undeveloped centres or subsystems showing a greater capacity to adapt themselves to new opportunities, each shift instituting a larger, more elaborate system of trade. This inbuilt tendency for organisational shifts to disclose themselves as geographical shifts was especially true of a societal system in which institutional forms of adaptation were anchored to specific blocks of space even at a local level. It is by highlighting this geographical component that the geographer can make a contribution to the debate over societal change. In a sense, it balances conflict-models of change by admitting the possibility of a quite opposite form of change, a sort of conflict-avoidance model. Yet such a contrast misleads. By their very differences, mature, highly-adapted systems and new, emergent systems of trade themselves became the basis of conflict, as when the patrician groups who dominated Flemish towns like Bruges by the fourteenth century used their power to destroy the equipment and livelihood of cloth-workers who had emerged in the surrounding countryside and whose freer conditions of work conferred greater responsiveness to market opportunity (Nicholas, 1971, pp. 78, 85 and 110).

Turning from hypotheses to case-studies, we can identify a number of shifts in the controlling centres of European trade and the flows which fanned out around them taking place over the late medieval and early modern periods. With each decentring, wrote Braudel, there occurred a recentring, as if the 'world-economy' could not 'live without a center of gravity, without a pole'

(Braudel, 1977, p. 85). In each case, we can perceive an organisational advancement, with a larger network of movement and a more complex organisation of trading activity. What began in the tenth and eleventh century with an individual merchant, perhaps in the company of other merchants, trading between fairs and markets and carrying goods and silver with him, a self-contained agent of exchange, evolved, by the sixteenth and seventeenth centuries into an infinitely more elaborate system, with bankers, merchants, shippers, broggers, packmen, finance houses, bills of exchange, credit notes, stock exchanges, joint-stock companies and so on. The upsurge of each new system, and its almost inevitable adaptation at a higher scale and level of organisation, testifies to the fact that, sooner or later, change was deflected to previously peripheral sites which, by virtue of being less organised, had the greater potential for adapting to new ideas and opportunities. Taking the more significant shifts in turn, the foremost system of trade back in the twelfth and thirteenth centuries was that based on the cloth-producing towns of Flanders, notably Bruges, Ghent and Ypres but including minor towns like Osterburg. The prime markets for Flemish cloth were the rapidly-emerging towns of northern Italy, with producers and consumers being linked via the fairs of Champagne. In a world of small dealers and consumers, and long-distance movements, commercial gathering-points like the Champagne fairs were a necessity if the search costs involved in trade were not to outweigh the gains. However much sustained by a particular trade, there would always have been a tendency for the activity of such fairs to broaden as dealers of all kinds took advantage of its peculiar concentration of information and contacts, with the principle of trade=information=more trade ruling the day. In fact, for a time, the Champagne fairs became the great emporium of west European trade. By the mid-thirteenth century, its conjunction of flows earned it a status as a finance centre, its prices and equivalencies being used as a yardstick elsewhere. Yet the bustle of the thirteenth century gave way to stagnation and decline in the fourteenth century. Instead of buying Flemish cloth, Italian cities like Milan and Florence, began to produce cloth themselves. The Flemish industry stagnated and what it did produce no longer had the same market in Italy. The corresponding growth of the Italian cloth industry brought with it whole new patterns of trade. Subverting supplies of English and Spanish wool that had previously sustained the Flemish industry, and expanding the demand for such supplies, the Italian industry made greater use of sea-borne traffic. But like all shifts in trade, we are dealing with a jump in the volume of trade so that we can also speak of an absolute increase in overland trade too. Now though, trade between northern and southern Europe became increasingly funnelled through the emergent fairs at Lyons not those of Champagne, a shift that enabled Italian merchants to secure their position. Their growing control over the cloth trade led to a broadening control over trade generally, as profits from the one were reinvested in a broader and broader range of activity. This deepening Italian control over trade was ramified by a whole series of innovations that left Venetian, Genoan and Florentine merchants and bankers pre-eminent throughout Europe. New business techniques like double-entry bookkeeping raised efficiency, whilst others, like *contratti di commenda*, served to draw more funds into trade and to encourage a wider range of trade (Cipolla, 1976, pp. 183–5; Braudel, 1974, pp. 357–72). Such innovations can be seen as deriving from the increased scale of trade and the consequent need for a more ordered system. Merchants moved from 'poop to desk' said Kedar (Kedar, 1976, p. 122) meaning that it was no longer a case of merchants single-handedly controlling all aspects of trade. Specialised roles and services began to appear, the shipper becoming separate from merchant and the merchant from the banker. As their activities expanded, merchants and bankers began establishing subsidiary agents and finance houses in outlying centres of the system, slowly threading together a vast interconnected network of flows and information, all focused on northern Italy and its particular needs. By the fifteenth century, Italian merchants and bankers were well-established in most regional centres of trade, like Antwerp, Bruges and Seville, whilst at Lyons, the new trading junction between north and south, 143 out of 169 finance houses operating there during the mid-sixteenth century were Italian.

Yet the more highly organised Italian trade became and the more it adapted to even local conditions, then the more likely was it that with any fundamental shift in the nature of trade, whether through new resources or techniques, the intitiative would pass to a new area of control. With the discovery of the New World and the opening up of a trade route to the East Indies around Cape

Horn, there opened up just such a change in the map of opportunities. To an extent, Italian finance houses, especially Genoese bankers, were involved in the early ventures to exploit these new opportunities commercially. Faced with the closure of its traditional sources of sugar in the Levant, they funded early ventures to the West Indies in the hope of securing alternative supplies (Verlinden, 1972, pp. 625–46; Pike, 1966, pp. 48–83). However, the real initiative in exploiting these new opportunities lay with the Spanish and Portuguese. As events turned out, their expeditions to the New World succeeded in flooding Europe with precious metals, thereby triggering off a vast inflationary spiral over the sixteenth century, and the rapid build-up of their fleet of galleons – boats of Basque origin that were better suited to Atlantic traffic than Italian ships – gave them a shipping capacity second to none, yet they failed to establish themselves as the organising focus for a new European economy. Instead, the locus of control for a new, emergent system of trade developed in the northern part of the Hispano-Netherlands world, at Antwerp. During the early fifteenth century, Antwerp was no more than a minor seasonal fair operating in the shadow of nearby Bruges. By the early sixteenth century, it had become the centre which energised the rapidly-forming Atlantic Economy. Chaunu's description of the latter as moving from 'nothingness to being' (cited in Wallerstein, 1974, p. 170, footnote 25) over the early sixteenth century is just as apt when applied to Antwerp, a centre which 'underwent the processes of rise, expansion, maturity and decadence with peculiar intensity' (Van Der Wee, 1963, vol. II, p. 52). Its location enabled it to draw together the strands of four separate subsystems, all of which experienced growth over the early sixteenth century: the Atlantic trade (including the Americas and the East Indies), the vigorous trade emanating from upper Germany, the rapidly growing export of cloth from England and last but not least, the trade generated by a now successful Dutch industry (Van Der Wee, 1963, p. 177). Accompanying its response to these opportunities and the vastly-extended scale of trading activities which they induced were 'a stream of qualitative innovations' (Van Der Wee, 1963, p. 191) in business organisation. Merchants began trading all-year round and not just during the seasonal fair. Foreign merchants were welcomed. An exchange was built as a meeting-place for merchants and a new port was constructed. Building on their direct experience of Italian banking technique, the merchant community of Antwerp now added their own refinements. New techniques, like discounting bonds with long-term credit, were combined with low-interest loans to fuel a rapid build-up of speculative investment in trade (Van Der Wee, 1963 pp. 355–60). The attraction of funds into trade was also facilitated by the formation of joint-stock companies, perhaps the single most important development in business organisation over the early modern period. Antwerp's role as the organising centre of European trade came to an abrupt end when the war with Spain disrupted trade over the late sixteenth century.

The baton passed to Amsterdam. Again, this was a centre whose sixteenth century background was modest but 'suddenly . . . the city was there' (Barbour, 1950, p. 17). Its growth involved a rapid adaptation to the opportunities being unfolded by the continued expansion of trade with the Americas and East Indies. Amsterdam's special achievement however, was in diverting trade (especially Asian trade) from overland routes to their own maritime fleet and in penetrating the Baltic at the expense of the Hanseatic towns, an invasion of space which enabled it to co-ordinate not just the trade between Europe and Asia, but also, that between northern and southern Europe. Again, as a comparatively underdeveloped system growing rapidly, Amsterdam was able to shape its institutional development to the needs of the times. Like Antwerp before it, it contributed substantially to the forward development of business organisation. Limited-stock companies, a true stock exchange, a commodity market and a futures market all sprang up (Van Houtte, 1977, pp. 208–9; Kriedte, 1983, p. 87). Combined with low interest credit, they sucked vast amounts of capital, including a great deal from small investors, into trade (Barbour, 1950, p. 75). It became a port suffused with the spirit of speculative capitalism, with everyone trying to buy cheap and sell dear (Barbour, 1950, p. 75). The city was particularly-well suited to speculative dealing in commodities. Its trading links with the East and West Indies, northern and southern Europe, gave its merchants unrivalled access to a wide range of complementarities. By 1675, it reportedly dealt in 491 different commodities (Kriedte, 1983, p. 87). With its extensive warehousing and storage facilities, it could always guarantee ships a return cargo, a fact which established its reputation as a great trans-shipment port.

Just as trading systems could adapt through growth, using areas of 'unused freedom' to institute radical change, so also, do we have the corollary of systems which, in becoming highly complex and hyperadapted, had, in the process, lost the freedom to adapt easily to new changes in base conditions. Obviously, we need to see this in purely relative terms. In becoming more complex and more specifically adapted to the conditions of one phase, the controlling centres of each transient system were less capable of responding to any radically new configuration of opportunities compared with other less well-adapted centres or sub-systems. In fact, when we survey the literature, it provides many instances of dominant centres losing ground simply because, in becoming hyperadapted to one set of market conditions, they had forfeited their freedom to respond easily when these conditions changed. A few examples need suffice. Thus, when faced with the loss of their prime markets and sources of wool supply during the fourteenth century, Flemish towns became notoriously more rigid and defensive, more hostile to change than responsive to it (Van Houtte, 1966, pp. 38–40; Nicholas, 1971, p. 343). External pressures caused by changes in the structure of the European economy became fused with internal conflicts between craftsmen and patricians and between town and countryside, plunging Flemish towns into stagnation at a time when trading systems elsewhere were growing (Van Houtte, 1966, p. 40). In time, this was also to be the epitaph on the Italian city-states which took their place. After an initial phase of growth and adaptation, they in turn became 'an economically backward and depressed area' by the end of the seventeenth century (Cipolla, 1952, p. 178). Having become what Cipolla describes as a mature economy, they found themselves operating in a market system in which a new equilibrium prevailed (Cipolla, 1952–3, pp. 186–7). The necessary adjustments required, though, were inhibited by a whole gamut of institutional restraints from gild and state regulations to the high cost-structure of Italian industry by the early modern period (Cipolla, 1952–3, pp. 182–3). Increasingly constrained by the inflexibility of its institutional structures in a changing world, the verdict of historians is that it missed out on two great opportunities for change: the crises of the fourteenth and sixteenth centuries, when the Black Death and unrestrained price inflation threatened traditional relationships and values (Romano, 1974, p. 195). The same growing maladaptation appears in discussion of individual states. The controls governing Venetian trade, for example, became increasingly defensive and restrictive during the fifteenth and sixteenth centuries, even to the extent of blocking attempts by 'northerners' from trading in their port, a policy quite opposite to the open access enjoyed by traders in northern ports like Antwerp and Amsterdam (Sella, 1968, pp. 94–5). Venice also illustrates this further point: maladapted systems did not necessarily decline when faced with more strongly developing rival systems. It was a matter of relative performance. Some, like Venice, simply found themselves standing 'still in an expanding world' (Sella, 1968, p. 104). In northern Europe, the Hanseatic towns faced similar problems of adjustment by the fifteenth and sixteenth centuries. In becoming a highly structured system of trade, with an elaborate set of place-specific privileges, they became less and less 'adaptable to new conditions' (Dollinger, 1970, p. xix). Key organising centres like Lubeck manifest these problems through their increasingly inflexible organisation, being increasingly dominated by a closed 'circle' that was cut 'off from the outside world' (Rörig, 1967, p. 124). The experience of Spain offers us a different case. Its response to the opportunities of the New World was to export its internal problems. Frustrated by the decline of feudal privilege in the Peninsula, its nobility turned to the colonies, recreating variants of the coerced labour systems that had provided them with their economic base at home. In effect, they 'externalised' the problems of Spanish society (Kriedte, 1983, p. 42).

Over the fourteenth and fifteenth centuries, the tendency for change to skirt round the institutional rigidity of trade also began to work itself out in the relationship between town and country. As the gild structure of towns became more elaborate and as gilds enveloped themselves in a mesh of petty regulations regarding their conditions of work and trade, their behaviour acquired different goals. They became less concerned with exploiting new opportunities and more concerned with defending those to which they had already adapted, becoming, as Hibbert put it, 'defensive in outlook' (Hibbert, 1963, p. 182). He went on to liken them to Mesozoic reptiles, slowed down by the weight of their own defences and the 'entrenched specialization of their structure' (Hibbert, 1963, p. 228; see also, Langton and Hoppe, 1983, p. 33; Olson, 1983). Relatively speaking, not only did less-adapted urban systems have greater scope for radical change compared with more-adapted systems, but by the same token, non-urban communities, or at least those not bound by the restraints of finely-developed customary tenure, also found themselves with more 'unused freedom'. As the medieval period drew to a close, some countryside areas began to exploit this greater freedom by developing a range of industrial crafts and trades. Free from the oppressive control of the urban gilds, these newer rural-based trades were able to establish new routines of production and, by cheapening their product, to undercut urban industries. However, we cannot ascribe the growth of rural production solely to their greater freedom of adaptation to changing market opportunities. When we look more closely at where rural industry developed, we find it developed in particular kinds of environment, or the more marginal environments that were colonized vigorously from the twelfth century onwards. In character, these were mainly pastoral environments made up of hill pasture, forest, heath and marsh, the areas 'where commercial grain farming was impossible' (Langton and Hoppe, 1983, p. 25; see also, Thirsk, 1961, pp. 70–88; Kriedte, 1981, p. 14).

Their ecologically varied habitats provided a ready supply of industrial raw materials: timber, leather, bone, wool, dyes and ores. In trying to explain why these areas had need of adjustment to new types of economy, we must also keep in mind the sorts of community which inhabited them. They were free communities, beyond close feudal control. Almost inevitably, their inheritance customs favoured partibility, the spreading of livelihood between all male heirs. Over time, holdings that began small and marginal became even more so. Filling the slack periods in the farming calendar with a simple trade, one that exploited the wider potential of the local environment, provided a logical step forward.

Faced with the early growth of rural industry over the thirteenth, fourteenth and fifteenth centuries, many towns tried to obstruct it (Nicholas, 1971, pp. 78–9: Langton and Hoppe, 1983, p. 33). The real problem though, was the increasingly institutionalised nature of production within towns as much as the freer context in which rural production was growing. By the sixteenth century, their balance of advantages and disadvantages had become plainly visible to producer and merchant alike. When industrial output began to surge forward from the late sixteenth century onwards, it was the rural artisan working from his cottage or smallholding as much as the urban craftsman who sustained it. By the seventeenth century, we find livestock-woodland and open-pasture districts throughout western Europe sharing in this development, each exploiting a local resource and a local product. As these areas became penetrated by merchant capital and organised into large, coherent systems of production, markets became energised via a welter of regional specialisms, from needles and cutlery to serges and hosiery (Thirsk, 1961, pp. 70–88; Jones, 1968, pp. 58–71; Mendels, 1972, pp. 247–8; Kellenbenz, 1974, pp. 48–72; Kriedte, 1981, p. 23; Dodgshon, 1983, pp. 55–6; Langton and Hoppe, 1983, p. 25; Houston and Snell, 1984, pp. 473–92). Much has been written about how the concern of such cottagers and smallholders with sustenance rather than profit and their consequently cheap labour, enabled merchants to gain substantially from the differential profit of buying goods cheap in marginal areas and selling them dear in core areas (see, for example, Medick, 1976, pp. 299–300). However, we must not overlook the all-important fact that being able to opt into industrial production by cheapening both costs and products was not an option open to highly-regulated, mature urban economies in the sixteenth and seventeenth centuries. Although largely impelled by subsistence crises, it was an adjustment that only marginal, less-adapted areas could have made.

The Decline of Feudalism: A Case Study

In this final section, I propose to explore the whole notion of change at the margins by looking in detail at a specific problem in a specific context: the decline of feudalism in England. My discussion will fall into three parts: first, I want to demonstrate how the spread of freedom can be seen to follow a distinct geographical pattern. Second I will consider whether this represents a decline of feudalism or simply a case of feudalism adjusting itself to new opportunities in space. Third (and finally) I want to consider how the spatial contrasts so created provided just as potent a basis for conflict as the tensions internalised within particular feudal relations.

Feudalism: the Geographical Basis of its Decline

In an early attempt to chart the decline of feudalism geographically, Page posited that commutation of feudal tenures and the spread of money-rents first began in the south-east. The irradiation of commercial activity from London was seen as the *primum movens* (Page, 1900, p. 43). It was Gray, with his fine eye for regional variations, who undermined this argument. Anxious to correct the geographical bias in Page's analysis, with its exclusive reliance on manorial extents for the south-east and ecclesiastical extents at that, Gray sampled evidence from a wider area and a wider range of sources for the period 1333–42. His conclusions introduced a new perspective, for he found that out of 110 manors in the north Midlands and the north of England, only four still had labour-services being rendered. The situation was only marginally different in other parts of the Midlands. By contrast, those sampled for eastern and southern counties showed labour-services still being exacted on a fair proportion of manors. Although primarily concerned with exposing what he saw as Page's false chronology, with its stress on the Black Death as its turning-point, Gray was mindful of the way that his data inverted what hitherto had been the standard geography of commutation since it revealed that, overall, money-rents were prevalent sooner in the north and west of the country than in the south and east – a case of the periphery seemingly being more progressive than the core (Gray, 1914, pp. 625–56).

Gray's work itself was later challenged by Kosminsky. The latter argured that Gray had failed to take into account the fact that money-rents in the north and west – the *redittus assisae, auxilium*, etc. – had originated by means other than by the commutation of labour services. The crude balance between money-rents and labour-services, therefore, could not be used to measure the progress of commutation. Rather what was needed was a more restricted but discerning study of those villeins whose basis of tenure had been *ad opera*, or as Kosminsky phrased it, a study of the extent to which the estate's demand for labour had been covered by the services of villeins. Only through this more discriminating analysis can the paradox of commutation proceeding more quickly in the north and west than in the south and east be seen in its proper terms (Kosminsky, 1934–5, p. 28). To some extent though, this takes too formal a view of the matter. Kosminsky himself admitted the importance of rents-in-kind to northern and western estates, with areas like Northumberland having as much as 36 per cent of their rents paid in this form. To doubt the feudal nature of such payments, even though they probably evolved out of the tribute and hospitality owed by tribesmen to their chief, and to ignore the fact that they were equally subject to a process of conversion is misleading. However, even allowing for the way his discussion tries to filter out money-rents which did not result from the commutation of labour-services, and for the fact that his own analysis was based on the geographically-restricted coverage of the hundred rolls, he still endorsed Gray's broad contrast between the freer, more monetised relationships of the north and west and the ongoing importance of villeinage and labour services in the south and east. In fact, he enlivens the rather flat, uniform appearance of Gray's contrast by adding association to it. Thus, labour services were seen by him as surviving most strongly on the older, larger estates (especially those of the church) in areas which, paradoxically, were thickly populated and contained the major urban centres of industry and trade, centres whose trading activities were widely monetised (Kosminsky, 1934–5, p. 40). Money-rents, meanwhile, at least within the area covered by the hundred rolls, were more likely to be found on newer, smaller, more peripheral estates, where production was for the local market, where there was an emphasis on pastoral products, where there was an abundance of smallholders, where there were already freeholders as well as in what he termed 'backward' areas. 'How are we to explain' he asked of Gray's conclusions (before confirming them himself) 'the greater speed of commutation in the most economically backward part of England and the survival of a natural economy, in the shape of labour services, in the areas of most active money turnover?' (Kosminsky, 1934–5, p. 27, see also, p. 40).

Kosminsky goes on to add an extra dimension to the problem, one germaine to much recent thinking. Again basing his conclusions on the hundred rolls, he found that free tenures could be locally important even in areas where villeinage was traditionally strong, like the southern and eastern Midlands. Manors were to be found encircled by free tenures and though they were, *in toto*, nowhere near as extensive as in the north and west of England, nevertheless, they could form 'far more than a "narrow fringe" around the typical elements of the manor, the demesne and villein land' (Kosminsky, 1956, p. 131). In other words, to the macro-scaled contrast delineated for us by Gray, he added a new micro-scale contrast between the manorial core of estates and the free tenures of the periphery, with the former held for labour-services and the latter for cash.

More recent work has served to confirm that Kosminsky was right in seeing the contrast between villeinage and free tenures at two levels, the national and local. In regard to the former, Hilton, reviewing current opinion, has confirmed that the spread of money-rents at the expense of labour-services made quicker progress in the north and west than in the south and east (Hilton, 1975a, p. 139). It is still easier, given all the published work now available, to find studies of northern and western estates – like those of Bolton Priory or the Duchy of Cornwall – on which money-rents predominated around 1300. Particularly revealing are those es-tates which were sprawled across these opposite divisions of the country. When we look at those like the Percy estates or the Honour of Mowbray, there are clear signs that demesne farming and service obligations persisted more strongly in the south and east. Recent work has also confirmed that within the south and east, it was the peripheral and marginal areas that underwent the transition to free tenures and cash-rents first. Hilton, for instance, found that in the Cotswolds, it was the smaller manors of the scarp rather than the larger manors of the plateau that experienced commutation first. In terms of ecological character, the former were of a livestock-woodland type, whilst the latter were largely arable and geared to demesne production (Hilton, 1975a, p. 139). Similarly, in the Lincolnshire portion of the Honour of Mowbray, it was the old-established and highly-fertile Isle of Axholme that we find still given over to demesne production, using labour-services, at a time when the peripheral fen areas were being apportioned out into freeholds and cash-bearing tenancies (Green-way, 1972, p. xlviii).

However, the most important conclusion of more recent work has been the realisation that, quite apart from the contribution of commutation and what are loosely termed ancient freeholds, the presence of freeholds held for cash-rents in the north and west of the country or the more marginal and peripheral areas of the south and east owed much to the *de novo* creation of such tenures by assarting over the twelfth, thirteenth and fourteenth centuries. It was a link which Hilton saw as 'commonplace' (Hilton, 1969, p. 17). Postan too, thought 'colonisation played a highly important part in spreading free land tenure' though, aware of the way that twelfth-century colonisation on the Glastonbury Abbey estate still used such land to create customary tenements, he cautioned against too great an emphasis on the 'emancipating effects of colonisation' (Postan, 1973, p. 286). Exceptions there probably were but the fact remains that innumerable local and regional studies have vouched for its emancipating effects. Naturally, the connection between assarting and freeholds is more abundant for those parts of the country where waste survived after 1086 in great quantities. It is well attested, for instance, by the freeholds created in upland areas like the Pennines or Dartmoor. It is particularly well-documented for the large regional wastes or Forest areas which lay strewn across the north and west Midlands and which were subjected to much colonisation over the twelfth, thirteenth and fourteenth centuries, like the Forest of Arden and Cannock Chase (see, for example, Roberts, 1968, pp. 101–13).

Although the gross amount of land involved was smaller, the link between assarting and freeholds also holds true for the south and east once we reach the twelfth century. The interstitial areas of waste that survived in between manors often acquired a peripheral belt of freeholds: this was the freehold 'fringe' which Kosminsky found when studying the hundred rolls. Some of it formed small pieces of assart appendaged to customary tenements but distinguished from the tenure of the latter by being free-land held for a cash-rent. Other parts, however, were incorporated into entirely separate holdings that were distinguished physically as well as tenurially from customary tenements. In addition to this manorial 'fringe' of cash-bearing freeholds, there also developed more extensive systems of freehold created as colonisation pushed more deeply into the large remaining waste areas like the Kentish and Sussex Weald and the Chilterns (Du Boulay, 1966, p. 117; Moore, 1965, p. 35; Brandon, 1969, pp. 145–8). Elsewhere, Miller has shown how Ely Abbey used land newly-reclaimed from the Fens to endow large number of small, rent-paying tenancies over the twelfth and thirteenth centuries (Miller, 1951, p. 120). It was, he suggested, the prime means by which the Abbey raised its cash revenues over these centuries. In a later discussion, he portrayed this use of assart to establish cash-paying freeholds as a widespread phenomenon, widespread both within the rapidly-changing land-scapes of the Fens and in other waste areas tamed by the husband-man over these centuries (Miller, 1971, p. 5; see also, Dodgshon, 1975b, pp. 331–5).

Viewed overall, the spread of cash-rents and freeholdings, and with them, the spread of personal freedom, had a consistent geographical basis to it. Everywhere, it tended to be the more marginal or peripheral areas, whether measured absolutely or relatively, that underwent such transitions first. Their peripheral or marginal status can be defined in terms of physical distance or environmental quality. In terms of the former, they were the areas most remote from centres of political power or manorial control (Kosminsky, 1934–5, p. 42). Somewhat surprisingly, they also tended to be the areas remote from the great centres of population and trade. As regards environmental quality, they tended to be the least fertile types of land, those which would not be classed as arable today. They fall into Thirsk's livestock-woodland or open-pasture types of habitat. Thus far, what I have said is implicit in much of what has been written about the spread of freedom and money-rents. Admittedly, it is by no means the main thrust of what has been written about their spread, but it is what impresses the geographer most.

The Core-Periphery Structuring of Feudal Relations: A Matter of Decline or Adjustment?

On the face of it, we can interpret the pattern of change outlined in the previous section as a case of change occurring more easily where it mattered least or where it involved least disruption, that is, on the margins. This would help us to understand why change occurred where it did but it tells us nothing about why it occurred when it did. Was it simply because the whole concept of demesne production using labour-services became economically unattrac-tive? There were certainly secular swings in the importance of demesne production, largely because of shifts in the price of grain. Given the institutional rigidities surrounding customary ten-ements, a rigidity that could work in the tenant's favour as well as against him (Hatcher, 1981, p. 15), it is understandable why some lords may have found it easier to accommodate the changing viability of demesne production by making adjustments at the margins. The areas of 'unused freedom' represented by peripheral areas of weak manorialism or colonisable waste enabled lord–peasant relationships to be changed more easily. We can identify situations, though, when this sort of explanation is patently not sufficient. Surveying the English countryside over the thirteenth century, a number of scholars have noted a curious paradox, with, in some areas, labour services being exacted to a greater degree than before and villeins being defined as unfree and yet, in other areas, the trend of change was towards money-rents and personal freedom. This paradox acquires more coherence when we set these trends in their spatial context and see the longer survival and reactivation of villeinage and labour-services more as core-phenomena and the spread of money-rents and freedom more as a peripheral one. Such contrary trends alert us to the fact that when lords decided it was time to dismantle demesne production, it was not simply a matter of lords suddenly deciding a change was needed but of finding that their efforts made greater progress on the margins because that is where change was easier. These supposed core- and peripheral areas of the manorial system appear at times to have been subject to different sets of influences. To put this another way, part of the explanation of why change occurred needs to be seen in relation to why it occurred where it did. We can only appreciate why so many feudal lords exploited the lower opportunity costs offered by change in peripheral areas if we also accept that special conditions could prevail in these areas which made a change in the nature of lord–peasant relationships not just easier but more attractive.

We can tease out what these special conditions may have been by exploring the problem in two ways. First, we need to take cognisance of all the different considerations that could affect the manor as a unit of demesne production. As explained in the previous chapter, the manor provided the means whereby lords and their retinue could be directly supported. If the manor began as a self-contained natural economy, it did not remain as such for long. With the growth of markets, it became geared to market production, a fact which allowed the amount of demesne and service-bearing tenements on each estates to grow dramatically. In time, this orientation towards market production became its prime role. I have already made the point that once tied to marketing, demesne production became exposed to new, potentially destabilising factors because of long-term variations in the profitability of agricultural produce. However, there were other ways in which its character could be exposed to the pressure for change. A crucial development was the change which took place in the broad tenurial context of demesne production. Initially, we have to envisage a situation in which estates were constituted locally or, at most, regionally. The regional basis of the early Saxon kingdoms would itself have imposed limitations on the physical spread of estates. With their fusion into the English state came the possibility of land-owners having a property interest that touched widely-scattered corners of the realm. In fact, large, dispersed estates were already evident by 1086 (Hilton, 1975b, p. 42). Lennard talked of the 'great estates being curiously widespread', a factor which he felt contributed to the political integration of the country (Lennard, 1959, p. 33). Amongst the examples which he cited were the estates held by the Earl of Chester and the Count Mortain, both of whom held land in twenty different counties (Hilton, 1975b, p. 28). Others can be seen developing over the eleventh, twelfth and thirteenth centuries, such as those comprising the truly vast Duchy of Lancaster estate and the equally dispersed Honour of Mowbray. It was less a feature of ecclesiastical estates which followed an obvious segmentation principle but a few, such as Westminster Abbey, could still be described as highly scattered. The 'colonial' predicament of Wales provided many windfalls of land for the Anglo-Norman nobility. Like the Earl of Lincoln (the de Lacy family) who acquired the Honour of Denbigh, these windfalls formed sizeable but distant outshoots of systems of property whose main *loci* was within the south and east (for general comment, see Elias, 1982, p. 75).

I want to suggest that the emergence of these supra-regional estates introduced new parameters into the problem of demesne farming and villeinage. Decisions on how best to deploy the resources of the estate would now be taken in relation to a larger, more diverse portfolio of opportunities. The fact that some areas were more suitable than others for demesne production may not have mattered much if they functioned in relative isolation, but it would have mattered acutely once their differences in potential were set on the same scale of judgement. In short, estates which began life as localised systems of lordship and functioned as locally bounded systems of production and consumption, now found themselves drawn into supra-regional systems of landholding in which their capacity for exploitation was rated differently. Many northern and western parts of the country, for instance, would have been seen as less suited to demesne production once they became part of a national system of landholding. Relatively speaking, costs would have been higher than in the south and east simply because demesnes were smaller, yields lower, population more scattered and local urban consumption less. By converting labour services to cash, lords were able to transfer these higher opportunity costs onto the peasant. The fact that demesne production was weakly developed in northern and western areas would have made this conversion easier. Of course, to talk solely of demesne production ignores the fact that many tenants in these areas held their land on the basis of rent-payments in kind. Once such payments no longer sustained local lords and their retinue, then arguably, they would have been subject to the same unfavourable comparison with estates in the south and east as local demesne production. Viewed from a centre of decision-making in the heart of England, the peripheral component of supra-regional estates would have been seen as better suited to the production of cash rents rather than grain. A clear example of such logic being applied is provided by those parts of the Lordship of the Isles which fell into the hands of the Scottish king in the late fifteenth century. As soon as they became part of a system of lordship based on Edinburgh, albeit only temporarily, their customary grain-rents were converted to cash-rents.

The second way of approaching this problem is by looking at the ecology of manorialism. As Lennard was so anxious to stress, the better, more fertile land was already settled by 1086. The sort of land into which colonisation pushed during the eleventh, twelfth and thirteenth centuries was everywhere less fertile, less suited to arable and, therefore, to demesne production. Needless to add, this would have applied just as much to the interstitial areas of waste that still survived between manors in the south and east, to the large areas of heath and forest that survived in the south and east, as well as to the large areas of upland waste that remained in the north and west. The combination of poorer land being worked at a greater distance from manorial centres would have meant diminishing returns for any system of demesne production. But there was a further, more important point about the ecology of late colonisation. The land now being colonised offered a distinct type of resource-mix compared with areas of old-established arable land. These newer areas were of Thirsk's livestock-woodland or open-pasture type. To utilise them for an extension of demesne based on villein service was hardly to strike the best bargain, for the yield – relative to the inputs of labour – would have been poor. However, by contracting cash-based tenures, feudal lords enabled tenants to spread the burden of rent across a range of resources: arable, pasture and woodland. By doing so, they not only fostered subsystems based on a variety of new and more generalised adaptations, but ones that were capable of yielding far more feudal rent in marginal environments than could be yielded by demesne cultivation. Seen from this point of view, it is difficult to talk of a crisis of feudalism in these areas. What we are witnessing in these peripheral areas during the eleventh, twelfth and thirteenth centuries is an adaptation to new cicumstances which secured the lord's position rather than eroded it.

Some support for this view can also be gained by looking at the pattern of borough-creation. Hypothetically, it could be reasoned that if the creation of a system of monetised rents and dues in peripheral areas is to be taken as an alteration in the terms of feudalism, but not a concession by it, then we can expect lords to have established points of exchange where tenants could transform available resources into the cash needed to meet their obligations. In a society where lords controlled both rents and markets, we can reasonably expect some co-ordination between the two. In fact, the pattern of borough-creation shows that the need for co-ordination between the two may not have been lost on those who planned such affairs. The areas which acquired the densest network of boroughs lay to the north and west of the country. Thus, we have the further paradox that the areas with the highest population and greatest volume of trade, like East Anglia or the east Midlands, had fewer boroughs than, say, the south-west. Beresford and Finberg saw this contrast in terms of land quality, concluding that it was the least fertile parts of the country that had the most boroughs (Beresford and Finberg, 1973, p. 51). Admittedly, when ordinary market towns are taken into account, the pattern of provision is equalised. Recent work on such markets suggest that counties like Suffolk stand up favourably in comparison with counties like Devon when the problem is phrased in terms of ordinary markets as well as boroughs (Britnell, 1981, p. 210; Everitt, 1967, p.497). However, when we weigh the provision of markets against the size of local population, the conclusion must still be that peripheral areas were well-provided with markets. This logical association between market-provision and cash-rents suggests an analogy with the ideas of Smith. She made the point that even where entrepreneurs did not directly control factors of production, they could still appropriate a surplus through their control over the marketing system. The evolution of feudal control in the north and west of England enabled lords to control both the factors of production and the marketing system (Smith, 1976, p. 310).

The Decline of Feudalism: A Geographical Conflict?

If the distinction argued between core- and peripheral areas developed out of an adjustment in the terms of feudalism when faced with expansion, then when can we talk of its decline? The gist of the argument to be presented here is that once these core- and peripheral areas were integrated within the same market system, the disequilibrium caused by their differences worked against the regulated economies of the core. It is at this point that we can speak of a feudal system based on the manor and demesne production truly being dismantled. Implicit in many discussions of how the feudal system declined is the notion that once the growth of trade and the regular use of money had breached the traditional bonds between lord and peasant, then further decline was progressive and cumulative. Money rents and villeinage, said Harvey, were incompatible, the appearance of the one acting as a solvent of the other (Harvey, 1977, p. 239). This, though, would only be a sufficient explanation if the decay of feudalism was a process sustained entirely by changes from within its core-areas. Not only can we see money-rents and free tenures appearing widely in peripheral areas before core-areas, but – no less meaningful – they appeared as a rational response to new environments and the problems posed by peripheral locations, not as an attempt to dismantle an established system because it had ceased to be relevant to the times. Instead, we can argue that a more critical point in the decline of feudalism may have been when the wholly separate conditions of the periphery and those of the core were merged through the growth of more-integrated marketing systems.

It must be stressed that my discussion of this aspect is not put forward as a comprehensive review of the way that feudalism declined, but merely as a review of the way that the spatial structure of its decline may yield insights into the processes involved. Moving my argument forward, it is basic to what I am trying to say that conditions in the periphery could only affect those of the core if the two interacted through trade, exposing production functions in the latter to those of the former. In fact, there are good reasons why the two should become so linked. The more important is the quite different resource endowment of the two areas. In core-areas, the economy of both lord and peasant rested on grain-cropping. Peripheral and marginal areas, meanwhile, boasted a farming system in which arable farming was less important and pastoral farming more so. In addition, peripheral and marginal areas had a wide range of other resources: these included the basic industrial raw materials of the medieval period, such as wool, leather and timber. Some areas also possessed minerals. Such products were generally traded as raw materials or semi-finished products, with many peasants supplementing their income with a part-time trade or craft. When these differing resource endowments are taken into account, it requires little imagination to see the two sectors of the feudal domain – core and periphery – as possessing the sort of complementarity that we associate with upland and lowland, chalk and cheese, river and wold (see especially, Jones, 1981, p. 90; Langton and Hoppe, 1983, pp. 30–1). Such complementarity, of course, is the very stuff of trade. In reality, the greater flows tended to be from the north and west to the south and east, from the areas with the greatest variety of exploitable resources and the greater adaptability to prevailing opportunities of trade to the areas of greatest demand and, initially, industrial activity. It this interaction that prompted Hilton to remark that merchants made their profits out of the trade of 'isolated areas' or what he calls the 'backwards elements of the economy' (Hilton, 1952, p. 35) and what Jones had in mind when he talked about the market economy being a product of the non-market world (Jones, 1981, p. 102).

Any discussion of the interaction between core and periphery must at some point consider the terms of trade between them. Was it based on an elaborate system of equivalencies or did it involve principles of negative reciprocity with one side getting the better bargain? To answer this question, we need to remind ourselves again of the rigidities built into medieval prices. Men, said Postan, 'came to expect goods to exchange at constant ratios' (Postan, 1972, p. 225; see also, Everitt, 1967, p. 486). We can see this as a pricing system governed by equivalencies, with neither side trying to overturn the customary value of a good in relation to other goods. In other words, it was seen as a direct exchange of use-values. In the first instance, money entered transactions not because it established a pricing system that could be flexible but because it gave flexibility to the range of goods that could be equated. It is sometimes said that a further feature of early agricultural markets was the narrow range of goods involved. Arguably, this would be a more appropriate characterisation of rural markets in the core-areas of English feudalism. In peripheral areas, there are reasons to expect a different, more improvised situation. Taking the system of markets as a whole, the range of goods involved was more diverse, more innovative and more difficult to standardise in terms of quantity and quality. In the second place, the sort of economies that were starting to flourish by the late medieval period had no traditional framework to retard them. Indeed, their foundation called for initiative and enterprise not conservatism. Many of the products now being traded in and out of such areas could have not been covered by a traditional price because there had been no tradition. In fact, when Postan concedes the possibility of peasants being dependent on marketing and the prices set in the market-place, the examples which he cites are products of the periphery rather than the core (Postan, 1972, p. 226; see also, Slicher Van Bath, 1963, p. 33). The whole question of medieval prices must be seen in relative terms. Even prices that were subject to customary valuations or to strict regulation could vary on occasion. As Farmer found in his study of agricultural prices over the late twelfth and early thirteenth centuries, they could vary enormously from year to year so much so that it becomes difficult to disentangle short- and long-term variations (Farmer, 1956–7, p. 43; see also Postan, 1972, pp. 226–7). But even allowing for such price movements, it would still be reasonable to argue that the wider range of products and the lack of any customary restraint on prices in peripheral areas probably allowed for a greater amplitude of price variations and for an easier penetration of true price-fixing markets. However, with the major urban markets being in core areas and given the high trans-shipment costs to be overcome in order to reach them, we can expect this freer movement of prices, to have depressed rather than raised prices, to have transferred the location costs onto the peasant rather than consumer, especially if the peasants involved were more concerned with use-values than exchange values, more with supply rather than demand economics or with trying 'to maximize the gross product, not the net profit' (Medick, 1976, p. 298, see also, Dodgshon, 1983, pp. 46–59). Indeed, goods produced in peripheral areas were generally of a cheaper quality or type compared with the equivalent products of core-areas. Above all, labour and material costs were far lower in peripheral areas. By underpricing their labour, they could reach out to more-distant markets. In the process, they also provided the prospect of a differential profit, a profit that was to prove so attractive to mercantile capital in the seventeenth and early eighteenth centuries, enabling merchants to buy cheap and sell dear to their gross advantage.

Helping to buttress further the growing system of negative reciprocity between core and periphery may have been the social differences and distances between them. It has long been accepted by anthropologists that trade for gain is more likely to develop between social groups who see themselves as different, without common interest. As a distinction based on villeinage and freedom, it is possible to argue that core- and peripheral areas were sharply divorced in character, at least where they were constituted as separate communities. Indeed, as I mentioned earlier, there is an extensive literature on the subject. Where closely juxtaposed, as they must have been with many newly-colonised forest areas in the south and east, then, as Hilton has pointed out, their differences could lead to social tensions (Hilton, 1969, pp. 19–20). But we also need to know about their economic tensions. Bloch once wrote a paper in which he argued that the forms of payment used in medieval exchange – money or kind – varied with the closeness of the ties between lord and peasant. Interestingly, he saw the use of money as more likely where relationships were not customarily defined, that is, where their relationship had no traditional framework of reference (Bloch, 1967, pp. 230–43). Clearly, such conditions were most likely to be found on the periphery of the feudal system. If a valid presumption, we would need to see the contractual status of those peasants on the edge of the system as subject to a spatially- and socially-progressive decline in favour. It would of course make sense of a conversion to money-rents that initially had greater moment on the fringes of the system if, instead of being a progressive trend, it was perceived by lords as a conversion down, a mark of social distance. As in a system of negative reciprocity, the periphery may well have been seen as the 'unsocial extreme' in the context of the early Middle Ages.

For the geographer, the physical and social distance between core and periphery may have an additional significance. Their latent integration created new levels of market activity. In addition to earlier systems of local and international trade, one now had the slow emergence of interregional or national systems of trade. For Polanyi, what really mattered about these emergent national systems was not the complementarities of resource-endowment which it exploited, but the fact that it also brought areas producing broadly similar kinds of product – albeit under widely differing conditions of work, labour-cost and resource-availability – within the same arena of market activity. As this interaction gathered pace, regional economies would have been forced to compete with each other, to adjust to the equilibrium set by the region with the most favourable production functions.

National integration then, could lead ultimately to competitive trading markets (Polanyi, 1944, p. 60). Yet arguably, these early moves towards a national system of marketing need not have altered the peasant's relationship with his local market. Despite the increasing amount of peasant involvement with marketing throughout the sixteenth and seventeenth centuries, many peasants in peripheral areas would still have been concerned above all else with securing livelihood and, therefore, with use-values. The links now being established between markets, though, were probably charged with a growing interest in exchange values. We can typify this situation by using Marx's 'circulation of commodities' formula. The peasant produced commodities to raise money to buy more commodities ($P-M-P$). The merchant meanwhile used money to buy commodities to raise more money ($M-C-M$). Once we fix the different levels at which these values operated within the growing hierarchy of market organisation, we can see how they worked together. As a relation between the producer and his local market, the peasant's quest for use-values may have been aided but not yet transformed by the insertion of intermarket links in which the merchants quest for exchange-values was paramount.

Logically, it was those who controlled the flows between markets, who could take advantage of their separation in time and space, that gained most from any differences in price between them. With their complementarity and differential price structure, the slowly-evolving system of trade between core and periphery over the closing centuries of the medieval period would have enabled the merchants, broggers, chapmen and packmen who regulated such trade to gain from their imbalance. However, this still leaves us with the question of how the rapidly-expanding freedom of the one affected the other? Was it through the pressure which the freer conditions of peripheral areas could exert on the more inflexible price structure of core-areas? Perhaps, but even if the two sectors were locally-juxtaposed, such conflict could not have worked itself out directly or simply if farm production was based on contrasting habitats so that each yielded a different basket of produce. In fact, it was their role as growing centres of craft-production that enabled peripheral areas to compete directly with core-areas, slowly squeezing the older but fettered industries that were to be found in its urban centres and contributing substantially to the malaise that afflicted the urban economy over the sixteenth century. An alternative line argument is to ask whether changes in peripheral areas affected tenurial relationships in core-areas because lords saw the benefit to be gained from redefining their entire role in the system as that of *rentiers*? There were not the same gains to be made in core-areas by converting all feudal services and obligations into cash. Doing so did not extend the burden of rent from a narrow, arable sector out over a vast untapped reserve of non-arable resources to anything like the same degree as in peripheral areas. However, there was a substantial gain of a different sort to be made. By commuting services into cash, and above all by establishing a system of flexible economic rents that could be uprated with the trend of market prices, land-rents in core-areas could be made to bear the full price of their locational advantage within an evolving national system of markets. The sharp inflation of land-rents in the sixteenth century would have helped to pressurise core-areas into such a change, for it would have accentuated the problems of allowing any form of customary evaluation to survive at a time of rapidly changing values, particularly if the cash rents of peripheral areas were able to maintain their real value. There is certainly sufficient support for the idea that the struggle between lords and peasants over commutation was as much about the desire of lords to force customary tenements into the market-place as about the desire of the peasantry to free themselves from personal ties and obligations.

I have not attempted here to offer a comprehensive review of the way that English feudalism declined. Rather has my purpose been the much narrower one of making the geographical basis of its decline more explicit. The crux of my argument is that its later course of development possessed a geography which, in the words of D'Arcy Thompson, was a map of its tensions (Thompson, 1961, p. 11). This geography is the inverse of what might be tacitly assumed, with the shift towards cash-rents and personal freedom seemingly making greater progress in peripheral and marginal areas than in the core-areas of feudalism. Given the progressive tag normally attached to the monetisation of lord–peasant relations, this pattern would seem to be a mirror-image of what we might expect. As a map of the tensions involved though, it is a pattern which suggests that we cannot take our reading of the processes involved for granted. The apparently vigorous shift into cash-rents and personal freedom along the geographical edge of feudalism can be seen as an adaptation permitted by its growth into areas of 'unused freedom', not as a collapse through failure. Conceivably, the true start of its decline may have been when the forces activated within these peripheral areas, through their very success, swept like some great backwash of change over the institutional framework of core areas themselves. This offers what is very much a looking-glass sort of perspective on feudal decline, an inverse image, and it may be that Carr's strictures on the logic of Charles Lutwidge Dodgson, alias Lewis Carroll, to the effect that 'the Dodgsonian mode is not the mode of history' (Carr, 1964, p. 105) is an appropriate riposte to it. However, it is not inconsistent with those concepts of societal change which concede a critical role to less-organised peripheral areas, and which see the geographical structuring of the processes involved as having an intrinsic part to play in the whole process of societal change. As an idea, it compares closely with Harvey's notion of the 'spatial fix'. Is it possible, asked Harvey in a discussion of recent colonialism, that civil society tried to solve its inner contradictions by undergoing 'an outer transformation through imperialism, colonialism and geographical expansion?' (Harvey, 1981, p. 2). The answer I have tried to give in the foregoing chapter is yes, but that we need to see such change through expansion as operating in both a relative and absolute sense, both within and without state systems.

9
Taking Space to Market

The replacement of regulated markets by price-fixing or competitive markets set in motion a narrower, more insistent restructuring of space. In being taken to market, space was allocated to those uses or users that yielded the highest rent. In whatever terms we choose to see it – as location, resource, structure or activity – it became capitalised, treated as something that could be taken to market and sold at the highest bid-price, its price being used to balance levels of consumption with levels of supply. In the process, it became predominantly ordinated and configured through economic forces, or as Polanyi might have put it, something embedded in economy. There are, of course, other ways of construing the spatial order that was ushered in by early capitalism. In a recent study, for instance, Harvey was quite specific in his abandonment of price-fixing markets as the central, integrating mechanism of capitalism, a mechanism that permeated his conceptualisation of the capitalist city in an earlier study (Harvey, 1973, pp. 261–74), preferring instead to recouch his analysis as a problem of capital and its spheres of circulation (Harvey, 1982, p. xiii). In a text that tries to tease out and extend the ideas with which Marx dealt in his treatise on capital, he follows the latter in seeing capitalist profit as arising out of the relations between capital and wage labour, more especially the differential between the value of labour power and the value that labour-power produces, and not as something created through market exchange (Harvey, 1973, p. 23). Harvey accepts that competitive markets determine the price of commodities but not that they create, in themselves, the surplus value on which capitalist profit is based. In a sense, his displacement of the market mechanism from a central to an accessory role within capitalism reflects his interest in the nature of capitalism at large. In reply, I would argue that when we reduce the problem to those spheres which had to do with the way that capital is configured in space, directed to those areas or sectors in which it will give the

287

highest return, then we are dealing with the nature and operation of price-fixing markets. In other words, if we wish to construct a geography of capitalism as opposed to a model of capitalism in its entirety, then the bid-price mechanism must loom large in our considerations.

The emergence of such markets was a prolonged affair. They were not legislated into existence overnight or given a ready-made domain of operation, but evolved slowly, both in a geographical and organisational sense. How their activity was broadened must represent our first line of enquiry. In exploring this problem, we need to consider the way in which their orbit was extended so as to integrate more space at, first, an international and, second, national level. Third we need to examine the way in which they spread through an ever-widening array of commodities, pricing each according to what the market was prepared to bid. The prising-open of land- and labour-markets to a freer bid-price mechanism was especially critical, for control over rents and wages provided a means by which the volume (as opposed to the range) of goods could be pressurised into expansion, the one by being increased and the other by being devalued. Fourth, the expansion of price-fixing markets into new areas of space and new sectors of operations precipitated scalar problems for the organisation of trading activity. Although I propose to explore these scalar problems in relation to metropolitan centres, where they were most acutely felt, they were problems that ultimately affected market systems generally. Fifth, no examination of how price-fixing markets emerged would be complete without consideration of the way in which their scalar growth induced changes in their organisation. In fact, the institutional character of price-fixing markets experienced the same sort of evolutionary trends that affected societal systems at large, with a progressive differentiation, then hierarchisation of roles and functions, integrating national and international space into a single, continuously expanding system. Yet this progressive elaboration, with competitive markets penetrating into more and more space and more and more commodities, does not mean we can treat them as a simple innovation, one that spread neatly and tidily along a single frontier of change, integrating one new regional cell after another into what became a national, then an international space economy, in the manner described by Gras (1926, pp. 89 *et seq.*). Different sectors and different levels expanded more quickly than others. Different spheres of opportunity and different lines of communication were penetrated more quickly than others, so that its early spread was in a selective, spatially non-continuous fashion (see Figure 9.1). Clouding the picture further, the evolving or deepening organisation of price-fixing markets meant that their effects were layered, with crude, undressed forms of free market being the first institutional form to spread and sophisticated, highly structured forms succeeding them. Armed with this sort of view, the geographer's natural task of sectorising space into areas controlled through price-fixing markets and areas without such markets, becomes an elusive goal. Even in a well-documented country like Britain, the widely-differing views about when regional economies became integrated into a national space-economy illustrate the difficulties of trying to arrive at a gross statement.

As a second broad line of enquiry, we also need to explore the effect that price-fixing markets had on the structuring of space and spatial order. I want to argue that the spatial order produced by price-fixing markets passed through successive but temporary equilibria, each attuned to a particular scale of market activity (cf. Pollard, 1981, p. 30). At one level, we can see this as a simple problem of relaxation-time, or how long it took for the structures produced under one set of market conditions to change into those consistent with an ensuing set. At a higher level, though, it needs to be seen in relation to all the issues raised by the mobility of capital and the effect which this had in fluxing the use of space. Running through my discussion of these themes will be a stress on the fact that whilst we can speak of price-fixing markets as slowly establishing themselves as the prime determinant of spatial order by the mid-nineteenth century, it does not follow that we can speak of real-world systems of spatial order given coherence or integrated through the equilibrium conditions of a single market. The reason why is of the essence to any understanding of how price-fixing markets produced spatial order. Put simply, space had to be referred to price-fixing markets if the latter was to have an allocative effect on how it was used. This was a process in time as well as space. It depended on the decisions and transactions of countless individuals who could only respond to market pressures and opportunities in a way that was marginal rather than substantial and in a way that was intermittent rather than continuous. For

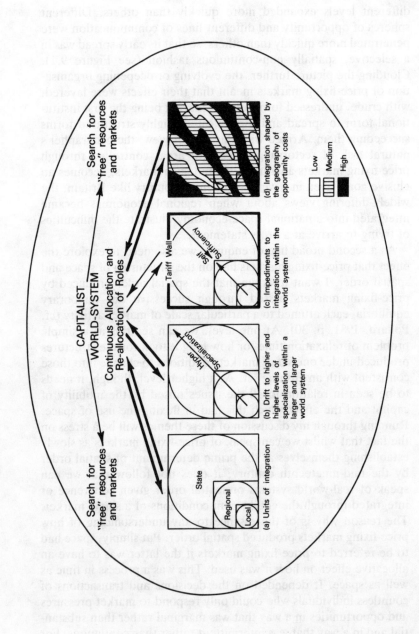

CAPITALIST WORLD-SYSTEM

Continuous Allocation and Re-allocation of Roles

Search for "free" resources and markets

Search for "free" resources and markets

(a) Units of integration

State

Regional

Local

(b) Drift to higher and higher levels of specialization within a larger and larger world system

Hyper specialization

(c) Impediments to integration within the world system

Tariff Wall

Self Sufficiency

(d) Integration shaped by the geography of opportunity costs

Low

Medium

High

this reason, the ability of price-fixing markets to produce a wholly compatible spatial order was a slow, cumbersome affair. Given the intrinsic tendency for market conditions to change in a regular cyclical way, to adjust to successive equilibria, this relatively sluggish adjustment of spatial order caused the landscape to evolve through a succession of partial, incomplete adjustments. If we define compatibility between price-fixing markets and spatial order as a condition in which the latter is so organised as to yield the highest possible rent under a given set of market conditions, then real-world spatial order could only approach such a degree of compatibility, or efficiency (Berry, 1973, p. 493) but never reach it. It was a system of spatial order that was always becoming, yet always liable to be overtaken by a change in the equilibrium of markets, a change that projected new parameters of supply and demand over the landscape. In effect, the idea of a landscape wholly integrated through price-fixing markets is no more than a mirage of capital. The reality is always of a landscape compounded of successively-formed and superimposed market conditions, one that must be decomposed into these different dimensions if it is to be effectively understood.

I propose to develop such ideas by looking at the effect which price-fixing markets had on the spatial ordering of factory, town and farm. In each case, Britain provides the main source of illustration. Driven forward by its pioneering industrial, urban and agricultural revolutions, Britain was the first country in Europe to experience the large-scale reorganisation of its spatial order through the institution of competitive markets. Transformed by industrial capitalism, new technologies and the factory system, its industrial economy established radically new parameters of production. It cannot be said to have originated an international system of raw-material supply and product-distribution, but it did

---

FIGURE 9.1 *Price-fixing Markets and the Economic Integration of Space*

NOTE With the emergence of a world-system of price-fixing markets, the organisation of space becomes an economic process that envelops and even transcends political space. This drift to a global system of economic integration via economic specialisation develops at each level of state order, the local, regional and national, the whole process being advanced or retarded by the geography of opportunity costs, costs that could be varied by natural factors (such as navigable rivers) or residual political barriers (for instance, tariff walls).

magnify the scale of flows involved considerably. Many of the peculiarly spatial problems experienced by industrial capitalism, such as the greater place-specificity, and with it, the reduced adaptability to change, conferred by the novel build-up of investment in fixed as opposed to circulating capital, are first apparent in a British context. As the first urban-industrial society if not the first society with large urban centres, British towns were the first to show how price-fixing markets could impose their own sense of order on urban space. As I intend to show, this is far from being a straightforward point. It was not simply a case of cities being differentiated into different sectors via the bid-price mechanism once they reached a certain population. Other factors need to be taken into consideration, such as the outward expansion of cities in space and the generalisation of its inhabitants into simpler, broader groups or classes. Generally speaking, these other variables have received considerable attention of late from British historical geographers, making the socio-genesis of the British industrial town the most studied in Europe. Propelled by the demands of, first, London, and then, its rapidly growing system of industrial towns, it also created a network of food supply that spread its tentacles out not just over many parts of Britain, but also, over many parts of western and northern Europe and, eventually, out as far as the Americas, Africa and Australasia: the first truly global system of spatial interaction.

The Broadening of Price-Fixing Markets

Price-fixing markets expanded by subjecting an ever-wider range of resources over an ever-wider area to competitive pricing. By their very nature, price-fixing markets were always inclined to expand. Their lack of regulation enabled individuals living on the margins of subsistence to circumvent strict controls over prices, quality, conditions of work and so on, thus opening up petty production to a far greater pool of labour. Hovering above them, merchants seeking to capitalise on the exchange value of commodities saw free markets as a means whereby they could create for themselves an ever-broadening circle of capital plus interest, simply by buying where labour and commodities were cheap and selling where they were dear. Once provided with an area of the economy in which exchange could take place freely, merchants would naturally have worked to broaden it, compounding their interest as capital after each cycle of investment.

During the early growth of free markets, such expansionary forces would not have proceeded unchecked but would have come up against all the custom and rigidity that surrounded older regulated markets. While we can talk of price-fixing or supply–demand–price markets being established locally or sectorally by the close of the medieval period, it was not until the nineteenth century that we can speak of societies and their spatial order being widely and securely embedded in economic processes (Polanyi, 1968 pp. 26–37; Harvey, 1973, pp. 242–3; Braudel, 1977, pp. 40–1). In other words, we still have to ask how they breached the areas or sectors in which they first developed.

At an abstract level, it involved a change from the idea that money-making was a vice, a potential source of disorder if not controlled, to the idea prevalent by the early eighteenth century that it could be beneficial to society, even an activity out of which order could arise (Hirschman, 1977, especially pp. 41–2 and 56; cf. Thompson, 1971, p. 90). By the time Adam Smith was writing in the late eighteenth century, money-making had become something justified on its own terms, that is, an activity that was economically rather than politically advantageous (Hirschman, 1977, pp. 82–3). However, to understand the eventual occlusion of regulated markets, we need to understand more than just the inner workings of price-fixing markets and how they vented the needs and problems of commercial capitalism. We need to relate them to the historical conditions and opportunities that unfolded over the sixteenth, seventeenth and eighteenth centuries, for these historically-determinate conditions and opportunities were decisive in triggering the final shift into a *laissez-faire* economy. We can group the factors involved under two broad headings: those which raised the general level of trade and spatial interaction and those which concentrated it on specific organising centres.

The First World-System?

As regards the first group of factors, we can identify a critical phase of change starting in the sixteenth century, when, after a phase of stagnation, trade began to recover and grow rapidly. The opportunities presented by the opening-up of the New World, the establishment of sea-routes to the Orient and the quickening of flows between western Europe and the Baltic played a crucial part in this energising of trade. They injected a wider, more diverse range of goods, afforded scope for new forms of trading organisation and agreements and tapped distant areas of supply whose forceful exploitation posed no threat to the social order of the European states. In fact, from the very outset, the colonies were seen as a source of exchange, not of use-values. Their shift into systems of production based on coerced labour can be seen as part of their adaptation to trade at a distance, the tyranny of man over man being used to offset the tyranny of distance. State-systems responded to the new opportunities opened up by this growth in overseas trade by evolving mercantilist policies that were designed to secure the trading interests of the state as a whole. In effect, they took the privileges and monopolies that had hitherto existed at the level of the town and create an additional layer at the level of the state itself. This new level of regulation took two forms. First, trade with key areas became channelled through privileged companies. Select spheres of Dutch trade were monopolised by the Dutch East India Company (1602) and the Dutch West India Company (1621), whilst comparable spheres of English trade were monopolised by the English East India Company (1600), the English Hudson Bay Company (1670) and the Royal African Company (1672). Second, the European states sought to surround themselves with a wall of protectionist measures. These could amount to little more than tariffs on imported goods: this is how the German states and France responded. In the case of England, the measures enacted went further. Anxious to create a closed relationship with its colonies, it passed a series of Navigation Acts throughout the 1660s, 1670s and 1690s that weighted the terms of colonial trade in its favour and restricted such trade to English ships and ports. Not surprisingly, the second half of seventeenth century saw a massive expansion of English maritime trade and shipping, a system and capacity 'created out of nothing', though its rate of growth paled a little towards the close of the century (Davis, 1962, pp. 2–23). Between 1572 and 1629, the tonnage of English shipping grew from 50 000 tons to 115 000 tons, an expansion largely sustained by an expansion in coastal traffic. By 1686, the surge in overseas trade had pushed the total to 340 000 tons. After a temporary decline in tonnage around 1700, the momentum of growth recovered with tonnage reaching 1 055 000 by 1788

(Davis, 1962, p. 27), a twenty-fold increase since the late sixteenth century. Even before the end of the seventeenth century, the size of the English merchant fleet and the value of trade being handled surpassed that of the Dutch, and English hegemony over international trade had started to replace Dutch hegemony (Wallerstein, 1980, pp. 75 *et seq.*). During the eighteenth century, it consolidated this position (Rostow, 1975, pp. 116–17). With such a scalar growth, we can hardly be surprised if it transcended traditional institutions of trade, spawning new, more efficient forms, more efficient in the sense of being able to cope more effectively with the quickening pulse of trade activity.

Not unreasonably, the growth of regulated trade between countries, or mercantilism has been seen as a means of providing the more centralised states that emerged over the sixteenth and seventeenth centuries with an economic identity. An equally fertile source of inspiration is likely to have been the concern by state rulers to encourage industrial production. To this extent, it can be seen as a shift in emphasis when compared with medieval policies which attended more to the way that goods were distributed between consumers. This is a shift on which Dobb especially, laid great stress. What mattered most to mercantilist thinking, he argued, was net profit: this could be achieved by a shift in the terms of trade (Dobb, 1946, pp. 200–4; Wallerstein, 1980, pp. 37–8). Noting the way in which the regulated systems of internal trade inhibited such a shift in the context of internal trade, or at least those sectors that were regulated, he saw their effort as directed towards the great areas of new opportunity that now opened up through trade with the colonies (Dobb, 1946, p. 210). Speaking specifically of England, he saw mercantilist policy as working towards a 'dependent' relationship between colonies and the metropolitan economy, one rigged and endorsed through state policy, in which low-cost raw materials and agricultural produce were exchanged for relatively high-cost manufactured goods (Dobb, 1946, p. 207, cf. Wallerstein, 1980, p. 71). By the end of the eighteenth century, this concern with the rate of profit gave way to an equal concern with further expanding the volume of trade at these rates (Dobb, 1946, p. 218). This phasing has a bearing on how price-fixing markets spread. The initial growth of colonial trade tended to extend the regulated conditions of medieval trade, with carefully defined monopolies over who could trade with whom and on what terms. Yet despite this regulated framework, considerations of the national interest, together with the speculative nature of such trade, was used – from the very outset – to legitimate high profit rates for those companies privileged to take part in it. However, when attention turned to expanding the volume of such trade to still greater levels, it would have seemed far easier to achieve this goal by dismantling its regulated and monopolistic nature and allowing it to expand through the open and easy attraction of fresh investment than by trying to force more trade through the fettered and inflexible institutions of early colonial trade. In this sense, its sequence of development might be contrasted with that of national trade, with the dismantling of trade regulation being contributory to, rather than a consequence of, its rapid scalar growth.

The Integration of National Space

Matching the growth of overseas trade was a build-up of internal trade. For Polanyi, this was to prove a powerful solvent of regulated trade since it involved spheres of trade that acted alongside and, in time, became interwoven with regulated forms. There can be no disputing this point. In essence though, it simply activated the same forces and pressures which we have noted in respect of overseas trade, with areas of opportunity being used to establish new forms of relationship, new customs of trade, and with their subsequent success in an overall system of expanding trade helping to undermine regulated forms. Taking a closer look at how internal trade expanded, the key factor, around 1500 was still the high, prohibitive cost of inland transportation. Apart from lowering costs of production by finding cheaper reserves of raw material or labour, trade over any distance – interregional trade – could only develop if transport costs were lowered through improvements in transportation. In the event, what we see taking place is a succession of improvements spread out over the early modern period, each prompted by the strains and limitations gradually imposed on trade by its growth under existing systems, each lowering the real cost of transport and each, in consequence, allowing a further scalar jump in the volume of trade. Although both geographers and historians have talked freely about the break-up of regional isolation and the creation of integrated national economies as if this occurred suddenly and decisively, the reality is that the pace of regional integration progressed through a series of upward-moving but broken curves, some admittedly steeper than others, but each set in motion by a significant change in the opportunity costs of trade to which the volume of trade then worked to adapt itself. Indeed, with writers like Elias talking of early state-systems being slowly integrated through a rising tide of interregional flows and interaction and others seeing this as the achievement of the Industrial Revolution, we can hardly see the problem otherwise. In truth, we have no means by which we can calibrate degrees of spatial integration except in gross terms.

Mention has already been made of the basic fact that medieval trade moved with less resistance and significantly less cost over water than over land. The appetite of towns and the needs of its craftsmen could reach out further and draw in more if it could do so via navigable rivers (or coastwise) than if it was forced to use pedlars, pack-horses and carts. Estimates of their respective costs suggest that by the sixteenth and seventeenth centuries, the cost of transporting goods by land could be as much as four or five times greater than transporting them by river, but that the more circuitous route taken by rivers lowered the differential to only a two-or threefold difference (Willan, 1964, p. 119; Pawson, 1977, pp. 22–3; Chartres, 1977a, p. 43). Naturally, different countries had differing potentials in this respect. France, for instance, has an excellent network of navigable rivers that were widely used over the late medieval period for the transport of goods and passengers, with boatmen on some rivers, such as the Seine and Loire, organising themselves into powerful syndicates. However, apart from the problem of high, exorbitant tolls, the prime difficulty for France was that whilst rivers like the Rhone and Seine struck deep indland, they did not provide the basis for a nationally-integrated network, tending instead to channel flows outwards rather than inwards (Price, 1983, p. 11). Although by the seventeenth century attempts were being made to breach the various watersheds with canals, like the early attempt to link the Seine and Loire via the Loing valley, and although the Canal du Midi provided an ambitious link between the Atlantic and Mediterranean, there still remained large areas beyond water-borne access and still no facility for moving goods by river between the north and south of the country. Indeed, lacking this 'early' form of natural connectivity, France remained notoriously disintegrated from an economic point of view until the coming of the railways in the mid-nineteenth century. Holland and England were better served. The former had a river network that criss-crossed the countryside and, through its polder land reclamation, had acquired considerable expertise in the engineering of river improvements and canals. With the surge of inland transportation over the seventeenth century, the rate of return from improvements in water-borne transport rose accordingly, triggering a massive investment over the middle decades of the century, but especially between 1630–60. Rivers were widened and new canals built, including an extensive network of *trekvaarts*, narrow canals intended primarily for passenger use between the major towns (de Vries, 1974, pp. 206–7: de Vries, 1978, pp. 56–64). The sum effect was that by the late seventeenth century Holland had a more complete network of interregional waterways than any other European state, a network that supported a regular and sizeable flow of people between all the major nodes of its urban system (de Vries, 1978, pp. 347–9).

England too, possessed a good river network. Faced with a surge in inland trade over the seventeenth century, it also looked to improve its river-based system: the 1095 km of navigable rivers which it had in 1660 was extended to 1536 km by 1700 and 1856 km by the 1720s (Willan, 1964, p. 133). Yet whilst key areas of its economic space were within reasonable distance of a waterway by the 1720s, it would greatly overstate the degree of connectivity provided by navigable rivers if we saw them as providing a sufficient basis for the integration of national space (Fullerton, 1975, p. 8; Freeman, 1980, p. 27). Significant improvements in road transport both complemented and competed with this extension of inland waterways, helping to lower the cost of moving goods to river-ports and providing alternative, more direct routes. The importance of road transport in raising levels of intra- and inter-regional movement, especially over the seventeenth and eighteenth centuries, has been strongly highlighted by recent studies (see, for example, Freeman, 1980, p. 19). Between the 1660s and the 1760s, when the growing interconnectedness of the English industrial economy began to place severe demands on all forms of transportation, the waggon capacity on English roads rose dramatically from around 30 cwts to six tons, lowering costs at a time when prices were increasing (Albert, 1972, p. 181; Chartres, 1977a, p. 40). One estimate is that between 1500 and 1700, the capacity of English road transport grew three- or four-fold (Chartres, 1977a, p. 40). The upswing in the growth rate of English industrial output after 1740 and even more so after 1780 created demands, or rather rewards, for a still more efficient and more connected system. The market response was the development of turnpikes, roads maintained and improved through the levying of tolls. From their beginning in the 1690s, the number of turnpikes trusts increased rapidly from 143 in 1750, to 519 in 1770 and 942 in 1836, accounting in all for 35 185 km of road by 1836 (Pawson, 1977, p. 114). Although there was a tendency for turnpikes to emphasise the connectivity of London, it is important to keep in mind a point stressed by Freeman. Addressing the suggestion made by Wrigley that the Industrial Revolution, with its shift from organic to inorganic resources, introduced a need for moving large quantities of low-value materials like coal along a limited number of basic routes – a need met by canals and later, by railways (Wrigley, 1962, pp. 1–16) – he tries to balance it by drawing out the needs of a growing national market. In the early stages of the Industrial Revolution, the diffused nature of the latter required a system capable of distributing small quantities of goods and produce over a wide area, a requirement satisfied only by roads (Freeman, 1980, p. 19; Chartres, 1977b, p. 78; Turnbull, 1977, p. 26). As this network of better roads developed, new patterns of transportation developed. Better roads meant that more traffic was transferred from pack-horse to waggons, whilst the carrier services that had first emerged during the late medieval period were able to realise a new potential, covering the landscape with a dense, reticulated network and providing a regular service in goods and market information not just between market towns and their hinterlands, but also, between towns (Pawson, 1977, pp. 30–40; Chartres, 1977b, p. 77). In a study based on the period 1637–1715, Chartres found that the number of carrier services more than doubled (Chartres, 1977b, p. 86). Over the eighteenth century, growth was fitful over the first half but gathered fresh pace towards the close, with, for example, the number of carriers and services working out of London and those operating around Manchester more than doubling, 1772–97 (Turnbull, 1977, pp. 29–30). Between 1800 and 1880, the number of carriers and, *pari passu*, services doubled yet again, a growth that was as marked after the coming of the railways as before, a continued growth that can be ascribed to their ability to sustain local, small-scale flows and to function as a feeder service (Everitt, 1976, p. 196). Indeed, more than any other change, it was the carrier that breached the isolation of local space, for it made local trade both cheaper and more predictable, and above all, possible.

Transport had an constantly evolving character. The needs of trade over the sixteenth and seventeenth centuries had primarily been for a system of transport that could cope with collecting and distributing relatively small quantities of materials or goods to and from petty producers scattered over the countryside or could reach down to the individual farm (Wrigley, 1962, pp. 1–16). Far from disappearing, this scale of need actually expanded with industrial-isation, as the needs of consumers scattered over a wide area were satisfied. However, as Wrigley observed, the changes of the eighteenth century witnessed a gradually enhanced demand for the transport of large quantities of cheap, bulky commodities like coal between a more limited range of points (Wrigley, 1962, p. 7). Canal construction was taken up as the response, attracting vast sums of investment and yielding high rates of profit during the late eighteenth and early nineteenth centuries with the local schemes of the eighteenth century giving way to schemes floated on the London capital market by the nineteenth century (Fullerton, 1975, pp. 14–15). Bound up with their appeal as a source of investment was their effect in halving the cost of transporting commodities like coal, thereby encouraging greater flows over greater distances. It is this facility for transporting bulky raw materials that explains why as much early investment was directed at building canals within or between major industrial areas like Lancashire and the Black Country as with establishing links between them and the London market (Moyes, 1978, pp. 409–13).

By the 1830s, the pressure for still further improvement was answered by the development of the railways, a system that allowed for a more flexible system, easier construction, faster speeds and greater volumes. Again, its patent advantage led to a rapid increase in investment. As with turnpikes and canals before them, this increase was greatly facilitated during the early phases of its diffusion by high rates of return on capital: the one acting as a magnet for the other. Also like turnpikes and canals, the railway network first developed as a radial system fanning out of London towards other major urban centres and as a system of linkages within the major industrial regions: the reticulation of inter-regional routes outside London, though, followed quickly. By 1880,

28 800 km had been laid and only the outer edges of national space remained to be connected. Despite the assertion that the social savings from the development of railways were modest rather than spectacular (Hawke, 1970, pp. 6–23), study after study has highlighted the way in which the connectivity conferred by the railway, the degree of accessibility which it opened up between regions, wrought fundamental changes in what could be taken in and out of regions. The principle of comparative advantage now began to operate with brutal effect on production systems everywhere. Reaping the benefits from adopting larger and larger scales of production, the more successful industrial centres were able to command national as well as international markets. The manufacture of agricultural implements is a good illustration here for it was an activity that, prior to the railways, was widely diffused, a by-product of innumerable small forges and blacksmiths. With the accessibility afforded by the railways, a dramatic thinning in the number of producers occurred, a process that eventually culminated in the collapse of local rural producers over the 1850s, 1860s and 1870s when railway penetration and local carrier-services gave the larger manufacturers access even to the most remote recesses of the countryside. Greater accessibility into the countryside, though, also meant greater accessibility out of it. For those prepared to adjust to new more market-orientated systems or to new roles within a more enlarged system, the railway proved decisive. What had been the privilege of those farmers close to market centres or those whose handicap of distance was lessened by proximity to canal, river or sea, now became open to a far larger population of producers. Areas hitherto removed from the pull of urban markets, like west Wales (Howell, 1977, pp. 119–27) now found themselves drawn – or pushed through the instrument of rent-inflation – into a market response.

The coming of the railway compressed space throughout western Europe. For a country like France, it was the first real opportunity for market activity to foster a nationally-integrated economy, to transform the self-sufficiency or marginal specialisation of its regions into a system of interlocking, interdependent economies (Price, 1983, p. 291). Over the middle decades of the nineteenth century, 12 000 km of railway were constructed. Like a web woven around a spider, it was a network that emphasised the centrality of Paris.

The development of inland transportation systems, 1500–1900, provide a positive measure of how trade developed within nation states over this period. Their progressive improvement provided a more capable, efficient and cheaper system of moving goods, people and ideas at all the different scales – the local, regional and national – at which economies were now becoming functionally integrated. We can see such improvement as something that both responded to and acted upon the gathering tide of internal trade, a constant adjustment in the face of new demands, each adjustment establishing a higher capacity and, therefore, a new propensity for trade. The structures of spatial interaction that slowly emerged out of these developments are dealt with later. All I am concerned with here is to record the growing facility and volume of internal trade. Like the growth of international trade over the same period, it undermined the insular worlds of regulated trade. The more trade grew, the more space became interconnected and interdependent and the more regulated and unregulated forms of trade became interwined. As this fusion occurred, the greater success of unregulated forms would have contributed substantially to the final dissolution of regulated forms that we see over the seventeenth and eighteenth centuries.

The Broadening Content of Trade

Bound up with the geographical and scalar expansion of trade was an increase in the range of goods and commodities being brought to market. It is·a fact that many of the industries that flourished over the sixteenth and seventeenth centuries were not covered or restrained by any form of customary regulation. The manufacture of products like gunpowder, bricks, linen, paper, refined sugar and the vast range of new metalware products that now began to find their way into the market-place were all new and, for this reason, without any tradition of control. As Coleman has pointed out, the declining importance of regulation owed much to 'the practical difficulties of applying an ancient policy to a changed structure of output' (D. C. Coleman, 1977, p. 179). In effect, the regulated sector of trade was being by-passed by a more dynamic unregulated sector. Even textiles, the most carefully administered of medieval trades, did not escape this problem. Much of the growth that we see taking place over the sixteenth and seventeenth centuries involved new products in areas that lay outside older production centres. The problem was partly caused by the inflexible nature of regulations that had a strong place-specific component written into them. Confronted with the burgeoning growth of new textile products in countryside areas, and more seriously, the latter's freedom to adapt product-quality or labour rates to the run of the market, older urban centres were well-nigh impotent. Despite the Statute of Artificers in 1563 restricting all cloth-production to authorised boroughs, urban centres were powerless to stop the broadening of the industry, both as regards its location and product. However, we need to draw a distinction between the ordinary craftsman, with his apprentice and journeyman, and those who, by the sixteenth century, had begun to take on a more entrepreneurial role and who – though part of the urban community – were attracted by the cheap labour of the countryside (Unwin, 1904, p. 11; Dobb, 1946, pp. 129–30). Just as Kisch found in a highly relevant study of Cologne, when faced with the ossifying effect of urban regulations, such would-be merchants 'rushed forth over the city walls in order to galavanize the inhabitants of an unencumbered countryside' (Kisch, 1972, p. 298; see also Kisch, 1964, p. 523), taking advantage of the fact that rural production was more adaptable to new market opportunities (Kisch, 1972, p. 517). It was this urban control of rural production that fostered the simple division of labour between town and country which was to prove such a feature of areas like East Anglia, with rural areas engaged in preparing and spinning the wool and urban areas being responsible for weaving and the finishing trades.

Having an equally important bearing on the growth of free markets was the fact that many of the industries that we see growing over the sixteenth, seventeenth and early eighteenth centuries evolved a closer more responsive relationship to market trends. We find them searching out a market niche for themselves either by cheapening their product, devising new ones or by creating a new style or type of established product. In fact, this proved to be an age of product innovation, an age when staple industries like textile production and the metal trades experienced a dramatic diversification. This diversification was a feature of most rural industrialising regions in western Europe but it was one most sharply accented in England. If we compare the geography of textile production in 1500 with that in 1700, we find that much of the geographical broadening that had taken place had involved the innovation of a wide array of local cloths, including serges, worsteds and 'new draperies', narrowcloths, medleys, linen and hosiery. A particularly fine description of how the metalware trades of the Black Country were diversified over the late seventeenth and early eighteenth centuries has been published by Rowlands. Driven forward by an expanding home market, a rapidly expanding colonial market and, in time, by its successful invasion of European markets, the output of metalwares from the Black Country grew impressively, surging strongly from the 1660s onwards (Rowlands, 1975, p. 129). Its growth owed much to its responsiveness to a widening market for basic goods such as harnesses, axes, scythes, pots and pans, candlesticks, nails, etc., and to the flourishing market now opening up for 'decencies' like buckles, pins, fine locks, metal toys, tinderboxes and fenders, a responsiveness that mixed product innovation with a willingness to use new materials such as brass, japanned tin. As part of this evolving response, more and more of the industry passed under the control of 'gentlemen manufacturers', men who perceived that new markets could be exploited or secured by anticipating and marketing fashionable goods, fashionable in the sense that demand for them was buoyant and in the sense that they satisfied a prevailing taste (Rowlands, 1975, p. 154; see also, Jones, 1973, pp. 198–226; McKendrick, 1982, pp. 1–2 and 9). With this elaboration, the web of geographically-mapped specialisms became still more intricate, different villages and communities being associated with different products or styles. It was a shift towards a more geographically-elaborate system of industrial production that affected many other areas. Out of it was born the geographical complexity that some have rightly seen as a notable feature of pre-industrial England (see, for example, Langton, 1979, p. 52).

Of immense significance to the development of price-fixing markets was their broadening into commodities that were not ordinarily produced for market: these were what Polanyi called the commodity fictions of land and labour. He considered the opening up of a free market in land to have been a product of the late eighteenth century and the changes in manufacturing technique ushered in by the factory system and mechanisation. These led to a build-up of fixed capital (see pp. 321–3). As industry became more dependent on fixed capital investment, more committed to heavy investment in specific blocks of land, industrialists moved to force land into the market-place. To protect their investment and to ensure the continued expansion of production, they needed to be able to bid for land. This is a valid statement of how the large-scale industrialisation of the late eighteenth and nineteenth centuries contributed to the onset of a free market in land but it tells us little about how such a market actually originated. Above all it ignores the shifts towards a freer market in land that can be seen in both the countryside and the town in the medieval period. A central weakness of Polanyi's reasoning here is that he has a sense of space but not of location. He ignores the implications of the fact that if the supply of land is finite, the supply of 'good' or 'desirable' locations is even more so. What stressed the customary evaluation of land was the greater value which consumers now began to place on some land above others, and their willingness to bid up for it. We can identify broad locations in both the country-side and the town in which this was happening even by the end of the medieval period, though I would question whether we can talk of anything like a finely-worked gradient of values. More general stress on any customary evaluation was also exerted by the sixteenth-century price-revolution. Bound by customary rents at a time of rapid price inflation, many landlords – both urban and rural – pressurised old-established leaseholds into the market-place. The sheer scale of price-inflation would have been a source of considerable disequilibrium as rents and prices chased each other. Finally, any attempt to improve land by building or re-building on it would have provided a basis for renting space on a more selective basis. This may have been a factor in the early appearance of an active land-market in Italian towns like Venice and Florence, for site-improvement was a strong feature by the fourteenth century. In England, a similar adjustment of urban rents would have followed the improvement, or what Vance calls the capitalisation, of urban land (Vance, 1971, p. 107) over the seventeenth century, when timber-framed and fire-prone buildings were replaced in town-centre locations by larger, stone-built dwellings: those in London, were built up to five storeys, a density of use that may have been designed, in part, as a trade-off against higher rents per acre. Yet however much we stress the precocious nature of land-markets, we must not hurry their development too quickly. Substantive studies of the problem still find it possible to speak of an imperfectly developed land-market as late as the mid-nineteenth century. This was true even in England. The

306 The European Past

problem, as Thompson discovered, was that although land was generally sold by auction to the highest bidder, the amount of land changing hands was not sufficient to foster a single or centralised market or the specialised jobbers and dealers handling a continuous flow of business (Thompson, 1957, p. 285). Lack of integration was accentuated by the fact that the price of land was not tested regularly or evenly in the market-place, as if it was a true commodity produced for sale. A welter of factors, from the monopoly control and idiosyncratic policies of particular landlords to the vagaries of different leasehold systems, could intervene here. Between sales or lease agreements, its value could soon lose touch with market conditions unless inflation or improvement was covered by an advancing rent. So entrenched had a free-market mentality become in other spheres by this point that some contemporaries viewed this imperfect operation as 'an affront to harmony and symmetry, a nagging flaw in the perfection of the structure of markets' (Thompson, 1957, p. 285).

The penetration of price-fixing markets into labour was no less vital in the evolution of a spatial order shaped in its outlines by market forces. We can frame this development in terms of three overlapping sets of relationship. First, there was the emergent relationship between capital and hired labour, the very essence of capitalism as a system of production. As an organisational adjustment that introduced greater coherence into what had been a differentiated but weakly-integrated system of production, we can see the penetration of merchant capital into the purely domestic system of production and the establishment of putting-out systems as bound up with the increasing scale of production and not just as a reorganisation without growth. This is not to insist on the necessity for merchant capital but only to note that any scalar increase in production, any gains to be made from a more elaborate division of labour, would have required greater system coherence as a precondition of growth. If not the merchant capitalist, then other low-level forms of system management would have been imperative. Of course, like Brenner, we could argue that the penetration of merchant capital into domestic systems of production, the creation of a new class-relationship based on surplus labour, was itself a precondition for growth, the cause not the consequence of market-enlargement. The expansionary nature of capitalism makes this a plausible line of argument. However, capitalist appetite for profit was not the only dynamic at work. We can speak of burgeoning markets that were not created out of merchant capitalism but which stand as an exogenous, independent variable to which merchant capitalism responded.

As an intermediary between producer and consumer, merchants were very much concerned with the exchange value of goods and the profit that could be made by buying in a low-cost area and selling in a high-cost one (Hobsbawm, 1964, p. 344; Medick, 1976, pp. 299–300). To this end, wage differentials were crucial. From the moment of their first appearance, merchants who controlled putting-out systems were concerned to find reserves of cheap labour, reserves that were invariably a function of social and physical environments whose economies were marginal. The immediate concern of such labour was with livelihood. It was this minimal concern with use-values that provided the merchant with the potential for differential profit. However, it was a differential profit that was only sustained if merchants preserved the subsistence wage or basis of labour. Although the disruption caused by the sixteenth-century price-revolution is thought to have helped the real value of wages to advance a little, this advance was soon eroded by the resurgence of industrial growth over the late seventeenth century. There began a sustained 'pauperisation' of labour (Kriedte, 1983, p. 97), a depression of wage-rates which some see as worsened rather than relieved by the onset of the Industrial Revolution (see, for example, Hobsbawm, 1964, pp. 64–104; Foster, 1977, p. 21). Initially, the factory system had the effect of generalising the industrial labour force, replacing the rich variety of trade that characterised earlier phases with a uniform rating of status and wages. Only in the 1840s, when, as Tribe put it, the scale of factory production reached the point at which it had meaning as a new system of production (Tribe, 1981, p. 114), do we find the industrial labour force being redifferentiated and acquiring a more graded appearance with the emergence of a more-tiered system of skills and control (Foster, 1977, pp. 212–38; Gregory, 1978b, pp. 302–4). This was a significant step for we cannot expect a crude grading of class groups (unskilled, semi-skilled, skilled and lower middle) to be mapped into the land-market of late-nineteenth-century industrial towns if such gradings were not matched by a differential system of rewards and statuses in the first place. Any such grading would, of course have been supplemented by the impact which the deregulation of wages must have had on those trades which remained organised on a workshop basis or which were not affected by either mechanisation or new forms of work-routines though in these areas the suggestion that the worker's own calculation of his wage remained for long 'a customary and not a market calculation' (Hobsbawm, 1964, p. 347) would have been an important factor. By the 1850s and 1860s, evolving union-organisation or worker-rights, not just in Britain but in other industrialising areas of Europe, restored the ability of labour groups to bargain over their conditions of work and remuneration (Hobsbawn, 1964, p. 356).

Criss-crossing with these broad changes in the relationship between capital and labour were the contrasts and ultimate conflicts between urban and rural labour, or to put it another way, between the regulated forms of the urban gild structure and the freer forms of the countryside. Through its cheaper wage-rates, no less than its cheaper-quality products, the growth of industry in the countryside was a challenge to the gild-protected trade of the town. The problem for the latter was that privileges were spatially specific. They could exercise control over free tradesmen within their bounds but had no direct power over those outside. The different parts of Europe tackled the problem in different ways. In England, fruitless attempts were made during the sixteenth century to restrict cloth-production to the boroughs whilst even the system of wage-assessments introduced to regulate the price of labour on a county – as opposed to urban – basis does not appear to have been strictly observed though assessments for different trades were made down to the early nineteenth century (Minchinton, 1972, pp. 26–7). Faced with this threat, the whole apparatus of control and regulation customarily exercised by the urban economy began to disintegrate. By the eighteenth century, if not earlier, tolls and customs were collected erratically (Clark, 1981, p. 19; Everitt, 1967, pp. 502–6). More serious, the gild system was progressively enfeebled as a basis for trade regulation. In a sense, this decline can be extended back to the emergence of gild companies, combinations of different trades or crafts. The earliest Company was that formed in 1345 by the pepperers, canvas-dealers and spicers of London (Kramer, 1927, p. 2). By the late sixteenth or early seventeenth century, such Companies were to be found in most provincial towns. In the case of Wallingford and Faversham, these omni-gilds had incorporated all trades. Like Kramer, we can see this upward integration into companies as a defensive move, an

attempt not only to exert more influence on market affairs
(Kramer, 1927, p. 21) but also, to squeeze out the increasing
number of outsiders or 'foreigners' to be found practising a trade
actually within towns (Kramer, 1927, pp. 39–40 and 89–90) and to
tighten their monopolistic control (cf. Unwin, 1904, p. 37–8). This
was a particularly acute problem in rapidly-growing towns like
London whose new suburban areas lay outside the strictly defined
domain of gilds (Kellett, 1958, pp. 381–2). Despite such belated
adjustments, the gild system had lost its real effectiveness by the
eighteenth century though we still find foreigners being prosecuted
for practising a trade and gild privileges remained intact (see
Kramer, 1927, p. 142; Kellett, 1958, p. 393; Clark, 1981, p. 19;
Palliser, 1972, pp. 111–2).

It is sometimes said that the success of industry in England over
the seventeenth and eighteenth centuries owed a great deal to the
generally freer atmosphere in which industry developed, at least in
rural areas. On the continent meanwhile, the longer survival of the
gilds retarded such growth. That there were differences of chronology in the way that gilds declined is beyond dispute. This had as
much to do with the ability of governments to act on gild power as
with their willingness to do so. Gilds were weakened most quickly
where central authority was strongest but it mattered that governments saw it as in their interest (Milward and Saul, 1973, p. 36). In
France, for instance, seventeenth-century policy actually multiplied the number of gilds. So assertive was royal authority that
areas where rural industry developed under free conditions, such
as the metal-working district of Pays d'Ouche, became organised
into gilds, or combinations as they were called in France (Zeller,
1950, p. 134; Coornaert, 1946, p. 125). The greater vigour of
industry outwith the gilds though, continued to undermine that
within (Clout, 1977, p. 451). By the late eighteenth century,
changes in government policy reversed the trend, with gilds being
suppressed temporarily in 1776 and finally abolished in 1791. The
role of central authority in determining their moment of decline is
thrown into sharp relief by the experience of the Flemish towns.
So long as they were ruled at a distance, gilds remained strong,
stifling the growth of its cloth industry at a time of rapid change
elsewhere: this survival was in spite of attempts by the Austrian
Emperor to suppress their power. Yet once Belgium was overrun
by France and given firmer, closer authority, gilds, as in the

310   *The European Past*

Republic, were easily abolished (Milward and Saul, 1973, pp. 87–8). What we are faced with is the political acknowledgement that whilst tolls and tariffs at a state level worked to the advantage of home industry, its regulation at a local or town level did not.

The Metropolitan Effect

The overall increase in the scale of trade, its broadening into new areas and spheres of activity, was not the only aspect of the problem that we need to consider. A great deal of the stress exerted on regulated forms of trade stemmed from the fact that the scalar growth of trade was not spread evenly. When we survey how it was organised geographically, we find that a dominant feature of its growth until at least the early nineteenth century was its strong focus on and articulation around metropolitan centres (Dobb, 1946, p. 207).

There were two interlocking reasons why metropolitan centres emerged so prominently. The first stemmed from their enhanced role as the political centre of state systems which were being ordered into a more centralised, coherent system. The sixteenth and seventeenth centuries formed an age when centralised states came more to the fore in Europe, the diffused, segmented power structures of the feudal state giving way to the more pinnacled form of absolute monarchs and the centripetal state. In the process, control over the great organs of state, the judiciary, exchequer, church and military became more focused, controlled through centralised bureaucracies. Such developments were not only a source of growth in themselves but generated secondary, ancillary forms of growth. As foci of opportunity and of a national information network, they naturally became the destination for an increasing groundswell of townward migration. The sixteenth and seventeenth centuries actually saw metropolitan centres increasing their position of dominance within their respective urban hierarchies, with relatively few provincial rivals of any size (De Vries, 1981, p. 99).

The dominance accorded to metropolitan cities by the centralisation of government was reinforced by the growth of overseas trade. By its diffused and speculative nature, the early build-up of overseas trade, especially colonial trade, favoured a concentration of control on particular centres where flows of vital information and finance together with storage and shipping facilities could be maximised. To these, metropolitan centres could add other locational advantages, including scope for close contacts between merchants and state rulers, easier legitimation of new trading links, greater security, and a buoyant demand for products and produce. In fact, so important was the coherence which metropolitan centres injected into early trade that, as noted in the case of Amsterdam they acted as trans-shipment centres and not just centres of consumption or production. The control functions which Amsterdam had exercised over international trade with such distinction during the seventeenth century had passed to London by the eighteenth century, a shift which owes as much to the need of international trade for a centre of maximum information, as it does to any seizure of initiative by English merchants.

This leads directly to a point which is of central importance to any discussion of why regulated markets gave way to free markets. The scalar growth of trade stressed regulated markets in different ways. The manner in which it brought older, tradition-bound centres of trade into contact with newer, freer, unregulated areas of trade is one. So too is the overall volume of trade, a volume and degree of spatial interaction that increased progressively if not continuously. However, the potency of such factors was all the greater for being so strongly articulated around a select number of dominant centres. As the organisational focus for this asymmetrical growth of trade, metropolitan centres not only reaped the gains of trade, they also bore its heavy impact on older institutional structures of trade. Time and time again, we read of how regulated forms of trade in such centres were overwhelmed by the sheer volume of goods being handled, the number of individuals involved and the number of transactions needed. In short, the rapid growth of metropolitan markets, and their vital role at the centre of these greatly-enlarged networks of trade, meant that they were the points in the system at which the stresses on regulated forms of trade were sharply felt, points at which the inability of regulated forms to cope with a sizeable increase in trade were likely to be highlighted, points at which the disequilibrium created by the scalar growth of trade was likely to be acutely experienced and points at which newer forms of trade were likely to be brought into direct and competitive confrontation with regulated forms.

Implicit within this last point is the notion that regulated trade was not only a residual feature of feudalism, it was also an adaptation to a particular scale of trading activity. Any significant expansion in this activity was bound to bring such growth into conflict with the institutional basis of trade itself. What we find is that the gradual assertion of free markets at the expense of regulated markets brought about a change in the prevailing organisation of trade. Indeed, it might be argued that the replacement of a closely-specified system with an open system of trading activity, not only encouraged more trade through its release of any constraints over profit-rates, making scarcity rather than labour the ultimate determinate of value, it was a prerequisite of growth. By this, I mean that free markets, whilst not the only solution, were able to cope with the quickened, enlarged and distended patterns of trade now emerging in a way that regulated systems could not. It is instructive to compare this reading of the problem with that offered by North. He saw the switch from regulated to self-regulating markets as bound up with the search for a more efficient system in face of the scalar growth of trade. So long as it occurred within the framework of regulated markets, with its stress on face-to-face dealings between producer and consumer and on the open inspection of all goods, any sizeable increase in the scale of markets raised transaction costs. By shifting to free markets, society was able to reverse this rising curve of transaction costs (North, 1981, p. 159). My quibble with North here is not over the role of transaction costs, but over how we read the extent to which it was a politically-designed act of change. As already argued, the nursery for free markets was in the freer, unregulated conditions of socially-free, peripheral areas, both within and beyond nation-states. The greater adaptability of these peripheral areas, their higher profit-margins from a mercantile point of view, enabled them to compete more successfully when trade began to surge forward in the sixteenth and seventeenth centuries, spurred on by a demand that emanated largely from core-areas. When governments came to dismantle or suppress the institutional trappings of regulated trade within their own national domains in the eighteenth and early nineteenth centuries, they were, in effect, acting on a revolution already in progress. We can see this upwelling of unregulated trade in peripheral areas, and its successful penetration into core-areas, as a dysfunction of regulated trade. As an open, unfettered system, the unregulated systems of trade that had grown up around regulated systems were more capable of making the organisational adjustments needed to cope with the long scalar growth that set in during the sixteenth and seventeenth centuries.

Coping With Spatial Interaction

We can typify these adjustments as taking the form of greater differentiation and elaboration in the organisation of trade. Different branches of trade, different commodities, acquired institutional separation. Contemporary political economists saw efficient markets as ones in which information about all sellers and buyers could somehow be brought together, maximised around a single point of exchange. The idea of a market exchange dealing in a specific commodity such as cotton, wool and corn was the outcome (Westerfield, 1915, pp. 334–6). In the process, the idea that all goods should be openly displayed before sale receded, replaced by the idea of sale by sample, as inevitable consequence of the growing volume of goods involved in trade and the need to trim costs by speeding throughput. More importantly, the creation of a permanent exchange dealing in a specific product dealt a blow at the wholesaling functions of periodic fairs and markets. This was part of a general trend towards more continuous forms of marketing, with the retailing functions of markets and fairs being also threatened from the late eighteenth century by a sharp increase in the number of provincial shops and stores, a form of outlet that could cope more easily with a greater volume of more regular sales (Westerfield, 1915, pp. 336–7; see also, Scola, 1975, p. 154; Shaw and Wild, 1979, especially pp. 279–80).

The supply of capital for trade also became increasingly specialised and sophisticated, with leading exchange banks like the Wisselbank of Amsterdam (1609) and the Bank of England (1694) both quickening and extending the flow of capital by refining standard techniques of banking practice, taking deposits, discounting bills, issuing credit notes against deposits and, in the case of the latter, issuing bank notes against its own reserves. What had emerged by the end of the seventeenth century is the embryo of a new metropolitan banking system that not only provided a security over transactions but offered a multilateral system of transactions between merchants and dealers, one that matched the regular and complex flows of goods between them. But in so far as trade also had a strong provincial component, there was also a need for a system of credit that reached out to the provinces. Studies of eighteenth-century growth areas like Lancashire suggest that local adaptations quickly emerged, with merchants making extensive use of bills of exchange to support an elaborate system of short-term regional credit (Anderson, 1970, pp. 90–1). In time, the profits of such activity led to a network of provincial banks often outgrowths from the credit-funding role of merchants. By its very nature though, finance could not be bound by geography (cf. Powell, 1915, p. 252). As it developed, the provincial networks of banks and credit – at least the more successful, for it is an area where some have talked of a Darwinian process of natural selection applying (Powell, 1915, pp. 302 and 320–1) – became integrated upwards and articulated around dominant metropolitan systems (Kindleberger, 1978, p. 72). By the nineteenth century, we are dealing with international centres of finance and vast, distended networks of finance which moved investment funds freely across national boundaries, as when English and Belgium capital was invested in the development of the Ruhr. This ultimate integration and co-ordination of local circuits of credit within still larger circuits, and their organisation through a few dominant nodes can be taken as an essential feature of credit capital, an entelechy of its very workings (Kindleberger, 1978, pp. 66–134). To maximise its returns once it had been disaggregated from what Powell called entrepreneurial capital (Powell, 1915, pp. 248–54), credit capital needed an elaborate hierarchy of sensors, a means of concentrating and handling information about local developments at an international level. Only in this way could its innate mobility work to full effect, seeking out new opportunities and 'riding triumphantly on the crest of the booms as they come' (Powell, 1915, p. 250). As the institutional framework of banking and finance evolved, credit became easier and signally cheaper than it had been over the medieval period, a sign not just of the greater opportunities for speculative investment, but also, of the greater certainty of return. From its early origins in Antwerp, the whole notion of the joint-stock company with transferable shares developed further. What began as temporary associations of capital took on permanent form, drawing the distinction between dividend and working capital and raising new capital by issuing shares: these permanent-stock companies became a notable feature of English trade over the seventeenth century, with a veritable explosion in number over the closing decade. In London as in Amsterdam and later Paris, the buying and selling of company shares moved from being an activity of shareholders meeting in coffee houses to being an activity of dealers and brokers clustered around formally-designated stock exchanges.

As well an increasing degree of differentiation between markets, there also occurred an increasing specialisation of roles within each market. Again, part of the reason for this was the increased volume of trade and the increasing distance across which trade now flowed. The elaboration of trade, with more and more middlemen separating themselves functionally, was bound up with the very origin of price-fixing markets. The 'longer these chains become', wrote Braudel, 'the more successful they are at freeing themselves from the usual regulations and controls and the more clearly the capitalist process emerges' (Braudel, 1977, p. 53). The longer or more complex the chains, the more Westerfield's 'new kind of man' found a place, 'correlating and establishing a mutual interdependence between specialized producers and consumers' (Westerfield, 1915, p. 124). We can see this elaboration taking place at all levels of trade: international, national and regional. It was a logical development in the case of international trade, with producer and consumer being increasingly separated by a complex network of trading companies, shippers, dealers, wholesalers and the like. The intervention of middlemen is especially well-documented in respect of national trade. Trade after trade – in textiles, leather-working, the various branches of metal-working – became organised through merchants. In such trades, craftsmen or artisans no longer interacted via the market-place but dealt with a motley band of merchants, chapmen and broggers who provided the raw materials and bought back the finished product, or as increasingly happened over the seventeenth century, paid them a wage of piece-rates. Regional trade did not escape these trends. The provisioning of towns, always the most supervised of market activities, became no less elaborated through the separation of farmer and consumer. Of course, the idea of farmers actually coming to market was always likely to be threatened once really large cities emerged. We see it first in the case of London. Over the seventeenth and eighteenth centuries, control of its corn trade passed gradually into the hands of a varied community of hoymen, corn-mongers, broggers, factors, millers and mealmen; a corn exchange solely for dealers and millers was established in 1750; and more and more grain and flour was sold in shops as opposed to open market (Gras, 1926, pp. 184, 196–9; Baker, 1970, pp. 132–6; Thompson, 1971, pp. 87 and 93). By the eighteenth century, private bargaining between individuals or open bidding at auctions was commonplace (139; Everitt, 1967, pp. 506 *et seq.*) and more and more grain was sold by sample rather than in the pitching markets (Thompson, 1971, p. 87), though the threat of riots by the poor could still force grain into local markets if, during times of scarcity, dealers tried to move grain to more lucrative markets (Thompson, 1971, p. 125). Just how radical these changes were can be gauged from the strenuous attempts made to exclude middlemen and any sort of private dealing during the medieval period. The rise of middlemen though, did not affect all forms of farm produce. By their special demands on speed of delivery, fruit and vegetables were still brought to market and sold by farmers until the nineteenth century. Similar trends affected provincial cities by the end of the eighteenth century, with the different forms of produce acquiring different markets and their marketing slowly changing from a direct sale between farmer and consumer to a sale involving the intervention of middlemen, wholesalers and shop-keepers, with more and more produce being sold initially to wholesalers and more and more sales to the consumer being handled by shops rather than in centralised open markets, though the latter often continued in use alongside shop outlets (see, for example, Blackman, 1963, pp. 88–9; Scola, 1975, pp. 153–7; Shaw, 1982, p. 174).

The Price of Landscape: Price-Fixing Markets and the Production of Spatial Order?

Although the idea that price-fixing markets emerged as mature, dominant institutions by the mid-nineteenth century features strongly in work by economic historians, the strong empirical tradition established by historical geographers working on the nineteenth century has taken a more equivocal view of it as a dominant explanatory variable. It certainly figures in discussions of the forces shaping the spatial order of the countryside, but has been given a more subdued role in the extensive analyses carried out by geographers working on the nineteenth-century town and is accorded a rather anonymous role in discussions of the industrial economy, for ever being couched in other terms. I want to argue that this somewhat mixed treatment arises in part from a failure to see the relationship between price-fixing markets and spatial order as something dynamic, a relationship continually being transformed rather than one that works towards a single stable form. The idea that price-fixing markets produce coherent or complete landscapes, the sort modelled by Christaller, von Thünen and Weber, is valid only if we freeze our images of market society. To do so, however, is to lose sight of an essential fact about market-dominated societies.

Quite apart from the failure of individuals, be they farmers, industrialists or urban property developers, to command perfect knowledge of market conditions, or to seek optimum solutions, a prime weakness of normative or equilibrium models is that they assume a stable world. In actuality, base conditions are continually changing. This has two consequences. To start with, it means that real-world landscapes are never those predicted by such models. At best, they are always in a state of becoming, but never actually produced. How quickly such adjustments proceeded depended on how frequently different uses of land or different resources were forced into the market-place. For some, this was on an annual cycle. For others, it might take generations before space or resources could be reallocated (cf. Harvey, 1982, p. 393). Yet even where market-involvement was regular and capital circulated quickly, the variable response of individuals could be equally potent in advancing or retarding the rate of adjustment. The sum effect was that any ongoing adjustment to a particular set of market conditions was gradual. In no way can the one be seen as an instantaneous product of the other. Invariably, what we find is that long before such adjustments had reached anything like completion or had created a price-efficient landscape, that is, one that yielded the highest rent under a given set of market conditions, these conditions had moved inexorably forwards or backwards. Instead of a single coherent system of spatial order, we are faced with a patchwork of incomplete adjustments, each orientated towards a particular conjunction of market circumstances, some – like anciently-formed rocks – bearing the mark of a past magnetic north, but all bearing testimony to the innate tendency of markets to turn eventually.

Geography and Industrial Capitalism

Latterly, the flux surrounding price-fixing markets and their continual resetting of what constituted the optimum use of space and resources has found a prominent place in general discussions of capitalism by geographers. Whereas nineteenth-century political economists tended to view any discrepancy between the way that resources should be allocated and the way that they actually were allocated as a dysfunction of the market mechanism, a sign of their immaturity, the drift of recent thinking has been to see it as an essential part of the way market capitalism worked. We can approach this view of capitalism through the ideas of Schumpeter. For him, the inherent 'instability' of what he called market or competitive capitalism derived from the nature of technological innovation. The diffusion of innovations occurs in clusters, so that we need to see technological development as a fitful or discontinuous process. Each phase of innovation begins as a phase of depression, brought on by the dislocation effects of new technologies. However, the high profit-ratios offered by new technologies draws investment, so that, as innovations diffuse, depression gives way to a phase of prosperity. Of course, as innovations spread, profit-rates level off. Individual industrialists begin the search for still newer technologies and the whole 'business' cycle begins again, each cycle moving pendulum-like between equilibrium and disequilibrium (Schumpeter, 1971, especially pp. 37–40; Schumpeter, 1939, especially pp. 46–104).

Recent discussion of these business cycles has tended to couch them in terms of the crises which accompanied the switch from growth to stagnation. These crises have been particularly well-studied in relation to the Lancashire cotton industry. In a pioneering attempt to apply some of the concepts of organisation theory to a specific historical problem, the sociologist, Smelser, has described how the structure of industrial output and the family division of labour both underwent a shift towards a more differentiated or specialised form over the late eighteenth and early nineteenth centuries. Central to his thesis is the proposal that this shift towards greater differentiation occurs in phases. Each phase is set in motion by specific disequilibrating conditions. Although Smelser himself does not make the comparison, his ideas can be aligned alongside those of Schumpeter, for his disequilibrating conditions arise when the general adoption and growing obsolesence of 'old' industrial organisation in an area combine with a poor or more competitive market to precipitate a crisis (Smelser, 1959, pp. 3–4). Smelser's approach differs in so far as he emphasises the fact that each new phase of investment and innovation leads to greater differentiation, to a more specialised system of production, but, like Schumpeter, he sees the switch from decline to renewed growth as punctuated by tensions and crisis for both capital and labour. For capitalists, it was a choice between bankruptcy or risking new forms of investment. For labour, it was a threat of starvation or adopting the new work practices and conditions demanded by new systems of manufacturing (Smelser, 1959, pp. 225–64). More recent work by Foster (Foster, 1974) and Gregory (Gregory, 1984, pp. 68–117) – the former based on a sample study of Oldham and the latter on a study of the region as a whole – has emphasised the degree to which the experience of the industry over the late eighteenth and early nineteenth centuries was one of regular crises. Both stress the need for seeing these crises in place-specific or contextual terms, with each community being an individual arena within which the conflict between capital and labour could take a different form and within which the response to crises could take a different course. To the extent that they are saying that the relation between capital and labour was cast and solidified around specific locations and that – through the inertia which this spatial configuration necessarily imposed on the disposition of social and technological resources – this affected how communities coped with crises, then we are in agreement. However, my prime concern is to emphasise how this commitment of social and technological resources to a particular form in a particular place could divert change into wholly new spatial adaptations. This was appreciated by Schumpeter. Surveying the nineteenth-century experience, he reminds us that new technologies were rarely innovated within the context of established firms, but more usually involved the establishment of new firms or sites, a fresh start that, in the process, brought about a progressive shift of activity in space (Schumpeter, 1971, p. 40). In other words, the locational adjustments that characterised the Lancashire cotton industry over the late eighteenth and nineteenth centuries (see, for example, Farnie, 1979, pp. 277–323) were as much a manifestation of the search for new more flexible locations in the face of a changing economic and technological environment as crises were a manifestation of the loss of such flexibility by old, set locations.

Put simply, the gist of my argument here is that crises of capitalism can only be fully understood if they are seen as arising out of the fact that the economy is, in part, a space economy. To develop this point further, we need to make the distinction between circulating and fixed capital, between what was bound up in stock and materials and what was embodied in plant or equipment. A characteristic of industry prior to the industrial revolution was its emphasis on circulating as opposed to fixed capital. This not an imbalance we should overstress when dealing with the purely domestic systems of the medieval period, for the low capitalisation of some trades would have rendered any such imbalance insignificant if not liable to be changed by normal fluctuations of account. With the spread of merchant capitalism over the sixteenth and seventeenth centuries and the emergence of extensive putting-out systems, their distinction became more emphatic. Entrepreneurs built up large commercial enterprises whose capital consisted primarily of raw material, semi-finished and finished products moving through the various stages of production via scattered craftsmen and artisans and whose gross value far exceeded the plant and equipment involved. What is also worthy of note is the fact that with the growth of putting-out systems, circulating and fixed capital actually became disaggregated into two separate if interacting circuits. Although entrepreneurs did provide the credit needed by craftsmen and artisans to purchase the tools and equipment and although some forms of putting-out involved the selling of materials and the buying back of the finished or processed good, the sort of system that eventually emerged established only a loose coupling of circulating and fixed capital.

This has an important bearing on the mobility of capital. At the end of each period of account or cycle of production, circulating capital was available for reinvestment and, if required, redirection. Naturally, this conferred a high degree of mobility on circulating capital, enabling it to be moved relatively easily between products, industries and locations. It is in relation to this mobility that we can appreciate how the industrial map of England was virtually redrawn between 1500–1700. Southern industries, like the Wealden iron industry and the East Anglian cloth industry experienced what Jones has called a progressive east–west dieback

(Jones, 1968, pp. 58–71) whilst Midland and northern areas witnessed a veritable eruption of industrial activity (see also, Thirsk, 1970, pp. 167–76). The same period saw a comparable shift of industry from Flanders northwards to Brabant and ultimately Seeland (Van Der Wee, 1975, pp. 203–21), whilst similar processes of deindustrialisation and industrialisation affected southern and northern France respectively (Mendels, 1972, pp. 247–8; see also Houston and Snell, 1984, p. 490). In effect, the predominance of circulating capital helped to make the relationship between industrial activity and location a generalised relationship, one that could easily be revised.

Starting in the late eighteenth century, the Industrial Revolution wrought a far-reaching change in the balance between these two forms of capital. The adoption of new technologies and the establishment of the factory system brought a rise in the general level of fixed capital. It was not a dramatic rise, at least not during the early stages of change. This was true even of the cotton industry. Until the 1790s, some decades after its 'take-off', its fixed capital needs remained relatively modest, with machines still largely made of wood, water-wheels rather than steam engines and a fair proportion of its early 'factories' being mills converted from other uses (Chapman, 1971a, pp. 59 and 75). However, the abandonment of Arkwright-type production and the adoption in its place of mule spinning from the 1790s onwards led to larger, more mechanised, steam-powered factories, with the proportion of fixed capital rising to as much as 50 per cent by the 1820s and even higher once integrated spinning and weaving mills began to make their appearance over the 1830s and 1840s (Chapman, 1971a, p. 80; Deane and Cole, 1967, p. 263; Gattrell, 1977, p. 103). More typically, we are dealing with industries in which the proportion of fixed capital rose to between a quarter and a third of all capital (see, for example, Gregory, 1982, pp. 94–5). In fact, it has been suggested that up to 1830 the main feature of change was the increasing proportion of firms with modest fixed capital ratios rather than any striking change in the ratio of fixed capital within the more advanced firms (Pollard, 1964, p. 302; Crouzet, 1972, p. 39). This is understandable for it was only from the 1830s onwards that really large-scale industrial complexes emerged, with large units of production and greatly expanded outputs (Deane and Cole, 1967, p. 277; Tribe, 1981, pp. 114–5). Reinforcing this shift towards higher fixed capital ratios was the gathering investment in mining (Dobb, 1946, pp. 139–40; Flinn, 1984, p. 199) and public utilities (Deane, 1972, pp. 103–4). Canals and railways, in particular, reified enormous sums in the form of fixed or relatively fixed plant, the latter consuming 10 per cent of national capital, mostly in a fixed form, by 1885 (Deane and Cole, 1967, p. 271). Taking an overview, we can see this shift towards fixed capital as introducing a new factor into the problem of location. Quite simply, it created obstacles to the free movement of capital.

In such circumstances, capital clearly had to seek ways of freeing itself from the potential anchor provided by fixed capital if it was to combat the equalisation of profit rates that came with the more general adoption of new technologies. Because fixed capital was place-specific, this can be seen as an intrinsically geographical problem. It is a problem that Harvey has considered. Capitalists innovate for gain but as production over an area approaches any kind of equilibrium, then the more likely it is that some will 'seek to disrupt the basis of that equilibrium through technological change' (Harvey, 1982, p. 393). He sees this equalisation as achieved not simply by technological innovation but by the rents levied on location, so that innovation becomes traded-off against location. The problem then becomes one of how to free embodied capital so as to redirect it towards new technologies and to recapture the high profits that came from establishing new production functions. This is anything but a straightforward problem. Different technologies have different turnover rates. Moreover, the linkages that inevitably develop between activities make it difficult to isolate one block of investment from another so that 'the barriers to the reorganization of production multiply to a corresponding degree' (Harvey, 1982, p. 394). The nineteenth-century Black Country metal-working trades provide a good illustration of how interconnected and interdependent an industrial region could become, from the quarries and mines that provided the ore, coal and limestone through to the furnaces, mills and forges that produced the sheets, rods, bars and castings for the innumerable small workshops which turned out everything from nails to locks and from pans to horse-bits, all supported by a complex network of roads, canals and rails and tied together via wholesalers, agents, chapmen and carters (for a detailed study of intra-regional linkages, see Moyes, 1979, pp. 39–56). Nor should we restrict the build-up of investment solely to specifically-located networks of economic relations. Each local or regional system of industry revolved around communities whose labour skills and whose web of social relations were equally adapted to the specific economic environment in which they lived and worked (cf. Gregory, 1982, p. 21). This fixed social capital no less than that embodied in machines and factories opposed any facile, spontaneous movement of capital (Harvey, 1982, p. 403).

To overcome this potential geographical inertia, capital devised elaborate systems of credit that were not so geographically tied. This had the effect of creating a circuit of capital that profited from fixed capital yet could more easily separate itself from it (Harvey, 1982, pp. 265 and 269; see also, Pollard, 1963, pp. 81–2 and 87). The place and moment of separation was accomplished by massive devaluations. The value of what is invested in fixed capital is written off or, in reality, transferred as a burden on to others. The corresponding devaluation of social capital, a process that necessarily occurs in specific contexts, is seen by Harvey as having a crucial role in the formation of crises. In other words, in order to maintain its profit margins, capital is constantly investing and then disinvesting in specific socio-economic environments. I have no disagreement with Harvey on these points of argument. What Dobb called the 'self-defeating tendency inherent in the process of capital accumulation' (Dobb, 1946, p. 282) has been widely recognised as an innate characteristic of capitalism and not some unfortunate malfunction (see also, Schumpeter, 1971, p. 37; Mandel, 1978, p. 30; Wallerstein, 1983, p. 70).

However, to link it in more closely with what I have argued in this book, the search by capital for new forms of technological investment can be seen as a problem of adaptation. Whether we see them in terms of fixed capital or social capital, the resultant systems of local or regional activity represent complex adaptations. The more new innovations diffuse, the more elaborate these adaptations and interrelationships tend to become. But as such systems approach the equalisation of profit, as they matured, their capacity to adjust to new opportunities becomes diminished. Part of the dilemma stems from what economists call 'technological interelatedness'. As an industrial area develops, its activities become more intricately linked, not just in the sense that one supplies the other, but equally in the sense that the throughput between the different stages has to be consistent in terms of scale, material needs and so on. Change in one is not divisible from change in the total system. Unlike a newly-developed industrial area, 'modernization for the established enterprise or country is limited by the extent to which the necessary changes can be made to "fit" the existing system' (Frankel, 1955, p. 301). What this means is that once the industrial development of an area is under way, we cannot see further innovation as occurring in a 'disembodied' way (Mokyr, 1976, p. 153; Robson, 1973, pp. 221–4). As the freedom to adapt becomes exhausted, then change, the shift to new better-practice technology has to cope with 'the dead hand of the past' (Jervis, 1947, p. 116), the entrepreneur becoming 'more limited by history' (Habakkuk, 1962, p. 218). In this sort of situation, capitalists will see investment in new technologies and the establishment of any new labour systems associated with them as more easily accomplished in new environments, so that we can hardly be surprised if each new phase of investment and innovation seeks out the freedom of new economic and social environments (see especially, Pollard, 1981, p. 20; Wallerstein, 1983, p. 70; Olson, 1982, pp. 98–9). Construed in this way, the history of capitalism should read as a series of locally- or regionally-specific investments, each moving through a cycle of innovation, adaptation, then crisis as capital moves on to areas of unused freedom.

The idea of industrialisation developing through a series of place-specific adaptations is not alien to what has been written about the industrial revolution. It is, for instance, consistent with the stress that scholars like Pollard and Langton have placed on seeing industrialisation as being, in essence, a regional process. Pollard talks of new ideas and innovations reverberating around within regions with the shared institutions and facilities, social capital, material resources, demonstration effect and external economies that operated within regions all serving to heighten the place-specific nature of the industrialising process (Pollard, 1981, pp. 19–20). Langton follows a similar line, seeing attempts to interpret industrialisation through national aggregates as fruitless: the vital dynamics of change were those which combined around specific locations and regions (Langton, 1972a, p. 54). In so far as they are suggesting that successful industrialisation represented an elaborate and self-reinforcing adaptation of new commercial and technological possibilities to the complex of opportunities offered by particular locations or regions, then I am in absolute agreement with them. Given what I said in the previous paragraph though, I would add that we must not overlook the fact that, increasingly, as capital markets became organised, eruptions of regional or local activity need to be seen as overlain by a higher, more national and ultimately international circuit of capital that sought to engage and disengage from such place-specific investment as new break-through opportunities offering higher profit rates presented themselves (Wallerstein, 1983, p. 70). To an extent, such a view vitiates the whole question of whether industrialisation developed as an instance of balanced or unbalanced growth by simply allocating different functions to the different levels, the regional and national (Hartwell, 1971, pp. 185–200). It also supposes that sooner or later, the hyperadaptation of mature industrialised regions or complexes will deflect new investment. This too, is consistent with what has been written about the Industrial Revolution. Whether we talk about the broad changes in production techniques from the late medieval period onwards (=handicrafts–putting out–factory production and mechanisation) or simply about the changing phases of organisation within factory production during the late eighteenth and nineteenth centuries, there are those who see each phase as involving a different mesh of techniques, work practices and labour control (see, for example, Mandel, 1978, pp. 42–3; Pollard, 1981, p. 20). As investment was built up, both within the firm and within the region, it moved increasingly towards inertia through the interrelatedness of activity and the consequent difficulty of making selective changes without disturbing the total network of relations. The replacement of one phase of investment by another, the exploitation of one set of historically-specific opportunities by another, involved a comprehensive adjustment, one that reached out and touched the structure of social as well as economic relations. It is this roundedness of adaptation and, in consequence, the comprehensive nature of any change by replacement, with all its costs of disruption, that explains why each phase of change carried with it a probability of change through the exploitation of new areas. During industrialisation, Mokyr tells us, 'discontinuity is one of the conditions for spectacularity' (Mokyr, 1976, p. 27). Arguably, the problem became more acute with each phase. As the Industrial Revolution ran its course, and new investment created larger complexes and more elaborate networks of interrelatedness between industrial activities, the problem of diminished adaptability grew apace. This is particularly well shown in Landes' work. Each new area was an area of new opportunity, allowing industrialists to establish a more up-to-date system of production, to reap the benefits of being a 'latecomer' (Landes, 1969, p. 230; see also, Trebilcock, 1981, pp. 48–9). Subsequent change is towards a more elaborate system. With an eye on late nineteenth-century German industrialisation, Landes allows for ·much accretionary growth in this process of ramification, with firms constantly adding extra facilities and capacity to existing sites. In time though, he sees 'the matrix of past arrangement becoming ever more confining, and at each stage of equipment or addition to plant the gap between "best possible" and "best practicable" grew' (Landes, 1969, p. 301; see also, Habakkuk, 1962, 218; Mokyr, 1976, pp. 153–5). Ongoing adjustments were of course always possible even within mature systems. The problem was that they were increasingly less easy to make, placing greater stress on revolutionary change. Thus, references to the adaptability of the cotton industry during the early stages of its growth (Chapman, 1971a, p. 73) and to its ongoing adjustments over the first half of the nineteenth century contrast with the 'problems' it manifested by the second half of the century, when, as one mill-owner had put it in the 1840s, they had to stick with 'their money in old concerns' (Gattrell, 1977, pp. 116–7). Landes himself provides a splendid review of the attempts to maintain the growth momentum of established industries during the late nineteenth century, with the‘ introduction of what he calls new logistics of production, like the standardisation of parts and assembly-line techniques. At the same time, the costs of investing in entirely new, 'best possible' systems of production rose with each new phase of innovation. Taking a theoretical view, Ames and Rosenberg see this as increasing the possibility that as the complexity of industrial systems increases, then sooner or later, the costs of adopting entirely new systems will become too great for less-developed areas, or areas with the opportunity, to make a response. How do we decide, they quip, 'which frog leaps last' and thereafter enjoys permanent economic leadership (Ames and Rosenberg, 1971, p. 428). The answer, of course, is that the mobility of credit capital is always preserved.

The extent to which the general adaptation of regional economic systems lowered their responsiveness to radically new systems of production and raised the attractiveness of new locations is borne out by what actually happened during the Industrial Revolution. References to the changing industrial map of Europe over the sixteenth and seventeenth centuries, with each new phase of change mapping itself into space in a different way from earlier phases, can be matched by identical reference for industrial change over the eighteenth and nineteenth centuries. Each phase of innovation and adjustment disturbed the geography of production, as more adaptable newcomers leap-frogged their way past older areas of production. To a degree, these locational shifts were bound up with the specific needs of new innovations, such as when coal replaced water or charcoal as a source of power. The extent to which water power survived after the invention of the steam engine and charcoal furnaces survived long after the pioneer use of coke in all parts of western Europe, though, shows that much depended on the place-specific nature of industrial activity and the continuing ability of particular areas to maintain their competitiveness by continuing to adapt within themselves.

A good illustration of how the Industrial Revolution, no less than the sixteenth and seventeenth centuries, witnessed a continuing movement of capital in space is provided by the British iron and steel industry. For the iron industry, the Industrial Revolution began with the development of coke smelting. Although available in 1709, the substitution of coke for charcoal did not gather momentum until the second half of the eighteenth century. The reasons for this delayed response has been clarified by Hyde. Until the 1750s, charcoal-smelters produced better-quality pig-iron at a cheaper cost than coke-smelters. Once costs had moved in favour of coke-smelting, a crossover which occurred during the 1750s, new investment was directed towards coke-smelters. Only where labour and charcoal costs were competitive did charcoal-smelters survive. Some even survived until the very end of the century before the gap between their 'best practicable' and the 'best possible' practice became too great. The earliest response to the opportunities opened up by coke-smelting was in the area around its point of initial development, Coalbrookdale. For a few decades thereafter, Shropshire and Staffordshire became the foremost centre of British iron production. By the 1780s, production functions in the industry had altered yet again with the introduction of Cort's puddling process, an innovation which enabled the blast-furnace (producing pig-iron) and finery-furnace (producing bar-iron) to be linked directly, effecting a considerable saving in fuel, though, a plausible case has recently been presented for seeing the new techniques of putting and stamping as the critical innovation of this phase. What is not in dispute is the fact that new investment at this point was directed largely to south Wales. By the 1790s, the area had become the leading producer of both pig- and bar-iron in Britain. The next phase of adjustment came in the 1820s and 1830s after the development of Neilsen's hot-blast technique. This recycled waste gases back into the furnace, enabling it to reach higher working temperatures. It proved of particular advantage to the Clyde Valley where local reserves of coal and ore had proved difficult to use without high working-temperatures. To this however, it added the extra bonus of producing a cheaper pig-iron than any earlier method. Investment in the Clyde Valley was quick to capitalise on the new possibilities and, for a few decades, the area took over the mantle of being Britain's leading producer of pig-iron. This geography of production survived no longer than earlier patterns. Around 1850, further refinements rather than any single innovation meant that the amount of coal needed to produce of a ton of pig-iron fell below the amount of ore needed. It now made more economic sense to direct new investment in iron production towards the ore-fields. The response was that the phase of investment that built up over the third quarter of the nineteenth century established the ore-fields of Cleveland and later the Jurassic scarp of the east Midlands as the major centres of iron-smelting (Hyde, 1977, especially pp. 23–41, 76–108, 121–3 and 146–53; see also Roepke, 1956; Birch, 1967, especially pp. 145–77).

Comparable adjustments worked their way through the steel industry in the second half of the nineteenth century. A simple succession of innovations – the Bessemer converter, the open-hearth furnace and the basic process – changed production functions and, in the case of the basic process, permitted new resources (phosphoric ores) to be used. As with pig- and bar-iron output, the response to these innovations displayed interesting spatial variations. Briefly, investment in the Bessemer converter was fairly widespread, being built up rapidly in the traditional steel districts around Sheffield, in the heamatite ore districts of Furness, the nascent engineering district of south Lancashire and, to a lesser extent, in south Wales. The latter, responding to the broadening opportunities of steel production somewhat later, tended to concentrate its investment on open-hearth furnaces, combining its response with a shift towards coastal sites where ore could be imported more cheaply. Its superiority in steel production, though, was shortlived, being outstripped by the heavy investment made after 1879 in basic open-hearth furnaces in areas like Cleveland and the Clyde Valley. This tendency for new innovations to be more widely adopted in some areas than others was matched by a tendency for the different areas to tap new areas of demand that opened up during these decades: including steam engines, rails, metal-clad ships and other branches of heavy engineering. By establishing a close relationship with a particular sphere of demand, the different production areas were able to build up their capacity quickly and to reap important scale benefits. Inevitably, it emphasised the cyclical nature of such regional success.

Comparable shifts of new investment have been seen as a feature of industrialisation on the continent, a largely nineteenth-century affair (see, for example, Landes, 1969, p. 226; Pollard, 1981, p. 20; Trebilcock, 1981, p. 49). For a time, industrial output managed to expand using traditional methods, so that one finds French textile production continuing to grow using domestic operatives and Belgium iron production continuing to expand using charcoal as a smelter fuel. By the 1830s though, after the ending of the Napoleonic Wars had exposed continental markets to British technology as well as a flood of cheaper goods, the switch of investment towards new, more productive technology gathered pace. In France, earlier, more-diffused systems of textile production gave way to an investment in massive, more productive mills, notably in Alsace and Normandy (Clout, 1977, p. 477). Likewise, scattered centres of iron production in areas like Champagne, Franche-Comte and Nivernais gave way to investment in large coastal centres, like Boulogne and Calais and, by the 1850s, to a massive build-up of investment in both iron and steel production in the ore-fields areas of Lorraine (Clout, 1977, p. 476; Landes, 1969, p. 226). German investment followed similar shifts in space, the most spectacular adjustment being the redirection of investment, accompanied by its enormous scalar growth, from old-established iron areas of Sauerland and Seigenland to the Ruhr over the 1850s and 1860s. Each new cycle of investment brought modernity and, therefore, a temporary advantage. This is well shown by Wrigley's survey of the various parts of the Austrasian coalfield. As the coal-fired economy took shape over the nineteenth century, the Austrasian coalfield became the location for a range of activities from metal-working to textiles. Each new forward movement of technology though, imposed a new regional pattern of industrial activity (Wrigley, 1961, p. 37). Viewed overall, the history of the coalfield over this vital century is one of new areas first emulating and then overtaking older areas as each new phase of investment used the opportunity to make a fresh adaptation to new technologies and their precise locational needs (Wrigley, 1961, p. 68).

This constant remapping of market advantage from one new area of investment to another also surfaces in the vigorous debate over whether Britain, as the first to industrialise, carried a handicap. Historians and economists commenting on the problem stress the way in which countries like Germany and France were able to avoid many search or experimental costs and were able to invest in what, for the mid-nineteenth century, was more up-to-date technology, as contemporary wonder at the size of say, the cotton-mills of Mulhouse or the ironworks of the Ruhr makes clear. This more direct adaptiveness, always a freedom of the latecomer, was particularly evident in Germany. Its rapid successs over the third quarter of the nineteenth century owed a great deal to the possibilities of a large tariff-free market created by the Zollverein in 1834 and to the way railways and German nationalism conspired to turn these possibilities into a reality. However, equal stress must be placed on the way it designed institutional structures that were more in keeping with market needs. The creation of investment banks over the 1850s and 1860s poured large quantities of capital into new plant. Its new educational emphasis on producing scientists and technologists also yielded immense dividends, as the lead which it soon took in technologies like chemicals, engineering and electricity discloses (Kemp, 1969, p. 114; Landes, 1969, p. 229).

Price-Fixing Markets and Urban Space

The question of whether price-fixing markets, especially those operating in respect of land and labour, played a dominant or muted role in the organisation of urban space has been widely debated. Although some have pleaded for their formative influence on urban layouts (Harvey, 1973; Rodger, 1982), the drift of much recent writing on the nineteenth-century town, at least in Britain, has been to stress their individual rather than regimented form. What emerges from this recent work is a stress on the varied behavioural and socio-cultural influences that could affect urban layouts and the way accidents of site or history, or the monopolistic control of individual landlords, could personalise their character, whilst some have even tried to despatialise the town altogether by calling for a purely class-orientated approach. By arguing here in favour of a more defined role for price-fixing markets, I do not wish to underplay the role which behavioural and socio-cultural variables played or to imply that site influences can be taken for granted. Rather is my intention to show that price-fixing markets are relevant at a particular level of generalisation and that, far from these other variables vying alongside price-fixing markets for explanatory effect, they act within the broad framework established by the latter and, therefore, at a lower, more specific level.

The penetration of urban land by price-fixing markets meant that its value became set by exchange rather than use. Put simply, the notion of exchange value can be seen as the rent determined by the bid-price mechanism. Its precise composition involved three different kinds of rent: differential, monopoly and absolute rent. Differential rent was that paid for the utility or desirability of particular locations. This had a profound impact on urban space because it introduced a sense of ordination, with central locations being more valued than others. Monopoly rent is the surcharge levied where there are particular pressures constraining the supply of land. Where these were physical constraints, then such monopoly rents clearly represented a scarcity value, pure and simple. However, it could also arise through a deliberate manipulation of supply by dominant landlords and developers hoarding land or controlling how it was developed. This has been shown to be a potent feature of many towns, shaping the 'aristocratic' estates of west London, like Bloomsbury and Grosvenor, and middle-class suburban estates like that developed by the Calthorpe family at Edgbaston in Birmingham, to the industrial and worker-housing sponsored by the Bute family's near-monopoly control of Cardiff (Cannadine, 1980, pp. 41, 76 and 94–123). Absolute rent is that attributable to the pressure of demand or capital on particular locations. Reviewing these various forms of rent, Harvey (1973, pp. 179–82) has stressed the need for seeing them as compounded together, with the different proportions altering in step with changes in the nature of capitalism. Tentatively, he suggests the possibility that early industrial towns were dominated by differential rents. However, with the rise of monopoly capitalism over the late nineteenth century, he sees monopoly and absolute rents as becoming relatively more significant though he allows for the possibility that such forms may have been important as early as the eighteenth century in those cities where commercial functions like banking, insurance, etc. – activities whose productivity could not be measured – were concentrated. In reply, one could argue that monopoly rents were probably a prominent feature of many early industrial towns simply because so much of their urban space was in the hands of a dominant landlord.

Whilst I have no quibble with the compounded nature of rent as defined by Harvey, I would question whether we can link it so neatly or directly to prevailing forms of capitalism. In his scheme of things, the dependent nature of urban rents caused him to see urban form as a secondary phenomenon. Yet if we are forced to select a single factor which, more than any other, nurtured the growth of a price-fixing market in urban land, then a case can be made out for seeing the scalar growth of towns as a more potent influence on both the unshackling of urban rents and on their subsequent character and movement. As noted in Chapter 7, land-rents had already started to move more freely in the larger towns as early as the fourteenth century. The centripetal growth of metropolitan centres like London and Paris would have advanced this process further over the sixteenth, seventeenth and eighteenth centuries, their population being inflated by large influxes of migrants. De Vries has suggested that from being less than one would expect from a study of the rank-size distribution of urban systems, by the mid-seventeenth century, Paris, London and Amsterdam became greater than one would expect (De Vries, 1981, pp. 93–4). Their growth at this point was impressive. In terms of absolute size, though, their real take-off was over the nineteenth century, with London growing from 900 000 to over 6 million, and Paris from 0.5 million to 2.5 million by 1900. Yet, as De Vries has shown, the provincial urban system of Europe was now growing so quickly that it tended to lessen the singular dominance of metropolitan centres (De Vries, 1981, p. 94). The overall degree of change is conveyed by the proportion of total population living in cities. In 1800, about 20 per cent of Britain's population lived in towns. By 1900, the figure was closer to 80 per cent (Law, 1967, p. 131; Lawton, 1978, pp. 330–47).

Such sustained scalar growth affected urban land-markets in two ways. First, it pressurised and, ultimately, collapsed any residual restraints on the customary control of land prices. Second, through the sheer numbers that now made up the urban community, it created an imperative for new expressions of social differentiation. Class differences provided this basis, sorting large numbers into simpler categories of meaning, a system compatible with the large impersonal nature of the industrial town and the divorce of interest between capital and labour. Amongst the questions we need to ask are how a free market in land affected the development of the town as a whole and how, at a more specific level, the bid-price mechanism was used as the agency by which emergent differences between uses and classes were mapped into space. Following on from this is the further question of when such segregation became a prominent feature of the industrial town. We can see this not just as a question of chronology, but equally, as a question of whether there was a particular size of population or scale of urban space at which the major uses or social classes territorialised themselves.

Viewing the problem at a general level, the penetration of free markets into urban land, into labour, and into commodity production cannot be said to have created the periodicity that characterises urban growth. In all probability, urban growth has always been phased in step with the course of developments in the economy as a whole, give or take some lag due to problems of relaxation-time. What we can maintain is that as free markets spread into these sectors of life and economy, and as the movement of the economy became impregnated with the cyclical rhythms of capitalism, then we can expect the phasing of urban growth, its repetitive succession of growth and standstill, to have become more pronounced. Work by Parry-Lewis suggests that the notion of a house-building cycle can be vouched for as long ago as the eighteenth century (Parry-Lewis, 1965, pp. 10–41). By the nineteenth century, the data is sufficiently detailed to enable us to link such periodicities with the general boom and slump conditions within the economy as a whole. Phases of house-construction correlate with phases of economic growth (Parry-Lewis, 1965, pp. 186–210). The sharpness of these movements varied in relation to the growing specialisation of urban economies. Strong signs that the generalised nature of the medieval economy was giving way to a more specialised economy are apparent by the seventeenth century, after urban economies had recovered from their depression of the sixteenth century (Clark, 1981, p. 17). By the nineteenth century, functional differentiation was well-established, especially amongst the newer industrial towns that had filled out the urban hierarchy (Robson, 1981, pp. 114 *et seq.*). Tied to the fortunes of a single industry, functionally-specialised towns tend to show a greater variability of growth (Robson, 1981, p. 122; see also pertinent comments of Carter, 1978, pp. 378–84). Indeed, as with their economies, we can expect opportunities for adaptation to have become more and more diminished with time, so that their growth phases would have become less and less spectacular with time, as capital for growth increasingly sought out new opportunities elsewhere. 'The rise and fall of particular places' writes Robson 'is a function of the individual patterns of investment, disinvestment and reinvestment in given locations' (Robson, 1981, p. 127), a conclusion that clearly matches the history of urban growth with the history of technological change (see also, Robson, 1973, pp. 131–85 and 214–28).

Broken down into different spurts of expansion, each phase of urban growth tended to be associated with a different pattern of income, different tastes and possibilities in building styles and with different transport technologies. The effect which this could have on urban layouts has been demonstrated in an American context by Adams's excellent study of mid-western cities, with each phase imprinting the constraints of prevailing transport technology and prevailing taste in building styles into urban layouts (Adams, 1970, pp. 37–63). Despite the relevance of Adams's work, we have no comparable study of European towns. However, the phased nature of urban growth over recent centuries is well-appreciated. So too is the way each phase contributed its own style to the evolving townscape (Summerson, 1945, p. 24; Lawton, 1972, p. 213). Each phase of growth was separated by a phase of standstill. In some cases, the divide between the two was marked in the landscape by a fixation line, a line which symbolised the static limits of the town during the slumps in building activity. By the mid-nineteenth century, such slumps may have witnessed a changed in usage rather than actual standstill. In a study based on Glasgow, 1846–1914, Whitehand demonstrated how, during building slumps when land-values were lower, institutional users of land (such as hospitals, cemeteries) – invariably the more extensive users of land – took the opportunity of acquiring land, so that as one moves out of the city one moves through successive belts of housing and institutional uses (Whitehand, 1972, pp. 39–55).

The dynamic behind booms in housebuilding can only be fully grasped once we realise that such phases were associated with higher rents and land-values. This is what attracted the speculator. In an upwardly-spiralling market, those competing for land were forced to bid upwards: the speculator – to use Westerfield's phrase – dealt as much in a 'time market' (Westerfield, 1915, p. 349) as in a space market, meaning that his risk was in anticipating these demands in both time and space. However, his driving concern was with ability to pay not with social need, so that we can find phases and places where increases in the housing stock and increased demand did not match, an imbalance that invariably prolonged the life of older, 'obsolete' properties. During Liverpool's rapid growth over the first half of the nineteenth century, the number of houses built did not satisfy demand from the flood of migrants or make up for those overrun by expansion of city-centre commerce or for those cleared under pressure from early Improvement Acts (Lawton, 1972, p. 209) so that lower-income groups were forced into overcrowded housing around the city centre and landlords were able to draw far higher rents than the quality of housing stock or location alone would dictate (Pooley, 1982, pp. 213–22). In central London, sharply-escalating land-values made it impossible by the late nineteenth century to find houses that 'could be let at rents the working man could afford' (Wohl, 1971, pp. 27–8). This rising cost of rent was a general problem over the nineteenth century, one estimate being that house-rents rose from 5 per cent of GNP in 1800 to 8 per cent by mid-century and 9 per cent by the end of the century, the shift after 1850 disguising a sharp rise between 1880 and 1900. As Englander has recently pointed out, the increases born out of this 'age of unfettered capitalism' affected the lower-paid far more acutely than the better-paid since rent accounted for a larger proportion of their pay (Englander, 1983, pp. 5–6). The provision

of mortgages and new transport technologies by the close of the
nineteenth century enabled the better-paid to abandon the inner
city for the surburbs, but for a time, the lower-paid were en-
trapped by a growing inability to afford either rents or transport
costs. Only with the introduction of the Cheap Trains Act of 1883
and the all-too-slow spread of subsidised housing was this market
failure answered. Other forms of geographical variation can be
found. In Scotland, the generally lower wages of the average
industrial worker coupled with the way in which feu tenure operated to raise development costs, meant that the average town-
dweller paid more for less land than his English counterpart: the
outcome was a more intensive use of land as the typical Scottish
tenement bears witness to (Rodger, 1983, p. 208).

Turning to the question of how a free market in land acted to
differentiate space within the city, the land-value surface established through the competitive marketing of land affected the
problem at gross rather than specific level. Other things being
equal, urban land-value surfaces peaked in the central, more
accessible parts of the town and declined outwards, slowly along
major routeways but more rapidly in the relatively inaccessible
interstitial areas. In theory, uses and users of land were sifted and
sorted across this surface by their willingness or capacity to bid for
the different locations. If we were dealing with a perfectly uniform
and circular city, we would expect commercial (banks, insurance,
shops, etc.) and industrial users, those capable of yielding the
highest rent, to bid most successfully for town-centre locations. In
terms of ability to pay, middle-class groups were those next-best-
placed to bid in the land market, followed by lower middle-, upper
working- and lower working-class groups. The weakness of this
scheme is that it fails to take account of the fact that different users
were capable of making different adaptations to the land market.
In essence, the land-value surface constituted a utility index,
measuring the accessibility and, therefore, the economic advantage of different locations. Industry, commerce and retail outlets
are certainly concerned with the marginal productivity of different
locations. However, residential users are concerned with matters
of desirability as much as with productivity or the sum-cost of
particular locations, more so in a growing industrial town. The
extent to which these wider issues could distort the problem is
dramatically illustrated by the way in which middle-class groups,

confronted with the expansion of town-centre commerce, shops and industrial workshops over the early nineteenth century, began to relocate themselves to the periphery of English towns. As a process, we can see this relocation taking place in London by the 1690s and in cities like Manchester and Liverpool by the 1830s and 1840s. It was an option which enabled the middle-class to trade off larger plot-size against lower land-values and pleasanter surrounds against the higher cost of commuting. The higher commuting-cost from living further out from city centres obviously became a factor only as urban growth pushed out far beyond the confined space of the pre-industrial town (see, for example, Wohl, 1971, pp. 29–34). It was not such an easy solution for low income groups. They could trade high rents against high-density living. In fact, developers sometimes found that by building cheaply and densely they could derive a greater profit from working-class housing than from middle-class housing. In many towns though, the real problem for low-income groups was the failure of the housing market to provide a supply of cheap housing anywhere, forcing them into the shift of adopting the inner-city housing stock abandoned by the middle-class, offsetting high rents with multiple tenancy.

Despite much empirical work, there is little consensus over when we talk of British towns being organised around social-class districts. A number of studies have revealed signs of an incipient segregation into rich and poor districts by the sixteenth and seventeenth centuries (see, for example, Phythian-Adams, 1979, pp. 161–3). Such a simple contrast, based on the extremes of society, had become widespread by the early nineteenth century. Yet although prefigured in this spatial repulsion of rich and poor, any finely-worked differentiation of towns on a class basis was unquestionably a development of the nineteenth century. There is much in what Vance says about the prior need for the generalisation of housing, that is, the separation of housing and employment, a severance that forced the great mass of workers into the open market for housing (Vance, 1971, pp. 112–13). In the context of the nineteenth century, this market for workers' housing was increasingly dominated by rented accommodation, enabling the relationship between land-values and demand to be fairly well-tuned. Long leases, though, could reintroduce rigidities into the land market (see, for example, Cannadine, 1980, pp. 76 and 122), a factor which partly explains why capital continually sought to create newly-set rents on the suburban periphery of towns. Vance's stress on the role played by the land-developer is also relevant, for along with the landlord, it was the developer who injected a speculative element into the housing market of the industrial town. Studies of suburban development, like Dyos's pioneering work on Camberwell, show a townscape being created by the pushy risk-taking of numerous small speculators (Dyos, 1961, pp. 124–6). Almost inevitably though, such changes in practice took advantage of – indeed, were allowed by – the disequilibrium caused by the sudden and large-scale growth of towns over the nineteenth century. In other words, like the generalisation of housing, the land-developer was both a cause and a consequence of the increasing scale of towns. This scale could be measured in terms of population. Pooley, for instance, has pointed to the strong appearance of both class-based and ethnic segregation in what were fairly compact industrial towns by the 1830s and 1840s, but he is careful to note that it was developed at a street or court rather than a district level and that it involved what, for the time, were the largest towns (Pooley, 1982, pp. 202–3). As Pooley's work with Lawton on Liverpool has ably shown, the scaling-up of such patterns to a district level was part of the process by which the city *in toto* was scaled-up, a process in full movement by the middle decades (the 1850s, 1860s and 1870s) of the century. However, some prefer a simpler, tidier treatment, linking the elaborate differentiation of urban space on a socio-cultural basis to the introduction of mass transit systems over the late nineteenth century. This is very much the view upheld by Ward. Although acknowledging that a crude distinction had emerged between upper middle-class and working-class districts by the middle decades, Ward reserves the more detailed elaboration of this pattern until the closing decades when new transport technologies opened up vast new reserves of land for the developer (Ward, 1975, pp. 135–51; see also comments of Pooley, 1984, pp. 134–5). In London, large-scale commuting began with the introduction of working-men's rail fares in the 1850s and 1860s. Elsewhere, such possibilities were only tapped with the introduction of the horse-drawn tram and, later, the electric tram, from the 1890s onwards (Lawton, 1972, p. 216). Comparison of town plans before and after this great social revolution show the extent to which it triggered-off an explosion of town growth, a growth made all the more dramatic by the fact that the greater pool of cheap land now opened up was used to support a more extensive use of space. Running through all this mammoth scalar expansion of cities over the nineteenth century was a tendency for finer scales of differentiation to emerge within the broader zonation produced by the ability of different income-groups to bid for different locations. For this reason, we find that as the scale of the zones so produced expanded, a still-finer adjustment involving different ethnic, cultural or status groups emerged within them. This finer grouping had the function of mediating between new migrants and the wider urban complex, helping to scale a vastly-increased flow of information and opportunities down to the level of the individual. Just as larger scale brought with it a finer level of differentiation to the residential areas of the town, so too can we detect a finer differentiation of space within city-centres, with the gross character of the early central business district being sifted and sorted into a clearer and larger array of functional sectors, a process of elaboration that started sooner and went further in larger cities like London (Carter, 1983, pp. 164–7).

Towns, no less than industry, were a focus of capital investment and, like industry, they have always experienced problems caused by the rigidity of fixed capital in the face of changing needs and opportunities. In an ideal world, the growth of cities would involve a form of allometric growth, with its different zones expanding in step with the total expansion of the city. In reality, of course, this is far from being the case. Each new phase of expansion has to take existing conditions as its starting-point, adjusting to, rather than supplanting, them. Whilst we can find instances, even before the comprehensive redevelopment schemes of modern times, of towns layouts being radically metamorphosed, like Paris in the nineteenth century by the vision of a ruler or government, there are many examples of town plans resisting change. Even when most of the city had been razed to the ground in London's Great Fire of 1665, Wren's plans for a new baroque capital could not surmount the resistance of individuals possessive of their old property rights. Generally, the conservatism of existing structures must have been increased further when, over the sixteenth and seventeenth centuries, timber-framed buildings of many southern England towns were replaced by more fire-resistant stone, a building material that also allowed for greater height (Clark and

Slack, 1972, pp. 148–9). The racking up of town-centre values by sheer pressure of growth over the eighteenth and nineteenth centuries was countered by substitution, with centre-sites being improved upwards. In fact, even by the mid-seventeenth century, London was said to have numerous five- and six-storey buildings in its centre. In effect, the whole drift of change was against change! The capital improvement of sites, especially in city-centres slowly became something to be accommodated by each new phase of development rather than something that could be reduced to a *tabula rasa* in a fresh beginning. During the take-off in urban growth over the second half of the nineteenth century, the problem of having to deal with inherited structures in the housing market – structures attuned to different market conditions – was solved by the development of a filtering process. As the city expanded outwards, its older housing stock, especially its larger middle-class houses around the inner city, underwent a devaluation in value and status, moving gracefully down the social hierarchy. Although we know that middle-class hand-me-downs were not the only way in which low-income groups were housed, it was a way in which capital no less than the middle class adjusted itself in space when need arose.

Feeding the Masses: From Locality to Continentality

The history of European farming from the sixteenth century onwards is one of continuous adjustment to a higher and higher level of market organisation. The debate over the way that this came about can be considered at different levels. At its most basic, it is a debate about whether the growth of commercial production stemmed, in the first instance, from a change in landlord–peasant relations, a change that created a capitalist class of farmers, eager to profiteer from urban markets, or whether the whole process was primarily demand-induced, with the developing appetite of large and growing towns bringing about a shift from subsistence to commercial and then, as an eventual adaptation, to specialised farms. Such divisions of interpretation are not necessarily helpful. Landlords may have conspired through enclosure and amalgamations to produce larger, more efficient farms whose surplus beyond subsistence made marketing a logical development. They may also have forced up rents in expectation of what could be made by marketing surplus produce. Such developments though, could only take effect if an urban market existed, the scale of that market determining the degree of commercialisation and specialisation. In other words, we need to see each as a condition of the other, each as a possibility of the other, rather than one as the consequence of the other. This mutually-supportive relationship means that the scalar growth of towns over the period 1500–1900 was both a cause and a consequence of the considerable changes in tenure, farm layout, new crops, breeds, tools and rotations over the same period, with any disequilibrium in one being ultimately corrected or magnified by a response from the other (cf. Merrington, 1976, pp. 170–95). It would be absurd to see this as an intimately sensitive relationship, but equally, not to envisage any reciprocation would be no less absurd, for it would suppose that capitalist farming alone could create its own demand or that towns – by themselves – were able to force subsistence farmers into producing what they did not need to produce. There is also a strong case for seeing transport technologies as a co-partner, for they provided the means by which any change in relationship between towns and their food supply could be realised.

At risk of over-complicating my point, it could be argued that whilst the coexistence of a class of capitalist or market-oriented farmers and expanding urban markets may have been instrumental in marrying-off surplus rural production to urban demand; nevertheless, once established, the latter became the dominant force in the relationship. Once farmers marketed produce, we can expect them to have shown an increasing responsiveness to market needs, continually seeking to adapt within the limitations of their farms' physical resources. Because of the number of potential producers and consumers involved, the relationship between farm production and market demand was capable of being a finely-tuned adaptation. Perhaps more importantly, the regularity with which farm produce was marketed meant that farmers were in a position to respond quickly to changes in the profitability of particular produce. Of course, farmers did not perceive and, therefore, did not respond to, market opportunities in any uniform way. Overall, though, we can expect farmers to move or to be moved towards the average rate of profit for a region. Seen thus, the pace of change would be set by the needs of market development.

If we look at England around 1500, we find that its towns,

London included, still had local or, at most, regional systems of supply (Everitt, 1967, pp. 490–502). Over the next four centuries, this system of local markets was transformed by the progressive imposition of larger and larger circuits of trade until, by the end of the nineteenth century, we can speak of a vast international network of food supply. To an extent, this process of broadening involved the coalescing of adjacent markets, as growing urban centres reached out to a wider hinterland of supplies. However, we obscure the true dynamics of the situation if we fail to appreciate that the needs of those urban centres which dominated the urban hierarchy expanded ahead of other centres. Put simply, this meant that the market system grew asymmetrically, from being organised around local markets to being organised around the larger regional centres, then provincial centres, then the metropolitan centre and, finally, a dominant international centre. This sort of coherent, graduated scale of trade expansion runs through a number of discussions (see, for example, Unwin, 1904, p. 9; Gras, 1926, pp. 89–94). The geographer needs to tread warily at this point. Whilst accepting that we are dealing with the ultimate emergence of international systems that integrated national, regional and local systems into a large interdependent system and that the burgeoning growth of metropolitan centres served as the draw-thread by which the whole was pulled together, it does not follow that it was a system of spatial integration that was achieved by a spatially-continuous expansion, local space giving way to regional space and regional to national. In reality, its precise course of development was shaped in detail by all sorts of circumstance or opportunity cost, such as easy accessibility and trading monopolies, though its progressive, accelerating rate of spatial integration is not in dispute.

London provides the best-documented example of this market expansion. It is generally agreed that the needs of London had already fostered a regional hinterland of specialised farming by the sixteenth century (Fisher, 1934–5, pp. 53–4). This compares well with other capitals, like Amsterdam and Paris, which had also fostered specialised rural production by this point (De Vries, 1974, p. 155) In the case of London, Gras talks of a von Thünen landscape starting to take shape around it, with intensive systems of market-gardening and fruit-growing, using hired labour and the city's night-soil, developing on smallholdings around the edge of the city, then a zone of grain farming and, further out, systems of stock production (Gras, 1926, p. 77). The growing scale of its market growth can be measured through its grain needs, its consumption of 165 000 quarters in 1534 expanded eightfold to 1 468 000 quarters by 1696. Just as the area of market-gardening and fruit-farming expanded outwards under pressure from the same increase in demand, so also can we expect the zone producing grain for the London market to have pushed still further out. Whereas over the sixteenth century, grain had been brought into London from the upper Thames valley and from Kent via the Thames, by the end of the seventeenth century, it was being drawn from a much wider area, with coastal areas of Sussex now participating and, more importantly, large areas of East Anglia and even south Yorkshire. In East Anglia, the easy shipment of grain down rivers like the Ouse to Kings Lynn enabled the needs of the capital to penetrate deep inland (Gras, 1926, pp. 107–8). Semi-perishable produce like cheese and butter were also being drawn from further afield, with supplies being shipped from as far north as Yorkshire, Durham and Northumberland (Fisher, 1934–5, p. 50). In fact, by this date, London's system of food supply had become truly national for its stock needs were answered by flows of cattle from peripheral regions like Wales, Ireland even the Highlands of Scotland. Such droves were of lean-stock, the cattle being fattened in the Midlands, Essex and along the Thames marshlands before being sold to London's butchers (Fisher, 1934–5, pp. 56–7).

By the early nineteenth century, the population of London sustained an international network of supply. The capital was now surrounded by a wide area of intensive farming, supplying daily supplies of vegetables, fruit and milk. The scale of its grain needs, meanwhile, had grown so considerably that it now needed supplies from abroad. Peet has represented its supply area as divided into an inner and an outer zone. The former was a zone supplying semi-perishable produce: livestock, butter, cheese and preserved meat. By the early nineteenth century, such produce was being shipped not only from as far away as Ireland, but also, across the North Sea, from area like Friesland, Oldenburg and Holstein (Peet, 1972, p. 15). Beyond, lay a zone of grain production: the cheaper grains were being drawn from along the east coast of Britain, now from areas as far north as north-east Scotland, and from the more easily accessible parts of Holland, north-west

Germany, Jutland and southern Sweden. Still further out, high quality grain was being shipped to London from areas like eastern Europe, tapping the catchments that fed grain down the Oder and Vistula to the Baltic, the Ukraine via the Volga and even small quantities from across the Atlantic (Peet, 1972, pp. 7–9). There was even a still-more-distant production zone, supplying products like tallow and hides from areas as remote as Siberia and South Africa.

During the 1830s and 1840s, a series of coincidental changes set in motion an adjustment to a still-larger scale of market organisation. The rapid development of railways and sharp falls in the costs of shipping had the effect of greatly lessening the friction of distance over land and sea alike. Railways not only made it easier to move bulky commodities like grain and wool from otherwise remote, interior production-zones, it opened up vast reservoirs of low-rent land which helped to depress their opportunity costs still further. Transatlantic shipping costs, meanwhile, fell to under a third of their former levels (North, 1958, pp. 537–47). In Britain, the abolition of the Corn Laws in 1846 created an open market at all price-levels and enabled producers over a much wider area to compete in its grain-markets. Making this new potential a matter of necessity, population doubled over the century and rates of urbanisation in Britain reached their peak over the 1840s, 1850s and 1860s. At the same time, a new elasticity of demand emerged with rising real incomes allowing a broadening of diet. Driven forward by this sharp upward inflexion of demand and facility, patterns of agricultural production were gradually reformulated so as to involve a vastly-increased catchment. These new patterns were apparent by the 1860s and 1870s. Although London continued to form the price-basing point for the system, the effective core of the system now became the whole complex of industrialising cities growing up rapidly not just in Britain but in north-west Europe generally, the whole forming a vast aggregate metropolis. Around it, farming systems everywhere shifted towards more intensive forms, based on market-gardening and livestock products, maximising their proximity to the metropolitan core. In Britain, the shift out of grain into more intensive systems was under way by the 1850s and 1860s. The Great Depression of the 1880s, when cheap grain began flooding into Europe in vastly-increased quantities, confirmed what the more perceptive farmers had earlier realised, that home-produced grain could no longer compete with imported grain. Farmers on the heavier soils especially, were forced to lay down acre after acre to grass, whilst even light-soil farmers now regarded grain as a source of cattle-feed. The production of fatstock though, was itself undergoing changes. At the start of the nineteenth century, one still had a supply system whereby the northern and western areas of Britain acted as stock-rearing areas and the Midlands and south-east fattened them for the London market. By the middle decades of the nineteenth century, producers as far north as Yorkshire found it possible to fatten stock, both for local industrial towns and for London. By the second half of the century, with the development of both railways and refrigeration, former suppliers of lean-stock like Aberdeenshire were now able to supply fatstock and carcases, the latter heralding the decline of Smithfield market (Blackman, 1975, pp. 60–1; Perren, 1975, pp. 385–7). As this broadening occured, livestock producers in the south-east turned more and more to milk production. Encouraged by the railway companies, farmers as far west as Wiltshire and as far north as Derbyshire were producing milk for the London market by the 1880s (Atkins, 1977–8, pp. 208–26). As part of the same pattern of readjustment, specialised zones of intensive farm production were expanding in other parts of north-west Europe by the third quarter of the nineteenth century, with coastal areas of Holland shifting more wholeheartedly into market-gardening and in one of the more notable examples of adaptation at this point, Danish farmers shifting into dairy products. As with London, the hinterland areas immediately around other metropolitan centres saw not only a marked shift into systems of commodity production that maximised their proximity to large and growing centres of demand but also a withdrawal from those products that had become part of an international system of supply, such as grain and wool. The experience of Paris, for example, mirrors that of London. With the construction of railways and the changing price-structure of produce, grain production in proximate areas like, naturally, the Ile de France declined in favour of more intensive systems of farming and those producing perishable produce. So too did wine production, replaced by better quality and now more accessible areas like Bourgogne. Paris's milk-shed spread out to over 200 km and areas which previously produced lean-stock, like Berry, now produced fatstock (Price, 1983, pp. 290–343). Like Britain's Great Depression, this *crise d'adaptation* can be seen as the systemic adjustment between different market structures, one drawn on a far-larger scale than the other.

Beyond this greatly-expanded inner zone of intensive farm production, and directly bound up with its expansion, there now existed extensive areas of grain production, one that increasingly provisioned the whole of metropolitan Europe. The main sources by the late nineteenth century were the mid-West, Eastern Europe and Russia, areas which used low land-rents or coerced-labour systems as the basis for the production of cheap grain. Beyond these grain-producing zones lay others producing wool and hides. As early as the 1830s and 1840s, improvements in shipping had enabled countries like Australia to supply products like wool and hides, provided producer costs were kept to an absolute minimum (Broeze, 1975, especially pp. 587–8). In time, though, refrigeration enabled these distant areas of economic space to opt into meat production, with countries like Argentina producing beef and New Zealand, mutton (see Grigg, 1974, pp. 241–55).

Although concerned ostensibly with the evolving pattern of farm production, Peet appreciated the wider context in which these changes occurred. In this respect, his conclusions anticipated those of Wallerstein: thus, he stresses the role played by free-labour systems in western Europe and coerced systems in eastern Europe and the fact that core and peripheral areas were increasingly allocated the contrasting roles of industrial and agricultural producer respectively. The difference between them is one of chronology. For Wallerstein, the complementarity between the core of the European world system and its periphery was already apparent by the end of the 'long' sixteenth century (Wallerstein, 1974, pp. 155 and 275). There can be no doubting the fact that connections had certainly developed between the different parts of his world-system by the sixteenth century, but the supposition that such areas were already functionally or systemically interdependent is questionable. To assume this is to discount the significance of all the institutional and technological changes of the eighteenth and nineteenth centuries and the way that they both permitted and demanded larger and larger scales of market activity as a condition or consequence of their development. To put this another way, spatial integration has to be realised through the marginal growth of economic activity towards progressively larger scales of activity. It is not sanctioned by the still-feeble flows that linked core and periphery over the sixteenth century. The idea of a European world-system as defined by Wallerstein may have been a possibility by the end of the 'long' sixteenth century, but it was not yet a fact. The value of Peet's work is that it demonstrated in respect of farm production that the market-integration of metropolitan Europe and areas like eastern Europe was a gradual affair, something to be argued through in evolutionary terms rather than just assumed and something that became a fact only in the nineteenth century (see also, Schlebecker, 1960, pp. 187–208).

The Value of Space

How can we summarise the effect which price-fixing markets had on space and spatial order? In answering this question, I do not wish to offer a rounded definition but to pick out those aspects which highlight the differences between the market-based system of spatial order which had matured by the mid-nineteenth century, and prior systems. It has been said that the spatial order of market-based societies is pivoted around the concept of private property. With this in mind, the progressive clarification of property rights which North and Thomas note as occurring over the early modern period is clearly important, though arguably, they exaggerate the extent to which this clarification involved a shift from communal to several property (for example, in North and Thomas, 1973, pp. 150–1). The sharper definition of property rights, whether in land or its resources, made it easier to market them and, as North and Thomas emphasise, lowered transaction costs. However, it was only part of the pressures leading to systemic change over the early modern period. The vast scalar growth of trade – with its dramatic broadening of the areas and commodities involved, its overwhelming increase in the number of transactions, the greater distances over which regular flows were now moving and the increasing complexity of such movements – stressed the organisation of regulated trade. Slowly, new dominant forms of trade evolved, forms whose character was determined through new conditions of trade rather than imposed by legislation or customary notions of 'just price' and 'reasonable profit'. For this reason, we can see these new forms as self-organising, having the means of evolving their own institutional forms, their own checks and balances. In saying this I do not mean to resurrect the belief of nineteenth-century classical economists in 'an economy operating according to laws of its own, *independent of man's conscious will*' [my italics] (Dobb, 1946, p. 200). That would be absurd. A capitalist society may play according to economic rules but, in the final analysis, it can choose to validate these rules or, as North put it, to specify a particular pattern of wealth distribution and to frame an underlying structure of property rights (North, 1981, p. 205). In other words, these rules are not given but are something arrived at through practice and the successive, accumulating actions of governments and individuals, with each new form generating new institutional structures which, under pressure from continuing growth, gradually subdivided into a complex mesh of more specialised, institutional functions. To this extent, we must accept Gregory's point, made in relation to the West Riding woollen industry, that the structures of a capitalist or market-determined society 'were not determinate projections of the fully formed intentions of clothiers' or any other kind of capitalist but need to be seen as the product of 'a continuous movement effected through the bounded activities of reflexive human subjects' (Gregory, 1982, p. 18).

There is an important paradox to be drawn out here. On the one hand, the clarification of property rights, their clearer prescription, led to a closed, more exclusive sense of property and, therefore of space. More and more, property became something as much to be owned and exchanged as to be used (cf. Vance, 1971, p. 107). On the other hand, the clearer specification of land and resources as commodities led – in another sense – to a more open, integrated concept of space. Just as the institutional forms associated with 'freer' forms of trade became more elaborate through becoming more specialised, so also, did the organisation and use of space become more elaborate through becoming more specialised. It has been widely acknowledged that specialisation produced major gains in output, both in industry (Unwin, 1904, p. 9) and agriculture (Wrigley, 1978, p. 301). Invariably, this specialisation had a spatial component. Towns and whole districts became specialised, their degree of specialisation developing in direct proportion to the overall scale of production. This shift towards more specialised uses of space was under way by the sixteenth and seventeenth centuries, but was injected with a much higher impetus once production and demand began to be transformed from the late eighteenth century onwards. Its gross effect was to prise 'regional' space open. What some see as the self-sufficiency and closure of medieval towns and regions now gave way to an increasing degree of interregional and interurban connectedness and, ultimately interdependence. We are still in no position to calibrate this opening-up of regional space precisely. Larger medieval towns were already showing some signs of specialisation by the thirteenth and fourteenth centuries though the medieval norm was still one of generalised economies. Other towns and areas became specialised to varying degrees over the sixteenth and seventeenth centuries. However, despite these early shifts toward specialisation, some historians have still been impressed by the degree to which regions lived within themselves, even as late as the eighteenth century. 'Most economic decisions' wrote Deane of early eighteenth-century Britain, 'were taken in relation to the conditions of the regional market, and as between one region and another, the quality and levels of economic activity and the character and direction of economic change varied substantially' (Deane, 1965, p. 17). On the continent, some commentators see the 'semi-autarkic' nature of industrial regions, each with a wide rather than a specialised array of trades, as persisting everywhere until well into the nineteenth century (Pollard, 1974, pp. 7–35; Kindleberger, 1964, p. 27). Such generalisations may overstate the case for the late persistence of relatively-impervious, regional systems of industrial activity, but at least they help to highlight the real difficulty of assessing when generalised systems gave way to specialised ones. The problem we face here has two dimensions. To adapt Adams's ideas, different spaces have first to be identified, then co-ordinated and, finally, integrated. It is a gradual process involving stages and we must avoid the mistake of confusing the achievement of interconnectedness with the more advanced state of interdependence. In addition, we must recognise that spatial interdependence could be forged at different scales, with both the character and degree of specialisation having to be adjusted accordingly. Although I do not believe its emergence was a geographically-coherent or continuous trend, the ultimate pattern towards which the processes of specialisation and integration worked was the European world-system defined for us by

Wallerstein. However, we must enter this caveat. As a definition of the way the European world-system was differentiated and activated, Wallerstein's system is convincing. As an historically-framed process of growing spatial interdependency – as opposed to interconnectedness – it is not. The linkages which we see being threaded through the different parts of Europe from the sixteenth century onwards, did not produce the kind of complementarity which lies at the heart of his 'world system' until much later. Like others, I would not date its floresence earlier than the nineteenth century. Only at this point do we have the scale of flows and degree of areal specialisation to warrant its description as a European world-system made up of specialised, interlocking parts.

Price-fixing markets cannot be said to have given rise to spatial nodality, but they did transform its meaning. Space became contoured into locations of differing accessibility. The notion of accessibility in this context needs to be seen in terms of its marginal utility, the cost-saving from being in one location rather than another. It might be the point at which access to the greatest number of producers or consumers was maximised or at which distance from a particular resource was minimised. Considered in relation to the nineteenth century, the cost-gradient created by demand, pure and simple, would have been progressively flattened as new transport technologies opened up reserves of cheap land and as some users (that is, higher-income groups) adjusted their adaptation so as to take advantage of the larger and physically more-desirable sites that were now open to development. However, other factors worked in the opposite direction. Once 'best' locations were utilised, further development would have been forced to bid-up on these locations or make do with less favourable ones: the drift of development, therefore, was always towards the saturation of 'best' locations and, therefore, to the pressurising of their locational rent.

If we are forced to choose a feature that above all else distinguished the spatial order incepted by price-fixing markets, then a strong case can be made for seeing it as the tension that emerged between fixed and circulating capital. The build-up of investment in fixed capital – a build up which escalated significantly over the eighteenth and nineteenth century – introduced a strong element of place-specificity into investment, one that threatened the mobility of capital. This place-specificity of fixed capital, its close adaptation to a particular set of technological, locational and socio-cultural opportunities, was further accentuated by the increasing scale and elaboration of urban–industrial complexes. The problem for capital was that as urban–industrial complexes matured, as investment in particular innovations accumulated in an area, then rates of profit averaged out. Yet the more adapted capital became to a place-specific set of conditions, the more this adaptation lowered its ability to respond to the opportunities offered by new production functions or new market conditions. In these circumstances, radical change, the rejuvenation of profit rates, was seen as a matter of preserving the mobility of capital so as to make a fresh adaptation in space. To this end, we find capital markets evolving a more complex form over the eighteenth and nineteenth centuries, differentiating out a circuit of credit or speculative finance which, through devices like share capital, dividend and the fixed depreciation of plant, was able to preserve its freedom to respond to new opportunities. As Braudel observed, only capital had real freedom of movement. Faced 'with inflexible structures ("those of material life and no less of ordinary economic life"), it is able to choose the areas where it wants and is able to meddle, and the areas it will leave to their fate' (Braudel, 1974, p. 445), a freedom which it continually employed to seek out fresh adaptations leaving real-life forms behind like some exuviated cast. It is this constant revolutionising of activities in space, as free capital sought to maximise the advantages of a free market, that lies at the centre of any understanding of how price-fixing markets transformed the character of space and spatial order during the eighteenth and nineteenth centuries.

10
Evolutionary Spatial Systems: A Summary of the Problem

The idea that societal systems have evolved over time permeates much anthropological writing. Only 'a real flat-earther' says Goody, could maintain otherwise (Goody, 1971, p. 20). This accepted, the problem becomes one of how this evolutionary shift should be formulated. Concerned ostensibly with the organisation of society in space, my approach to this formulation has been deliberately slanted. Yet if what I have argued reads like a general history of societal systems, then this is because the history of spatial systems is not a problem we can detach from the organisational issues that surround this wider problem. Indeed, the case for seeing the spatial organisation of society as a central rather than a marginal factor in its evolutionary development is a strong one. It is a case that has been restated time and time again by anthropologists. For them, the problem of societal evolution is about the growing scale and organisational complexity of society, aspects that have an intrinsically-spatial dimension.

That societal systems have evolved into larger and larger forms is an indisputable conclusion. However, if we are to sustain this scalar growth as an ongoing process, we must appreciate that changes in the bases of societal integration were inextricably connected with it, the one supporting the other. Indeed, we could argue that significant jumps in the scale of societal integration are unlikely to survive if there are not corresponding adjustments in the nature of societal integration. Over time, integration in the lead systems of societal order – by 'lead', I mean those manifesting the most elaborate form of organisation and the greatest degree of energy-capture – shifted from being based on kinship and religion, through politically-structured processes to forms in which economic processes predominated. Although we can find exceptions to this course of development at a specific level, it is one that holds reasonably firm at a general level.

352

For some, the main source of contention is over the part accorded to state-systems. At the outset, state-systems were structurally coincident with societal systems, the one serving to delimit the other. However, the mistake is to presume that since state-systems survive, then so must their accordance with societal systems. The long evolutionary homeostasis that some would attach to the state as the context for a particular kind of societal system was broken by the rise of price-fixing markets and the emergence of 'global' or transnational systems of economic integration in which, to use Polanyi's phrase, society was embedded in the economy or, as Powell phrased it, 'the economic frontier no longer corresponds with the political' (Powell, 1915, p. 252). The quibble over chronology apart, the achievement of Wallerstein is in demonstrating how, with the 'modern' world-system, different countries acquired roles within a wider system of societal integration, so that a country's inner social, political and economic character is only explicable within this wider supralocal system of capital relationships, a view now accepted by some human geographers as essential to any understanding of contemporary world order.

Implicit within this stress on the scalar growth of societal systems is acceptance of the fact that such systems also evolved towards greater organisational complexity, though some would see this as a form of developmentalism not evolutionism (Blute, 1979, pp. 49–50). We can generalise this drift towards organisational complexity in two ways. First, society acquired an increasing hierarchy of control levels and functions as part of the means by which it coped with the increasing scale of socio-cultural integration. We can express these levels and functions in purely social terms, with the emergence of ever more elaborate élites and managerial groups: in economic terms through the higher concentration of wealth and control over its production: and geographically through the structuring of space into ever more elaborate hierarchies of order, with the homogeneous systems of early societal systems giving way to systems ordered around an increasingly tiered hierarchy of centres. Most anthropologists stop once they have nursed societal systems into the three-tiered systems associated with early state systems. Arguably, the rise of price-fixing markets added a fourth level, with the global economy that began to evolve after 1500 ordering itself around a sequence of centres that, in their day, were ranked higher than other metropolitan centres as markets and organising centres.

The second way in which societal systems became more elaborate was through the increasing specialisation of roles and functions: this took various forms. Vertically, it involved a growing differentiation of control or managerial functions, a trend most clearly expressed in the basic differentiation that emerged with the formation of early states between the spheres of the judiciary, exchequer, military and church. As societal systems became ranged into higher levels of control, so also were their different spheres of control: the latter being the means by which the former was achieved. Where change involved the integration or amalgamation of societal systems into larger systems, we can expect the different spheres of control to have evolved upwards in step with the overall structure of the system. Alternatively, where primary differentiation occurred in response to the needs of a larger system, then it is likely to have been instituted at the apex of the system and adjusted downwards. Whether adjusted upwards or downwards, each sphere of control faced an identical problem, that of establishing a network of authority that linked the control functions of the core to the outer limits of the system. The common solution was to territorialise the system, conferring a similar slice of responsibilities on each segment. In other words, whilst we can talk about control functions being differentiated, and whilst this emphasised the distinction between core and periphery, the different spheres of control that emerged tended to organise space on the principle of segmentation rather than differentiation.

In the very long term, the differentiation of space has relied more on straightforward economic specialisation. As communities and regional sub-systems became more specialised and their degree of self-sufficiency more marginal, there necessarily occurred an increase in spatial complementarity, interconnectedness and interdependence. It was a process set in motion by the earliest ranked societies, with a simple but far-reaching differentiation of specialist craftsmen from farmers, and later, town-dwellers from country-dwellers. The subsequent advance of this trend involved both the broadening of specialisation through the introduction of new products and activities and the intensification of specialisation through the fragmentation of production systems. The advancing rate of specialisation meant also, that the scale at which the total system of complementarities, interconnections then interdependencies operated, also grew. We can see all these interlocking trends towards increasing scale and complexity as a more or less continuous process, at least at the level of general evolution. However, they must always be seen as operating within a context in which the nature of societal integration also underwent change, with each new form of integration releasing new potentials in terms of the system's scale, organisational complexity and coherence. But in noting those aspects of the problem that manifest a consistent trend, it does not follow that each new 'phase' of societal integration followed naturally from the previous one or that they represent the only means by which societal systems of a certain scale could be sustained.

Turning to the question of how changes in the nature of societal systems were brought about, our prime concern must be with elucidating its geographical dimensions, or with determining whether its ordering in space was an essential part of why it occurred. That some changes need have no intrinsically-spatial component is not disputed. However, the character of others, including some that were vital to the whole course of societal evolution, can only be understood when we establish how they were mapped into space. Two lines of argument would seem important here. First, there are signs that some change was by an aggregative process, with previously-independent societal systems being forged through alliance and interaction into a larger systems, evolving higher forms of organisation that consolidated this larger scale of integration (see Figure 10.1). Second, there is support for a form of societal change that exploits the greater freedom to make pattern-breaking adaptations offered by the geographical colonisation of new or peripheral areas. Again, in stressing the 'external' nature of such change, or seeing it as something that goes around the edge of society, I am not trying to weaken the case for dialectical change. After all, we could see such change as a means of 'externalising' inner conflicts, a general form of Harvey's so-called spatial fix. What I am trying to highlight is a factor that I feel deserves more stress, that is, the problem of seeing the different levels of societal development as adaptations, a commitment of social and physical resources to a particular form of use and organisation. The problem of existing in a material world means that new adaptations, new responses to changing conditions or to the possibilities released by new technologies, are more likely to occur on the edge rather than in the core-areas of society or its subsystems (see Figure 10.1). For this reason, we can expect society always to have a greater propensity for changing from without. In reality, this meant, as Sahlins and Service reasoned, that particular forms of societal order did not carry the baton of societal advancement indefinitely so that we cannot expect it to have always been located in the same place. Lead and laggard areas were continuously being remapped (see Figure 10.2). This is what Ekholm, Friedman and Rowlands have in mind in their suggestion that societal evolution has been sustained through a constantly shifting geography of core and peripheral areas. For them, it provides the basis for an epigenetic view of the way societal systems evolved, or rather, did not evolve, for under such a scheme, societal order is continuously reproduced in the form of core–periphery systems. Whilst accepting their point the core and peripheral areas were being continuously remapped, I would argue that such an emphasis glosses a point that deserves greater emphasis. Peripheral areas of society, defined socially or geographically, offer the greater scope for changing the established order of things or responding to new opportunities. It is in these areas that we are most likely to find examples of evolutionary transcendence, that is, a change that goes beyond the possibilities of the existing system. It is for this reason that we can also expect changes in societal organisation to be underpinned by changes in spatial order (cf. Butzer, 1980, pp. 517–23). With these substantive changes in societal order came not only new centres of control, but also, new bases of integration.

Seeing societal change in this way helps to overcome the criticisms that have been levelled at organisational approaches to societal evolution. The main thrust of this criticism has been directed at the fact that it contains no inbuilt theory of change. Worst still, in order to accommodate change, the whole concept of homeostasis, with societal systems working towards a state of

FIGURE 10.1   *The Geographical Dimensions of Societal Change*

NOTE   Expansion into areas of unused freedom enables new adaptations to be established. These new adaptations can be integrated either as new peripheral subsystems for established systems (Path *A*) or by the upward integration of previously independent systems (Path *B*). The variety of adaptations now being integrated into a single system caused the creation of still higher levels of control which, through their novelty or pioneering nature, could be suitably adapted to the expanded and more varied needs of the system.

357

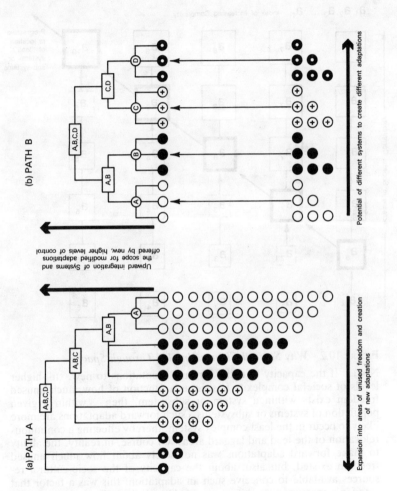

(a) PATH A

Expansion into areas of unused freedom and creation of new adaptations

Upward integration of Systems and the scope for modified adaptations offered by new, higher levels of control

(b) PATH B

Potential of different systems to create different adaptations

358

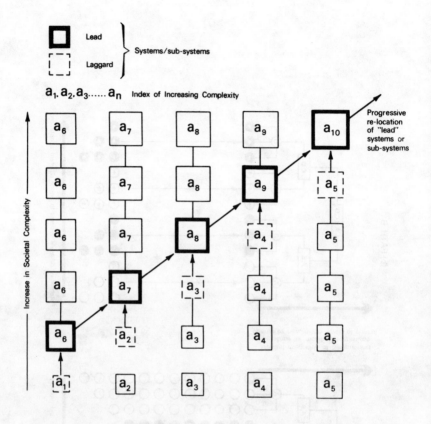

FIGURE 10.2 *Why Societal Change Unfolds Through Space*

NOTE If the capacity to make forward adaptations to new, still-higher levels of societal complexity is seen as a function of how much unused freedom exists within a system or subsystem, then – within a given population of systems or subsystems – such forward adaptations are more likely to occur in the least complex system, thereby effecting a continuous relocation of the lead and laggard areas. Of course, in reality, the ability to make forward adaptations was not solely about how much unused freedom existed, but also, about the capacity of the socio-cultural resources available to conceive such an adaptation: this was a factor that acted in a contrary way, shifting the likelihood of qualitative change back towards the more complex systems.

equilibrium, has to be put aside so as to enable new conditions and goals to become operative.

Compounding matters, many evolutionary schemes have tended to construe change as something immanent within societal order, a progressive, linear adjustment towards greater complexity that occurs entirely within societal systems and which is driven forward by mechanisms that are latent within it and, therefore, internal to it. Seen thus, an evolutionary view of societal order is clearly beset with serious contradictions, as writers like Bock (Bock, 1963, especially pp. 234–5) and Nisbet (Nisbet, 1969, p. 283) have both noted. Accepting that a significant amount of societal change has come about through growth into 'areas of unused freedom' circumvents these problems. It does so because it establishes logical circumstances in which the pressure for growth or change – with all its potential for making more opportune and successful adaptations – could by-pass the control functions that regulated existing societal systems or subsystems within acceptable limits. The extent to which this counters stock criticisms of evolutionary schemes is shown by the way it allows for a closer comparison with Nisbet's own ideas. In an argument designed to confine the study of societal change to the analysis of specific events, Nisbet stresses the importance of seeing stability as the normal condition of societal systems. Nothing, he declared, 'is more obvious than the conservative bent of human behaviour, the manifest desire to preserve, hold, fix, and keep stable' (Nisbet, 1969, pp. 270–1). We are in agreement here. However, whereas Nisbet uses this tendency for societal systems to conserve themselves as support for his view that change, in consequence, can only derive from events that, in effect, intrude into this stability of pattern, shattering its steady-state (see also, Butzer, 1980, p. 517), I would see it as something that deflects change, a reason why new forms have tended to germinate more easily on the periphery of older ones. Nor is my suggestion that change to old-established forms frequently developed from the integration and interaction with newer forms entirely at odds with what Nisbet has argued, for he himself saw change to old-established forms as frequently coinciding with the increased spatial interaction that came from invasions, explorations, migrations and the opening-up of new trade routes (Nisbet, 1969, p. 280). A less negotiable difference is that whilst he stresses the need to see change through historically- and geographically-specific events, I would argue that such a perspective can actually

be used to strengthen an organisational approach since it shows
how the consistency of such an approach is preserved if the course
of societal evolution is taken as a succession of ever more-complex
forms that shift as much through space as through time.

By way of a final conclusion, some comment is needed on how
the ideas presented here compare with ideas on biological evolution. Growth metaphors borrowed from the natural sciences have
long been used to guide thinking about societal development.
Inevitably, Darwin's theory of evolution proved an especially
fruitful source of analogues, with many attempts to fit societal
evolution into the same sort of framework. Latterly, however, the
idea that such analogues have a value has been treated more
sceptically. Opponents of linear evolutionary schemes of societal
development have been quick to point out that even the natural
sciences have moved away from models which presumed the
transformation of species *in toto* or of lineages through time,
classical anagenesis, as the vital dynamic of evolution. Such a
position of argument, though, merely redefines the question without trying to answer it. What we need to know is whether ideas on
societal evolution can be compared in any way with these newer
models of biological evolution. Given the sort of argument already
outlined for societal evolution, the answer must be that whilst
there are points of similarity, one is more impressed by the
differences.

Thus, as an instance of similarity, we might take Gould's concept of punctuated equilibrium: this postulates that the most
significant evolutionary changes occur by means of branching
speciation, or bifurcation, rather than through anagenesis and that
whilst these critical changes take place quickly, the pattern of
speciation so formed tends then to move into a long phase of stasis
(Gould, 1982, p. 83, see also, Blute, 1979, pp. 49–50). Clearly, a
model of branching speciation is broadly consistent with an argument that stresses the greater ease with which societal systems can
'speciate' in peripheral areas than experience a revolutionary
transformation of their core-areas. Such a comparison, though,
leaves out other vital areas in which no such similarity can be
established. Thus, even Gould has acknowledged that whilst biol-
ogists are generally agreed over the dominant and, for some,
exclusive role of natural selection in negatively filtering-out less-
adapted forms, nevertheless, Larmarckian ideas – with their stress
on species making a direct and, therefore, positive adaptation to

environment – have more significance in the context of cultural evolution. Likewise, cultural geographers – both determinists and possibilists – have tended to uphold a Lamarckian approach by seeing cultural forms as a positive or creative adaptation to particular environments (for critical review, see Campbell and Livingston, 1983, pp. 267–87). Of course, there can be no denying that some form of selection has played a part in societal evolution, enabling more successful systems or sub-systems to gain ground at the expense of less-successful ones, but what is distinctive about societal evolution is the facility which it displays for creative as opposed to selective adaptation, for extending the range of possibilities by acquiring new cultural traits rather than working out solutions within a finite range of choice (for a different emphasis, see Kirch, 1980, p. 39; Wenke, 1981, p. 111). This is not just another way of saying that human culture is essentially additive and that its ability to accumulate information endows it with greater evolutionary potential. What we are confronted with is a human capacity to alter the manifest form of evolution. This has come about through the increasing scale of societal systems and the drift towards a single, global system. In the process, the level at which key pattern-breaking adaptations were instituted has shifted from a system to a sub-system level. To put this another way, the early stages of societal evolution can be seen in terms of whole systems leap-frogging each other towards greater complexity. With the rise of complex, hierarchical world-systems, we approach the possibility of a single, linear course of development at a system level. Societal evolution at a general level ceases to be the most successful adaptation amongst a population of systems and becomes the specific evolution of a single system. At the same time, the dynamics of societal change become refocused around the most successful adaptation to prevailing conditions amongst the many and varied subsystems, conditions that are continually shifting. Once we couple the evolutionary implications of the drift towards a single, incorporated system with the radical changes which have taken place in the bases of societal integration, then clearly, we are dealing with a form of evolution in which some of the vital processes have changed both qualitatively and quantitatively through time and a form which has no obvious analogue amongst models of evolutionary biology. As I have tried to demonstrate, it is one that a spatial perspective can do much to illuminate.

Bibliography

Adams, J. S. (1970) 'Residential Structure of Mid-Western Cities', *Annals of the Association of American Geographers*, vol. 60, pp. 37–63.

Adams, R. M. (1966) *The Evolution of Urban Society* (Chicago: Aldine).

Adams, R. N. (1975) *Energy and Structure: A Theory of Social Power* (Austin: University of Texas Press).

Albert, W. (1972) *The Turnpike Road System in England 1663–1840* (Cambridge: Cambridge University Press).

Ames, E. and Rosenberg, N. (1971) 'Changing Technological Leadership and Industrial Growth' in Rosenberg, N. (ed.) *The Economics of Technological Change* (Harmondsworth: Penguin Books) pp. 413–39.

Anderson, B. L. (1970) 'Money and the Structure of Credit in the Eighteenth Century', *Business History*, vol. XII, pp. 85–101.

Anderson, P. (1974) *Lineages of the Absolute State* (London: New Left Books).

Andrewes, A. (1971) *Greek Society* (Harmondsworth: Penguin Books) First published by Hutchinson in 1967.

Aston, T. H. (1958) 'The Origins of the Manor in Britain', *Transactions of the Royal Historical Society*, vol. VIII, pp. 59–83.

Atkins, P. J. (1977–8) 'The Growth of London's Milk Trade, c.1845–1914', *Journal of Transport History*, new series, vol. 4, pp. 208–26.

Aymard, M. (1982) *Dutch Capitalism and World Capitalism* (Cambridge: Cambridge University Press).

Ayres, C. E. (1944) *The Theory of Economic Progress* (Chapel Hill: University of North Carolina Press).

Bahn, P. G. (1977) 'Seasonal Migration in South-West France During the Late Glacial Period', *Journal of Archaeological Science*, vol. 4, pp. 245–57.

Baker, A. R. H. (1979) 'Historical Geography: A new Beginning', *Progress in Human Geography*, vol. 3, pp. 560–70.

Baker, A. R. H. (1982) 'On Ideology and Human geography' in Baker, A. R. H. and Billinge, M. (eds) *Period and Place: Research Methods in Historical Geography* (Cambridge: Cambridge University Press) pp. 233–43.

Baker, A. R. H. (1984) 'Reflections on the Relations of Historical Geography and the Annales School of History' in Baker, A. R. H. and Gregory, D. (eds) *Explorations in Historical Geography* (Cambridge: Cambridge University Press) pp. 1–27.

Baker, D. (1970) 'The Marketing of Corn in the First Half of the Eighteenth Century: North-East Kent', *Agricultural History Review*, vol. 18, pp. 126–50.

Ballard, A. (1913) *British Borough Charters 1042–1216* (Cambridge: Cambridge University Press).

Barbour, V. (1950) *Capitalism in Amsterdam in the Seventeenth Century* (Baltimore: John Hopkins University Press).

Barraclough, G. (ed.) (1938) *Medieval Germany 911–1250, Essays by German Historians* (Oxford: Basil Blackwell) vol. 1.

Barrow, G. W. S. (1980) *The Anglo-Norman Era in Scottish History* (Oxford: Clarendon).

Bateson, G. (1972) *Steps to an Ecology of Mind: Collected Essays in Anthropology, Psychiatry, Evolution and Epistemology* (London: Intertext).

Beardsley, R. K. *et al.* (1962) 'Functional and Evolutionary Implications of Community Patterning' in Wagner, P. L. and Mikesell, M. W. (eds) *Readings in Cultural Geography* (Chicago: University of Chicago Press) pp. 376–98.

Bender, B. (1978–9) 'Gatherer–Hunter to Farmer: A Social Perspective', *World Archaeology*, vol. 10, pp. 204–22.

Beresford, M. W. and Finberg, H. P. R. (1973) *English Medieval Boroughs* (Newton Abbot: David & Charles).

Berger, R. M. (1980) 'The Development of the Retail Trade in Provincial England', *Journal of Economic History*, vol. 40, pp. 123–8.

Berry, B. J. L. (1973) 'A Paradigm for Modern Geography' in Chorley, R. J. (ed.) *Directions in Geography* (London: Methuen) pp. 3–21.

Biddle, M. (1976) 'Towns' in Wilson, D. M. (ed.) *The Archaeology of Anglo-Saxon England* (London: Methuen) pp. 99–150.

Binchy, D. A. (1970) *Celtic and Anglo-Saxon Kingship* (Oxford: Clarendon Press).

Binchy, D. A. (1975) 'Irish History and Irish Law II', *Studia Hibernica*, vol. 16, pp. 7–36.

Birch, A. (1967) *The Economic History of the British Iron and Steel Industry 1784–1879* (London: Cass).

Birdsell, J. B. (1968) 'Some Predictions for the Pleistocene Based on Equilibrium Systems Among Recent Hunter–Gatherers' in Lee, R. B. and de Vore, I. (eds) *Man the Hunter* (Chicago: Aldine) pp. 229–40.

Blackman, J. (1963) 'The Food Supply of an Industrial Town: A Study of Sheffield's Public Markets, 1780–1900', *Business History*, vol. V, pp. 83–97.

Blackman, J. (1975) 'The Cattle Trade and Agrarian Change on the Eve of the Railway Age', *Agricultural History Review*, vol. 23, pp. 48–62.

Bloch, M. (1962) *Feudal Society* (London: Routledge & Kegan Paul) 2nd edn.

Bloch, M. (1967) *Land and Work in Medieval Europe* (London: Routledge & Kegan Paul).

Blum, J. (1978) *The End of the Old Order in Rural Europe* (Princeton: Princeton University Press).

Blute, M. (1979) 'Sociocultural Evolutionism: An Untried Theory', *Behavioral Science*, vol. 24, pp. 46–59.

Bobek, H. (1962) 'The Main Stages in Socio-Economic Evolution From a

Geographical Point of View' in Wagner, P. L. and Mikesell, M. W. (eds) *Readings in Cultural Geography* (Chicago: University of Chicago Press) pp. 218–47.

Bock, J. E. (1963) 'Evolution, Function and Change', *American Sociological Review*, vol. 28, pp. 229–37.

Boserup, E. (1965) *The Conditions of Agricultural Growth: The Economics of Agricultural Change Under Population Pressure* (London, George Allen & Unwin).

Bourdieu, P. (1977) *Outline of a Theory of Practice* (Cambridge: Cambridge University Press).

Boussard, J. (1968) *The Civilization of Charlemagne* (London: Weidenfeld & Nicolson).

Bowsky, W. M. (1981) *A Medieval Italian Commune: Sienna Under the Nine, 1287–1355* (Berkeley: University of California Press).

Boyle, A. (1977) 'Matrilineal Succession in the Pictish Monarchy', *Scottish Historical Review*, vol. LVI, pp. 1–10.

Bradley, R. J. (1980) 'Subsistence, Exchange and Technology – A Social Framework for the Bronze Age in Southern England c.400–700BC' in Barrett, J. and Bradley, R. J. (eds) *The Later British Bronze Age*, BAR British Series, vol. 83(i), part i, pp. 57–75.

Bradley, R. J. (1984) *The Social Foundations of Prehistoric Britain* (London: Longman).

Brandon, P. T. (1969) 'Medieval Clearance in the East Sussex Weald', *Transactions of the Institute of British Geographers*, no. 48, pp. 135–53.

Branston, B. (1955) *Gods of the North* (London: Thames & Hudson).

Braudel, F. (1974) *Capitalism and Material Life 1400–1800* (London: Fontana).

Braudel, F. (1975) *The Mediterranean and the Mediterranean World in the Age of Philip II* (London: Fontana) vol. 1.

Braudel, F. (1977) *Afterthoughts on Material Civilization and Capitalism* (Baltimore: John Hopkins University Press).

Brenner, R. (1977) 'The Origins of Capitalist Development: A Critique of Neo-Smithian Marxism', *New Left Review*, no. 104, pp. 25–92.

Brewer, J. (1982) 'Commercialization and Politics' in McKendrick, N., Brewer, J. and Plumb, J. H. (eds) *The Birth of a Consumer Society* (London: Europa) pp. 197–262.

Britnell, R. H. (1978) 'English Markets and Royal Administration', *Economic History Review*, second series, vol. XXXI, pp. 183–96.

Britnell, R. H. (1981) 'The Proliferation of Markets in England 1200–1349', *Economic History Review*, second series, XXXIV, pp. 209–21.

Broeze, F. J. A. (1975) 'The Cost of Shipping: Shipping and the Early Australian Economy', *Economic History Review*, second series, XXVIII, pp. 582–97.

Brown, A. L. (1973) *Origins of English Feudalism* (London: George Allen & Unwin).

Brown, G. Mackay (1973) *An Orkney Tapestry* (London: Quartet Books).

Brown, J. C. (1982) *In the Shadow of Florence: Provincial Society in Renaissance Pescia* (Oxford: Oxford University Press).

Burgess, C. (1980) *The Age of Stonehenge* (London: Dent).

Butlin, R. A. (1982) *The Transformation of Rural England c.1580–1800: A Study in Historical Geography* (Oxford: Oxford University Press).

Butzer, K. (1980) 'Civilizations: Organisms or Systems', *American Scientist*, vol. 68, pp. 517–23.

Butzer, K. (1982) *Archaeology as Human Ecology* (Cambridge: Cambridge University Press).

Byrne, F. J. (1971) 'Tribes and Tribalism in Early Ireland', *Ériu*, vol. 22, pp. 128–66.

Campbell, J. A. and Livingstone, D. N. (1983) 'Neo-Lamarckism and the Development of Geography in the United States and Great Britain', *Transactions of the Institute of British Geography*, new series, vol. 8, pp. 267–94.

Cannadine, D. (1980) *Lords and Landlords: the Aristocracy and the Towns 1774–1967* (Leicester: Leicester University Press).

Cannadine, D. (1982) 'Residential Differentiation in Nineteenth-Century Towns: From Shapes on the Ground to Shapes in Society' in Johnston, J. H. and Pooley, C. G. (eds) *The Structure of Nineteenth-Century Cities*. (London: Croom Helm) pp. 235–51.

Carneiro, R. L. (1962) 'Scale Analysis as an Instrument for the Study of Cultural Evolution', *South-western Journal of Anthropology*, vol. 18, pp. 149–69.

Carneiro, R. L. (1967) 'On the Relationship Between Size of Population and the Complexity of Social Organization', *South-western Journal of Anthropology*, vol. 23, pp. 234–43.

Carneiro, R. L. (1970) A Theory of the Origin of the State, *Science*, no. 169, pp. 733–8.

Carneiro, R. L. (1974) 'A Reappraisal of the Roles of Technology and Organization in the Origin of Civilization', *American Antiquity*, vol. 39, pp. 179–86.

Carneiro, R. L. (1978) 'Political Expansion as an Expression of the Principle of Competitive Exclusion' in Cohen, R. and Service, E. R. (eds) *Origins of the State: the Anthropology of Political Evolution* (Philadelphia: Institute for the Study of Human Issues) pp. 205–23.

Carr, E. H. (1964) *What is History?* (Harmondsworth: Penguin Books).

Carter, H. C. (1978) 'Towns and Urban Systems 1730–1900' in Dodgshon, R. A. and Butlin, R. A. (eds) *An Historical Geography of England and Wales* (London: Academic Press) pp. 367–400.

Carter, H. C. (1983) *An Introduction to Urban Historical Geography* (London, Edward Arnold).

Chadwick, H. M. (1905) *Studies in Anglo-Saxon Institutions* (Cambridge: Cambridge University Press).

Chapman, S. D. (1971a) 'Fixed Capital Formation in the British Cotton Manufacturing Industry' in Higgins, J. P. P. and Pollard, S. (eds) *Aspects of Capital Investment in Great Britain 1750–1850* (London: Methuen) pp. 57–107.

Chapman, S. D. (ed.) (1971b) *The History of Working-Class Housing: A Symposium* (Newton Abbot: David & Charles).

Chapman, S. D. (1972) *The Cotton Industry in the Industrial Revolution* (London: Macmillan).

Charles-Edwards, T. M. (1971) 'Some Celtic Kinship Terms', *Bulletin of the Board of Celtic Studies*, vol. XXIV, pp. 105–22.

Charles-Edwards, T. C. (1972) 'Kinship, Status and the Origins of the Hide', *Past and Present*, no. 56, pp. 3–33.

Charles-Edwards, T. C. (1976) 'The Distinction Between Land and Movable Wealth in Anglo-Saxon England' in Sawyer, P. H. (ed) *Medieval Settlement* (London: Edward Arnold) pp. 180–7.

Chartres, J. (1977a) *Internal Trade in England 1500–1700* (London: Macmillan).

Chartres, J. (1977b) 'Road Carrying in England in the Seventeenth Century: Myth and Reality', *Economic History Review*, second series, XXX, pp. 73–94.

Cipolla, C. (1952) 'The Decline of Italy: The Case of a Fully-Matured Economy', *Economic History Review*, second series, vol. V, pp.178–87.

Cipolla, C. (1976) *Before the Industrial Revolution: European Society and Economy, 1000–1700* (London: Methuen).

Claessen, J. J. M. and Skalnik, P. (1978) 'The Early State: Theories and Hypotheses' in Claessen, J. J. M. and Skalnik, P. (eds) *The Early State* (The Hague: Mouton) pp. 3–29.

Clanchy, C. T. (1979) *From Memory to Written Record: England 1066–1307* (London: Edward Arnold).

Clark, G. (1965) 'Traffic in Stone Axe and Adze Blades', *Economic History Review*, second series, XVIII, pp. 1–28.

Clark, G. (1975) *The Earlier Stone Age Settlement of Scandinavia* (Cambridge: Cambridge University Press).

Clark, G. (1983) *The Identity of Man* (London: Methuen).

Clark, P. (ed.) (1976) *The Early Modern Town: A Reader* (London: Longman).

Clark, P. (1981) 'Introduction: English County Towns 1500–1800 in Clark, P. (ed.) *County Towns in Pre-Industrial England* (Leicester: Leicester University Press).

Clark, P. and Slack, P. (eds) (1972) *Crisis and Order in English Towns 1500–1700* (London: Routledge & Kegan Paul).

Clarke, D. L. (1968) *Analytical Archaeology* (London: Methuen).

Clarke, D. L. (1972) 'A Provisional Model of an Iron Age Society and Its Settlement System' in Clarke, D. L. (ed.) *Models in Prehistory* (London: Methuen) pp. 801–69.

Clarke, D. L. (1976) 'Mesolithic Europe: the Economic Basis' in Sieveking, G. de G., Longworth, I. H. and Wilson, K. E. (eds) *Problems in Economic and Social Archaeology* (London: Duckworth) pp. 449–81.

Clout, H. D. (1977) 'Industrial Development in the Eighteenth and Nineteenth Centuries' in Clout, H. D. (ed.) *Themes in the Historical Geography of France* (London, Academic Press) pp. 447–82.

Cohen, M. N. (1977) *The Food Crises in Prehistory*. (New Haven: Yale University Press).

Cohen, R. (1978) 'State Origins: A Reappraisal' in Claesen, H. J. M. and Skalnik, P. (eds) *The Early State* (The Hague: Mouton) pp. 31–75.

Cohen, R. and Service, E. R. (eds) (1978) *Origins of the State: The Anthropology of Political Evolution* (Philadelphia: Institute for the Study of Human Issues).

Coleman, D. C. (1977) *The Economy of England 1450–1750* (Oxford: Oxford University Press).

Coleman, E. R. (1977) 'People and Property: the Structure of a Medieval Seigneury', *Journal of European Economic History*, 6, pp. 675–702.

Coles, J. M. (1971) 'The Early Settlement of Scotland: Excavations at Morton, Fife', *Proceedings of the Prehistoric Society*, vol. XXXVII, pp. 284–366.

Collis, J. (1971) 'Markets and Money' in Hill, D. and Jesson, M. (eds) *The Iron Age and Its Hill Forts* (Southampton: University of Southampton Monograph Series) no 1, pp. 97–103.

Coorneart, E. (1970) 'French Guilds Under the Old Regime' in Cameron, R. (ed.) *Essays in French Economic History* (Homewood, Illinois: American Economic Association) pp. 123–7.

Corfield, P. (1972) 'A Provincial Capital in the Seventeenth Century: The Case of Norwich' in Clark, P. and Slack, P. (eds) *Crisis and Order in English Towns 1500–1700* (London: Routledge & Kegan Paul) pp. 263–310.

Crouzet, F. (1972) 'Editor's Introduction' in Crouzet, F. (ed.) *Capital Formation in the Industrial Revolution* (London: Routledge & Kegan Paul) pp. 1–69.

Cunliffe, B. (1974) *Iron Age Communities in Britain* (London: Routledge & Kegan Paul).

Cunliffe, B. (1976) 'Hillforts and Oppida in Britain' in Sieveking, G. de G., Longworth, I. B. and Wilson, K. E. (eds) *Problems in Economic and Social Archaeology* (London: Duckworth) pp. 343–58.

Cunliffe, B. (1978) *Hengistbury Head* (London: Elek).

Dalton, G. (ed.) (1968) *Primitive, Archaic and Modern Economies: Essays of Karl Polanyi* (Boston: Beacon Press).

Dalton, G. (1975) 'Karl Polanyi's Analysis of Long-distance Trade and His Wider Paradigm' in Sabloff, J. A. and Lamberg-Karlovsky. C. C. (ed.) *Ancient Civilization and Trade* (Albuquerque: University of New Mexico Press) pp. 63–162.

Darby, H. C. (1956) 'The Clearing of Land in Europe' in Thomas, W. L. (ed.) *Man's Role in Changing the Face of the Earth* (Chicago: University of Chicago Press) pp. 183–216.

Darvill, T. C. (1979) 'Court Cairns, Passage Graves and Social Change in Ireland', *Man*, vol. 14, pp. 311–27.

Davidson, H. R. Ellis (1964) *Gods and Myths of Northern Europe* (Harmondsworth: Penguin Books).

Davies, R. R. (1978) *Lordship and Society in the March of Wales 1282–1400* (Oxford: Clarendon Press).

Davies, W. and Vierck, H. (1974) 'The Contexts of Tribal Hidage: Social Aggregates and Settlement Patterns', *Frümittellterliche Studien*, vol. 8, pp. 223–93.

Davis, R. (1962) *The Rise of the English Shipping Industry* (Newton Abbot: David & Charles).

Davis, R. (1973) *The Rise of the Atlantic Economies* (London: Weidenfeld & Nicolson).

De Roover, R. (1958) 'The Concept of the Just Price: Theory and Economic Policy', *Journal of Economic History*, vol. XVIII, pp. 418–38.

De Rosa, L. (1979) 'Property Rights, Institutional Change and Economic Growth in Southern Italy in the XVIIIth and XIXth Centuries', *Journal of European Economic History*, vol. 8, pp. 531–51.

De Vries, J. (1974) *The Dutch Rural Economy in the Golden Age, 1500–1700* (New Haven: Yale University Press).

De Vries, J. (1978) 'Barges and Capitalism: Passenger Transportation in the Dutch Economy', *A. A. G. Bijdragen*, no. 21, pp. 33–398.

De Vries, J. (1981) 'Patterns of Urbanization in Pre-Industrial Europe', in Schmal, H. (ed.) *Patterns of European Urbanization Since 1500* (London: Croom Helm) pp. 77–109.

Deane, P. (1965) *The First Industrial Revolution* (Cambridge: Cambridge University Press).

Deane, P. (1972) 'Capital Formation in Britain Before the Railway Age', first published 1961, reprinted in Crouzet, F. (ed.) *Capital Formation in the Industrial Revolution* (London: Methuen) pp. 94–118.

Deane, P. and Cole, W. A. (1967) *British Economic Growth 1688–1959* (Cambridge: Cambridge University Press) 2nd edn.

Dennell, R. (1983) *European Economic Prehistory: A New Approach* (London: Academic Press).

Dickinson, R. E. (1962) *The West European City: A Geographical Interpretation* (London: Routledge & Kegan Paul).

Dillon, M. (1962) *Lebor Na Cert: The Book of Rights* (Dublin: Irish Texts Society).

Dobb, M. (1946) *Studies in the Development of Capitalism* (London: Routledge & Kegan Paul).

Dobzhansky, T. (1970) *Genetics of the Evolutionary Approach* (New York: Columbia University Press).

Dodgshon, R. A. (1975a) 'Scandinavian Solskifte and the Sunwise Division of Land in Eastern Scotland', *Scottish Studies*, vol. 19, pp. 1–14.

Dodgshon, R. A. (1975b) 'Infield–outfield and the Territorial Expansion of the English Township', *Journal of Historical Geography*, vol. 1, pp. 327–45.

Dodgshon, R. A. (1977) 'The Modern World-System: A Spatial Perspective', *Peasant Studies*, vol. VI, pp. 8–19.

Dodgshon, R. A. (1980) *The Origin of British Field Systems* (London: Academic Press).

Dodgshon, R. A. (1981) *Land and Society in Early Scotland* (Oxford: Clarendon Press).

Dodgshon, R. A. (1983) 'Agricultural Change and Its Social Consequences in the Southern Uplands 1600–1780' in Devine, T. M. and Dickson, D. (eds) *Ireland and Scotland 1600–1850.* (Edinburgh: J. Donald) pp. 46–59.

Dodgshon, R. A. (1986a) 'Symbolic Classification and the Making of

Early Celtic Landscape', *Cosmos*, vol. 1, in press.

Dodgshon, R. A. (1986b) 'West Highland Chiefdoms 1500–1745: A Study in Redistributive Exchange' in R. Mitchison and P. Roebuck (eds) *Scotland and Ireland: A Comparative Study of Development* (Edinburgh: J. Donald, in press).

Doehaerd, R. (1978) *The Early Middle Ages in the West: Economy and Society* (Amsterdam: North Holland).

Dollinger, P. (1970) *The German Hansa* (London: Macmillan). Original German edition first published in 1964.

Du Boulay, F. R. H. (1966) *The Lordship of Canterbury: An Essay on Medieval Society* (London: Nelson).

Duby, G. (1968) *Rural Economy and Country Life in the Medieval West* (London: Edward Arnold).

Duby, G. (1974) *The Early Growth of the European Economy: Warriors and Peasants from the Seventh to the Twelfth Century* (London: Weidenfeld & Nicolson).

Duby, G. (1977) *The Chivalrous Society* (London: Edward Arnold).

Dudley, D. (1975) *Roman Society* (Harmondsworth: Pelican Books).

Duffy, P. J. (1981) 'The Territorial Organization of Gaelic Landownership and its Transformation in County Monaghan, 1591–1640', *Irish Geography*, vol. 14, pp. 1–26.

Duncan-Jones, R. (1965) 'An Epigraphic Survey of Costs in Roman Italy', *Papers of the British School at Rome*, vol. 3, pp. 189–306.

Duncan-Jones, R. (1974) *The Economy of the Roman Empire. Quantitative Studies* (Cambridge: Cambridge University Press).

Durkheim, E. and Mauss, M. (1969) *Primitive Classification*, translated with introduction by R. Needham (London: Cohen & West). Original French edition first published 1903.

Dyer, C. (1980) *Lords and Peasants in a Changing Society: The Estates of the Bishopric of Worcester 680–1540* (Cambridge: Cambridge University Press).

Dyos, H. J. (1961) *Victorian Suburb: A Study of the Growth of Camberwell* (Leicester: Leicester University Press).

Earle, P. (ed.) (1974) *Essays in European Economic History 1500–1800* (Oxford: Clarendon Press).

Ehrenberg, V. (1969) *The Greek State* (London: Methuen) 2nd edn.

Eisenstadt, S. N. (1963) *The Political Systems of Empires* (New York: Free Press of Glencoe).

Eisenstadt, S. N. (1964) 'Social Change, Differentiation and Evolution', *American Sociological Review*, vol. 29, pp. 375–86.

Ekholm, K. (1977) 'External Exchange and the Transformation of Central African Societies' in Friedman, J. and Rowlands, M. J. (eds) *The Evolution of Social Systems* (London: Duckworth) pp. 115–36.

Ekholm, K. (1980) 'On the Limitations of Civilization: the Structure and Dynamics of Global Systems', *Dialectical Anthropology*, vol. 5, pp. 155–66.

Ekholm, K. (1981) 'On the Structure and Dynamics of Global Systems', pp. 241–61 in Kahn, J. S. and Llobera, J. R. (eds) *The Anthropology of Pre-Capitalist Societies* (London: Macmillan).

Eliade, M. (1954) *The Myth of the Eternal Return or, Cosmos and History* (Princeton: Princeton University Press). Original French edition published in 1949.

Eliade, M. (1958) *Patterns in Comparative Religion* (London: Sheed & Ward).

Eliade, M. (1973) *Australian Religions: An Introduction* (Ithaca: Cornell University Press).

Elias, N. (1982) *State Formation and Civilization, vol. 2, The History of Manners* (Oxford: Blackwell). Original German edition published in 1939.

Ellison, A. (1981) 'Towards a Socioeconomic Model for the Middle Bronze Age in Southern England' in Hodder, I., Isaac, G. and Hammond, N. (eds) *Pattern of the Past: Studies in Honour of David Clarke* (Cambridge: Cambridge University Press) pp. 413–38.

Englander, D. (1983) *Landlord and Tenant in Urban Britain 1838–1918* (Oxford: Clarendon Press).

Evans, E. E. (1973) *The Personality of Ireland: Habitat, Heritage and History* (Cambridge: Cambridge University Press).

Everitt, A. (1967) 'The Marketing of Agricultural Produce' in Thirsk, J. (ed.) *The Agrarian History of England and Wales, vol. IV, 1500–1640.* (Cambridge: Cambridge University Press) pp. 466–592.

Everitt, A. (1973) 'Town and Country in Victorian Leicestershire: the Role of the Village Carrier' in Everitt, A. (ed.) *Perspectives in English Urban History* (London: Macmillan) pp. 213–40.

Everitt, A. (1976) 'Country Carriers in the Nineteenth Century, *Journal of Transport History*, N. S. vol. III, pp. 179-202.

Everitt, A. (1979) 'Country, County and Town: Patterns of Regional Evolution in England', *Transactions of the Royal Historical Society*, fifth series, vol. 29, pp. 79–108.

Farber, H. (1978) 'A Price and Wage Study for Northern Babylonia During the Old Babylonian Period', *Journal of the Economic and Social History of the Orient*, vol. 21, pp. 1–51.

Farmer, D. L. (1956-7) 'Some Price Fluctuations in Angevin England', *Economic History Review*, second series. vol. IX, pp. 34–43.

Farnie, D. A. (1979) *The English Cotton Industry and the World Market* (Oxford: Clarendon Press).

Ferguson, J. (1980) *Greek and Roman Religion: A Source Book* (Park Ridge, New Jersey: Noyes Press).

Finberg, H. P. R. (1974) *The Formation of England 550–1042* (St Albans: Paladin).

Finley, M. I. (1970) 'Aristotle and Economic Analysis', *Past and Present*, no. 47, pp. 3–25.

Finley, M. I. (1973) *The Ancient Economy* (London: Chatto & Windus).

Finley, M. I. (1978) 'The Ancient City: From Coulanges to Max Weber and Beyond', *Comparative Studies in Society and History*, vol. 19, pp. 305–27.

Fischer, W. (1973) 'Rural Industrialization and Population Change', *Comparative Studies in Society and History*, vol. 15, pp. 158–70.

Fisher, F. J. (1934–5) 'The Development of the London Food Market 1540–1640', *Economic History Review*, vol. 5, pp. 46–64.

Flannery, K. V. (1976) 'The Cultural Evolution of Civilizations' in Richerson, P. J. and McEvoy, J. (eds) *Human Ecology: An Environmental Approach* (North Scituate, Massachusetts: Duxbury Press) pp. 96–118.

Fleckenstein, J. (1978) *Early Medieval Germany* (Amsterdam: North Holland).

Fleming, A. (1971) 'Territorial Patterns in Bronze Age Wessex', *Proceedings of the Prehistoric Society*, XXXVII, pp. 138–66.

Fleming, A. (1972–3) 'The Genesis of Pastoralism in European Prehistory', *World Archaeology*, vol. 4, pp. 179–91.

Fleming, A. (1973) 'Models for the Development of the Wessex Culture' in Renfrew, C. (ed.) *The Explanation of Culture Change: Models in Prehistory* (London: Duckworth) pp. 571–85.

Fleming, A. (1978) 'The Prehistoric Landscape of Dartmoor, part 1, South Dartmoor', *Proceedings of the Prehistoric Society*, vol. 44, pp. 97–123.

Flinn, M. W. (1984) *The History of the British Coal Industry* (Oxford: Clarendon Press) vol. 2.

Foley, R. (1977) 'Space and Energy: A Method for Analysing Habitat Value and Utilization in Relation to Archaeological Sites', in Clarke, D. L. (ed.) *Spatial Archaeology* (London: Academic Press) pp. 163–87.

Foster, J. (1974) *Class Struggle and the Industrial Revolution* (London: Methuen).

Fowler, P. J. (1983) *The Farming of Prehistoric Britain* (Cambridge: Cambridge University Press).

Fox, C. (1932) *The Personality of Britain* (Cardiff: National Museum of Wales).

Fox, R. (1967) *Kinship and Marriage: An Anthropological Perspective* (Harmondsworth: Penguin Books).

Fox, R. G. (1976) 'Lineage Cells and Regional Definition in Complex Societies' in Smith, C. A. (ed.) *Regional Analysis, vol. 11, Social Systems* (New York: Academic Press) pp. 95–121.

Frankel, M. (1955) 'Obsolesence and Technological Change in a Marketing Economy', *American Economic Review*, vol. 45, pp. 296–319.

Freeman, A. M. (ed.) (1944) *Annála Connacht: The Annals of Connacht.* (Dublin: Institute for Advanced Studies).

Freeman, M. J. (1980) 'Road Transport in the English Industrial Revolution: An Interim Reassessment', *Journal of Historical Geography*, vol. 6, pp. 17–28.

Fried, M. H. (1975) *The Notion of a Tribe* (Menlo Park, California: Cummings).

Friedman, J. (1975) 'Tribes, States and Transformations' in Bloch, M. (ed.) *Marxist Analyses and Social Anthropology* (London: Maleby Press) pp. 161–202.

Friedman, J. (1982) 'Catastrophe and Continuity in Social Evolution' in Renfrew, C., Rowlands, M. J. and Segraves, B. A. (eds) *Theory and Explanation in Archaeology* (London: Academic Press) pp. 145–96.

Friedman, J. and Rowlands, M. J. (1977) 'Notes Towards an Epigenetic Model of the Evolution of Civilization' in Friedman, J. and Rowlands, M. J. (eds) *The Evolution of Social Systems* (London: Duckworth) pp. 201–76.

Friedrich, P. (1966) 'Proto-Indo-European Kinship', *Ethnology*, vol. 5, pp. 1–36.

Frier, B. W. (1977) 'The Rental Market in Early Imperial Rome', *Journal of Roman Studies*, vol. 67, pp. 27–37.

Fullerton, B. (1975) *The Development of British Transport Networks* (Oxford: Oxford University Press).

Gall, P. L. and Saxe, A. A. (1978) 'The Ecological Evolution of Culture: The State as Predator in Succession Theory' in Earle, T. K. and Ericson, J. E. (eds) *Exchange Systems in Prehistory* (New York: Academic Press) pp. 255–68.

Gamble, C. (1978) 'Resource Exploitation and the Spatial Patterning of Hunter-gatherer: A Case Study' in Green, D., Haselgrove, C. and Spriggs, M. (eds) *Social Organization and Settlement* (Oxford: British Archaeological Reports, International Series) no. 47, part 1, pp. 153–85.

Gamble, C. (1980) 'Information Exchange in the Paleolithic', *Nature*, no. 283, pp. 522–3.

Gamble, C. (1981) 'Social Control and the Economy' in Sheridan, A. and Bailey, G. (eds) *Economic Anthropology* (Oxford: British Archaeological Reports, International Series) no. 96, pp. 187–213.

Ganshof, F. L. (1971) *The Carolingians and the Frankish Monarchy: Studies in Carolingian History* (London: Longman).

Ganshof, F. L. and Verhulst, A. (1966) 'Medieval Agrarian Society in Its Prime: France, The Low Countries and Western Germany' in Postan, M. M. (ed.) *The Cambridge Economic History of Europe, vol. I, The Agrarian Life of the Middle Ages* (Cambridge: Cambridge University Press) pp. 290–339.

Gattrell, V. A. C. (1977) 'Labour, Power, and the Size of Firms in Lancashire Cotton in the Second Quarter of the Nineteenth Century', *Economic History Review*, second series, XXX, p. 95–139.

Georgescu-Roegen, N. (1971) *The Entropy Law and the Economic Process* (Cambridge, Massachusetts: Harvard University Press).

Giddens, A. (1981) *Contemporary Critique of Historical Materialism, vol. 1, Power, Property and the State* (London: Macmillan).

Giddens, A. (1984) *The Constitution of Society* (Cambridge: Polity Press).

Gill, S. D. (1982) *Beyond 'The Primitive': The Religions of Non-literate Peoples* (Englewood Cliffs: Prentice-Hall).

Gimbutas, M. (1982) *The Goddesses and Gods of Old Europe 6500–3500BC: Myths and Cult Images* (London: Thames & Hudson) 2nd edn.

Gledhill, J. and Larsen, M. (1982) 'The Polanyi Paradigm and a Dynamic Analysis of Archaic States' in Renfrew, C., Rowlands, M. J. and Segraves, B. A. (eds) *Theory and Explanation in Archaeology* (New York and London: Academic Press) pp. 197–229.

Godelier, M. (1975) 'Modes of Production, Kinship and Demographic

Structures' in Bloch, M. (ed.) *Marxist Analyses and Social Anthropology* (London: Malaby Press) pp. 3–27.

Goldthwaite, R. A. (1980) *The Building of Renaissance Florence: An Economic and Social History* (Baltimore: John Hopkins University Press).

Goody, J. and Watt, I. (1962–3) 'The Consequences of Literacy', *Comparative Studies in Society and History*, vol. 5, pp. 304–45.

Goody, J. (1976) *Production and Reproduction. A Comparative Study of the Domestic Domain* (Cambridge: Cambridge University Press).

Göransson, S. (1961) 'Regular Open Field Pattern in England and Scandinavia', *Geografiska Annaler*, XL111B, pp. 80–101.

Gottfried, R. S. (1982) *Bury St Edmunds and the Urban Crisis: 1290–1539* (Princeton: Princeton University Press).

Gould, S. J. (1982) 'The Meaning of Punctuated Equilibrium and Its Role in validating a Hierarchical Approach to Macroevolution' in Milkman, R. (ed.) *Perspectives on Evolution* (Sunderland, Massachusetts: Sinauer Associates) pp. 83–104.

Grant, M. (1980) *The Etruscans* (London: Weidenfeld & Nicolson).

Gras, N. S. B. (1926) *The Evolution of the English Corn Market* (Cambridge, Massachusetts: Harvard University Press).

Gray, H. L. (1914) 'The Commutation of Villein Services in England Before the Black Death', *English Historical Review*. XXIX, pp. 625–56.

Greenway, D. E. (ed.) (1972) *Charters of the Honour of Mowbray 1107–1191* (Oxford: Oxford University Press) British Academy: Records of Social and Economic History, new series, no. 1.

Gregory, D. (1978) *Ideology, Science and Human Geography* (London: Hutchinson).

Gregory, D. (1980) 'The Ideology of Control: Systems Theory and Geography', *Tijdschrift voor Economische en Sociale Geografie*, LXXI, pp. 327–42.

Gregory, D. (1982) *Regional Transformation and Industrial Revolution: A Geography of the Yorkshire Woollen Industry*. (London: Macmillan).

Gregory, D. (1984) 'Contours of Crisis? Sketches for a Geography of Class Struggle in the Early Industrial Revolution in England' in Baker, A. R. H. and Gregory, D. (ed.) *Explorations in Historical Geography* (Cambridge: Cambridge University Press) pp. 68–117.

Griaule, M. and Dieterlen, G. (1954) 'The Dogon' in Forde, D. (ed.) *African Worlds* (London: RIIA) pp. 83–110.

Grierson, R. (1959) 'Commerce in the Dark Ages: A Critique of the Evidence', *Transactions of the Royal Historical Society*, fifth series, vol. 9, pp. 123–40.

Griffeth, R. and Thomas, C. G. (eds) (1981) *The City-State in Five Cultures* (Santa Barbara and Oxford: ABC–Clio).

Grigg, D. B. (1974) *The Agricultural Systems of the World* (Cambridge: Cambridge University Press).

Grigg, D. (1982) *The Dynamics of Agricultural Change* (London: Hutchinson).

Habakkuk, H. J. (1962) *American and British Technology in the Nineteenth Century* (Cambridge: Cambridge University Press).
Hallam, E. M. (1980) *Capetian France 987–1328* (London: Longman).
Hallpike, C. R. (1979) *The Foundations of Primitive Thought* (Oxford: Clarendon Press).
Halstead, R. (1981) 'From Determinism to Uncertainty: Social Storage and the Rise of the Minoan Palace Culture' in Sheridan, R. and Bailey, G. (eds) *Economic Archaeology* (Oxford: British Archaeology Reports, International Series) no. 96, pp. 187–213.
Halstead, P. and O'Shea, J. (1982) 'A Friend In Need is a Friend Indeed: Social Storage and the Origins of Social Ranking' in Renfrew, C. and Shennan, S. (eds) *Ranking, Resource and Exchange: Aspects of the Archaeology of Early European Society* (Cambridge: Cambridge University Press) pp. 92–9.
Harner, M. J. (1970) 'Population Pressure and the Social Evolution of Agriculturalists', *South-western Journal of Anthropology*, vol. 26, pp. 67–86.
Harpending, H. and Davis, H. (1977) 'Some Implications for Hunter–gatherer Ecology Derived from the Spatial Structuring of Resources', *World Archaeology*, vol. 8, pp. 275–86.
Harris, D. R. (1977) 'Settling Down: An Evolutionary Model for the Transformation of Mobile Bands into Sedentary Communities', in Friedman, J. and Rowlands, M. J. (eds) *The Evolution of Social Systems* (London: Duckworth) pp. 401–17.
Harris, M. (1980) *Cultural Materialism. the Struggle for a Science of Culture* (New York: Vintage Books).
Hartwell, R. M. (1971) *The Industrial Revolution and Economic Growth* (London: Methuen).
Harvey, B. (1977) *Westminster Abbey and Its Estates in the Middle Ages.* (Oxford: Clarendon Press).
Harvey, D. (1973) *Social Justice and the City* (London: Edward Arnold).
Harvey, D. (1981) 'The Spatial Fix – Hegel, Von Thunen and Marx', *Antipode*, vol. 13, pp. 1–12.
Harvey, D. (1982) *The Limits of Capital* (Oxford: Blackwell).
Harvey, P. D. A. (1974) 'The Pipe Rolls and the Adoption of Demesne Farming in England', *Economic History Review*, second series, vol. XXV11, pp. 345–59.
Hatcher, J. (1969) 'A Diversified Economy: Later Medieval Cornwall', *Economic History Review*, second series, vol. XXII, pp. 208–27.
Hatcher, J. (1981) 'English Serfdom and Villeinage: Towards a Reassessment', *Past and Present*, no. 90, pp. 3–39.
Hawke, G. R. (1970) *Railways and Economic Growth in England 1840–1870* (Oxford: Clarendon Press).
Hawkins, J. D. (1979) 'The Origins and Dissemination of Writing in Western Asia' in Moorey, P. R. S. (ed.) *The Origins of Civilization* (Oxford: Clarendon Press) pp. 128–66.
Heers, J. (1974) 'The Feudal Economy and Capitalism: Words, Ideas and Reality', *Journal of European Economic History*, vol. 3, pp. 609–53.

Heers, J. (1977) *Family Clans in the Middle Ages: A Study of Political and Social Structures in Urban Areas* (Amsterdam: North-Holland) Original French version published in 1974.

Henderson, R. N. (1972) *The King in Every Man: Evolutionary Trends in Onitsha Ibo Society and Culture* (New Haven: Yale University Press).

Herlihy, D. (1958) *Pisa in the Early Renaissance: A Study of Urban Growth* (New Haven: Yale University Press).

Herlihy, D. (1959) 'The History of the Rural Seigneury in Italy, 751–1200', *Agricultural History*, pp. 58–71.

Herlihy, D. (1967) *Medieval and Renaissance Pistoia: The Social History of an Italian Town, 1200–1430* (New Haven: Yale University Press).

Hiatt, I. R. (1968) 'Ownership and Use of Land Among the Australian Aborigines' in Lee, R. B. and de Vore, I. (eds) *Man the Hunter* (Chicago: Aldine) pp. 99–102.

Hibbert, A. B. (1953) 'The Origins of the Medieval Town Patriciate', *Past and Present*, no. 15, pp. 15–27.

Hibbert, A. B. (1963) 'The Economic Policies of Towns' in Postan, M. M., Rich, E. E. and Miller, E. (eds) *The Cambridge Economic History of Europe, vol. III, Economic Organization and Policies in the Middle Ages* (Cambridge: Cambridge University Press) pp. 157–229.

Hicks, J. (1969) *A Theory of Economic History* (Oxford: Oxford University Press).

Higgins, J. P. P. and Pollard, S. (1971) *Aspects of Capital Investment in Great Britain 1750–1850* (London: Methuen).

Higgs, E. S. and Jarman, M. R. (1969) 'The Origins of Agriculture: A Reconsideration', *Antiquity*, vol. XLIII, pp. 31–41.

Hilton, R. H. (1952) 'Capitalism – What's in a Name', *Past and Present*, vol. 1, pp. 32–43.

Hilton, R. H. (1967) 'Some Problems of Urban Real Property in the Middle Ages' in Feinstein, C. H. (ed.) *Socialism, Capitalism and Economic Growth* (Cambridge: Cambridge University Press) pp. 326–37.

Hilton, R. H. (1969) *The Decline of Serfdom in Medieval England* (London: Macmillan).

Hilton, R. H. (1975a) *The English Peasantry in the Later Middle Ages.* (Oxford: Clarendon Press).

Hilton, R. H. (1975b) *Bond Men Made Free* (London: Temple Smith).

Hilton, R. H. (1982a) 'Towns in Societies – Medieval England', *Urban History Yearbook*, pp. 7–13.

Hilton, R. H. (1982b) 'Lords, Burgesses and Hucksters', *Past and Present*, no. 97, pp. 3–15.

Hirschman, A. O. (1977) *The Passions and the Interests: Political Arguments for Capitalism Before Its Triumph* (Princeton: Princeton University Press).

Hirshler, E. E. (1954) 'Medieval Economic Competition', *Journal of Economic of History*, vol. XLV, pp. 52–8.

Hobsbawm, E. J. (1964) *Labouring Men: Studies in the History of Labour* (London: Weidenfeld & Nicolson).

Hocart, A. M. (1941) *Kingship* (London: Watts).

Hocart, A. M. (1970) *Kings and Councillors: An Essay in the Comparative Anatomy of Human Society*, with introduction by R. Needham (Chicago: Chicago University Press). First edition published in 1936.

Hodder, I. (1978) 'Social Organisation and Human Interaction' in Hodder, I. (ed.) *The Spatial Organisation of Culture* (London: Duckworth) pp. 199–269.

Hodder, I. (1979) 'Pre-Roman and Romano-British Tribal Economies' in Burnham, B. C. and Johnson, H. B. (eds) *Invasion and Response: The Case of Roman Britain* (Oxford: British Archaeological Reports, International Series) no. 73, pp. 189–96.

Hodder, I. (1984) 'Archaeology in 1984', *Antiquity*, vol. LVIII, pp. 25–32.

Hodges, R. (1978a) 'Ports of Trade in Early Medieval Europe', *Norwegian Archaeological Review*, vol. II, pp. 97–101.

Hodges, R. (1978b) 'State Formation and the Role of Trade in Middle Saxon England' in Green, D., Haselgrove, C. and Spriggs, M. (eds) *Social Organization and Settlement* (Oxford: British Archaeological Reports, International Series) no. 47, part II, pp. 439–53.

Hodges, R. (1982) *Dark-Age Economics. The Origins of Towns and Trade AD600–1000* (London: Duckworth).

Hodgett, G. A. J. (1972) *A Social and Economic History of Europe*. (London: Methuen).

Homans, G. C. (1964) 'Bringing Men Back In', *American Sociological Review*, vol. 29, pp. 809–18.

Hopkins, K. (1980) 'Taxes and Trade in the Roman Empire (200BC–AD400)', *Journal of Roman Studies*, vol. 70, pp. 101–25.

Hoskins, W. G. (1964) *Provincial England: Essays in Social and Economic History* (London: Macmillan).

Houston, R. and Snell, K. D. M. (1984) 'Proto-Industrialization? Cottage Industry, Social Change and Industrial Revolution', *Historical Journal*, vol. 27, pp. 473–92.

Howell, D. W. (1977) *Land and Politics in Nineteenth-Century Wales* (London: Routledge & Kegan Paul).

Hughes, D. O. (1975) 'Urban Growth and Family Structure in Medieval Genoa', *Past and Present*, no. 66, pp. 3–28.

Hughes, D. O., (1977) 'Kinsmen and Neighbors in Medieval Genoa' in Miskimin, H. A., Herlihy, D. and Udovitch, A. L. (eds) *The Medieval City*. (New Haven: Yale University Press) pp. 95–111.

Hugh-Jones, C. (1979) *From the Milk River: Spatial and Temporal Processes in North-west Amazonia*. (Cambridge: Cambridge University Press).

Humphreys, S. C. (1969) 'History, Economics and Anthropology: the Work of Karl Polanyi', *History and Theory*, vol. 8, pp. 165–212.

Hyde, C. K. (1977) *Technological Change and the British Iron Industry 1700–1870* (Princeton: Princeton University Press).

Innis, H. A. (1972) *Empire and Communication*, revised by M. Q. Innis (Toronto: Toronto University Press). First edition published in 1950.

Isaac, G. L. (1972) 'Early Phases of Human Behaviour: Models in Lower Paleolithic Archaeology', pp. 167–99 in Clarke, D. L. (ed.) *Models in Archaeology* (London: Methuen).

Jackson, A. (1971) 'Pictish Social Structure and Symbols Stones', *Scottish Studies*, vol. XV, pp. 121–40.

Jarman, M. R. (1972) 'A Territorial Model for Archaeology: a Behavioural and Geographical Approach' in Clarke, D. L. (ed.) *Models in Archaeology* (London: Methuen) pp. 705–33.

Jensen, J. (1982) *The Prehistory of Denmark* (London: Methuen).

Jervis, F. R. J. (1947) 'The Handicap of Britain's Early Start', *The Manchester School*, vol. 15, pp. 112–22.

John, E. (1960) *Land Tenure in Early England* (Leicester: Leicester University Press).

John, E. (1966) *Orbis Britanniae* (Leicester: Leicester University Press).

Johnson, G. A. (1982) 'Organizational Structure and Scalar Stress' in Renfrew, C., Rowlands, M. J. and Segraves, B. A. (eds) *Theory and Explanation in Archaeology* (New York and London: Academic Press) pp. 389–421.

Johnson, J. H. and Pooley, C. G. (eds) (1982) *The Structure of Nineteenth-Century Cities* (London: Croom Helm).

Johnston, R. J. (1984) 'The World is an Oyster', *Transactions of the Institute of British Geographers*, new series, vol. 9, pp. 443–59.

Jolliffe, J. E. A. (1954) *The Constitutional History of Medieval England* (London: A. & C. Black) 3rd edn.

Jones, A. H. M. (1964) *The Later Roman Empire AD284–602* (Oxford: Blackwell).

Jones, E. L. (1968) 'The Agricultural Origins of Industry', *Past and Present*, no. 39, pp. 58–71.

Jones, E. (1973) 'The Fashion Manipulators: Consumer Tastes and British Industries, 1660–1800' in Cain, L. P. and Uselding, P. J. (eds) *Business Enterprise and Economic Change* (Kent, Ohio: Kent State University Press) pp. 198–226.

Jones, E. L. (1974) 'Institutional Determinism and the Rise of the Western World', *Economic Inquiry*, vol. 12, pp. 114–24.

Jones, E. L. (1981) *The European Miracle* (Cambridge: Cambridge University Press).

Jones, G. R. J. (1976) 'Multiple Estates and Early Settlement' in Sawyer, P. H. (ed.) *Medieval Settlement* (London: Edward Arnold) pp. 15–40.

Jones, P. J. (1954) 'An Italian Estate, 900–1200', *Economic History Review*, second series, vol. VII, pp. 18–32.

Jones, P. J. (1965) 'Commune and Despots: The City State in Late Medieval Italy', *Transactions of the Royal Historical Society*, fifth series, vol. 15, pp. 71–96.

Jones, P. J. (1966) 'Medieval Agrarian Society in its Prime: Italy' in Postan, M. M. (ed.) *The Cambridge Economic History of Europe, vol. 1, The Agrarian Life of the Middle Ages* (Cambridge: Cambridge University Press) pp. 340–431.

Kedar, B. Z. (1976) *Merchants in Crisis: Genoese and Venetian Men of*

Affairs and the Fourteenth-Century Depression (New Haven: Yale University Press).

Kellenbenz, H. (1974) 'Rural Industries in the West From the End of the Middle Ages to the Eighteenth Century' in Earle, P. (ed.) *Essays in European Economic History* (Oxford: Clarendon Press) pp. 45–88. Article first published in French, 1963.

Kellett, J. R. (1958) 'The Breakdown of Gild and Corporation control over the Handicraft and Retail Trade in London', *Economic History Review*, second series, vol. X, pp. 381–94.

Kemp, T. (1969) *Industrialization in Nineteenth-Century Europe* (London: Longman).

Kiernan, V. G. (1980) *State and Society in Europe 1550–1650* (Oxford: Blackwell).

Kindleberger, C. P. (1964) *Economic Growth in France and Britain 1851–1950* (Cambridge, Massachussetts: Harvard University Press).

Kindleberger, C. P. (1978) *Economic Response: Comparative Studies in Trade, Finance and Growth* (Cambridge, Massachussetts: Harvard University Press).

Kirby, D. P. (1967) *The Making of Early England* (London: Batsford).

Kirch, P. V. (1980) 'The Archaeological Study of Adaptation, *Advances in Archaeological Method and Theory*, vol. 3, pp. 101–56.

Kisch, H. (1964) 'Growth Deterrents of a Medieval Heritage: the Aachen-area Woollen Trades before 1790', *Journal of Economic History*, vol. XXIV, pp. 517–37.

Kisch, H. (1972) 'From Monopoly to *Laissez-Faire*: the Early Growth of the Wupper Valley Textile Trades', *Journal of European Economic History*, vol. 1, pp. 298–407.

Koebner, R. (1966) 'The Settlement and Colonization of Europe' in Postan, M. M. (ed.) *The Cambridge Economic History of Europe, vol. 1, The Agrarian Life of the Middle Ages* (Cambridge: Cambridge University Press) pp. 1–91.

Kosminsky, E. A. (1934–5) 'Services and Money Rents in the Thirteenth Century', *Economic History Review*, vol. 5, pp. 24–45.

Kosminsky, E. A. (1955) 'The Evolution of Fuedal Rent in England from the XIth to the XVth Centuries', *Past and Present*, no. 7, pp. 12–36.

Kosminsky, E. A. (1956) *Studies in the Agrarian History of England in the Thirteenth Century* (Oxford: Blackwell).

Kramer, S. (1927) *The English Craft Gilds: Studies in their Progress and Decline* (New York: Columbia University Press).

Kriedte, P. (1981) 'The Origins, the Agrarian Context and the Conditions in the World Market' in Kriedte, P., Medick, H. and Schlumbohm, J. (eds) *Industrialization Before Industrialization* (Cambridge: Cambridge University Press) pp. 12–37. Original German edition published in 1977.

Kriedte, P. (1983) *Peasants, Landlords and Merchant Capitalists, 1500–1800* (Leamington Spa: Berg) Original German edition published in 1980.

Kristiansen, K. (1982) 'The Formation of Tribal Systems in Later European Prehistory: Northern Europe, 4000–500BC' in Renfrew, C., Rowlands, M. J. and Segraves, B. A. (eds) *Theory and Explanation in*

Archaeology (New York and London: Academic Press) pp. 241–80.
Landes, D. S. (1969) *The Unbound Prometheus: Technological Change and Industrial Development in Western Europe from 1750 to the Present* (Cambridge: Cambridge University Press).
Langton, J. (1972a) 'Coal Output in South-West Lancashire 1590–1799', *Economic History Review*, second series, XXV, pp. 28–54.
Langton, J. (1972b) 'Potentialities and Problems of Adopting a Systems Approach to the Study of Change in Human Geography', pp. 125–79 in *Progress in Geography*, vol. 4.
Langton, J. (1975) 'Residential Patterns in Pre-Industrial Cities: Some Case Studies from Seventeenth-century Britain', *Transactions of the Institute of British Geographers*, no. 65, pp. 1–27.
Langton, J. (1977) 'Late Medieval Gloucester: Some Data from a Rental of 1455', *Transactions of the Institute of British Geographers*, new series, vol. 2, pp. 259–77.
Langton, J. (1979) *Geographical Change and Industrial Revolution: Coal-mining in South Lancashire 1590–1799* (Cambridge: Cambridge University Press).
Langton, J. and Hoppe, G. (1983) *Town and Country in the Development of Early Modern Europe* (Norwich: Historical Geography Research Series) no. 11.
Law, C. M. (1967) 'The Growth of Urban Population in England and Wales, 1801–1911', *Transactions of the Institute of British Geographers*, no. 41, pp. 125–43.
Lawton, R. (1972) 'An Age of Great Cities', *Town Planning Review*, vol. 43, pp. 199–224.
Lawton R. (1978) 'Population and Society 1730–1900' in R. A. Dodgshon and R. A. Butlin (eds) *Historical Geography of England and Wales* (London: Academic Press) pp. 313–66.
Leach, E. R. (1961) *Pul Eliya: A Village in Ceylon* (Cambridge: Cambridge University Press).
Lee, R. B. (1972) '!Kung Spatial Organization: An Ecological and Historical Perspective', *Human Ecology*, vol. 1, pp. 125–47.
Lennard, R. (1959) *Rural England 1086–1135* (Oxford: Clarendon Press).
Leroi-Gourhan, A. (1968) *The Art of Prehistoric Man in Western Europe* (London: Thames & Hudson).
Lévi-Strauss, C. (1969) *The Elementary Structures of Kinship*, (London: Eyre & Spottiswoode) 2nd edn. First French edition published in 1949.
Lévi-Strauss, C. (1972) *The Savage Mind* (London: Weidenfeld & Nicolson). First French edition published in 1962.
Lévi-Strauss, C. (1973) *Totemism*, translated by R. Needham and with introduction by R. Poole (Harmondsworth: Penguin Books). First French edition published in 1962.
Lewis, N. and Reinhold, M. (eds) (1966) *Roman Civilization: Sourcebook II: The Empire* (New York: Harper Torchbooks).
Lewis, P. (1969) *A Numerical Approach to the Location of Industry* (Hull: University of Hull Occasional Papers in Geography) no. 13.
Littlejohn, J. (1963) 'Temne Space', *Anthropology Quarterly*, vol. 101, pp. 1–17.

Lopez, R. (1956) 'The Economics of Land Transport in the Middle Ages', *Past and Present*, no. 9, pp. 17–29.

Lopez, R. (1976) *The Commercial Revolution of the Middle Ages, 950–1350* (Cambridge: Cambridge University Press).

Lopez, R. and Raymond, I. W. (1955) *Medieval Trade in the Mediterranean World* (New York: Columbia University Press).

Loyn, H. R. (1962) *Anglo-Saxon England and the Norman Conquest* (London: Longman).

Loyn, H. R. (1971) 'Towns in Late Anglo-Saxon England: the Evidence and Some Possible Lines of Enquiry in Clemoes, P. and Hughes, K. (eds) *England Before the Conquest* (Cambridge: Cambridge University Press) pp. 115–28.

Loyn, H. R. (1974) 'The Hundred in England in the Tenth and Early Eleventh Centuries' in Hearder, H. and Loyn, H. R. (eds) *British Government and Administration: Studies Presented to S. B. Chrimes* (Cardiff: University of Wales Press) pp. 1–15.

Loyn, H. R. (1984) *The Governance of England 500–1087* (London: Edward Arnold).

Lyon, B. (1957–8) 'Medieval Real Estate Development', *American Historical Review*, vol. 63, pp. 47–61.

Macalister, R. A. S. (1921) *Ireland in Pre-Celtic Times* (Dublin: Maunsel & Roberts).

Macfarlane, A. (1978) *The Origins of English Individualism* (Oxford: Blackwell).

McKendrick, N. (1982) 'Introduction: The Birth of a Consumer Society: the Commercialization of Eighteenth-Century England' pp. 1–8 and 'The Consumer Revolution of Eighteenth-Century England', pp. 9–18 in Mckendrick, N., Brewer, J. and Plumb, J. H. (eds) *The Birth of Consumer Society: the Commercialization of Eighteenth-Century England* (London: Europa Publications).

MacNeill, E. (1907) 'Mocu, Maccu', *Eriu*, vol. 111, pp. 42–9.

MacNeill, E. (1911) 'Early Irish Population Groups', *Proceedings of the Royal Irish Academy*, vol. XXIX, pp. 59–114.

MacNeill, M. (1962) *The Festival of Lughnasa* (Oxford: Oxford University Press).

Macpherson, A. G. (1966) 'An Old Highland Genealogy and the Evolution of a Scottish Clan', *Scottish Studies*, vol. X, pp. 1–43.

Maczak, A. (1972) 'Agricultural and Livestock Production in Poland: Internal and Foreign Markets', *Journal of European Economic History*, vol. 1, pp. 671–80.

Maitland, F. W. (1897) *Domesday Book and Beyond* (Cambridge: Cambridge University Press).

Malecki, J. M. (1977) 'The Vistula and Poland's Trade in the XVIth and XVIIth Centuries', *Journal of European Economic History*, vol. 6, pp. 193–8.

Malinowski, B. (1926) *Crime and Custom in a Savage Society* (London: Kegan Paul, Trench & Trubner).

Malinowst, M. (1974) 'Problems of the Growth of the National Economy of central-Eastern Europe in the Late Middle Ages', *Journal of European Economic History*, vol. 3, pp. 319–57.

Mandel, E. (1978) *Late Capitalism* (London: Verso Books). Original German edition published in 1972.

Martin, M. (1716) *A Description of the Western Islands of Scotland*, reprinted 1934 (Stirling: Macleod).

Martin, R. D. (1973) 'Concepts of Human Territoriality' in Renfrew, C. (ed.) *Explanations of Culture Change* (London: Duckworth) pp. 427–45.

Mauss, M. (1966) *The Gift: Forms and Functions of Exchange in Archaic Societies* (London: Routledge & Kegan Paul). First French edition published in 1903.

Mayer, T. (1938) 'The Historical Foundations of the German Constitution' in Barraclough, G. (ed.) *Medieval Germany 911–1250: Essays by German Historians, vol. 11.* (Oxford: Blackwell) pp. 1–33.

Medick, H. (1976) 'The Proto-Industrial Family Economy: The Structural Function of Household and Family During the Transition from Peasant Society to Industrial Capitalism', *Journal of Social History*, vol. 10, pp. 291–315.

Meillassoux, M. (1972) 'From Reproduction to Production', *Economy and Society*, vol. 1, pp. 93–105.

Meillassoux, M. (1978) 'The Economy in Agricultural Self-Sustaining Societies: A Preliminary Analysis', pp. 127–57 in Seddon, B. (ed.) *Relations of Production: Marxist Approaches to Economic Anthropology* (London: Cass).

Meinhard, H. H. (1975) 'The Patrilineal Principle in Early Teutonic Kinship' in Beattie, J. H. M. and Lienhardt, R. G. (eds) *Studies in Social Anthropology* (Oxford: Clarendon Press) pp. 1–29.

Mellars, P. (1976a) 'Fire Ecology, Animal Population and Man: a Study of Some Ecological Relationships in Prehistory', *Proceedings of the Prehistoric Society*, vol. 42, pp. 35–46.

Mellars, P. (1976b) 'Settlement Patterns and Industrial Variability in the British Mesolithic', pp. 375–99 in Sieveking, G. de G., Longworth, I. H. and Wilson, K. E. (eds) *Problems in Economic and Social Archaeology* (London: Duckworth).

Mendels, F. (1972) 'Proto-Industrialization: The First Phase of the Industrialization Process', *Journal of Economic History*, vol. 32, pp. 241–61.

Merrington, J. (1976) 'Town and Country in the Transition to Capitalism' in Hilton, R. H. (ed.) *The Transition from Feudalism to Capitalism* (London: Verso) pp. 170–95.

Miller, E. (1951) *The Abbey and Bishopric of Ely* (Cambridge: Cambridge University Press).

Miller, E. (1963) 'The Economic Policies of Governments' in Postan, M. M., Rich, E. E, and Miller E. (eds), *The Cambridge Economic History of Europe, vol. III, Economic Organization and Policies in the Middle Ages* (Cambridge: Cambridge University Press), pp. 281–339.

Miller, E. (1971) 'England in the Twelfth and Thirteenth Centuries: An Economic Contrast', *Economic History Review*, second series, vol. XXIV, p. 1–14.

Milward, A. and Saul, S. B. (1973) *The Economic Development of Continental Europe 1780–1870* (London: Allen & Unwin).

Minchinton, W. E. (ed.) (1972) *Wage Regulation in Pre-Industrial England* (Newton Abbot: David & Charles).

Mokyr, J. (1976) *Industrialization in the Low Countries, 1795–1850* (New Haven: Yale University Press).

Moore, J. S. (1965) *Laughton: A Study in the Evolution of the Wealden Landscape* (Leicester: University of Leicester, Dept. of English, Local History Occasional Paper) no. 19.

Morris, R. J. (1979) *Class and Class Consciousness in the Industrial Revolution 1780–1850* (London: Macmillan).

Moyes, A. (1978) 'Transport 1730–1900' in Dodgshon, R. A. and Butlin, R. A. (eds) *An Historical Geography of England and Wales* (New York and London: Academic Press) pp. 401–29.

Moyes, A. (1979) 'Victorian Industrial Structure and Inter-Industry Relationships in the Potteries: A Framework and Exploratory Analysis', *The North Staffordshire Journal of Field Studies*, vol. 19, pp. 39–60.

Muir, R. and Taylor, C. C. (1983) *Visions of the Past* (London: Dent).

Needham, R. (1963) 'Introduction' in Durkheim, E. and Mauss, M., *Primitive Classification* (London: Cohen & West) pp. vii–xlviii.

Needham, R. (1969) *Symbolic Classification* (Santa Monica: Goodyear Perspectives in Anthropology).

Newson, L. (1976) 'Cultural Evolution: a Basic Concept for Human and Historical Geography', *Journal of Historical Geography*, vol. 2, pp. 239–55.

Nicholas, D. (1971) *Town and Countryside: Social, Economic and Political Tensions in Fourteenth-century Flanders* (Brugge: Rijksuniversiteit Te Gent).

Nisbet, R. A. (1969) *Social Change and History: Aspects of the Western Theory of Development* (Oxford: Oxford University Press).

North, D. C. (1958) 'Ocean Freight Rates and Economic Development 1750–1913', *Journal of Economic History*, vol. 18, pp. 537–47.

North, D. C. (1977) 'Markets and other Allocative Systems in History: the Challenge of Karl Polanyi', *Journal of European Economic History*, vol. 6, pp. 703–16.

North, D. C. (1981) *Structure and Change in Economic History* (New York: Norton).

North, D. C. and Thomas, R. P. (1973) *The Rise of the Western World: A New Economic History* (Cambridge: Cambridge University Press).

North, D. C. and Thomas, R. P. (1977) 'The First Industrial Revolution', *Economic History Review*, second series, vol. XXX, pp. 229–41.

Ogilvie, R. M. (1965) *A Commentary on Livy, Books 1–5* (Oxford: Oxford University Press).

Olson, M. (1982) *The Rise and Decline of Nations* (New Haven: Yale University Press).

O'Rahilly, T. F. (1946) *Early Irish History and Mythology* (Dublin: Dublin Institute for Advanced Studies).

Outhwaite, R. B. (1981) 'Dearth and Government Intervention in English Grain Markets 1590–1700', *Economic History Review*, second series, vol. XXXIV, pp. 389–406.

Owen, R. C. (1965) 'The Patrilocal Band: A Linguistically and Culturally Hybrid Social Unit', *American Anthropology*, vol. 67, pp. 675–90.

Page, T. W. (1900) *The End of Villeinage in England* (New York: American Economic Association).

Palliser, D. M. (1972) 'The Trade Gilds of Tudor York' in Clark, P. and Slack, P. (eds) *Crisis and Order in English Towns 1500–1700* (London: Routledge & Kegan Paul) pp. 66–83.

Pallottino, M. (1975) *The Etruscans*, sixth edition, translated by J. Cremona (London: Allen Lane).

Palmer, R. E. A. (1970) *The Archaic Community of the Romans* (Cambridge: Cambridge University Press).

Parry-Lewis, J. (1965) *Building Cycles and Britain's Growth* (Manchester: Manchester University Press).

Parsons, T. (1964) 'Evolutionary Universals in Society', *American Sociological Review*, vol. 29, pp. 339–57.

Parsons, T. (1966) *Societies: Evolutionary and Comparative Perspectives* (Englewood Cliffs: Prentice-Hall).

Parsons, T. (1977) *The Evolution of Societies*, edited with intro. by J. Toby (Englewood Cliffs: Prentice-Hall).

Pawson, E. (1977) *Transport and Economy: The Turnpike Roads of Eighteenth-Century Britain* (New York and London: Academic Press).

Peake, H. and Fleure, H. J. (1927–56) *The Corridors of Time* (Oxford: Clarendon Press) vols. I–X.

Peebles, C. S. and Kus, S. M. (1977) 'Some Archaeological Correlates of Ranked Societies', *American Antiquity*, vol. 42, pp. 421–8.

Peet, R. (1969) 'The Spatial Expansion of Commercial Agriculture in the Nineteenth Century: A Von Thunen Explanation', *Economic Geography*, vol. 45, pp. 283–301.

Peet, R. (1972) 'Influences of the British Market on Agriculture and Related Economic Development in Europe Before 1860', *Transactions of the Institute of British Geographers*, no. 56, pp. 1–20.

Perren, R. (1975) 'The Meat and Livestock Trades in Britain, 1850–70', *Economic History Review*, second series, vol. XXXVIII, pp. 385–400.

Phythian-Adams, C. (1977) 'Jolly Cities: Goodly Towns', *Urban History Yearbook* (Leicester: Leicester University Press).

Phythian-Adams, C. (1979) *Desolation of a City: Coventry and the Urban Crisis of the Late Middle Ages* (Cambridge: Cambridge University Press).

Pike, R. (1966) *Enterprise and Adventure: The Genoese in Seville and the Opening of the New World* (Ithaca: Cornell University Press).

Pirenne, H. (1925) *Medieval Cities* (Princeton: Princeton University Press). Pagination based on paperback edition (New York: Doubleday, 1956).

Platt, C. (1976) *The English Medieval Town* (London: Secker & Warburg).

Polanyi, K. (1944) *The Great Transformation*, with introduction by R. M.

MacIver (New York: Rinehart & Co.). Pagination based on paperback edition (Boston: Beacon Press, 1957).

Polanyi, K. (1968) Dalton G. (ed.) *Primitive, Archaic and Modern Economies* (Boston: Beacon Press).

Polanyi, K. (1977) Pearson, H. W. (ed.) *The Livelihood of Man* (New York and London: Academic Press).

Pollard, S. (1963) 'Capital Accounting in the Industrial Revolution', *Yorkshire Bulletin of Economic and Social Research*, no. XV, pp. 75–91.

Pollard, S. (1964) 'Fixed Capital in the Industrial Revolution in Britain', *Journal of Economic History*, vol. XXIV, pp. 299–314.

Pollard, S. (1973) 'Industrialization and the European Economy', *Economic History Review*, second series, vol. XXVI, pp. 636–48.

Pollard, S. (1974) *European Economic Integration 1815–1970* (London: Thames & Hudson).

Pollard, S. (1981) *Peaceful Conquest: The Industrialization of Europe 1760–1970* (Oxford: Oxford University Press).

Pollard, S. and Crossley, D. W. (eds) (1968) *The Wealth of Britain 1085–1966* (London: Batsford).

Pooley, C. G. (1982) 'Choice and Constraint in the Nineteenth-Century City: A Basis for Residential Differentiation' in Johnson, J. H. and Pooley, C. G. (eds) *The Structure of Nineteenth-Century Cities* (London: Croom Helm) pp. 199–233.

Pooley, C. G. (1984) 'Residential Differentiation in Victorian Cities', *Transactions of the Institute of British Geographers*, new series, vol. 9, pp. 131–44.

Postan, M. M. (1944) 'The Rise of a Money Economy', *Economic History Review*, vol. XIV, pp. 123–34.

Postan, M. M. (1966) 'Medieval Agrarian Society in its Prime: England' in Postan, M. M. (ed.) *The Cambridge Economic History of Europe, vol. 1, The Agrarian Life of the Middle Ages*, (Cambridge: Cambridge University Press, 2nd edn, pp. 548–632.

Postan, M. M. (1972) *The Medieval Economy and Society: An Economic History of Britain 1100–1500* (London: Weidenfeld & Nicolson).

Postan, M. M. (1973) *Essays on Medieval Agriculture and General Problems of the Medieval Economy* (Cambridge: Cambridge University Press).

Pounds, N. J. G. (1953) *The Ruhr: A Study in Historical and Economic Geography* (London: Faber & Faber).

Pounds, N. J. G. (1974) *An Economic History of Medieval Europe* (London: Longman).

Pounds, N. J. G and Ball, S. S. (1964) 'Core-Areas and the Development of the European States System', *Annals of the Association of American Geographers*, vol. 54, pp. 24–40.

Powell, E. T. (1915) *The Evolution of the Money Market: An Historical and Analytical Study of the Rise and Development of Finance as a Centralised, Co-ordinated Force* (London: The Financial News).

Power, M. J. (1972) 'East London Housing in the Seventeenth Century' in Clark, P. and Slack, P. (eds) *Crisis and Order in English Towns 1500–1700*. (London: Routledge & Kegan Paul) pp. 237–62.

Previté-Orton, C. W. (1926) 'Italian Cities Till c.1200' in Tanner, J. R., Previté-Orton, C. W. and Brooke, Z. N. (eds) *The Cambridge Medieval History, vol. IV* (Cambridge: Cambridge University Press) pp. 208–41.

Price, R. (1983) *The Modernization of Rural France: Communication Networks and Agricultural Market Structures in Nineteenth-Century France* (London: Hutchinson).

Prigogine, I., Allen, P. M. and Herman, R. (1977) 'Long-term Trends and the Evolution of Complexity' in Laszlo, E. and Bierman, J. (eds) *Studies in the Conceptual Foundations* (New York: Pergamon) pp. 1–26.

Prigogine, I. and Stengers, I. (1984) *Order Out of Chaos*. (London: Fontana).

Ramage, E. S. (1983) 'Urban Problems in Ancient Rome' in Marchese, R. T. (ed.) *Aspects of Graeco-Roman Urbanism* (Oxford: British Archaeological Reports, International Series) no. 188, pp. 61–92.

Randsborg, K. (1975) 'Social Dimensions of Early Neolithic Denmark', *Proceedings of the Prehistoric Society*, vol. 4, pp. 105–18.

Randsborg, K. (1980) *The Viking Age in Denmark* (London: Duckworth).

Raper, R. A. (1977) 'The Analysis of the Urban Structure of Pompeii: A Sociological Examination of Land Use' in Clarke, D. L. (ed.) *Spatial Archaeology* (New York and London: Academic Press) pp. 189–221.

Rapp, R. T. (1976) *Industry and Economic Decline in Seventeenth-Century Venice* (Cambridge, Massachusetts: Harvard University Press).

Rapp, R. T. (1979) 'Real Estate and Rational Investment on Early Modern Venice', *Journal of European Economic History*, vol. 8, pp. 269–90.

Rappaport, R. A. (1977) 'Maladaptation in Social systems' in Friedman, J. and Rowlands, M. J. (eds) *The Evolution of Social Systems* (London: Duckworth) pp. 49–71.

Redman, C. L. (1978) *The Rise of Civilization* (San Francisco: Freeman).

Reed, M. (1981) 'Economic Structure and Change in Seventeenth-Century Ipswich' in Clark, P. (ed.) *Country Towns in Pre-Industrial England* (Leicester: Leicester University Press) pp. 87–141.

Rees, A. and B. (1962) *Celtic Heritage* (London: Thames & Hudson).

Renfrew, C. (1972) *The Emergence of Civilisation: the Cyclades and the Aegean in the Third Millenium BC* (London: Methuen).

Renfrew, C. (1975) 'Trade as Action at a Distance: Questions of Integration and Communication' in Sabloff, J. A. and Lamborg-Karlovsky, C. C. (eds) *Ancient Civilization and Trade* (Albuquerque: University of New Mexico Press) pp. 3–59.

Renfrew, C. (1976) *Before Civilisation* (Harmondsworth: Penguin Books).

Renfrew, C. (1977) 'Space, Time and Polity' in Friedman, J. and Rowlands, M. J. (eds) *The Evolution of Social Systems* (London: Duckworth) pp. 89–112.

Renfrew, C. (1979) *Problems in European Prehistory* (Edinburgh: Edinburgh University Press).

Renfrew, C. (1982) 'Socio-economic Change in Ranked Societies' in Renfrew, C. and Shennan, S. (eds) *Ranking, Resource and Exchange* (Cambridge: Cambridge University Press) pp. 1–8.

Renfrew, C. (1984) *Approaches to Social Archaeology* (Edinburgh: Edinburgh University Press).

Renfrew, C. and Cooke, K. L. (eds) (1979) *Transformations: Mathematical Approaches to Culture Change* (New York and London: Academic Press).

Renfrew C. and Level, E. V. (1979) 'Exploring Dominance: Predicting Polities from Centers' in Renfrew and Cooke (1979) pp. 145–67.

Renfrew, C. and Shennan, S. (ed.) (1982) *Ranking, Resource and Exchange: Aspects of the Archaeology of Early European Society* (Cambridge: Cambridge University Press).

Reynolds, S. (1977) *An Introduction to the History of the English Medieval Town* (Oxford: Clarendon Press).

Reynolds, V. (1973) 'Ethology of Social Change' in Renfrew, C. (ed.) *The Explanation of Culture Change* (London: Duckworth) pp. 467–80.

Richards, M. (1964–5) 'The Significance of *Is* and *Uwch* in Welsh Commote and Cantref names', *Welsh History Review*, vol. 2, pp. 9–18.

Richards, M. (1965) 'Early Welsh Territorial Suffixes', *Journal of the Royal Society of Antiquaries of Ireland*, vol. XCV, pp. 205–12.

Rickman, G. (1980) *The Corn Supply of Ancient Rome* (Oxford: Clarendon Press).

Roberts, B. K. (1968) 'A Study of Medieval Colonization in the Forest of Arden, Warwickshire', *Agricultural History Review*, vol. 16, pp. 101–13.

Robson, B. T. (1973) *Urban Approach: An Approach* (London: Methuen).

Robson, B. T. (1981) 'The Impact of Functional Differentiation Within Systems of Industrialized Cities' in Schmal, H. (ed.) *Patterns of European Urbanization Since 1500* (London: Croom Helm) pp. 111–30.

Rodger, R. G. (1982) 'Rents and Ground Rents: Housing and the Land Market in Nineteenth-Century Britain' in Johnson, J. H. and Pooley, C. G. (eds) *The Structure of Nineteenth-Century Cities* (London: Croom Helm) pp. 39–74.

Rodger, R. G. (1983) 'The Invisible Hand: Market Forces, Housing and the Urban Form in Victorian Cities' in Fraser, D. And Sutcliffe, A. (eds) *The Pursuit of Urban History* (London: Edward Arnold) pp. 190–211.

Rodgers, H. B. (1956) 'The Market Area of Preston in the Sixteenth and Seventeenth Centuries', *Geographical Studies*, vol. 3, pp. 45–55.

Roepke, H. (1956) *Movements of the British Iron and Steel Industry – 1720 to 1951.* (Urbana: University of Illinois Press).

Rogers, J. E. Thorold. (1866) *A History of Agriculture and Prices in England, vol. 1259–1400.* (Oxford: Oxford University Press).

Rokkan, S. (1975) 'Dimensions of State Formation and Nation-Building: A Possible Paradigm for Research on Variations Within Europe' in Tilly, C. (ed.) *The Formation of National States in Europe* (Princeton: Princeton University Press) pp. 562–600.

Romano, R. (1974) 'Italy in the Crisis of the Seventeenth-Century' in Earle, P. (ed.) *Essays in European Economic History* (Oxford: Clarendon Press) pp. 185–98.

Rörig, F. (1967) *The Medieval Town* (London: Batsford). First German edition published in 1932.

Rosen, A. (1981) 'Winchester in Transition' in Clark, P. (ed.) *County Towns in Pre-Industrial England* (Leicester: Leicester University Press) pp. 143–95.

Ross, A. (1967) *Pagan Celtic Britain* (London: Routledge & Kegan Paul).

Rostow, W. W. (1975) *How It All Began: The Origins of the Modern Economy* (London: Methuen).

Rowlands, M. B. (1975) *Masters and Men in the West Midlands Metalware Trades Before the Industrial Revolution* (Manchester: Manchester University Press).

Rowlands, M. J. (1980) 'Kinship, Alliance and Exchange in the European Bronze Age' in Barrett, J. and Bradley, R. (eds) *The British Later Iron Age* (Oxford: British Archaeological Reports, British Series) no. 83, part 1, pp. 15–55.

Rowlands, M. J. (1982) 'Processual Archaeology in Historical Social Science' in Renfrew, C., Rowlands, M. J. and Segraves, B. A. (eds) *Theory and Explanation in Archaeology* (New York and London: Academic Press) pp. 155–74.

Russell, J. C. (1972) *Medieval Regions and Their Cities* (Newton Abbot: David & Charles).

Sahlins, M. (1968) *Tribesmen* (Englewood Cliffs: Prentice-Hall).

Sahlins, M. (1974) *Stone Age Economics* (London: Tavistock).

Sahlins, M. and Service, E. R. (1960) *Evolution and Culture* (Ann Arbor: University of Michigan Press).

Salmon, E. T. (1982) *The Making of Roman Italy* (London: Thames & Hudson).

Saunders, T. J. (1970) *Plato: The Laws* (Harmondsworth: Penguin Books).

Sawyer, P. H. (1977) 'Kings and Merchants' in Sawyer, P. H. and Wood, I. N. (eds) *Early Medieval Kingship* (Leeds: Leeds University School of History) pp. 139–58.

Sawyer, P. H. (1978) *From Roman Britain to Norman England* (London: Methuen).

Sawyer, P. H. (1982) *Kings and Vikings: Scandinavia and Europe AD700–1100* (London: Methuen).

Schlebecker, J. T. (1960) 'The World Metropolis and the History of American Agriculture', *Journal of Economic History*, vol. XX, pp. 187–208.

Schon, D. A. (1973) *Beyond the Stable State* (Harmondsworth: Penguin Books).

Schrire, C. (1972) 'Ethno-Archaeological Models and Subsistence Behaviour in Arnhem Land' in Clarke, D. L. (ed.) *Models in Archaeology* (London: Methuen) pp. 653–70.

Schumpeter, J. (1939) *Business Cycles: A Theoretical, Historical and Statistical Analysis of the Capitalist Process* (New York: McGraw-Hill).

Schumpeter, J. (1971) 'The Instability of Capitalism' in Rosenberg, N. (ed.) *The Economics of Technological Change* (Harmondsworth: Penguin Books) pp. 13–42. Article first published in 1928.

Scola, R. (1975) 'Food Markets and Shops in Manchester 1770–1870', *Journal of Historical Geography*, vol. 1, pp. 153–67.

Segraves, B. A. (1974) 'Ecological Generalization and Structural Transformation of Sociocultural Systems', *American Anthropologist*, vol. 76, pp. 530–52.

Segraves, B. A. (1982) 'Central Elements in the Construction of a General Theory of the Evolution of Societal Complexity' in Renfrew, C., Rowlands, M. J. and Segraves, B. A. (eds) *Theory and Explanation in Archaeology* (New York and London: Academic Press) pp. 287–300.

Sella, D. (1968) 'Crisis and Transformation in Venetian Trade' in Pullan, B. (ed.) *Crisis and Change in the Venetian Economy* (London: Methuen) pp. 88–105. Article first published in Italian, 1959.

Service, E. R. (1971) *Primitive Social Organization* (New York: Random House) 2nd edn.

Service, E. R. (1978) 'Classical and Modern Theories of the Origins of Government' in Cohen, R. and Service, E. R. (eds) *Origins of the State: The Anthropology of Political Evolution* (Philadelphia: Institute for the Study of Human Issues) pp. 21–34.

Shaw, G. (1982) 'The Role of Retailing in the Urban Economy' in Johnson, J. H. and Pooley, C. G. (eds) *The Structure of Nineteenth-Century Cities* (London: Croom Helm) pp. 171–94.

Shaw, G. and Wild, M. T. (1979) 'Retail Patterns in the Victorian City', *Transactions of the Institute of British Geographers*, new series, vol. 4, pp. 278–91.

Sherratt, A. G. (1972) 'Socio-Economic and Demographic Models for the Neolithic and Bronze Ages of Europe' in Clarke, D. L. (ed.) *Models in Archaeology* (London: Methuen) pp. 477–542.

Sherratt, A. G. (1980) *The Cambridge Encyclopedia of Archaeology* (Cambridge: Cambridge University Press).

Sherratt, A. G. (1981) 'Ploughs and Pastoralism: Aspects of the Secondary Products Revolution' in Hodder, I., Isaac, G. and Hammond, N. (eds) *Pattern of the Past: Studies in Honour of David Clarke* (Cambridge: Cambridge University Press) pp. 261–305.

Sherratt, A. G. (1982) 'Mobile Resources: Settlement and Exchange in Early Agricultural Europe' in Renfrew, C. and Shennan, S. (eds) *Ranking, Resource and Exchange: Aspects of the Archaeology of Early European Society*. (Cambridge: Cambridge University Press) pp. 13–26.

Sieveking, A. (1979) *The Cave Artists* (London: Thames & Hudson).

Silver, M. (1983) 'Karl Polanyi and Markets in the Ancient Near East: The Challenge of the Evidence', *Journal of Economic History*, vol. XLIII, pp. 795–829.

Simmons I. and Tooley, M. (eds) (1981) *The Environment in British Prehistory* (London: Duckworth).

Sinclair, T. A. (ed.) (1962) *Aristotle: The Politics* (Harmondsworth: Penguin Books).

Sjoberg, G. (1960) *The Pre-industrial City, Past and Present.* (Illinois: Free Press of Glencoe).

Slater, T. R. (1981) 'The Analysis of Burgage Tenements in Medieval Towns', *Area*, vol. 13, pp. 211–16.

Slicher Van Bath, B. H. (1946) 'Manor, Mark and Village in the Eastern Netherlands', *Speculum*, vol. XXI, pp. 115–28.

Slicher Van Bath, B. H. (1963) *The Agrarian History of Western Europe AD 500–1850* (London: Edward Arnold).

Smelser, N. (1959) *Social Change in the Industrial Revolution: An Application of Theory to the Lancashire Cotton Industry 1770–1840* (London: Routledge & Kegan Paul).

Smith, C. A. (ed.) (1976) *Regional Analysis, vol. II, Social Systems* (New York and London: Academic Press).

Smith, C. T. (1967) *An Historical Geography of Western Europe Before 1800* (London: Longman).

Smith, R. M. (1984) 'Modernization, and the Corporate Medieval Village Community: Some Sceptical Reflections' in Baker, A. R. H. and Gregory, D. (ed.) *Explorations in Historical Geography* (Cambridge: Cambridge University Press) pp. 140–79.

Smith, W. D. (1985) 'The Function of Commercial Centers in the Modernization of European Capitalism: Amsterdam as an Information Exchange in the Seventeenth Century', *Journal of Economic History*, vol. XLIV, pp. 985–1005.

Smyth, A. P. (1982) *Celtic Leinster: Towards an Historical Geography of Early Irish Civilization AD 500–1600* (Dublin: Irish Academic Press).

Snodgrass, A. (1980) *Archaic Greece: The Age of Experiment* (London: Dent).

Song Nai Rhee (1981) 'Sumerian City States' in Griffeth, R. and Thomas, C. G. (eds) *The City State in Five Cultures* (Santa Barbara and Oxford: ABC Clio) pp. 1–30.

Sopher, D. (1967) *Geography of Religions* (Englewood Cliffs: Prentice-Hall).

Sorensen, J. K. (1978) 'Toponymic Evidence for Administrative Divisions in Denmark in the Viking Age' in Anderson, T. and Sandred, K. I. (eds) *The Vikings* (Uppsala: University of Uppsala) pp. 133–41.

Stacey, E. (1906) *The Guilds of Florence* (New York: Benjamin Blom).

Stafford, P. A. (1980) 'The Farm of One Night and the Organization of King Edward's Estate in Domesday', *Economic History Review*, second series, vol. XXXIII, pp. 491–502.

Stanner, W. E. H. (1965) 'Aboriginal Territorial Organization: Estate, Range, Domain and Regime', *Oceania*, vol. XXXVI, pp. 1–26.

Starr, C. G. (1977) *The Economic and Social Growth of Early Greece 800–500BC* (New York: Oxford University Press).

Stenton, F. M. (1932) *The First Century of English Feudalism 1066–1166* (Oxford: Clarendon Press).

Stenton, F. M. (1947) *Anglo-Saxon England* (Oxford: Clarendon Press) 2nd edn.

Steward, J. H. (1955) *Theory of Culture Change: The Methodology of Multilinear Evolution* (Urbana: University of Illinois Press).

Strayer, J. (1970) *On the Medieval Origins of the Modern State* (Princeton: Princeton University Press).

Summerson, J. (1945) *Georgian London* (London: Pleiades Books).

Taylor, A. M. (1971) 'Evolution–Revolution: General Systems Theory and Society' in Gotesky, R. and Laszlo, E. (eds) *Evolution-Revolution: Patterns of Development in Nature, Society Man and Knowledge* (New York: Gordon & Breach) pp. 104–32.

Taylor, A. M. (1973) 'Some Implications of the Forrester Model' in Laszlo, E. (ed.) *The World System: Models, Norms and Applications* (New York: Braziller) pp. 29–68.

Taylor. C. C. (1983) *Village and Farmstead* (London: George Philip).

Taylor, P. J. (1982) 'A Materialist Framework for Political Geography', *Transactions of the Institute of British Geographers*, new series, vol. 7, pp. 15–34.

Thirsk, J. (1961) 'Industries in the Countryside' in Fisher, F. J. (ed.) *Essays in the Economic and Social History of Tudor and Stuart England in Honour of R. H. Tawney*. (Cambridge: Cambridge University Press) pp. 70–88.

Thirsk, J. (1967) 'The Farming Regions of England' in Thirsk, J. (ed.) *The Cambridge Agrarian History of England and Wales, vol. IV, 1500–1640* (Cambridge: Cambridge University Press) pp. 1–112.

Thirsk, J. (1970) 'Seventeenth-Century Agriculture and Social Change' in Thirsk, J. (ed.) *Land, Church and People: Essays Presented to H. P. R. Finberg, Supplement, Agricultural History Review*, vol. 18, supplement, pp. 148–77.

Thomas, C. (1963) 'The Interpretation of the Pictish Symbols', *Archaeological Journal*, vol. CXX, pp. 31–97.

Thompson, D'Arcy W. (1961) *On Growth and Form* (Cambridge: Cambridge University Press) abridged edn. First published in 1917.

Thompson, E. A. (1965) *The Early Germans* (Oxford: Clarendon Press).

Thompson, E. P. (1971) 'The Moral Economy of the English Crowd in the Eighteenth Century', *Past and Present*, no. 50, pp. 76–136.

Thompson, F. M. L. (1957) 'The Land Market in the Nineteenth Century', *Oxford Economic Papers*, new series, vol. IX, pp. 285–308.

Thompson, J. W. (1928) *Feudal Germany* (Chicago: University of Chicago Press).

Thrupp, S. L. (1933) 'The Grocers of London: A Study of Distributive Trade' in Power, E. and Postan, M. M. (eds) *Studies in English Trade in the Fifteenth Century* (London: Routledge & Kegan Paul) pp. 247–92.

Thrupp, S. L. (1948) *The Merchant Class of Medieval London* (Ann Arbor: University of Michigan).

Thrupp, S. L. (1963) 'The Gilds' in Postan, M. M., Rich, E. E. and Miller, E. (eds) *The Cambridge Economic History of Europe, vol. III,*

Economic Organization and Policies in the Middle Ages (Cambridge: Cambridge University Press) 2nd edn, pp. 230–80.

Tilly, C. (1975) 'Western State-Making and Theories of Political Transformation' in Tilly, C. (ed.) *The Formation of National States in Western Europe* (Princeton: Princeton University Press) pp. 601–38.

Topolski, J. (1974) 'Economic Decline in Poland from the Sixteenth to the Eighteenth Centuries' in Earle, P. (ed.) *Essays in European Economic History* (Oxford: Clarendon Press) pp. 127–42.

Topolski, J. (1981) 'Continuity and Discontinuity in the Development of the Feudal System in Eastern Europe (Xth to XVIIth Centuries)' *Journal of European Economic History*, vol 10, 373–400.

Trebilcock, C. (1981) *The Industrialization of the Continental Powers 1780–1914* (London: Longman).

Tribe, K. (1981) *Genealogies of Capitalism* (London: Macmillan).

Trigger, B. (1978) *Time and Traditions* (Edinburgh: Edinburgh University Press).

Tringham, R. (1972) 'Territorial Demarcation of Prehistoric Settlements' in Ucko, P. J., Tringham, R. and Dimbleby, G. W. E. (eds) *Man, Settlement and Urbanism* (London: Duckworth) pp. 463–75.

Tuan, Yi-Fu (1974) *Topophilia* (Englewood Cliffs: Prentice-Hall).

Turnbull, C. M. (1968) 'The Importance of Flux in Two Hunting Societies' in Lee, R. B. and de Vore, I. (eds) *Man the Hunter* (Chicago: Aldine) pp. 132–7.

Turnbull, C. M. (1976) *Man in Africa* (Newton Abbot: David & Charles).

Turnbull, G. L. (1977) 'Provincial Road Carrying in England in the Eighteenth Century', *Journal of Transport History*, new series, vol. IV, pp. 17–39.

Turner, F. J. (1921) *The Frontier in American History* (New York: Holt).

Ucko, P. J. (1962) 'The Interpretation of Prehistoric Anthropomorphic Figurines', *Journal of the Royal Anthropological Institute of Great Britain and Ireland*, vol. 92, pp. 38–54.

Unwin, G. (1904) Industrial Organization in the Sixteenth and Seventeenth Centuries (Oxford: Clarendon Press).

Unwin, T. (1981) 'Rural Marketing in Medieval Nottinghamshire', *Journal of Historical Geography*, vol. 7, pp. 231–51.

Usher, A. P. (1913) *The History of the Grain Trade in France 1400–1710* (Cambridge, Massachusetts: Harvard University Press).

Van Der Wee, H. (1963) *The Growth of the Antwerp Market and the European Economy (Fourteenth-Sixteenth Centuries), vol. II, Interpretation* (The Hague: Nijhoff).

Van Der Wee, H. (1975) 'Structural Change and Specialisation in the Industry of the Southern Netherlands, 1100–1600', *Economic History Review*, second series, vol XXVIII, pp. 203–21.

Van Houtte, J. A. (1966) 'The Rise and Decline of the Market of Bruges', *Economic History Review*, second series, vol. XIX, pp. 29–47.

Van Houtte, J. A. (1977) *An Economic History of the Low Countries 800–1800*. (London: Weidenfeld & Nicolson).

Vance, J. E. (1971) 'Land Assignment in Pre-Capitalist, Capitalist and Post-Capitalist Cities', *Economic Geography*, vol. 47, pp. 101–20.

Vance, J. E. (1977) *The Scene of Man: the Role and Structure of the City in the Geography of Western Civilisation* (New York: Harper & Row).

Verlinden, C. (1963) 'Markets and Fairs' in Postan, M. M., Rich, E. E. and Miller, E. (eds) *The Cambridge Economic History of Europe, vol. III: Economic Organization and Policies in the Middle Ages*, (Cambridge: Cambridge University Press) 2nd edn, pp. 119–53.

Verlinden, C. (1972) 'From the Mediterranean to the Atlantic', *Journal of European Economic History*, vol. I, pp. 625–46.

Wagner, H. (1975) 'Studies in the Origins of Early Celtic Traditions', Eriu, vol. 26, pp. 1–26.

Waley, D. (1952) *Medieval Orvieto: The Political History of an Italian City-State 1157–1334* (Cambridge: Cambridge University Press).

Waley, D. (1978) *The Italian City Republics* (London: Longman) 2nd edn.

Wallerstein, I. (1974) *The Modern World-System, Vol. I. Capitalist Agriculture and the Origins of the European World-Economy in the Sixteenth Century* (New York and London: Academic Press).

Wallerstein, I. (1979) *The Capitalist World-Economy*. (Cambridge: Cambridge University Press).

Wallerstein, I. (1980) *The Modern World-System, Vol. II: Mercantilism and the Consolidation of the European World-Economy 1600–1750*. (New York and London: Academic Press).

Wallerstein, I. (1983) 'Crises: The World-Economy, the Movements, and the Ideologies' in Bergesen, A. (ed.) *Crises in the World-System* (Beverly Hills: Sage) pp. 21–36.

Ward, D. (1975) 'Victorian Cities: How Modern?', *Journal of Historical Geography*, vol. I, pp. 135–51.

Webb, B. and S. (1904) 'The Assize of Bread', *Economic Journal*, vol. XIV, pp. 196–218.

Wenke, R. J. (1981) 'Explaining the Evolution of Cultural Complexity: A Review', *Advances in Archaeological Method and Theory*, vol. 4, pp. 79–127.

Westerfield, R. B. (1915) *Middlemen in English Business* (New Haven: Yale University Press).

Wheatley, P. (1969) *City as Symbol* (London: University College) inaugural lecture, 1967.

White, L. A. (1959) *The Evolution of Culture. The Development of Civilization to the Fall of Rome*. (New York: McGraw Hill).

White, L. A. (1975) *The Concept of Cultural Systems* (New York: Columbia University Press).

Whitehand, J. W. R. (1972) 'Building Cycles and the Spatial Pattern of Urban Growth', *Transactions of the Institute of Britain Geographers*, no. 56, pp. 39–55.

Wickham, C. (1981) *Early Medieval Italy* (London: Macmillan).

Willan, T. S. (1964) *River Navigation in England 1600–1750* (London: Cass).

Willetts, R. F. (1962) *Cretan Cults and Festivals* (London: Routledge & Kegan Paul).

Williams, G. A. (1963) *Medieval London: From Commune to Capital* (London: Athlone Press).

Wobst, H. M. (1974) 'Boundary Conditions for Paleolithic Social Systems: A Simulation Approach', *American Antiquity*, vol. 39, pp. 147–78.

Wobst, H. M. (1976) 'Locational Relationships in Paleolithic Society', *Journal of Human Evolution*, vol. 5, pp. 49–58.

Wohl, A. S. (1971) 'The Housing of the Working Classes in London 1815–1914' in Chapman, S. D. (ed.) *The History of Working-Class Housing* (Newton Abbot: David & Charles) pp. 15–54.

Wolf, E. R. (1982) *Europe and the People Without History* (Berkeley: University of California Press).

Wood, C. T. (1966) *The French Apangages and the Capetian Monarchy 1224–1328* (Cambridge, Massachusetts: Harvard University Press).

Wright, A. F. (1965) 'Symbolism and Function: Reflections on Changan and other Great Cities', *Journal of Asian Studies*, vol. 24, pp. 667–79.

Wright, H. (1978) 'Towards an Explanation of the Origin of the State', in Cohen, R. and Service, E. R. (eds), *Origins of the State: The Anthropology of Political Systems* (Philadelphia: Institute for the Study of Human Issues) pp. 49–68.

Wrightson, K. (1982) *English Society 1580–1680*. (London: Hutchinson).

Wrightson, K. and Levine, D. (1979) *Poverty and Piety in an English Village: Terling, 1525–1700*. (New York and London: Academic Press).

Wrigley, E. A. (1961) *Industrial Growth and Population Change: A Regional Study of the Coalfield Areas of North-West Europe in the Later Nineteenth Century*. (Cambridge: Cambridge University Press).

Wrigley, E. A. (1962) 'The Supply of Raw Materials in the Industrial Revolution', *Economic History Review*, second series, vol. XV pp. 1–16.

Wrigley, E. A. (1967) 'A Simple Model of London's Importance in Changing English Society and Economy 1650–1750', *Past and Present*, no. 37, pp. 44–70.

Wrigley, E. A. (1978) 'Parasite or Stimulus: The Town in a Pre-Industrial Economy' in Abrams, P. and Wrigley, E. A. (eds), *Towns in Societies* (Cambridge: Cambridge University Press) pp. 295–309.

Yellen, J. and Harpending, H. (1972–3) 'Hunter–Gatherer Populations and Archaeological Inference', *World Archaeology*, vol. 4, pp. 244–53.

Yengoyan, A. A. (1968) 'Demographic and Ecological Influences on Aboriginal Australian Marriage Sections' in Lee, R. B. and de Vore, I. (eds) *Man the Hunter* (Chicago: Aldine) pp. 185–99.

Zeller, G. (1970) 'Industry in France Before Colbert' in Cameron, R. (ed.) *Essays in French Economic History* (Homewood, Illinois: American Economic Association) pp. 185–99. First published in French 1950.

Zytkowicz, L. (1972) 'The Peasant's Farm in Poland from the 16th to the Middle of the 18th Century', *Journal of European Economic History*, vol. I, pp. 135–54.

Index

236–8, 253, 313, 315–16, 340–7
renders 211, 271
Foster, J. 319
France 170, 177, 184, 190–1, 217, 234, 248–50, 309–10, 321, 345
Frankish kingdoms 133, 173, 191
free markets 20–3, 197–9, 225, 284–5, 287, 351
  broadening range 281–2, 292–310
  competitive instrumentalities 246–7
  differentiation 313–16
  impact on space, summary of 347–51
  labour 306–8
  land 225–303, 284–5, 305, 330–40
  organisational needs 313–16
  temporary equilibria 289, 291, 317–47
  see also food markets
free tenures 253–59, 271–4
Freeman, M. J. 299
Friedman, J. 16–18, 73–4, 83, 111, 113–14, 116–17, 128, 240–1, 356
Friedrich, P. 78
Friesland 343
frontier, role of 35, 243, 251–9, 272–4
Fyn 163

Gaul 152, 199–202
Genoa 187, 237, 263–4
Germany 41–2, 101, 177, 190, 223–8, 248, 254–5, 294, 326, 344
  North German Plain 41, 70, 121
Giddes, A. 4–8, 17
gift exchange *see* exchange
gilds 217, 22–3, 232, 266–69, 309–10
  companies 308–9
  decline 308–10

differentiation 222, 232–3
regulations 266–9, 302–3, 308–10
Ghent 233, 259, 262
Gimbutas, M. 57, 84–5
Goody, J. 108, 352
Gould, S. J. 360
Gregory, D. 22, 319, 348
grain
  marketing 196–7, 219–21, 234, 253, 257, 343–7
  scarcities 197, 205, 219–20
Gras, N. S. B. 288, 342
Gray, H. L. 270–2
Great Plague 235, 266, 270
Greece 144–9, 151
Grigg, D. 1

Hamburg 213–4
Hamwik (Southampton) 203–4
Hanseatic League 21–4, 212, 217, 267
Harris, D. R. 36, 64–5
Harris, M. 2
Harvey, B. 279
Harvey, D. 21, 286–7, 322–3, 332
Hedeby 162, 203
Henge monuments 110, 122
Hengistbury Head (Dorset) 199–203
Heriod's *Work and Days* 196
Hibbert, A. B. 267
Hilton, R. H. 272–3, 280, 282
Hirshler, E. E. 246
Hocart, A. M. 119
Hodder, I. 200
Hodges, H. 203–8
Holland 70, 113, 294–5, 298, 295, 343, 345
Holocene 32–3, 36
Holstein 255
Hopkins, K. 201–2
Hudson Bay Company 294
Hughes, D. O. 187
hundred
  hundredal centres as early markets 211